Praise for *Most Honorable Son: A Forgotten Hero's Fight Against Fascism and Hate During World War II*

"In *Most Honorable Son*, journalist-turned-historian Gregg Jones introduces readers to one of the most courageous airmen of World War II. A Japanese American gunner, Ben Kuroki not only flew a staggering fifty-eight combat missions over three continents in World War II, but also battled the racism and resentment so common on the home front at that time. In Jones's talented hands, readers will accompany Ben from the Nebraska farm fields to the heavens over North Africa, Europe, and Japan with pit stops in a Spanish prison and the internment camps in Wyoming and Idaho. This is an amazing story— and amazingly well told. Superbly researched, fast-paced, and heartfelt, this is narrative history at its finest."
—**James M. Scott, Pulitzer Prize finalist and author of**
Black Snow* and *Rampage

"*Most Honorable Son* is a WWII roller coaster of patriotism, perseverance, duty, dedication, and the bravery of bomber gunner Ben Kuroki—made more powerful by the hatred he endured at home as a Japanese American, despite completing fifty-eight missions against Germany and Japan. He never wavered, becoming a nationally known postwar opponent of prejudice and bigotry. An inspirational read that showcases the Greatest Generation's greatest legacy."
—**Scott McGaugh, *New York Times* bestselling author of**
Brotherhood of the Flying Coffin: The Glider Pilots of
World War II

"Ben Kuroki was championed as the first Nisei war hero of World War II, and this boy from Nebraska has long deserved a full-length biography. Gregg Jones has come through with a meticulously researched and compelling story that vividly captures the man behind the myth."
—**Frank Abe, filmmaker, *Conscience and the Constitution***

"There were very few Japanese Americans who served in the US Army Air Forces during World War II. But there was one who made the headlines back then. Gregg Jones meticulously recounts Ben Kuroki's amazing, death-defying journey through World War II. But this is not just about the first Japanese American war hero—it's about the other B-24 and B-29 fliers over Europe and the Pacific from the first raids against the Germans in France to firebombings of the major cities of Japan and the destruction of Hiroshima and Nagasaki. Along this journey we get a very different perspective of the Japanese American experience during the war from Kuroki, finding himself lauded by many though despised by some he thought were his own people."
—Bill Kubota, documentary filmmaker,
Most Honorable Son, **PBS, 2007**

"This story has it all: soaring drama, tragedy, and an unforgettable hero who struggles against foreign enemies and domestic prejudice. *Most Honorable Son*—prodigiously researched and expertly crafted—is an unforgettable work of history."
—Jonathan Eig, National Book Award long-list finalist and
New York Times **bestselling author of** *King: A Life*
and *Ali: A Life*

"*Most Honorable Son* is a gripping World War II story that speaks to us today—about the ravages of war and racism in America. Through meticulous research, Gregg Jones has created a vivid portrait of a Japanese American farm boy who changed history."
—Dale Maharidge, nonfiction Pulitzer Prize winner and author
of *Bringing Mulligan Home: The Other Side of the Good War* **and**
The Dead Drink First **podcast**

"With captivating detail and clarity, Gregg Jones brings to life Ben Kuroki's incredible military accomplishments, along with his deeply felt motivations and the complex challenges he faced. In the process, we gain a fuller appreciation for the intersection between the Nisei war heroes such as Kuroki and the draft resisters such as Yosh Kuromiya and the roles they have played in our Japanese American heritage."
—Susan Kamei, author of *When Can We Go Back to America? Voices*
of Japanese American Incarceration During WWII

"From page one, *Most Honorable Son* is hard to put down. Told with skill and aplomb, *Most Honorable Son* is an essential addition to the annals of the war by putting a spotlight on Ben Kuroki's overlooked heroism. Kuroki once said he looked Japanese but had the heart of an American. *Most Honorable Son* reminds us that America is everyone."
—**Kevin Maurer, *New York Times* bestselling author of**
No Easy Day* and *Damn Lucky

"Gregg Jones has penned an instant classic with *Most Honorable Son*, the story of Nebraska-born Japanese American Ben Kuroki, who through sheer determination found a way to fight for his beloved America after Pearl Harbor despite countless obstacles and racism. From ground-bound Army Air Forces clerk safely out of combat to a B-24 and B-29 bomber crewman, Ben Kuroki took part in some of the bloodiest air battles of World War II. Throughout his fifty-eight missions, he was captured and interned by Spanish forces, fought against every Axis power, and triumphed in his quest to prove his loyalty to the United States the night his crew bombed Tokyo. Gregg Jones has created a masterpiece with this biography of one of America's most unusual and transformative heroes of World War II. Not to be missed."
—**John R. Bruning, *New York Times* bestselling author of**
Indestructible* and *Race of Aces

"*Most Honorable Son* is a masterclass in history and biography. This book is a testament to the courage of one individual who defied stereotypes and racial attacks to serve his country in the greatest armed struggle the world has ever known. From Japanese internment camps in the United States to the fight for survival in the skies of Germany and Japan, Jones has produced a work that should be required reading for anyone who seeks to understand not only the individual motivations of just one member of the Greatest Generation, but also why they fought as a unified whole. This is history as it should be written."
—**Dr. Brian D. Laslie, Command Historian at the United States Air Force Academy and author of *Fighting from Above: A Combat History of the US Air Force***

"History is replete with forgotten stories. Gregg Jones has unearthed a key one, filling a significant void in WWII historiography and illuminating the American experience. Beautifully written, Jones takes the reader from the dusty farms of Nebraska to the flak-filled skies over Ploiesti and, later, the perilous air over Japan. Vivid and compelling, *Most Honorable Son* reveals a story of true courage: Ben Kuroki earned three Distinguished Flying Crosses, but this narrative also shows that some of the toughest battles are often fought at home."
—**Patrick K. O'Donnell, historian and bestselling author of**
The Indispensables* and *The Unvanquished

"*Most Honorable Son* is a poignant portrayal of the first Japanese American hero of World War II—a forgotten soldier who devoted his postwar life to combatting bigotry and hatred. Meticulously researched, Gregg Jones's labor of love brings Ben Kuroki alive, installing him to his rightful place in history while shedding light on a complex story of American valor."
—**Sally Denton, author of *The Colony* and *American Massacre***

"Gregg Jones has performed a public service with his rescue of the tale of Ben Kuroki from forgotten archives of World War II. This account of a Japanese American who flew fifty-eight combat missions on three continents is a compelling story of real patriotism and pure heroism. Kuroki's brave fight against racial prejudice and his courageous service as a gunner on perilous bombing raids will inspire and thrill readers. *Most Honorable Son* is an exciting book—and a truly important one."
—**Doug J. Swanson, author of *Cult of Glory: The Bold and Brutal History of the Texas Rangers***

MOST HONORABLE SON

A FORGOTTEN HERO'S FIGHT AGAINST FASCISM AND HATE DURING WORLD WAR II

GREGG JONES

CITADEL PRESS
Kensington Publishing Corp.
www.kensingtonbooks.com

CITADEL PRESS BOOKS are published by

Kensington Publishing Corp.
900 Third Avenue
New York, NY 10022

All Kensington titles, imprints, and distributed lines are available at special quantity discounts for bulk purchases for sales promotions, premiums, fund-raising, educational, or institutional use. Special book excerpts or customized printings can also be created to fit specific needs. For details, write or phone the office of the Kensington sales manager: Kensington Publishing Corp., 900 Third Avenue, New York, NY 10022, attn Sales Department; phone 1-800-221-2647.

10 9 8 7 6 5 4 3 2 1

First Citadel hardcover printing: August 2024

Printed in the United States of America

ISBN: 978-0-8065-4293-5

ISBN: 978-0-8065-4295-9 (e-book)

Library of Congress Control Number: 2024934888

To the memory of Ben Kuroki and Yosh Kuromiya
And other Americans of Japanese descent
Who fought for liberty and justice for all in World War II

CONTENTS

FOREWORD

By Naomi Ostwald Kawamura

Fully representing or encapsulating a people's collective experience poses inherent challenges. At Densho, a public history organization and digital archives dedicated to preserving, collecting, and educating about the history of the World War II incarceration of Japanese Americans, we actively strive to steward thousands of stories spanning generations, locations, and the diversity of wartime experiences of Americans of Japanese ancestry. These include survivors' firsthand experiences of forcible removal and incarceration, stories of families torn apart, businesses and homes lost, educational opportunities derailed, and individuals who either volunteered for military service or actively resisted the draft. Each narrative contributes to our understanding of this period in American history. Among these narratives, certain individual stories emerge that particularly illuminate the complexities of our shared past. Ben Kuroki is one such figure.

As a highly decorated soldier and patriot, Kuroki defied prejudice and stereotypes to carve out his place in a nation gripped by wartime hysteria. Kuroki's journey was marked by extraordinary challenges and achievements, which Gregg Jones details in this rich biography. Notably, as an aerial gunner, Kuroki was the only Japanese American to serve in air combat over Japan during the war. Despite facing discrimination and suspicion from fellow Americans and fellow soldiers, Kuroki became a decorated soldier, and his patriotism led him to become one of the most celebrated Japanese Americans of his time. However, his legacy remains complex.

As a Japanese American serving in the US military, Kuroki faced the challenge of reconciling his heritage with his unreserved allegiance to his country. Despite public recognition of Kuroki as a war hero, he became a divisive figure among Japanese Americans. Upon his return home, he was tasked to support the nation's military efforts with a tour to engage the 125,000-plus Japanese Americans who were unjustly incarcerated in America's concentration camps. While many Japanese Americans—especially young Nisei—viewed Kuroki as a hero, there were members of the Issei generation who particularly objected to Kuroki's dismissive attitude toward Japan and his failure to acknowledge the mixed emotions many Japanese Americans held about wartime Japan, where many had close relatives. Incarcerated Japanese Americans, in general, were also angered by Kuroki's failure to understand how their incarceration altered or shaped their views toward America (as Kuroki and his family, living in the Midwest, were outside of the exclusion area and thus not forcibly removed or incarcerated), something Kuroki himself later acknowledged. Without guidance, Kuroki's inability at that time to fully grasp the trauma from this experience likely exacerbated tensions between himself and the Japanese American community he intended to engage. This point also highlights the profound impact that forcible incarceration, rampant xenophobia, and discrimination had on the sense of identity and belonging held by Japanese Americans.

Jones admirably fulfills the essential task of illuminating Kuroki's life and role as one of the most prominent Japanese Americans in mainstream American consciousness during the war years while engaging in critical dialogue, particularly regarding Kuroki's stance on draft resistance. In addition, this biography challenges conventional narratives of the American patriot. Much like Daniel James Brown's *Facing the Mountain* (2021), Pamela Rotner Sakamoto's *Midnight in Broad Daylight* (2016), and Bradford Pearson's *The Eagles of Heart Mountain* (2021), Gregg Jones makes an important contribution to historical works aimed at a popular audience. Through *Most Honorable Son*, Jones not only shares Kuroki's unique story but adds to the complex landscape of the Japanese American experience during World War II.

In recounting Kuroki's story, we are compelled to confront timeless questions about patriotism and the response to injustice—questions that resonate with renewed urgency in our contemporary landscape. His journey prompts us to reflect on the complexities of loyalty, heritage, and resilience, offering profound insights into the human condition. Jones presents a sympathetic portrayal of a Japanese American patriot who navigated the complexities of national identity and belonging during a time of upheaval. As the events of World War II become increasingly a distant past, stories like this serve as a bridge to connect past struggles with current challenges and engage with issues that remain relevant today, while honoring the stories and individuals from the past that we give voice to, ensuring their legacies endure for future generations.

Naomi Ostwald Kawamura, PhD, is the executive director of Densho.

INTRODUCTION

By William Fujioka

Throughout the years, I've heard about Ben Kuroki, the Japanese American airman who fought in both the Europe and the Pacific campaigns during World War II. Reading *Most Honorable Son: A Forgotten Hero's Fight Against Fascism and Hate During World War II* by Gregg Jones gave me an intriguing insight into Kuroki's life and accomplishments. Ben Kuroki's bravery, heroism, and military record were truly exceptional. This book is also important for ensuring that others learn about the contributions of the many Japanese American soldiers who bravely fought during World War II while their families were forcefully removed from their homes and incarcerated behind barbed wire in concentration camps.

The Japanese American National Museum (JANM), located in the Little Tokyo community of Los Angeles, California, was established to preserve and share the history, journey, struggles, and contributions of individuals of Japanese heritage in America. The founders of JANM were Japanese American veterans of World War II and business leaders from Little Tokyo. JANM's current mission is to preserve the artifacts and stories of our community and retell these stories to ensure that what happened to Japanese Americans in 1942 would never happen to any other group. We pursue this goal each and every day.

The story of Japanese Americans in America is a classic immigrant story. Like all immigrants, the Issei (first generation in America) came to this country in the early 1900s with the hope for a better life for their families. Most came through the ports of entry on the West Coast and pursued their dreams by first working as laborers on farms, in factories and mines, and on railroads and fishing boats. Working on the railroad took many Japanese immigrants, like Ben Kuroki's father, to the Midwest states where they found opportunities in many industries, especially agriculture.

The Issei made significant contributions in such industries as agriculture, but it wasn't without great struggle due to the hardships they faced. Western states like California, Oregon, and Washington enacted alien land laws in the 1910s that prevented the Issei from owning land. They had to either lease the land they farmed or have their American-born children hold title to the land. In spite of this, from the West Coast to the Midwest Japanese American farmers flourished. By 1942, farms worked by Japanese immigrants were producing 40 percent of all produce consumed in America. For the Issei, the promise of a bright future in their adopted country was becoming a reality. As a group, they told their children to always honor their family and take great pride in being a citizen of the United States of America. The Issei believed that America gave their families great opportunities for success. Sadly, following the bombing of Pearl Harbor in December 1941 and the signing of Executive Order 9066 in February 1942, their lives were forever changed. EO 9066 resulted in the forced removal of over 125,000 individuals of Japanese heritage from their homes, who were then placed in concentration camps in desolate areas of America. EO 9066 was issued under the false claim of military necessity. However, many historians have established that it was driven by economics, racial animus, and xenophobia.

A significant fact is that two-thirds of the individuals incarcerated in the concentration camps were children and young adults who were born in this country. They were US citizens entitled to the rights, privileges, and protections afforded in the Constitution for all Americans. Sadly, the government failed these individuals. Another tragic fact is that while they were incarcerated behind barbed wire in the concentration camps, children and young adults were required to recite the Pledge of Allegiance every day in school. The pledge ends with the phase, "with liberty and justice for all." Many survivors of the concentration camps told me that the memory of saying the pledge haunted them their entire lives. As the survivors grew older, each and every time they said or heard the pledge, they were reminded of life behind barbed wire.

Despite the gross injustice of their forced removal and incarceration, many Issei still felt the need to prove their loyalty to the United States. When the opportunity arose, they encouraged their children to enlist in the armed services to demonstrate this loyalty. In time, over 33,000 Nisei (second-generation) men enlisted in the armed forces and fought in the Europe and Pacific campaigns.

I found Ben Kuroki's story to be extremely interesting because it was similar to but different from that of other Nisei men who fought during World War II. First, he grew up in Nebraska, and his family didn't suffer the injustice of losing their land, forced relocation, and incarceration experienced by so many other people of Japanese descent. Second, he started his military career in January 1942 prior to the signing of Executive Order 9066. The similarity was the racism and hatred he had to endure following the bombing of Pearl Harbor. As one of the few Japanese Americans in the Air Force, his ethnicity and questions regarding his loyalty to the United States were constantly highlighted. The majority of Nisei men who enlisted from the camps were assigned to the 100th Infantry Battalion and 442nd Regimental Combat Team. Both were segregated units comprising Japanese Americans who shared a common mission and bond. These men also suffered racism and hatred but found strength with their fellow Nisei soldiers.

A common theme among all Nisei soldiers was their Issei parents telling them to honor family by demonstrating their loyalty to the United States. This became their focus throughout their military careers. Most Japanese Americans can speak to the impact parental influence and family obligation had on their lives. The concept "honor your family" is truly the core of our existence.

Ben Kuroki and many others shared the belief that military service was the only way to prove that Japanese Americans were loyal to this country. As stated in this book, Kuroki truly believed that his "debt to the United States is greater than that of most of these other fellows."

I truly respect Ben Kuroki's actions as a member of the 93rd Bomb Group in Europe. This book tells the horrors of combat through his amazing bravery and dogged determination to prove his loyalty to the United States. It also describes the constant and pervasive racism Kuroki had to endure from other airmen. To complete thirty bombing missions in Europe is truly extraordinary. However, his decision to volunteer for bombing missions over Japan took his determination to a different level. I recognize that this decision was driven by his intense desire to demonstrate his loyalty. However, even the Issei who told their sons to enlist in the armed services had trouble with Ben Kuroki's participation in the bombing raids over Japan. The firebombing of cities throughout Japan targeted more than just military targets. The damage to nonmilitary entities and the injury of and death toll on civilians were devastating. The firebombing and subsequent use of the atomic bombs are very difficult for me to accept. I understand the premise that both hastened the end of the war, but the excessiveness and devastation were extremely tragic.

My father and one uncle were in the 442nd Regimental Combat Team and one uncle was in the Military Intelligence Service (MIS). Each one of them was a decorated veteran. To this day, the 442nd Regimental Combat Team remains the most highly decorated combat unit for its size and length of service in the history of the US military.

I asked my father and uncles why they fought for a country that took so much from our family and community. For context, my grandfather was one of the most prominent members of the Japanese American community.

Following the bombing of Pearl Harbor, he was arrested and charged—but never tried—as a war criminal. The US government took everything from our family. My father and uncles told me that they fought for their families' honor and to prove that they were loyal Americans. At the same time, they shared their anger at what was done to their families and community.

Another uncle was a proud dissident who refused to sign the infamous loyalty oath and became a "no-no boy." He refused to enlist in the military and protested because he strongly believed that what happened to the Japanese American community was unjust and a violation of every community member's civil rights. My family and uncle who stood up against the injustice were incarcerated at the Heart Mountain concentration camp located in a desolate area of Wyoming. This book has a segment that describes the hostility Ben Kuroki experienced when he visited Heart Mountain on a recruitment visit. It's possible that the dissidents who confronted him included my uncle and other family members. Prior to the war, my uncle was pursuing a degree at the University of Southern California. Due to his actions during the war, he wasn't allowed to finish his degree at USC.

There are thousands of stories of immense courage and bravery from the Japanese American community during World War II. This includes the many who were incarcerated in the concentration camps, the military veterans, and the dissenters. Each one proudly demonstrated the strength, resilience, and honor of our community.

Like many Sansei (third-generation) and Yonsei (fourth-generation) children, I owe my life and career to the strength of the Issei and the bravery of the Nisei—both those who fought in the armed forces and those who stood against the injustice to our community. The opportunities and successes that I've enjoyed in my life would not have been possible without the actions and sacrifices of those who came before me.

Ben Kuroki's life was both meaningful and impactful not only for the Japanese American community but for all Americans. His story deserves our profound admiration and respect. He truly was an exceptional person who addressed racism and hate with exceptional feats of bravery and honor. Thank you, Ben Kuroki.

William Fujioka is the chair of the Japanese American National Museum's board of trustees. He spent forty-four years in public service and was the first person of color to be appointed both as the city administrative officer of the City of Los Angeles and as the chief executive officer of the County of Los Angeles.

PROLOGUE

After a long and restless night, the Nebraska farm boy nervously made his way to the San Francisco hotel ballroom for his latest test of courage. In the twenty-six months since the Japanese attack on Pearl Harbor, twenty-six-year-old Ben Kuroki had faced death on countless occasions. He had survived thirty B-24 bombing missions in Europe and North Africa, including America's first attack on Rome and the suicidal smokestack-level raid on Adolf Hitler's Romanian oil fields at Ploiesti. He had survived an encounter with Moorish brigands, three months of Spanish captivity, and a failed escape attempt that ended with bullets whizzing around him. On his final raid in Europe, a German shell shattered his Plexiglas gun turret and barely missed his head. He had returned to America the first Japanese American war hero, and now he hoped to top that feat by becoming the first Japanese American airman to bomb Japan.

For all his good fortune to date, Ben's time in the army had been steeped in struggle and despair—the result of bigotry and racial discrimination that had confronted him from his first days in uniform. One of ten children born to Japanese immigrants, Ben was a high school graduate who seemed destined to spend the rest of his life growing potatoes and sugar beets with his father and brothers and trucking fresh produce back and forth to Omaha and the Rio Grande Valley. But the events of December 7, 1941, changed everything.

Nothing in his life had prepared Ben for the vitriol and suspicion that awaited him in the post–Pearl Harbor world beyond his remote corner of western Nebraska. Life was hard for the Kuroki children, but it was largely free of the prejudice and racial hatred that Shosuke and Naka Kuroki had encountered as Asian immigrants more than thirty-five years earlier. At tiny Hershey High School, Ben had been the popular vice president of his graduating class of fourteen students.[1] But after joining the Army Air Forces, he quietly cried himself to sleep some nights because of the racial epithets and ostracism that were staples of his daily life. When peers were given a crack at a bomber crew assignment, Ben was given weeks of kitchen duty and other menial tasks.

He endured it all. Even after he was assigned to a newly formed B-24 group that was being rushed through training to join the air campaign ramping up in Europe, he seemed destined to spend the rest of the war as a clerk. Twice before overseas deployment, a pair of bigoted sergeants plotted to leave Ben behind. Twice fair-minded white officers granted him a reprieve.

From the moment he set foot in Britain in early September 1942, Ben felt a new sense of acceptance. Within weeks, he had talked his way into gunnery training, and then onto a B-24 crew. Given the chance to fight, he distinguished himself as an aerial gunner. On his first combat mission, a crewmate suffered a near-fatal head wound only a few feet from him. Later that night, Ben accepted that he probably wasn't going to survive his tour.

Day after day, he conquered his fears to fly missions. He witnessed the death of good men and the disintegration of comrades shattered by combat stress. In December 1943, he returned home a decorated hero, celebrated in newspaper stories and radio interviews. Surely, he had done enough to silence the bigots who questioned his loyalty to America, or so he thought.

Ben spent the first weeks of 1944 at an Army Air Forces rest center in Southern California, awaiting his next assignment. In late January, he was scheduled to be interviewed by movie star Ginny Simms on her national NBC Radio show in Hollywood, only to be told at the last minute that he couldn't do it. It was too controversial to highlight the war record of a Japanese American, especially in California, War Department and NBC officials said.

Two days later, things took an even worse turn for Ben when stories about the Japanese maltreatment of American and Filipino prisoners of war appeared in newspapers across the country. Opportunistic politicians demanded that more than one hundred thousand West Coast residents of Japanese descent currently confined in interior camps be held for the duration of the war.

Against the backdrop of resurgent anti-Japanese hatred in America, Ben headed north to San Francisco. Before the atrocity stories broke, he had agreed to address the prestigious Commonwealth Club, one of San Francisco's most venerable institutions. Ben had planned to use the speech as a platform to speak out against continued anti-Japanese bigotry on the home front, but now he wasn't sure if he should raise this issue or even cancel the speech.

After a restless night, Ben slipped into his bemedaled dress uniform on the morning of February 4, 1944, and made his way to the ornate Gold Ballroom for the midday meeting of the Commonwealth Club. The hall was packed with more than seven hundred leading citizens. In the front row sat the bespectacled steel tycoon Henry Kaiser, Sr., whose seven huge shipyards on the West Coast had played a pivotal role in the previous year's military turnaround for Allied forces. Scattered throughout the audience were some of the country's most prominent politicians, entrepreneurs, educators, writers, artists, and journalists. Only one invited guest was a woman: the acclaimed photographer Dorothea Lange, who had documented the despair of Californians of Japanese descent as they were rounded up and herded into camps two years earlier.

After introductions were made, Ben stepped uncertainly to the microphone. Gazing out at the sea of strangers, he was sure he saw hate and hostility in their eyes. Panic welled in his gut. *What do they see? The face of the Bataan atrocities?* His voice shaking, he began to speak. "I'm a farm boy from Nebraska and I can't speak for all GIs, but I can speak for myself," he said.

There were no boos or catcalls, as he had feared. The audience hung on his every word. Faces he'd imagined as masks of hate now exuded warmth and empathy. Gaining command of the crowd and confidence with every word, Ben Kuroki began to tell his remarkable story—a saga of patriotism, courage, teamwork, and tolerance. A saga that was far from finished.

Chapter 1

FIT FOR SERVICE

Ben Kuroki gripped the wheel of the old truck as it rolled along the gravel road that connected the family's farm to the busy Lincoln Highway a mile-and-a-quarter to the south. It was Sunday morning, December 7, 1941, and he was headed into the town of North Platte for the sort of meeting he didn't usually attend. Twenty-four years of age, Ben had spent most of his life on the farm the family leased from a white landowner in the nearby village of Hershey. A federal law prevented Ben's parents, both immigrants from Japan, from becoming US citizens; a state law prevented them from owning land in Nebraska. That was the case in most farming states in the West, which had adopted "alien land laws" to prevent people who looked like Shosuke Kuroki from owning land.

As onerous as Nebraska's 1921 Alien Land Law could be, life in the Cornhusker state was better than what Sam—as a Swedish neighbor had begun calling Shosuke—had experienced in some of his previous stops, in California and Wyoming. Farming was hard work, but he loved it. It had gotten him away from the gambling habit he had developed in Wyoming, where he mined coal for the Union Pacific Railroad for a few years and maintained the company's rail lines in Wyoming and Nebraska, in all sorts of weather.[1]

Ben didn't share his father's love of farm life. In fact, Ben found a way to escape it. After graduating from Hershey High School in 1936, he saved some money from odd jobs and selling the pelts of skunks and raccoons he trapped. Ben and a partner bought a tractor-trailer rig for hauling produce. For about three years, they had been driving over to Omaha and down to the Rio Grande Valley in Texas, delivering Sam's potatoes and vegetables or the produce of other local farmers and returning with fruits or vegetables in season at their delivery point.

The meeting that Ben was headed to this morning wasn't about farming. A fellow from an organization that Ben didn't know much about—the Japanese American Citizens League—was in North Platte trying to organize the several dozen residents of Japanese ancestry to form their own chapter. Ben wasn't sure why, but he had agreed to listen to the fellow who had traveled from California by train. Ben didn't have deep feelings about his Japanese ancestry, but he would get to see old friends and learn more about the conflict between America and Japan that newspapers and radio newscasts were screaming about these days.

On either side of the gravel road lay fields where much of Ben's life had played out—irrigated expanses that in recent months had yielded bountiful harvests of potatoes, sugar beets, cabbages, and tomatoes. The Kuroki family was well-known in these parts for the size and quality of their fresh produce. They lived in a ramshackle one-story farmhouse just off the road, on the land they leased.

Ben had grown up in poverty, the sixth of ten children born to Sam and Naka Kuroki. His parents had emigrated separately to America in the century's first decade, and they had married in Wyoming in 1907, shortly after Naka's arrival. Steady work with the Union Pacific Railroad took Sam from California to Wyoming, where he hoped to realize his American dream. The newlyweds made their first home in Cheyenne, where Sam was a coal mine laborer, according to the 1910 federal census. The couple had taken on a boarder to supplement Sam's income. In Cheyenne, Naka gave birth to a son named Ichiro, who adopted the name of George, and a daughter named Fuji.

Around 1911, the family moved deeper into the Wyoming interior, to Hanna, where Union Pacific had its biggest coal mine. The work was no doubt a grueling adjustment for Sam, who had made a living selling silk sashes back in Japan, according to family lore. His coal-mining work was as dangerous as it was physically exhausting, with mine shafts subject to periodic explosions and cave-ins. Sam quit the mines around 1914 to act on his dream. As with the Wyoming move, the seeds had been planted by Sam's work for the Union Pacific Railroad. He had first laid eyes on the Platte River Valley's lush farmland during a stint with a railroad line crew, and it was there that Sam Kuroki hoped to raise his growing family in bucolic bliss.

FARMING WASN'T AS DANGEROUS as coal mining, but, as Sam discovered, it wasn't without perils. Gyrating prices, fickle markets, financial upheaval, assorted natural disasters such as wind- and hailstorms and droughts—these all became perilous forces for the Kuroki family on that plot of leased land near the town of North Platte. Naka had given birth to another two daughters, Shizuye (Cecile) and Yoshie (Wilma), and another boy, Atsushi (Henry), by the time that Ben entered the world on May 16, 1917.

By then the family was living outside of Gothenburg, an old Pony Express stop on the Platte River, about thirty miles downstream from North Platte. Sam kept moving the family farther west, following the river upstream, until finally the Kurokis put down roots a mile south of the North Platte River outside the village of Hershey. After delivering Ben, Naka gave birth to another three children in quick succession: Shitoshi (Fred), in 1919; Fusae (Beatrice) in 1921; and Minoru (William) in 1923. In 1926, a frail and exhausted Naka gave birth to her tenth child in eighteen years, a daughter they named Rose Marie (sometimes recorded as Rosemary in documents). Ben had been the first Kuroki child to not have a Japanese name; Rosie, as she was known, was the second.

The same year of Rosie's birth, the family marked another milestone when the oldest child, Ichiro—now known as George—graduated from tiny Hershey High School and entered the University of Nebraska in Lincoln. A fast runner, George held the South Platte Valley track record for the mile race for several years after his graduation, and he continued to compete for the Nebraska Cornhuskers track team. A sports columnist writing in the *Sunday Nebraska State Journal* newspaper in Lincoln once noted his admirable work ethic, but only after introducing him as "George Kuroki, a Jap from Hershey." The columnist had used what was then common shorthand for the word "Japanese"; Ben would grow to hate the word long before it was deemed an ethnic slur and retired from common usage.[2]

By the waning months of 1929, Sam Kuroki had earned a reputation in Lincoln County as a skilled and industrious farmer. At the same time, the Kuroki children were doing well in school, their lives largely integrated with those of their white classmates. There were one or two other Japanese families with children in the Hershey school and a few Mexican families, whose men worked as laborers on the local farms. George was in his third year at the University of Nebraska and the other children were scattered through the classes of the two-story Hershey school. Ninth-grader Atsushi—who now went by Henry—had brought great honor to his parents in the summer just passed by winning a medal for his essay on "Americanism" and for earning a spot on the American Legion junior baseball team. There was much to celebrate for Sam and Naka.

IN MANY WAYS, BEN'S CHILDHOOD was even more challenging than that of his siblings. Naka was so weak after giving birth to him that an extraordinary neighbor from a nearby farm became Ben's primary caregiver for weeks.[3]

A sweet, even-tempered baby who rarely cried, in that neighbor's recollection, Ben became a painfully shy child. His adjustment to school after the family's move to Hershey was traumatic. Ben was in the second grade when he first walked into the two-story building in Hershey that housed the classrooms for grades one through twelve. Ben was overwhelmed by the experience. When called on to answer a question in class, he would rise to his feet and stand mutely until classmates tittered and the teacher allowed him to sit.

The work that Ben and his siblings shouldered on the farm, like shoveling manure from the barn or digging potatoes, was drudgery. But as Ben grew in size and maturity and was entrusted with more demanding tasks, he developed confidence and self-assurance. By the time he was twelve, Ben was largely exempt from the menial farm chores that fell to the younger children; his developing physical strength allowed him to join the older boys and their father in the exhausting task of sacking, storing, or loading potatoes. By the time he was fourteen, Ben could handle a one-hundred-pound sack of potatoes with ease.[4]

Ben entered high school as the country sank into the despair of the Great Depression. It was during those years that his paralyzing childhood shyness became a distant memory and his personality fully emerged. He was humble, earnest, and soft-spoken in manner, but he also smiled easily and was warm and friendly. He had developed close friendships, a sense of humor, and a penchant for pranks—some of them bordering on obnoxious. He was a member of the basketball, baseball, and track teams, but he was an unexceptional athlete. By his junior year, he found that he enjoyed writing and he worked on the school's first yearbook. He also wrote the junior class "School Notes" column for the local newspaper.

Over several years, Ben had developed a close friendship with the most popular boy in his small Hershey High School class. From the time they were old enough to hold a shotgun, Ben and Gordon Jorgenson, or Gordy as he preferred, hunted ducks and pheasants together along the North Platte River. On one of their winter hunts, Ben crawled out on an ice sheet to retrieve some ducks they had brought down, only for the ice to give way. As Ben struggled for his life in the freezing water, Gordy extended the butt of his shotgun close enough for Ben to grab. He pulled Ben to safety and then built a fire to thaw him out.

By his senior year, Ben's status had risen such that he was elected the vice president of his fourteen-member graduating class; Gordy, to no one's surprise, was president. When he graduated from high school in 1936, Ben didn't have the money or inclination to attend college. He didn't know what he wanted to do with his life, except that he didn't want to spend it growing potatoes, sugar beets, and cabbages. Without any immediate alternatives, Ben worked on the farm and trapped fur-bearing animals along the North

Platte River to earn some money. He had learned to drive the family's old Chevrolet truck, and that nurtured an idea that he pitched to his father: He would buy a tractor-trailer rig with his trapping money and transport the family crops and those of other area farmers to markets in Omaha and beyond. Sam gave his blessing.

The life of a long-haul trucker turned out to be tougher than Ben had imagined. On his first trip in November 1938, Ben rolled out of Hershey with a load of his father's cabbages, bound for Omaha, 275 miles to the east. Ben and his partner made it into the city without incident, but then disaster struck. Ben's friend was at the wheel when a car ran a red light on a busy city street, forcing him to swerve to avoid hitting the vehicle broadside. The trailer tipped over, spilling nine tons of cabbages around a major Omaha intersection. The accident, written up in the Omaha newspaper and spread around the state in an Associated Press dispatch, foreshadowed further mishaps to come. Running on cheap tires, Ben had frequent blowouts. On another trip, Ben's partner fell asleep at the wheel, ran off the road, and tipped the trailer yet again; Ben smashed into the windshield and was lucky to walk away with only cuts and bruises.

With their truck out of commission, Ben and his partner borrowed money to buy another. They began venturing farther and farther from Hershey, making runs into Oklahoma and then Texas. In February 1940, Ben drove to south Texas to bring a load of fruit and vegetables back to wintry Nebraska to sell. With another year of driving under his belt, he repeated the Texas trip again in February 1941, dropping off a load of his father's potatoes in Oklahoma City before continuing to the Rio Grande Valley to fill his trailer with fresh citrus and vegetables.

Ben was helping his family with his trucking venture and had broadened his horizons beyond Nebraska, but there was a sense that life was leaving him behind. His five older siblings were set in their paths. His oldest brother, George, had been forced to drop out of the University of Nebraska and take over the farm when Sam suffered a heart attack; Ben's second brother, Henry, had earned his business degree at the University of Nebraska; four of Ben's sisters—Fuji, Cecile, Wilma, who were older than Ben, and his younger sister Beatrice—had found various jobs in Chicago. Ben's friend Gordy Jorgenson had married one of their Hershey High School classmates in January 1941 and now owned a Hershey service station; he and his wife were expecting their first child.

As Ben scratched out a living and contemplated his future, events far beyond America's shores suddenly loomed as a wild card. On September 16, 1940, in response to Hitler's conquest of much of Europe and Japan's expansionist activities in the Pacific, President Franklin Roosevelt implemented the first peacetime draft in US history. The Selective Training and Service Act of 1940 required men between the ages of twenty-one and forty-five to register for the draft and to serve at least one year in the armed forces if summoned.

In mid-November 1941, Ben received a letter from the army, ordering him to report for his physical examination—the final step prior to his induction for active military service. On November 19, 1941, eight days before Thanksgiving, Ben underwent his physical exam at an army facility in Grand Island, Nebraska. He was rated fit for service. Five years out of high school, unmarried, scraping out a meager living, Ben checked the mail each day for his army summons.

BEN REACHED THE PAVED LINCOLN HIGHWAY—US 30—and turned east. The road passed through flat farmland as the Platte River's north and south forks gradually converged. Approaching the western outskirts of the town, Ben came abreast of the five-mile-long Union Pacific rail switching yards that had put North Platte on the map. At the eastern edge of the switching yards, the highway suddenly curved at a forty-five-degree angle to the right. Off to the left a traveler might just catch a glimpse of the Second Empire–style mansion and ranch that had belonged to the Union Pacific's legendary hunter, William "Buffalo Bill" Cody. Ben slowed, made a right turn, crossed the railroad tracks, and entered downtown North Platte.

With a population of about twelve thousand, North Platte had been the "big city" for the Kuroki children growing up. Its two-story buildings seemed enormous and its maze of streets overwhelming to Ben and his younger siblings, Fred, Beatrice, Billie, and Rosie. On his initial trip into North Platte, Ben had seen a movie for the first time. His father had brought Ben and his two younger brothers with him when he had some business to handle in town, and he had bought movie tickets for Ben, Fred, and Billie so he would know where to find the boys when he was done. The movie was *All Quiet on the Western Front*, the screen adaptation of German writer Erich Maria Remarque's celebrated antiwar novel set in the shell-scarred trenches of Europe's Western Front during World War I.

Ben and his brothers found the war scenes scary, and during a climactic artillery barrage on the screen a thunderstorm hit North Platte. Inside the theater, the thunder of the shells blasting from the speakers was punctuated by hail stones pelting the roof above the terrified boys. Overcome by fear, Ben and his brothers bolted from the theater into the rain. Now, a decade after that searing experience, Ben faced the growing prospect of fighting in a real war.

Turning onto West 4th Street, Ben parked outside the Episcopal Church of Our Savior and made his way to the basement auditorium. Several dozen Japanese immigrants—Issei, they were called—and first-generation Japanese Americans—Nisei—began to fill the room. The meeting got underway around eleven o'clock.

At that moment, some thirty-six hundred miles to the west, it was six-thirty in the morning in Honolulu and day was breaking over the Hawaiian Islands.[5] A few minutes earlier, six aircraft carriers of the Japanese Imperial Navy, steaming two hundred miles from Oahu, had turned into the wind and launched a wave of fighter-bombers. As Ben and his friends settled into their seats in the church basement to hear a speaker talk about how the tensions between the United States and Japan might affect their lives, 183 Japanese military aircraft were about one hundred miles from the US Navy's base at Pearl Harbor and closing fast.

Chapter 2

"THIS IS URGENT"

A dapper dresser and a debonair ladies' man who loved to hear himself talk, Mike Masaoka had learned to command a room as a championship debater in high school and college back in Utah. The confidence he gained from years of success in pressure-filled competitions was evident as he addressed the fifty or so Japanese American farmers, agricultural laborers, and merchants on hand to hear him speak in the North Platte church basement on Sunday morning, December 7, 1941.

The gathering in the basement meeting hall of the Episcopal Church of Our Savior was the final stop of Masaoka's whirlwind tour of the Great Plains hinterlands in his role as national executive secretary of the Japanese American Citizens League (JACL). If everything went according to plan, he would wrap up his business in North Platte that afternoon, then catch a train for San Francisco, his home base these days.

The twenty-six-year-old Masaoka had departed California in late November with two goals: to assure local government officials in Colorado, Wyoming, and Nebraska that the people of Japanese descent in their areas were loyal and patriotic Americans, and to establish new JACL chapters to defend the interests of the region's Japanese American communities if the worst-case scenario became a reality. That scenario was war between the United States and Japan, which the Sunday morning newspapers suggested might be imminent after months of contentious negotiations.

Masaoka remained skeptical that the country of his birth would end up in a war with the country of his parents' birth, and he conveyed that sentiment to his audience. But even if the odds of war were remote, he said, it would be to the advantage of audience members to form local JACL chapters to defend their economic interests and civil rights. He explained how the JACL was cultivating relationships with government officials around the country to reassure authorities that people of Japanese ancestry would be loyal to America should there be a war with Japan.

He spoke with authority, and with his dark business suit, white shirt, necktie, and thick shock of wavy black hair, he looked the part of someone who knew what he was talking about. He prominently displayed a Stars and Stripes flag pin on the left lapel of his jacket to leave no doubt of his loyalties. For a Japanese American in the public eye, such a statement had become increasingly important as America's relations with Japan deteriorated.

In his comments in the North Platte basement, Masaoka was upbeat about the crisis, but there were things that he couldn't share with his audience. Like the fact that representatives of various federal government agencies and entities had summoned him to furtive meetings in recent weeks.

MASAOKA HAD BEEN SPEAKING about ninety minutes, pointing occasionally to a wall map to highlight locations where he hoped audience members would help form new JACL chapters, when two white men entered the room and approached the podium.

Masaoka was puzzled. He asked the men what they wanted.

"Are you Mike Masaoka?" one of the men asked.

"Yes," he impatiently replied.

"Would you mind coming outside with us for a minute?"[1]

Masaoka assumed the men were local newspaper reporters who wanted an interview, and their lack of manners irritated him. He asked them to wait outside until he was finished.

"This is urgent," one of the men replied. "I'm afraid it can't wait."

Without another word, the two men took Masaoka by each arm and escorted him from the meeting hall.

Puzzled, Ben and others filed upstairs and wandered out into the street to see if there was an explanation for Masaoka's abduction. That's when they heard the news. As Ben later recalled, "We went outside of the church building and heard the radio reports and said, 'My God, Pearl Harbor [has] been bombed by the Japanese.'"[2]

Chapter 3

"THIS IS YOUR COUNTRY"

Ben awakened to the most important decision of his life.

The shock of the radio reports announcing the Japanese attack on Pearl Harbor had raised questions that haunted him throughout that terrible day. How could he prove his patriotism to friends and neighbors? What could he do to dispel any suggestion that he felt a kinship with the Japanese airmen who carried out the Pearl Harbor attack? Should he enlist? He had passed his army physical eighteen days earlier and his induction notice might arrive any day, so he could wait for the army to act. Or he could take matters into his own hands. After all, the Marine Corps and the navy both had recruiting stations in North Platte.

He thought about this incessantly in the hours after racing home from the aborted meeting in North Platte's Church of Our Savior. The more he thought about it, the worse he felt. His parents had always taught him to never do anything that might bring shame on his family. Now, for the first time in his life, Ben felt shame because of his Japanese heritage. He was appalled by what he viewed as a dishonorable attack. On some level, he felt complicit because of his shared ancestry with the men who had bombed Pearl Harbor.

Whatever he felt or believed, he couldn't act without his father's permission.

Sam Kuroki had been in America for thirty-seven years, and yet he had never risen above second-class status because of his ancestry. Sam and Naka were painfully aware that America hadn't fully embraced them. And yet, they had embraced America without reservation, and that included teaching their children to celebrate the flag and their American citizenship.

When Ben asked his father what he should do, Sam didn't hesitate. "This is your country," Sam said. "Go ahead and fight for it."[1]

ONLY MINUTES AFTER THE FIRST Japanese bombs and torpedoes smashed into their targets at Pearl Harbor and Hickam Field, Americans of Japanese descent found themselves in the crosshairs of an ugly backlash. The FBI had spent months preparing a list of potentially "dangerous" or "disloyal" Japanese and Japanese Americans, and the agency's all-powerful director, J. Edgar Hoover, ordered his agents to start the roundup. Nationwide, more than seven hundred people of Japanese ancestry were arrested in the twenty-four hours following the Pearl Harbor attack.[2]

Fears of sabotage and spying by Japanese in America prompted authorities to post armed guards at defense plants, utilities, and bridges. The initial surge of fear intensified after false alarms of Japanese aircraft flying over West Coast cities, and saboteurs and spies on the ground. There were breathless stories about Japanese farm workers in Hawaii who supposedly had cut giant arrows in sugarcane fields to direct the strike force to Pearl Harbor and dockworkers and vegetable vendors who provided information on the location of American warships. Unconfirmed reports of Japanese spies and saboteurs photographing defense plants, utilities, and other key installations led the Justice Department to issue an order requiring all people of Japanese descent in America to turn in their radios and cameras to local police. Another Justice Department order froze the bank accounts of all people of Japanese descent.

In Nebraska, Ben had witnessed the opening moments of the government crackdown when Mike Masaoka was taken into custody and led from the North Platte church basement.

An even more shocking development occurred at the church later that Sunday. The beloved Reverend Hiram Hisanori Kano, who had helped arrange Masaoka's meeting in North Platte, emerged from the Church of Our Savior following an afternoon service and was arrested. Because his father was a prominent political figure in Japan, Kano was on a secret FBI list of potentially dangerous Japanese immigrants marked for arrest and confinement. On Monday morning, December 8, he was driven to Omaha and placed in FBI custody, and from there he was shipped to an internment camp in Louisiana. Kano would spend the next two years in government camps under armed guard.

The Kuroki family had experienced only sporadic incidents of bigotry in their decades in Nebraska, but a foul mood now swept the state. There were about 500 people of Japanese ancestry in Nebraska at the time, 400 of whom resided in the Platte River Valley. Among those 500, some 157 were immigrants and thus barred from citizenship, while 323, including Ben and his siblings, held birthright citizenship.[3]

In an incident illustrative of the vengeful mood of those days, several Nebraska newspapers published on their front page an Associated Press dispatch about an Omaha businessman who had offered a bounty to the first American aviator to bomb Tokyo—one of scores of such offers around the country. The article quoted the businessman, Rex J. Olson, as saying he would gladly reward that pioneering aviator with a $100 defense savings bond "provided he gets at least one dirty back-stabbing Jap."[4]

In the months ahead, the anti-Japanese backlash would result in the expulsion of tens of thousands of people of Japanese ancestry from the entirety of California and parts of Oregon, Washington, and Arizona. In Nebraska, the Kuroki family and other residents of Japanese ancestry would be allowed to remain in their homes, but only after being treated like the enemy spies and saboteurs that many believed them to be. They were fingerprinted and documented by agents of the Alien Registration Division. Their radios, cameras, and guns were seized, and travel was limited to a fifty-mile radius. Some Japanese residents buried or burned family heirlooms or Japanese-language letters they had received from loved ones in Japan for fear of raising suspicions if they were discovered by law enforcement authorities.[5]

In his quest to serve his country, Ben wouldn't be shielded from the prejudice and bigotry directed at American civilians of Japanese descent.

AT THE MARINE CORPS RECRUITING Station in North Platte, Ben and Fred presented themselves to the noncommissioned officer in charge. His name was Sergeant Williams, and he didn't know what to do with the two young Japanese American men. Williams told them to come back in a few days when the situation regarding the service of Japanese Americans was clearer, and sent them on their way. "All our friends in Hershey were all going in right and left, into the service, and we knew we were getting the runaround," Ben later recalled.[6]

When a day passed without word from the Marine recruiter, Ben forced the issue. He heard something on the radio about the Army Air Forces accepting recruits in the town of Grand Island, on the Platte River about 150 miles downstream. Ben got the recruiter on the phone and asked if his nationality would be a problem.

"Heck, no!" the recruiter replied. "I get two bucks for everybody I sign up."[7]

On Wednesday, December 10, Ben and Fred drove to the army's Grand Island recruiting station. The first radio bulletins announcing the Pearl Harbor attack had within minutes inundated Sergeant John Cook with a flood of applicants. He had to turn some away, including several grizzled World War I veterans; most of the men were already registered with Selective Service, and so he couldn't accept them without permission from their local board.

The two Japanese American brothers presented a thornier problem.

Sergeant Cook had told Ben to come on down, but he backtracked when the brothers presented themselves. Now Sergeant Cook told the Japanese American men that he needed to ask his superiors if he could accept their applications. The brothers drove back home to wait.

The following afternoon, Sergeant Cook notified Ben that his superiors had given him permission to accept the brothers for enlistment in the US Army Air Forces if they were willing to make the drive again. On Monday, December 15, Ben and Fred presented themselves at the Grand Island recruiting station for the second time. This time Sergeant Cook arranged for a local news photographer to be on hand to document the enlistment of the Japanese American brothers. As Ben and Fred pledged allegiance to the Stars and Stripes, the photographer snapped away. The image was published in several Nebraska newspapers.[8]

The Kuroki brothers had taken their army oath, but they again found themselves in limbo as they awaited orders for formal induction into the service. While they waited, anti-Japanese hysteria intensified across the country. Nearly every daily newspaper reported new arrests or allegations of Japanese spying or sabotage. On December 23, the *North Platte Telegraph* printed an Associated Press dispatch about a thirty-five-year-old Japanese man arrested in Scottsbluff, Nebraska, after he was unable to produce a passport when stopped by police. Under questioning, the man reportedly admitted that he had registered for Selective Service under a different name, compounding his problems.[9]

Far worse was the article that appeared in newspapers around the country in the final week of December. Written by correspondent Wallace Carroll of the United Press news service, the article opened with a sensational accusation: "A fifth column and espionage network, patiently organized over many years, paved the way for Japan's surprise blow at Pearl Harbor."[10] The article levied one unsubstantiated allegation after another to rationalize the lack of preparedness by American forces in Hawaii. Carroll asserted that in a recent reporting trip to Hawaii he had learned that "big arrows, pointing to military objectives, were reported to have been cut in the sugar cane on plantations in the islands a few hours before the Japanese struck." A local Japanese businessman had been arrested "for allegedly operating a short-wave transmitter during the Pearl Harbor attack," he claimed, and "Japanese vegetable dealers had an uncanny knack of knowing about movements in and out of port of units of the American navy because they delivered their produce to the ships."[11]

The article continued in that wildly speculative vein. Advertisements in local newspapers "may have contained coded messages to the fifth columnists." Additionally, Japanese expatriates had infiltrated Hawaii utilities, the post office, and telephone service as "ideal posts for spies"; Japanese proprietors of "small stores, restaurants and cafes" in Hawaii were actually spies working under the direction of Japanese army intelligence; and "local fishermen and seamen who knew the Hawaiian seas and coasts, hotel proprietors and employees, servants in private families and fresh produce dealers" were actually part of an extensive spy network run by Japanese naval intelligence, Carroll claimed.[12]

None of the allegations would ever be confirmed, but the cumulative effect of such reports on President Roosevelt was profound. Military and political pressure mounted on Roosevelt to do something about the "Japanese problem" at home.[13]

Against that increasingly ugly backdrop, Ben and Fred received their induction orders in the final week of December. They were to report to Fort Francis E. Warren in Cheyenne, Wyoming. In an outdoor ceremony there on January 6, 1942, the brothers officially began their army careers. They had barely learned to salute and stand at attention when they received orders to report to Sheppard Field, Texas, for basic military training.

On the long train ride to Texas, proudly wearing their uniforms, the Kuroki brothers were stunned by the racially tinged epithets, hostile comments, and suspicious looks directed their way by other soldiers. As dispiriting as the journey was, it was only the beginning of the ordeal that awaited Ben and Fred Kuroki.

Chapter 4

ALONE

Ben arrived in Texas in the vanguard of a chaotic effort to build the mightiest air force the world had ever seen. It was a bold quest by the ambitious air chief, General Henry "Hap" Arnold, to elevate American airpower to the pinnacle of the US defense pyramid. From the beginning, the quest was plagued by shortages of nearly every essential element: planes, high-octane aviation fuel, spare parts, recruits, qualified instructors, mechanics, facilities.

Far removed from Hap Arnold's world, Ben confronted his own problems.

His experiences during his induction in Wyoming and the train journey to Texas had been a harbinger of the hostility that awaited the Kuroki brothers in the army. Growing up in rural Nebraska, the brothers had only rarely encountered the sort of prejudice and bigotry unleashed by the Pearl Harbor attack. Now gratuitous insults and epithets became constants in their lives.

Some of the bigots took their cue from the hysterical news coverage and incendiary public statements by politicians and government officials.

President Roosevelt fueled the rising backlash on January 5 when the government reclassified all draft-age Japanese American men from the draft-eligible 1-A status to the ineligible 4-C. The army followed suit by discharging most Japanese Americans already in uniform or stripping them of their weapons and shipping them to Camp Robinson, Arkansas, to perform menial chores. From Roosevelt down to petty bullies at the local level, an unmistakable message was conveyed to the country: Even the American-born children of Japanese immigrants couldn't be trusted.

It was against this ominous backdrop that the Kuroki brothers began their Army Air Forces basic training on eight hundred acres of recently converted ranchland north of Wichita Falls, Texas.

NAMED FOR US SENATOR MORRIS SHEPPARD, a recently deceased Texas politician best known for writing the constitutional amendment that produced Prohibition, Sheppard Field had been conceived as an aviation mechanics school. Those plans suddenly changed during the Roosevelt administration's urgent defense buildup in the face of Axis military aggression. When army brass dedicated the base in mid-October 1941, Sheppard Field held an expanded brief as an Army Air Forces basic training center. At the time of the Japanese attack on Pearl Harbor, the service had some twenty-one thousand recruits enrolled at Sheppard Field and two other basic training centers. By late January 1942, the Army Air Forces had inducted another nineteen thousand new recruits, and they were scrambling to find a place for them all.[1]

Although each center's commander could determine the day-to-day schedule of basic training at the beginning of 1942, the course followed a set template over three to four weeks. On arrival at a basic training center, recruits underwent four to six days of processing that oriented the men to military life. There were lectures and films on military courtesy, the Articles of War, sex hygiene, war bonds, and life insurance. Medical personnel blood-typed and immunized recruits. Other instructors schooled the recruits on care of clothing and equipment and the basics of military drill. Finally, and perhaps most importantly, the men underwent a series of classification tests and interviews aimed at matching a recruit's intelligence and talents to a specific Army Air Forces need. Many of the men would be sent to a technical school for additional training in specialties that ranged from clerical work to gunnery.[2]

As the training got underway, Ben and Fred found themselves subjected to derogatory comments about "sneaky Japs" or "dirty Japs" or boasts about killing "Japs" in combat. No one talked to them in the barracks. A room would fall silent when they made their entrance.

The brothers decided they might stand out less if they didn't hang around together. They limited their interaction to mail call, when they would huddle to compare news from home. Their sisters Wilma and Fuji wrote upbeat letters about their lives in Chicago, but a missive from their brother Henry plunged them into despair. Henry described being harassed because of his ancestry and rejected by the army when he tried to enlist. The brothers sometimes lay awake at night in their bunks, consumed by their misery and crying into their pillows.[3]

About two weeks into basic training, without warning, Fred was transferred into a ground unit to dig trenches and perform other menial labor. Ben was on his own.[4]

BEN EXPECTED TO BE BOOTED FROM the air service any day. Unlike his peers, he drew the dirtiest assignments for days on end. "I didn't dare complain because I knew they were going to kick me out as quick as they did my brother," Ben recalled.[5]

As miserable as he was, Ben didn't break. And then, almost miraculously, he completed basic training. Around the first of February 1942, Ben received orders for his next assignment: the Army Air Forces clerical school at Fort Logan, Colorado, eight miles southwest of Denver.

In Colorado, Ben's life improved. He was lying in his top bunk shortly after arrival when the fellow below him struck up a conversation. The airman's name was Al Kuhn. Born in Hackensack, New Jersey, Kuhn had grown up in Bergen County, across the Hudson River from New York City. They were the same age and same build, close in height and weight. Kuhn had a handsome face and warm personality. His outlook on life was summed up by his senior quote in his high school yearbook: "I have a heart with room for every joy." Kuhn's sunny disposition had served him well in his work selling insurance for Globe Indemnity Co.

As he chatted with Ben, Kuhn never asked about his ancestry; it didn't seem to matter to him. For Ben, this kindhearted soul became his first real friend in the military. Kuhn introduced Ben to another Bergen County boy and another airman they had befriended. They invited Ben to join them on their outings off the base.[6]

Slowly, Ben began to feel he belonged in the Army Air Forces.

As BEN MEMORIZED RULES, REGULATIONS, and statistics as part of his clerical training, the anti-Japanese hysteria reached a peak in America. Japanese victories in the Pacific prompted panicked politicians and civic leaders at home to call for the removal of everyone with Japanese blood from the West Coast. On February 19, President Roosevelt obliged the mob by signing Executive Order 9066, empowering the armed forces to remove anyone deemed a security threat.

As the events on the West Coast played out, Ben completed his clerical training.

He and Al Kuhn were in a group of forty newly minted Army Air Forces clerks ordered to report to Barksdale Field, outside Shreveport, Louisiana. Crossing from Texas into Louisiana near the end of their journey, they had a layover as they changed trains. Ben encountered a sign over a toilet door: *For White Only.*

At a moment when more than 110,000 people of Japanese descent were about to be forcibly removed from their homes and locked into camps, Ben began the next uncertain chapter of his military career in the shadow of Jim Crow.[7]

Chapter 5

"ARE YOU AN AMERICAN CITIZEN?"

In the spring of 1942, Barksdale Field emerged as a crucial staging ground for Hap Arnold's plan to create an air force to bomb Nazi Germany into submission. Local residents began to see the first indications of Barksdale's new role as a training center for heavy bomber crews in February. After years of watching pursuit planes and light bombers zip across their steamy skies, the northwest Louisiana residents suddenly began seeing big B-24 Liberators and the occasional B-17 Flying Fortress landing, taking off, and droning overhead.

Barksdale's transition to training the vanguard of the heavy bomber crews that would carry out the high-altitude campaign against Nazi Germany began with the arrival of two newly formed B-24 units, the 44th and 98th Bombardment Groups. On March 1, 1942, they were joined by the B-24 crews of the 93rd Bombardment Group and the B-17 Flying Fortress crews of the 92nd Bombardment Group.

Taking to the skies in 1935, the B-17 had captured the public imagination with a series of high-profile missions and goodwill flights that established the aircraft as a glamorous demonstration of American power. When the ungainly B-24 made its debut in December 1939, it was inevitable that airmen and the public at large would compare America's two heavy bombers. The curvaceous B-17 boasted a classic profile with a single tail and broad 103-foot wingspan. The twin-tailed Liberator introduced a state-of-the-art tapered wing that measured 110 feet tip-to-tip and looked too thin to support a bulky fuselage that reminded some observers of a pregnant cow. Both heavy bombers generated nearly the same horsepower from four engines, but the B-24 initially had an edge in cruising speed and range. Wartime modifications would gradually narrow the gap.[1]

Over the next four years, the Liberator would prove itself a versatile bomber, patrol aircraft, and transport. The Flying Fortress would garner more media coverage and, fairly or not, a better reputation for combat survivability, especially in the European Theater of Operations (ETO). But the intense press scrutiny—and the fierce rivalry that developed between B-17 and B-24 crews—still lay in the future as Ben and his contingent of freshly minted clerks arrived at Barksdale Field in early April 1942.

At first, the clerks found themselves in a strange state of stasis. The Army Air Forces was struggling to induct and place tens of thousands of new recruits, and it took a few days to figure out what to do with another batch of clerks. After a week, all the new clerks except for Ben and one other man had been assigned to operational groups.

While he awaited his orders, Ben enjoyed watching the big twin-tailed Liberators as their crews went about their training. He had never seen America's celebrated heavy bombers up close, and he was thrilled by their size and power. Some of the clerks in Ben's cohort had hitched joy rides on the bombers, but Ben feared being suspected of nefarious aims, so he kept his distance. "It was the first time I ever saw a B-24 in the air and, my God, I thought that was about the most impressive thing I could think of," Ben later recalled. "As much as I was impressed by seeing them in flight, I didn't dare to go near one because I was afraid somebody would think I was trying to sabotage it."[2]

Ben could imagine flying into combat in one of those big bombers, but as a clerk seen as untrustworthy because of his ancestry, he could only dream. Then, after weeks of peeling potatoes on kitchen duty, a miracle: Ben was assigned to a heavy bomber group designated for duty with a new strategic bombing force in the United Kingdom.[3]

Ben's new outfit was the 409th Squadron, one of four combat squadrons comprising the 93rd Bombardment Group (commonly shortened to the 93rd Bomb Group). The group had been officially formed on March 1 and assigned to fly B-24 Liberators. In the vision of AAF planners, the aircrew—whether a solo fighter pilot or a ten-member B-17 or B-24 crew—would form the basic unit of each squadron. A squadron could range in size from 200 to 500 men at full strength, and each heavy bomber group would eventually become a combat force of about 2,200 officers and enlisted men, or so Hap Arnold's air strategists envisioned.[4] But by April the 93rd Bomb Group still consisted of only a skeletal force limited to commissioned officers in support roles and a growing cadre of pilots. There were no navigators, bombardiers, or enlisted men to fill out a ten-member B-24 crew, and no timetable for when they might arrive.

When Ben reported to the squadron headquarters for duty, a sergeant barked at him.[5]

"Are you an American citizen?"

All eyes in the room fell on Ben.

"Yes," Ben replied.

Instead of the snide comment that Ben had braced for, the sergeant turned and disappeared into the commanding officer's office. When he emerged, the sergeant was all business: He assigned Ben and another man to a barracks and told them to report to a Sergeant Smathers in the Communications Section.[6] And with that, Ben was a member of the 409th Squadron—for the moment.

A few days passed while the sergeant tried to figure out what to do with two more clerks for whom he had no work. Ben and the other new guy were assigned to be "teletype operators," even though the squadron had no teletype machines. Ben and the other teletype operators sat around and shot the bull during their duty hours for several weeks.

April gave way to May and the news on the war front worsened. Besieged US and Filipino troops on the Bataan Peninsula in the Philippines surrendered to the Japanese on April 9. On May 6, the last American and Filipino holdouts on Corregidor—the supposedly impregnable island fortress guarding the mouth of Manila Bay—fell to the Japanese.

The week following the Corregidor news, the men of the 93rd got word to prepare to move. Ben was summoned to the office of the squadron commander. He was so nervous that he couldn't stand still. "You're being transferred out of this outfit, Kuroki," the squadron commander said. "The order just came from group headquarters."[7]

Ben's eyes blurred with tears. "Is it because of my nationality, sir?" he softly asked.

The squadron commander eyed Ben carefully. Sensing an opening, Ben recounted his unhappy military career to date and begged to remain with the 93rd. Having made his case, Ben returned to his barracks. He packed and awaited the signed orders that would dash his dreams.

The orders never arrived, thanks to the sympathetic squadron commander.[8] When the 93rd boarded a train for Fort Myers, Florida, on May 15, 1942, Ben was still part of the group.

Chapter 6

"IN NO SENSE READY FOR COMBAT"

The 93rd Bomb Group's expedited training schedule called for the men to spend six weeks honing their aerial combat skills at the army air base in Fort Myers, Florida, followed by a deployment to England in July. But only days after Ben and his comrades reached their destination, an alarming development forced Hap Arnold to scrap the timetable.

German U-boat attacks had been a vexing problem for President Roosevelt even before America's entry into the war. In 1940, as Roosevelt tried to keep Britain afloat with weapons and other materiel, German submarines threatened to cut Winston Churchill's North Atlantic lifeline. In the second half of 1940, U-boats sank nearly three hundred Allied ships in the waters surrounding the British Isles. Jubilant German submariners dubbed those months the "Happy Time."

Immediately following Nazi Germany's declaration of war on the United States on December 11, 1941, the supreme commander of the German Navy's submarine service, Admiral Karl Dönitz, set in motion a plan to attack Allied shipping off America's East Coast. US military commanders rebuffed British and Canadian advice to enforce a nighttime blackout in East Coast cities and to implement a convoy system for shipping. The results were devastating.

Night after night, German U-boats sank Allied merchant ships silhouetted against the lights of East Coast cities. From January 13, 1942, until the time of their first withdrawal from American waters for logistical reasons on February 6, U-boats sank 156,939 tons of shipping without the loss of a single submarine. A second wave of German submarines supported by refueling tankers arrived within weeks and inflicted even greater losses. German submariners now celebrated their rampage in American waters as the "Second Happy Time."

In May, US military commanders belatedly employed a convoy system for merchant shipping along the East Coast. In short order, convoy escorts sank seven U-boats, prompting Admiral Dönitz to shift his submarines to the Caribbean and the Gulf of Mexico. On May 12, as the 93rd prepared to conclude its training in Florida, the German submarine

H-507 torpedoed the tanker *Virginia* in the mouth of the Mississippi River below New Orleans, with the loss of twenty-six crewmen. German attacks in the Gulf of Mexico and the Caribbean escalated.

With U-boat attacks threatening to disrupt the flow of oil from Texas and Louisiana ports to East Coast shipping hubs, military planners recommended deploying aerial patrols using Florida-based bombers. Shortly after Ben and his comrades arrived in Fort Myers, the 93rd Bomb Group was thrown into the fight against Hitler's U-boats.

THE 93RD'S PERSONABLE THIRTY-TWO-YEAR-OLD commander, Colonel Edward Julius Timberlake, Jr., a 1931 West Point graduate descended from a long line of army officers, would later recall Fort Myers as "hotter than hell" during the 93rd's stay. The rising late-spring heat was debilitating, but Ted Timberlake and his staff had an escape that was one of the privileges of their rank. While the enlisted men, both combat and support personnel, sweated in tents and swatted insects on the grounds of the Fort Myers air base, Timberlake and his aides spent their evenings in rented cottages along Fort Myers Beach, grilling seafood and steaks and sipping cocktails in the soothing sea breeze. Each day, Timberlake and his aides would awaken on their barrier-island paradise and commute ten miles inland to the air base.

The 93rd had taken over the Fort Myers base and adjacent Page Field from the B-24 Liberators of the 98th Bomb Group, an outfit that had been a step ahead of Timberlake and his men in the training pipeline. The 98th had trained at Barksdale just prior to the arrival of the 93rd, and then moved to Florida at the end of March to conclude their combat preparations at Fort Myers, where the air base was still under construction.

To make way for the 93rd at Fort Myers, the 98th crews and support personnel moved to Lakeland, Florida, one hundred miles to the north. The 98th had departed Fort Myers amid a swirl of intrigue. Security was still so lax in these early months of the war that the Fort Myers newspaper had reported freely on the presence of specific outfits at the local air base and their activities. Fort Myers *News-Press* coverage included reports on the Halverson Detachment, a group of twenty-three crews recruited from the 98th for a secret mission to bomb Axis oil refineries in Romania. The detachment was named for its commander, Harry Halverson, a rangy colonel from Iowa who had developed a passion for deep-sea fishing during his stay. As he led his men off on their clandestine endeavor only hours before the 93rd vanguard arrived, Halverson shared with a *News-Press* reporter his warm feelings toward Fort Myers. "Try to keep your city just like it is and try to give the new men the same fine treatment you accorded us," Halverson said.[1]

Fort Myers civic leaders did just that, lavishing the 93rd Bomb Group with an enthusiastic welcome. As Timberlake and his staff settled into the seaside cottages vacated by their recently departed comrades, the 93rd's crews set to work sharpening their combat skills.

While the men joked about the enervating heat that allowed monstrous mosquitoes to fly away with dazed victims, Ben wrestled with some of the same concerns he had harbored since the early days of his army experience. Would he ever earn the trust of his peers and his superiors in the 93rd Bomb Group? Would he ever get a shot to prove his patriotism in combat? Would he even make it out of Fort Myers with the group?

BEN'S FRIEND AL KUHN HAD ALSO ENDED up in Fort Myers, assigned to a service squadron camped on the air base. When duty hours ended, Ben could walk over to Al's tent to hang out. They would pitch horseshoes or explore the surrounding area, or sometimes just sit around and talk. Kuhn remained a vital source of support and comfort for Ben during these months.[2]

One day Ben and Al were among a group in an army six-by-six truck that was carrying a load of men to a day at the beach when the driver misjudged a turn. The truck rolled over and many of the men were seriously injured. Ben escaped with only cuts and bruises, but Al Kuhn sustained a serious head injury.[3]

Kuhn was hospitalized in Tampa, a hundred miles away. With the help of a chaplain, Ben managed to wrangle an emergency pass to visit him and was relieved to find his friend had regained consciousness and was rapidly improving. Al Kuhn made a complete recovery, and the accident only deepened their friendship.

The chaplain who drove Ben to Tampa had become another lifeline during these lonely months. James A. Burris was twenty-seven years old and a native of northwest Missouri. His father had been a Methodist preacher and James had spent his working years before the war doing pastoral and youth work with the Methodist Church and the Young Men's Christian Association (YMCA). A slightly built man with a long, angular face and piercing blue eyes, Burris had married at the age of nineteen and had two young children, a girl and a boy, back home in Missouri.[4]

Burris had been assigned to the 93rd at Barksdale, and had taken an interest in Ben's well-being. He had invited Ben for long talks following worship services, and the chaplain addressed head-on the prejudice and bigotry that the Japanese American airman had experienced. The conversations had been therapeutic for Ben, and his relationship with the Protestant chaplain enhanced his standing with the other men.[5] The truck accident also proved to be a bonding experience within the 93rd. Ben developed friendships with two men in the Communications Section, and noticed that other 93rd men began to warm to him.

Yet Ben found himself no closer to the action. He was reminded of that in June when two of the 93rd's crews struck the group's first blows of the war against Nazi Germany, earning credit for sinking a pair of German submarines in separate attacks.[6] The submarine encounters energized the 93rd's combat contingent, but the war still seemed distant to Ben. He remained in the Communications Section as a phantom teletype operator. Ben was underemployed—and increasingly vulnerable if the group whittled down its numbers before its overseas deployment.

When the 93rd reached the end of its six weeks of training at Fort Myers, Colonel Timberlake informed the men that their plans had changed. Until further notice, they would remain at Fort Myers and continue to fly submarine patrols over the Gulf of Mexico.

THE 93RD WAS STILL STUCK IN FORT MYERS on July 4 when news arrived from England that six British Douglas DB-7 Boston III light bombers crewed by Americans had joined with six RAF crews to bomb Luftwaffe airfields in the Netherlands. The modest raid had been ordered by Hap Arnold to make good on President Roosevelt's promise to Prime Minister Winston Churchill that US forces would be bombing the Germans by America's independence holiday. In reality, the raid was a publicity stunt, but it lifted home front morale.

In mid-July, the commander of the Eighth Air Force's fledgling bomber force, Brigadier General Ira Eaker, finally received 180 planes, including forty heavy bombers. But the gunnery skills of the crews proved appalling. Eaker discovered that the 97th Bomb Group gunners "had never fired at tow targets before." Furthermore, "the crews had done little flying at high altitude, the pilots were inept at formation flying and the whole outfit was lackadaisical, loose-jointed, fun-loving and in no sense ready for combat." Eaker sacked the commanding officer of the 97th and gave his replacement sixteen days to get the group ready for combat.[7]

The deficiencies of his new crews had shocked Eaker, but their lack of readiness was merely symptomatic of larger problems with the bomber crew training program back in the United States. In Florida, the 93rd Bomb Group was nearing the end of its training no better prepared than the B-17 crews that Eaker had deemed unfit for combat.

By early August 1942, Hap Arnold seethed over the sluggish efforts to launch the American daylight bombing campaign. From the factories tasked with producing B-17 and B-24 bombers to the hastily assembled specialty schools created to train pilots, navigators, bombardiers, flight engineers, radio operators, and gunners, missteps plagued the effort.

The 93rd Bomb Group's delayed deployment highlighted some of the problems. Every day the 93rd crews devoted to submarine patrols was a day they weren't practicing the skills they would need to survive in the skies over Europe.

On August 17, the Eighth Air Force finally mounted its first independent raid. A dozen B-17 Flying Fortresses of the 97th Bomb Group climbed into the skies over East Anglia and crossed the English Channel into enemy territory for the first time. Eaker accompanied the raiding party as an observer in a B-17 named *Yankee Doodle*.

Forty miles inland, the Flying Fortresses released their bombs on the railroad marshaling yards at Rouen, France, then headed for home. Back on English soil, a jubilant Eaker emerged from *Yankee Doodle*, shed his flying suit for his trademark tunic and hat, lit a cigar, and regaled reporters with his eyewitness account of the historic raid. The fact that the RAF had already mounted thousand-plane raids against Germany didn't dampen American newspaper coverage of the strike. "In Washington our hearts soared," Hap Arnold later wrote.[8]

THE HEARTS OF THE MEN IN THE 93RD Bomb Group were also soaring, for their long-awaited deployment was finally underway. On August 5, an advance group of 93rd crews led by Colonel Timberlake and his staff bade farewell to steamy Florida and flew north to Grenier Field, New Hampshire. There they awaited delivery of new B-24D bombers.

The rest of the group—aircrews, headquarters staff, and other ground personnel, including Ben—waited for the orders that would send them northward on the first leg of their journey to some unknown destination. In the meantime, newspaper stories about the combat debut of their B-17 brethren fueled visions of imagined glory within the 93rd.

When the balance of the 93rd forces finally received orders to proceed to Fort Dix, New Jersey, Ben was stunned to be informed that he was being transferred to another stateside outfit.

Once again, he tearfully pleaded his case, this time with Chaplain Burris and the 409th Squadron adjutant. "Where is it written in stone this kid can't go?" Burris asked the senior officers who would decide Ben's fate. The squadron adjutant, Lieutenant Charles F. Brannan, a twenty-two-year-old from Texarkana, Arkansas, asked the group adjutant if anything could be done. The group adjutant reached Colonel Timberlake by phone in New Hampshire and explained the situation involving Ben Kuroki.

Timberlake didn't hesitate.

"Bring him along," the 93rd commander decreed.[9]

Ben's quest to prove himself in combat remained alive.

Chapter 7

QUEEN OF THE SEAS

On August 22, 1942, Ben and the other 93rd air and ground personnel who still remained at Fort Myers boarded a northbound train for the first leg of their deployment. The train rolled from Florida into the Carolinas, on through Virginia, Maryland, Delaware, and into New Jersey. At a rail siding in Fort Dix, about fifty miles south of New York City, Ben and his comrades disembarked with their bags.

Throughout that summer, trains packed with military personnel had converged on the area as the buildup of American forces in Britain got underway. In June, the army opened a new processing facility—Camp Kilmer—in Raritan Township, twenty-five miles from Midtown Manhattan. Camp Kilmer would be a way station for personnel bound for Europe, a place where they would undergo final processing before boarding transport ships bound for Britain.

At Fort Dix, over several sultry August days, Ben and his 93rd comrades moved from one long line to another. They rolled up their sleeves for vaccinations, signed life insurance papers, boxed up personal effects for shipment to their families, and took possession of required clothing and equipment for the journey ahead. Once those tasks were accomplished, the 93rd men made the short journey to one of Midtown Manhattan's three eleven-hundred-foot "super piers" arrayed along the Hudson River waterfront from West 49th Street to West 52nd. Arriving at Pier 88, the 93rd men were astonished and excited to discover the identity of their transport.

Before the war, she was the crown jewel of the Cunard White Star Line fleet, ferrying well-heeled passengers between New York City and Southampton, England, on a weekly basis. Ben and his comrades were among more than eight thousand American soldiers and airmen who filed aboard the magnificent vessel, now repainted in muted bluish-gray wartime colors. Their long-awaited departure from America was thrilling in itself, but their anticipation soared after discovering they would make the perilous North Atlantic crossing in the world's largest and fastest ocean liner: the renowned RMS *Queen Elizabeth*.

The passage of the RMS *Queen Elizabeth* and her precious cargo would be assigned a convoy number that would be communicated to Britain in coded Allied communications, but the reality was that the men of the 93rd wouldn't be traveling by convoy. There were no fast destroyers or corvettes assigned to defend the *Queen Elizabeth*; the magnificent ship was on her own. The passage would pit the speed of the world's fastest ocean liner against the wiles of multiple U-boat wolf packs prowling the North Atlantic for prey.

On August 28, under the cover of darkness, the QE slipped her moorings and eased downstream into New York Harbor. Ellis Island and the Statue of Liberty loomed to port. Steaming past Sandy Hook, the great ship emerged into the Atlantic Ocean. A few miles out to sea, the captain turned his ship north. More than twenty hours of uneventful sailing brought the QE to Halifax, Nova Scotia, where she docked long enough to take on Canadian troops. From Halifax, she steamed northeast to Newfoundland, then turned east into the treacherous waters beyond.

Given her size, the QE's speed was all the more impressive. She measured 1,630 feet in length and 118 feet in width. The eleven thousand passengers now aboard were scattered among fourteen decks stacked inside the massive hull. To maintain order, each passenger was restricted to one of three living zones. Meals were an hours-long feat, with queues of men snaking along corridors and decks to await their turn in the cavernous restaurant. Troops messed in the ship's main restaurant in groups of two thousand, scheduled by color-coded cards. The kitchen staff prepared more than thirty thousand meals a day, which troops consumed using their own mess kits and utensils.[1]

Ben spent much of the voyage helping out in the galley. Given the warm weather, he preferred sleeping under the stars in a coil of the ship's lines rather than wedging himself into one of the claustrophobic three-tiered bunks below decks. The 93rd had been joined by several other contingents destined for duty with the Eighth Air Force in England, including the ground echelon of the 306th Bomb Group, a B-17 outfit, and the 3rd Photographic Group, which flew P-38 Lightnings. Other outfits making the passage included the 62nd Troop Carrier Group and the 67th Reconnaissance Group.

Ben was asleep in his topside coil of rope one night when someone shook him awake. It was a 93rd comrade who introduced himself as a fellow Nebraskan named Cal Stewart. A newspaper printer's devil and cub reporter before the war, Carroll (Cal) Stewart was assigned to the 93rd as a public affairs officer. Like many of the 93rd men, Stewart was miserably seasick during the voyage. One of the highlights of the passage for him was meeting Ben, and they became fast friends in the months ahead.[2]

For three days, the voyage proceeded without incident. On the final night at sea, a sudden vibration jolted the ship and threw some of the men from their bunks. The captain had been alerted to the presence of a U-boat wolf pack in the area, and so he swiftly executed a sweeping 360-degree maneuver to confuse any pursuers. After several anxious minutes, the alarm passed and the mighty ship continued on her eastward course.

On the late afternoon of Friday, September 4, the coast of Scotland came into view. Easing through the Firth of Clyde, the *Queen Elizabeth* dropped anchor off the Tail of the Bank, at the mouth of the River Clyde. From his vantage point on the RMS *Queen Elizabeth*, amid the gloom of a pelting rain and gathering darkness, Ben caught his first glimpse of the European war zone.

Chapter 8

"CHINAMAN BOY"

On the morning of September 5, 1942, in intermittent showers and patchy sunlight, Ben and his comrades were ferried ashore at Greenock, Scotland, on the south bank of the River Clyde. At the time, Greenock was a town of red-brick houses "scattered over the dark, heath-covered hills rising up from the river," one 93rd member recorded. Wearing helmets and lugging barracks bags, the last of the 93rd men shuffled into the town's central rail station at four-thirty in the afternoon. There, a Scottish band piped the Americans aboard a waiting train. Settling into their seats, the 93rd men were served dry buns and unsweetened tea "by smiling lassies with whom we flirted and tossed chocolate bars and gum as they passed beneath our windows."[1]

In the fading twilight, the train headed inland in a steady rain. "We looked out upon the cheerless, rain-soaked streets and houses of farms and villages and rocky hills that were racing by," the anonymous 93rd observer later wrote. "In a doorway amid a row of bombed houses along the track was a lonely old woman who waved to us as we raced by." They rolled through Glasgow, Scotland's most populous city, and east to Edinburgh, the capital, where they stopped for tea. Shortly after leaving Edinburgh in the early evening, the men heard air raid sirens and the train lurched to a stop. Defying orders on air raid protocol, the excited men rushed to the windows to see what an attack looked like. "Suddenly the whole countryside was illuminated by bright flares dropped from Jerry planes," the 93rd chronicler recorded. "It gave us a feeling of nakedness and that Jerry could see us looking out the windows."[2]

The flash of antiaircraft guns lit the night sky and the rumble of exploding bombs sounded in the distance. An enemy plane exploded in a red flash. Some of the men nervously joked that the Germans were "after us." A major anxiously made his way through the cars, asking if anyone had seen his helmet. "I did," teased a lieutenant. "Lewis pissed in it and I threw it out the window." Everyone laughed. The air raid ended and the train began to roll again.

As the night wore on, a chill seeped into the cars. Some of the men huddled close in the blue-lit compartments, trying to sleep. Others played cards. One recurring game of poker was dominated by a crafty sergeant who had repeatedly fleeced the same boys since leaving Florida.

Daybreak of Sunday, September 6, revealed the emerald English countryside, with its patchwork of farms, hedgerows, and country lanes. In the village of Alconbury, fifty miles north of London, the 93rd men exited the train with their bags. Their new home lay outside the village: a former RAF base, now designated Station 102.

BEN AND HIS COMRADES WHO HAD CROSSED the North Atlantic by sea were welcomed to the base by the vanguard of the 93rd combat crews who had arrived at Alconbury by air in new olive-drab B-24D bombers. Bad weather had delayed the crews in Newfoundland, and they had survived a harrowing all-night flight through even worse weather. Despite anxious moments, thirty-five of thirty-six combat crews who left Newfoundland found their way to Alconbury.

The one aircraft that didn't turn up was a B-24 named *Friday's Cat*, and it had disappeared without a trace in the hours before reaching Scotland. There was speculation that the missing boys had gone off course in stormy weather over the North Atlantic and had exhausted their fuel, or the pilot had experienced vertigo and drove the aircraft straight down to their deaths in the sea somewhere south of England. The men's squadron commander was a big-hearted lieutenant colonel named Addison E. Baker, a renowned stunt pilot in Ohio in the 1930s. Now one of Baker's first acts at Alconbury was writing condolence letters to the families of the ten missing men of *Friday's Cat*.

With an understrength roster of eighteen hundred men, including four hundred trained combat crewmen, the 93rd was the first American B-24 bomber outfit to reach England. More crews and planes were on the way. Ben and his comrades had arrived at a moment when General Ira Eaker, the Eighth Air Force bomber commander, was trying to build on three weeks of modest raids on targets in occupied France. Since leading his men on their combat debut to France on August 17, Eaker had lost ten B-17s—nearly one-quarter of his force—while logging ten bombing missions.

Eaker was filled with a sense of urgency, for he had recently been informed that the Eighth would be losing many of its fighters, bombers, and combat crews to the planned fall invasion of northwest Africa, now codenamed Operation TORCH. Eaker had been assured by Hap Arnold and army chief of staff General George Marshall that the Eighth would be left with enough bombers and crews "to continue some sort of strategic offensive," but Eaker was uneasy. The clock was ticking. But Eaker first needed to teach his new crews the survival skills they hadn't been taught in their truncated stateside training.

For the remainder of September, the 93rd's combat crews attended ground classes and flew practice flights. They learned how to take off in sequence, climb to an assigned rally altitude, then slip into a designated spot in twenty-four plane squadron formations circling above the countryside. More often than not, this feat would have to be accomplished in sloppy weather. There was much to learn, and the deficiencies in their training weren't lost on the 93rd men. "When we went over, we weren't trained at all," recalled Rollin Reineck, the navigator of a 93rd B-24 named *Jerk's Natural*. "All we had done was patrol over the Gulf. We had to learn to fly formations. We didn't have any training in high altitude bombing or anything of that nature."[3]

WHILE COLONEL TIMBERLAKE'S TOP priority was getting his aircrews ready for combat, his men were eager to reconnoiter their new surroundings.

For Ben, the countryside surrounding the base stirred memories of home. The group mess hall and the tents that served as temporary barracks for some of the 93rd men were surrounded by fields of sugar beets, one of the Kuroki family's specialties. Ben was struck by the small size of the farms and the lack of mechanization. In nearby fields, women harvested hay with hand tools and a horse-drawn cart. "It takes them a week to harvest this small patch," Ben remarked to one of his friends. "Back home we do it in a day."[4]

A little more than a mile away from the base lay the village of Alconbury, namesake for the RAF base established in this spot in 1938. The village and surrounding civil parish were home to about five hundred souls. Alconbury sat astride the ancient Great North Road as it ran from London, sixty-five miles to the south, to Edinburgh, Scotland, nearly three hundred miles to the north. Even closer to the air base was the hamlet of Little Stukeley, population two hundred. The pubs of Alconbury, Little Stukeley, and other nearby villages and hamlets introduced the curious American airmen to their exotic new world.

The staple beverage in the pubs was dark beer served at room temperature and consumed in prodigious amounts. It was an acquired taste for the American airmen, but the warm and hospitable company made the unfamiliar brew more palatable. In theory, the men and the village pub-goers spoke the same language, but the Americans could scarcely comprehend the heavily accented English spoken by locals. The airmen and their hosts were content to smile and nod and sip, satisfied they were among friends.

The base had been carved from an old farm, and the fields on which crops had grown for centuries were now crisscrossed by a triangle of intersecting runways. A perimeter track connected small hardstands on which the 93rd's Liberators were parked. The spires of nine country churches marked the location of Alconbury, Little Stukeley, and other villages and hamlets. The air base was located in the county of Huntingdonshire. To the west lay old manor houses and the occasional monastery, while to the east lay fertile fenland reclaimed from North Sea marshes in centuries past.[5]

Housing eighteen hundred American airmen posed a challenge to the 93rd commanders and their British hosts. Ben and many of the enlisted men found themselves sharing tents pitched under copses of old oaks. Many of the officers settled into prefabricated Nissen huts erected in an area known as Skunk Hollow, in the shadow of a thirteenth-century church where Chaplain James Burris presided over Protestant worship services as gray light streamed through lovely lancet windows. The plumbing was primitive—cold-water showers and squat toilets. The modest quarters were warmed by coal-burning heaters. A few dozen combat officers were housed in style three miles from the base in a gabled Elizabethan manor bearing the stately name of Upton House. Enlisted men housed on the manor grounds were relegated to tents.[6]

With a spirit of adventure and curiosity that belied the dangerous work that had brought them to England, the 93rd men began to explore the pubs and inns, churches, castles, and cemeteries of the ancient world they had suddenly entered. Among the many new friends that the 93rd men counted was the prominent British Conservative Party politician George Montagu—the Earl of Sandwich—and his Chicago-born wife, Alberta Sturges, Countess of Sandwich. The Earl and Countess warmly welcomed the American airmen into their castle-like mansion in Huntingdon.

It was the beginning of a beautiful friendship for the 93rd men as they prepared to join the fight to the death against Nazi Germany.

FROM THE MOMENT HE CAME ASHORE at Greenock, Ben had been struck by the lack of interest in his ethnicity by the locals he encountered in Scotland and England. There were no suspicious looks or raised eyebrows or offensive comments. It really seemed as if the people he met didn't care about his ancestry.

The same couldn't be said about his army comrades. His treatment by the men of the 93rd was far better than he'd gotten during his first months of military service, but Ben still faced the occasional offensive comment.

A drunk American spotted him in a bar and described him to an English friend as a "Chinaman boy" and a "good boy" who wasn't like "those lousy Japs" who were "being kicked out of California." Even close friends highlighted his heritage by giving him nicknames like "Hara-Kiri."[7] The incidents were rarer, but they made Ben cringe.

Still wary of giving his superiors any reason to ship him home, Ben stayed away from dances and parties. He felt most comfortable exploring alone or with a few friends. He shared the sense of wonder of most of his comrades as he savored his surroundings at Alconbury. He developed a taste for tea at the air base Red Cross Club. Venturing beyond Alconbury and other nearby villages and hamlets, he toured the old university town of Cambridge and took in his first ballet.[8] When Ben and his comrades were stuck on the base, they slept, wrote letters, played cards, shot craps, or sat around shooting the bull about life in general.

Ben had already made a name for himself by showing up at the flight line each morning to plead for a crew assignment. He didn't get his wish, but his eagerness was noted. He would watch as the bombers took off to practice formation flying or simulated bombing runs using live ordnance on imaginary targets in The Wash, the protected bay and estuary off the coast of East Anglia. He felt he was getting the runaround in his appeals for a crew assignment, and that tested Ben's patience. But he wasn't the only impatient man in the 93rd as September drew to a close. The combat crews were tired of training and eager for action.

On October 4, the 93rd crews were finally briefed for a mission. As the departure hour approached, the men were ordered to stand down because of bad weather. The disappointment among the aircrews and ground personnel was palpable.

The raid was rescheduled for the following day and the crews steeled themselves again, only to endure the disappointment of another cancellation because of bad weather. An officer in Ben's squadron noted the rising tension among the men as they awaited their first action. "Aircrews very anxious to get on a mission," the officer observed in the squadron diary.[9] The 93rd still hadn't crossed the English Channel into occupied enemy territory and they still hadn't faced a shot fired in anger. Yet the strain was already starting to weigh on some of the men.

Chapter 9

"HEY, THEY'RE SHOOTING AT US!"

On October 9, 1942, the 93rd finally made its long-awaited combat debut. The target was a locomotive manufacturing complex in Lille, France, about forty-five miles inland from Dunkirk. The crews were awakened in darkness, ate breakfast, then assembled for the pre-mission briefing. Intelligence officers apprised the men on expected enemy antiaircraft fire and fighter resistance. The weather officer covered visibility, cloud cover, and wind forecasts in the target area. But the climax was a rousing pep talk from group commander Ted Timberlake. "This is the day we've waited for and for gosh sake, fly a tight formation and put those bombs on target," Timberlake exhorted. "I know you Joes can do it."[1]

Rather than send his boys into combat with a speech and a pat on the back, Timberlake announced that he would lead the mission. When the briefing broke up, he climbed into a B-24 named for his baby daughter, *Teggie Ann*.

For Ben and other men watching from the ground, the tension built as ninety-six Pratt & Whitney engines around the airfield perimeter roared to life. The collective concern in the anxious hour that followed centered on whether the pilots could get their heavily loaded bombers into the air. A flare streaked from the control tower's viewing platform, and at 7:47 a.m. Timberlake revved his engines and released his brakes. *Teggie Ann* roared down the runway with a full fuel load and twelve five-hundred-pound bombs in her bay racks.

As Timberlake coaxed *Teggie Ann* into the sky, the other bombers followed at thirty-second intervals. With each aircraft near its maximum 62,000-pound gross weight, the pilots sweated the takeoff. One after another, the B-24s rose into the sky. Twelve minutes after *Teggie Ann* started the procession, the last Liberator on the runway disappeared into the mist.

On the ground, the sound of the Pratt & Whitney engines grew fainter and then disappeared entirely. For Ben and the hundreds of other 93rd men left behind, the vigil began.

AT 9:25 A.M., A LITTLE MORE THAN NINETY minutes after *Teggie Ann* took off, Timberlake's bombers made a successful rendezvous with seventy-five B-17s over East Anglia. With the Flying Fortresses leading the way, the strike force headed east over the English Channel. As the bombers climbed to twenty-four-thousand feet, the temperature outside the aircraft plummeted to minus fifty-five degrees Fahrenheit. Freezing winds whipped through the rear gunports of the B-24s and B-17s, punishing the waist gunners as they stood at their positions. Half-frozen men test-fired their weapons to make sure they were working and reported the results to the copilot.

The pilots had been instructed to turn back to base if any gun malfunctioned or a serious mechanical issue arose with the engines or hydraulic system. Ten miles from the French coast at Dunkirk, two of Timberlake's Liberators dropped out of the formation and turned back to Alconbury. Over the next few minutes, another five B-24s aborted for various reasons. With his force now down to seventeen B-24s, Timberlake pressed on.[2]

Most of the pilots had never flown a B-24 at maximum weight, and their heavily loaded aircraft presented a nerve-racking challenge. In their weeks of training in England, the pilots had practiced flying tight triangle-shaped formations comprised of three aircraft to concentrate their machine-gun fire against enemy fighters. Now the pilots struggled to tighten their formations without causing a midair collision.

As the B-24s arrived over the French coast, the sky erupted with black puffs. The men were so unprepared for aerial combat that the smudges puzzled many of them. "It was eerie and weird," said a 330th pilot from Iowa named John "Packy" Roche.[3] It was only after hearing a sound like gravel being tossed onto their bomber's aluminum skin that some of the men realized the puffs were exploding antiaircraft shells. In a 329th Squadron bomber named *Thunder Bird*, the twenty-three-year-old tail gunner shouted with astonishment over the crew intercom: "Hey, they're shooting at us!" Some of his crewmates at first thought he was joking, but the gunner was so shaken by the experience that he would never fly another mission.[4]

Within seconds of crossing into enemy-controlled airspace, the 93rd had learned the first of many hard lessons they would absorb in the weeks ahead: The bombers at the rear of a strike force faced greater peril than the vanguard as German gunners adjusted their fire. The black puffs had seemed harmless, and then two shells slammed into a B-24 named *Big Eagle*. Flames erupted from the number four engine and bomb bay, and *Big Eagle* fell into a death spiral. Five men parachuted from the crippled aircraft and five fell to their deaths. Among the survivors were the pilots, who were blown free when the bomber exploded. The pilots and two other men were taken prisoner by the Germans. Gunner Arthur B. Cox evaded capture and became the first American airman to escape to neutral Spain with the assistance of the French Underground.[5]

About twenty miles from Lille, Timberlake's group linked up with RAF Spitfires and RAF-operated P-38 Lightnings assigned to protect the B-24s from German fighter attacks in the target area. The escorts took up a position slightly above and behind Timberlake's force as the Fortresses began their final sprint to the target ahead.

The German fighter attacks began anew as the B-24s neared Lille. Six enemy fighters darted into Timberlake's formation and attacked the trailing B-24 formations nearly head-on. German Messerschmitt Me-109 and Focke-Wulf Fw-190 fighters swarmed the B-24s from all angles. B-24 gunners fired belts of .50-caliber rounds at the fleeting targets as the Spitfires and P-38s did their best to drive the enemy aircraft away from the bomber formation.

Bomber crewmen had been taught aviation shorthand to identify the relative position of threats using clock-face bearings and the vertical position relative to the horizon. Now the intercom system used by bomber crewmen to communicate with one another during flight crackled with shouts. "Me-109 at twelve o'clock high! Two Focke-Wulfs at six o'clock low!"

Timberlake's orderly formation disintegrated in the face of the attacks. Adding to the chaos, the B-17s that had dropped their bombs on the target were now on a collision course with the incoming Liberators. Timberlake banked to the south to avert disaster, and the B-24s sprinted to the target on an improvised route. Finally clear of the fighters, *Teggie Ann*'s bombardier toggled his load of bombs, and the other Liberators followed.

Suddenly six thousand pounds lighter, Timberlake banked hard to the west, and the battered Liberators fought their way home.

BACK ON THE GROUND, THE 93RD MEN described a harrowing battle that included forty to fifty clashes with German fighters. Under questioning by intelligence officers, the raiders claimed six enemy fighter kills, five probable kills, and another four enemy aircraft damaged.[6] The bombing had been excellent, the 93rd men reported, but strike photos revealed most of the group's bombs missed their targets—in many cases by hundreds of yards.

Allied press officers in London issued an exuberant communiqué that claimed a "devastating attack" and severe German fighter losses: a staggering forty-eight fighters shot down with certainty, with an additional thirty-eight probable kills and another nineteen enemy aircraft damaged, the communiqué claimed. The claims turned out to be grossly exaggerated, a common occurrence in Army Air Forces communiques in the months ahead.

While some men mourned the loss of the *Big Eagle* crew, many others celebrated the 93rd's combat blooding over beers and shots of whiskey on the base and at nearby pubs. There was a sense that the enemy fighter claims were inflated, but that didn't stop some of the men from predicting they would decimate the Luftwaffe fighter force in one or two more raids.[7]

The boasts belied the raid's sobering truths. Ten of their comrades had been blasted from the sky, and many others had narrowly avoided the same fate. Lille had proven that the big B-17s and B-24s, even in massed formations, were vulnerable to enemy flak and fighters. Some of them were going to get hurt, and some were going to die. In their hearts, the 93rd men knew they were in for a hard fight.

Chapter 10

"LOOK AT ME NOW"

The stories of courage, sacrifice, and survival that swirled through the enlisted ranks following the Lille raid intensified Ben's hunger to join a combat crew. Each of the squadrons still had a thin reserve of trained gunners who could fill losses, so Ben's appeals for a gunnery assignment went unanswered. For the time being, the closest Ben would come to combat was watching crews take off and land and listening to stories of comrades.

While Ben sought to put himself in harm's way, the Eighth Air Force received an urgent change of orders in mid-October. The directive came from General Dwight D. Eisenhower after a surge in Allied shipping losses from U-boat attacks in the North Atlantic. Eisenhower ordered the American B-17s and B-24s in England to shift their focus from industrial targets in France to German U-boat pens and maintenance shops along the southwest coast of occupied France.

Eisenhower's concerns went beyond the mounting shipping losses. D-Day for the Operation TORCH landings in northwest Africa was set for early November, and Allied convoys were preparing to head south from British ports with men and materiel. To shield the convoys from potentially devastating attacks, Eisenhower needed Ira Eaker's Eighth Air Force bombers to keep the German marauders bottled up in their French bases.

The onset of fall rains and fog complicated the Eighth's efforts to carry out Eisenhower's orders. Inclement weather put the 93rd out of action for twelve days following the Lille raid. Finally, on October 21, twenty-four 93rd Liberators took off to bomb the German submarine pens at Lorient. The B-17s leading the strike force bombed the target as planned, but a narrow weather window closed and the 93rd men made it only as far as the English Channel before they were ordered to return to Alconbury because of poor visibility.

Subsequent 93rd missions didn't even get that far. Four times in the final ten days of October the crews were briefed for missions that were canceled because of weather. The B-24s weren't equipped with radar, so the men could only bomb what they could see, and the autumn weather made it impossible to see much of anything from twenty thousand feet.

Four attempts were made to bomb the German submarine pens at Saint-Nazaire in the final days of October. Ground crews toiled all night in chilly, wet conditions to load the B-24s with bombs, and the crews were roused before dawn for final briefings, only to be told to stand down before takeoff. Another attempt was made to bomb Saint-Nazaire on November 1, with the same result. Frustration gnawed at the 93rd men.

On November 7, Ted Timberlake's crews again set out to complete only their second mission. Their target was the U-boat pens at Brest. Many of the fifty-six B-17s leading the strike force began experiencing mechanical malfunctions, and more than half eventually aborted the raid because of engine problems. Of the twelve 93rd B-24s that took off from Alconbury, only eight reached the target.

The Liberators faced intense antiaircraft fire in the seconds before and after they dropped their bombs, and as they turned for home, they were attacked by eighteen German fighters. The B-24 crews had no sooner fought their way out of that threat than twenty unidentified fighters closed on the formation near the French coast. The Liberator gunners opened fire and braced for a pitched battle. Suddenly, the leader of the fighters rolled into a

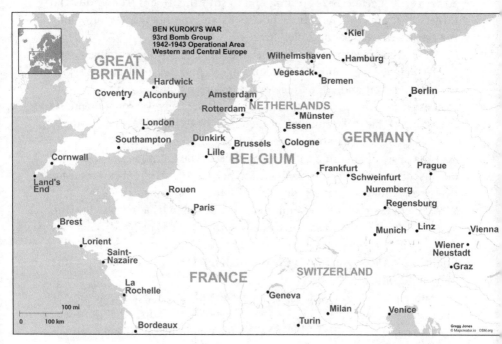

93rd Bomb Group, 1942–1943 operational area, Western and Central Europe

vertical bank and revealed his RAF insignia. The Liberators had mistaken a group of friendly Spitfires for enemy fighters. No harm was done in the brief encounter, and, in the gathering twilight, the fighters led the 93rd crews to an RAF base at Exeter, in southwest England.[1] The 93rd men were disappointed to learn from strike photos that their aim had been poor, but at least they didn't lose any men or planes. For the 93rd, mission number 2 was finally in the books.

On November 8, Allied troops stormed ashore in northwest Africa in the opening act of Operation TORCH. With the invasion underway and convoys carrying more troops and supplies through the North Atlantic waters off France and Spain, the Eighth Air Force stepped up its suppression raids on the German submarine pens. Twelve 93rd Liberators took off for Saint-Nazaire on November 9, and nine bombed the target. A scheduled raid on Bordeaux the following day was aborted due to weather, but nine 93rd bombers and five Liberators from the recently arrived 44th Bomb Group attacked Saint-Nazaire. Three B-17s were lost over the target. Once again, the 93rd avoided casualties.

As if the weather hadn't complicated his life enough, General Eaker now faced the loss of much of the force he had only recently acquired. Eisenhower had requested 1,698 planes for TORCH. About 1,200 of that number were to be drawn from Eaker's existing forces and the reinforcements supposedly headed his way. Among Eaker's losses to the TORCH diversion were his two most-experienced B-17 outfits.

The grim reality for Eaker's remaining bomber forces was they were expected to keep attacking German targets, no matter how small their numbers. Ted Timberlake's 93rd Liberators had enjoyed remarkably good fortune thus far, losing only one bomber on three raids against German targets in enemy-occupied France. Now a reckoning awaited Timberlake's B-24 crews as they prepared to mount even smaller raids against hardening German air defenses.

ALTHOUGH HE CHAFED IN HIS ROLE AS A CLERK, Ben reveled in the thrill of waking up each morning in England, with a front-row seat to the historic air campaign that was front-page news back home. He wasn't experiencing the alternating thrill and terror of combat, but Ben's daily life at Alconbury involved other adventures. There were quaint villages, ancient towns, and soaring cathedrals to explore, and the venerable university city of Cambridge lay only a half hour away. An even greater allure was London, only an hour's journey by train. For a farm boy from rural Nebraska, an exotic world beckoned.

On Friday, November 13, Ben and his comrades were ordered to assemble by squadron to await the arrival of a mystery guest. At 10:00 a.m., a black Daimler limousine rolled through the main gate of the base and eased to a halt. To the astonishment of Ben and the others, King George VI emerged from the back seat.

His Majesty had been escorted from the nearby train station by the commander of the Eighth Air Force, Major General Carl Spaatz, and Eaker, his bomber chief. Timberlake now ushered his distinguished guests into his office for conversation, a cup of tea, and Camel cigarettes. There was an awkward moment when the 328th Squadron commander, Major Addison Baker, climbed onto a table to snap a photograph and gave His Majesty a fright when the camera's flashbulb popped like a pistol shot.[2]

Afterward, Timberlake escorted King George to a waiting jeep for a guided tour of the flight line. The British monarch wore a royal-blue great-coat to ward off the damp chill, and he and Timberlake perched on an elevated rear seat as a sergeant from Detroit drove them to Timberlake's *Teggie Ann*. Climbing from the jeep, the 93rd commander and Major K. K. Compton escorted the monarch into the open bomb bay of the B-24. The king chatted with some of *Teggie Ann*'s gunners and asked questions about the various crew positions and responsibilities during a mission. Pointing to the twin .50-caliber machine guns in the top turret, the monarch quipped, "So that's what the Jerries don't like?"[3]

Emerging from the bomber, King George chatted a few more minutes with crew members and the ground crew chief. "How do you like the English weather, sergeant?" the king asked one of the men. Without missing a beat, Sergeant Norman Tussey, a twenty-eight-year-old sawmill worker from Blair County, Pennsylvania, replied, "I don't like it, sir."

Among the journalists on hand to document the king's first visit to an American base was *Life* magazine photographer Margaret Bourke-White, the first woman US authorities had accredited to work in a combat zone. For Ben and the 93rd men watching from a distance as King George and the other American and British dignitaries made their rounds trailed by Bourke-White, it was a day they would never forget. "If someone were to tell me I would be in England, I would have thought they were crazy," Ben wrote home. "But look at me now."[4]

THE DAY AFTER THE KING'S VISIT, THE 93RD was back in action. At 10:30 a.m., Major Baker, the 328th Squadron commander, led a force of thirteen bombers into the skies over England. Six of the aircraft were from Ben's 409th Squadron. Their target was La Pallice, the deep-water port of La Rochelle, France, and home base of the German Navy's 3rd U-Boat Flotilla. When the Liberators reached the target area, 320 miles southeast of

England's Cornwall coast, La Pallice and its submarine pens lay concealed beneath a blanket of clouds. The Liberators banked to the north and flew thirty minutes back up the coast to Saint-Nazaire. Under heavy enemy anti-aircraft fire, the B-24s released their bombs and headed for Cornwall. They passed at treetop level over Land's End at the far southwest tip of England, before landing safely at RAF Exeter.[5]

Six 93rd B-24s took off the following morning, November 15, to fly a diversionary sweep over the North Sea to draw enemy fighters away from a B-17 strike on German submarine pens on the Bay of Biscay. It was a quick and easy mission for Timberlake's boys. On November 17, twelve 93rd Liberators joined with thirty-one Flying Fortresses to strike the Saint-Nazaire submarine pens and a nearby power plant; the flak was heavy, but there were no fighters. Three B-17s were shot down over the target and twenty-two Flying Fortresses were damaged, but Timberlake's men escaped without casualties or the loss of an aircraft.

There was one close call involving some of Ben's friends from the 409th Squadron. The aircraft was named *Red Ass*, and only a few minutes from landing at Alconbury a mechanical problem caused all four engines to die. The pilot, a diminutive Tupelo, Mississippi, native named Jake Epting, took immediate action to revive the engines. In the process, he inadvertently rang the alarm used to signal the crew to abandon the aircraft. A few seconds later, Epting got his engines restarted and the crisis passed. When the pilot tried to raise his navigator over the intercom, the tail gunner informed Epting that the navigator and bombardier had parachuted from the plane. The men landed on an English farm not far from Alconbury, and the next day they sheepishly rejoined their comrades.[6]

On November 18, the 93rd put thirteen planes in the air to bomb the submarine pens at Lorient. Ben's friend and spiritual advisor, Chaplain James Burris, was allowed to accompany the crew of a 328th Squadron B-24 named *Bomerang*, a moniker derived from a mashup of bomber and boomerang. Burris wanted to understand what the stressed men he was counseling were experiencing, and so he stretched out on the flight deck and peered through the open bomb bay doors to watch the raid unfold. Shrapnel from bursting flak shells pierced the bomber's aluminum skin, and one chunk punched through the fuselage and whizzed by the chaplain's head.[7]

Nearby in the 93rd formation, the 328th Squadron crew of *Katy Bug* had an even worse time. The pilot, Lieutenant Al Asch of Beaverton, Michigan, had just been promoted from the copilot's seat. In the target area, a piece of flak ruptured the fuel tanks in the right wing and a stream of gas trailed from *Katy Bug* as Asch coaxed the bomber back across the English Channel. The enemy flak had damaged various controls, and Asch discovered that the nosewheel remained lodged in its well. The flight engineer and the bombardier lowered the wheel manually while Asch circled the field. Asch was only seconds from landing when the Alconbury control tower suddenly ordered him to abort to avoid a collision with a Liberator landing on the opposite runway. Asch applied full power, but the lowered flaps and landing gear made it impossible for him to generate enough speed to climb. He was perhaps one hundred feet above the field when his airspeed dropped to a hundred miles per hour and two starboard engines quit. On Asch's command, the wheels were retracted and he skidded the aircraft into a farmer's field. As the bomber careened across the uneven terrain, the bottom of the fuselage ripped away and the top turret collapsed into the interior, crushing his bombardier. Two gunners and the flight engineer also died in the wreckage of *Katy Bug*, but Asch and five others survived.[8]

On November 21, five days before Thanksgiving, Chaplain Burris conducted an open-air memorial service for the four dead men of *Katy Bug*. The next day, the men of the 93rd returned to action, this time bombing the submarine pens at Lorient. Leaving the target, the 328th Squadron crew of *Ball of Fire* was attacked by three Luftwaffe Junkers Ju-88 fighter-bombers. In the running battle that ensued, one of the gunners took a round in the stomach. Another round nearly severed the pilot's right arm before ripping into the copilot's right leg.

The navigator tied a tourniquet to the pilot's mangled arm to prevent him from bleeding out. The radio operator managed to remove the pilot from his seat while the copilot, blood spurting from his leg, kept *Ball of Fire* flying. Faint from loss of blood, the copilot asked the bombardier to help him fly the plane. The bombardier had completed only two months of pilot's training before failing the course, but he knew the rudiments of flying. With their radio shot out, the wounded copilot and plucky bombardier kept *Ball of Fire* in the air. They crossed the English Channel and safely landed *Ball of Fire* on an RAF field.[9]

By Thanksgiving Day, the 93rd had nine missions to its credit. Timberlake had lost only one plane in combat and another on a training flight. The 93rd's operational losses were the lowest of any of Ira Eaker's bomber groups, but casualties were mounting and the 93rd's reserve of spare gunners was nearly exhausted. Ben's pleas to join a crew as a gunner suddenly found a sympathetic audience.

Chapter 11

"ARE YOU SURE YOU KNOW WHAT YOU'RE DOING?"

Within weeks of arriving at Alconbury, Ben had sought the advice of a 93rd comrade whose path he hoped to follow. The comrade had arrived in England as a squadron first sergeant, with responsibilities that would have kept him on the ground and out of harm's way for the duration of the war. But the first sergeant wanted to fight. He requested reassignment to a combat crew as a gunner, and his request was granted. Ben approached the former first sergeant for advice on how he might do the same.

The newly minted gunner counseled Ben to talk to the head of the Armaments Section, a college-educated lieutenant from Iowa named Merlin D. Larson. "I want to prove my loyalty, sir," Ben told Larson. "I can't do it on the ground." Larson replied, "Are you sure you know what you're doing, Kuroki?" Ben said he did.[1]

The transfer was arranged, and Ben joined the Armaments Section. It was only the first step, but the new assignment allowed Ben to spend nearly every waking minute on the flight line. He helped load bombs into aircraft before missions, learned to clean and repair .50-caliber machine guns, and even got in some target practice with the fifties. He helped ground crews any way he could. He also chatted up combat gunners and their command pilots. But without formal gunnery training, Ben remained stuck on the ground.

For weeks, Ben cajoled Lieutenant Larson to send him to gunnery school, and for weeks Larson put off Ben's requests. In November, with the 409th Squadron facing an imminent need for replacement gunners, Larson relented. Ben was among a group of men assigned to the 93rd in various ground positions who were given physical examinations to test their flying fitness. The twelve men who passed, Ben included, were dispatched to a gunnery school near London.

The course lasted only five days and largely consisted of looking at pictures and models to sharpen aircraft recognition skills, learning to sight with the .50-caliber machine gun, then firing ten rounds—without ever leaving the ground. Some of the men fumed about the training, but Ben remained silent. If a sham gunnery course got him a spot on a combat crew, he wasn't going to complain.[2]

BACK AT ALCONBURY, BEN REDOUBLED HIS efforts to find a 409th Squadron pilot who would take him on. Openings were starting to occur more frequently now as gunners became combat casualties or succumbed to stress. Flying duty was entirely voluntary in the Army Air Forces, and a bomber crew member could opt out at any time. The first 93rd man to do so was Jack Stover, the tail gunner on the 328th Squadron crew commanded by Charles Murphy. Stover decided after one mission that aerial combat wasn't for him.[3] "In training in the States and everything, it was all glamor," recalled Art Ferwerda, a 93rd ground crew chief at Alconbury. "Once [men] started to get in the fighting part of it, the glamor stops."[4]

Another factor working in Ben's favor was the diversion of air combat forces to North Africa. Replacement crews that were supposed to fill the 93rd's combat losses were no longer arriving, and so it became clear to the group's senior officers that they would have to replace their casualties with men currently assigned to ground duties.

Ben had made a few close friends in the 409th Squadron and he was a familiar face to men throughout the 93rd, but the undercurrent of distrust because of his Japanese ancestry remained a concern for command pilots. The damp and dreary month of November 1942 drew to a close with Ben still in search of a crew.

ONE 409TH SQUADRON PILOT—A REDHEADED, freckle-faced twenty-five-year-old from Kansas City, Missouri—seemed sympathetic to Ben's plight. Richard L. Wilkinson—Wilkie to his B-24 comrades—had grown up under the roof of a man who was ahead of his time in many ways. Wilkie's father, J. L. Wilkinson, had been a gifted baseball player growing up in Iowa and became a star pitcher for Highland Park College while playing for professional and semiprofessional teams. Then an arm injury ended his career.[5]

At the age of thirty-five, a few years before the First World War, J. L. Wilkinson found his calling in the game he loved. He put together a women's professional baseball team that traveled around the Midwest by train, playing for two thousand fans in a collapsible covered grandstand. J.L. followed this feat in 1912 by cofounding a multiracial baseball team known as the All Nations. After the war, Wilkinson's All Nations team became the all-Black Kansas City Monarchs, a charter member of the Negro National League.[6]

J. L. Wilkinson had already distinguished himself with his barrier-breaking feats in professional baseball when the Great Depression arrived. Hard times threatened to cripple Black professional baseball, but J.L. hit on a solution to accommodate working fans who couldn't afford to catch a game during daylight hours: He bankrolled a portable lighting system that could be transported from town to town, allowing the Monarchs to travel the country playing night baseball. Wilkinson became a beloved figure among Black professional baseball players, sometimes bunking with coaches and players during road trips. His Monarchs would win ten league titles and two Negro League World Series crowns. One of those championships came in the fall of 1942 behind the power pitching of Monarch star Satchel Paige.[7]

Born in Des Moines in 1917, J.L.'s only son, Richard, was steeped in his father's values. When the family moved to Kansas City, young Dick Wilkinson's summers revolved around the Kansas City Monarchs and its Black players. In the late 1930s, after two years of college, Dick moved to Southern California. In July 1941, Dick was working as a bookkeeper for a multinational industrial company, the American Radiator and Standard Sanitary Corporation in Los Angeles, when he enlisted in the Army Air Forces. The following spring, Dick joined the newly formed 93rd Bomb Group at Barksdale Field, Louisiana.[8]

Wilkie, as he was quickly christened by his comrades, made his combat debut with the 93rd in the October 9 raid on the Lille locomotive works, and he burnished his résumé in the group's sporadic raids through the fall. Around the end of November, Wilkie found himself one gunner short for a mission. He was familiar with Ben Kuroki and the combat aspirations of the Japanese American gunner, and so Wilkie asked Ben if he was interested in filling a temporary vacancy on his crew. Ben jumped at the chance.[9]

Twice in the first days of December 1942, Ben took off with Wilkie's crew on missions, but both times the 93rd bombers were recalled over the English Channel because of bad weather. After the two aborted missions, Wilkie's regular gunner returned, and Ben resumed his search for a crew. But the landscape had shifted. Ben hadn't gotten credit for the aborted missions, but he had been initiated into the rituals of aerial combat. For the first time, he had donned his leather flight suit, attended a classified mission briefing, and climbed aboard a B-24 bomber cradling a .50-caliber machine gun.[10]

More importantly, a respected 409th Squadron pilot had broken the taboo that had made pilots reluctant to take the Japanese American gunner into combat.

Chapter 12

A BIG CHANCE

In the first week of December, Ben heard from a friend that the 409th Squadron pilot of *Red Ass*, Jake Epting, needed to replace a gunner who had taken himself off combat duty. Ben tracked down Epting to plead his case. Epting polled his men before giving Ben an answer. There were no objections.[1]

On Monday, December 7, 1942, the first anniversary of the Pearl Harbor attack, Ben's breakthrough was featured on the front page of the weekly 93rd Bomb Group newspaper, the *Liberator*. "Jap Gunner Gets 'Chance,'" announced the frontpage headline. "Born of full-blooded Japanese parentage near [Cozad], Neb., where his folks were farming, sturdy Ben looks like most Japanese; but inside he's different," the story declared.

The article was written by the *Liberator* editor, Cal Stewart, the Nebraskan who had introduced himself to Ben on the *Queen Elizabeth*. In his interview with Stewart, Ben described the discrimination he had endured during his military service. He also spoke of his hope to exact payback for the Pearl Harbor attack. "I've gone through a lot of hell because of that Pearl Harbor incident, and I've got a personal score to settle with them as well as their Axis partners," Ben said. "I'd just as soon be in the Far East pourin' it on them!"

Ben spoke passionately of his 409th comrades.

"About the dearest thing to Ben's heart is his squadron," Stewart wrote. He quoted Ben as saying, "You can tell them I wouldn't leave my outfit to fly for the King of England, and that's saying a lot!"

The article ended with a dramatic flourish by describing a resolute Ben "fastening his helmet as he strode away toward 'his' B-24 [for] his big chance."

BEN'S "BIG CHANCE" COINCIDED WITH news that electrified the 93rd. Because of inclement weather, the group had last completed a mission on November 23, and by early December the mood among the enlisted men and officers matched the foul weather. With one eye on the fighting in North Africa and one eye on Ted Timberlake's idle crews in England, US military commanders decided to temporarily reassign the 93rd to the tactical air campaign against German lines of supply in North Africa.

Three of the 93rd's four squadrons—the 328th, 330th, and 409th—received hasty orders to pack for a temporary assignment to some undisclosed location. Ben's name appeared on the orders, along with a promotion from private first class to sergeant—the rank bestowed on aerial gunners. His invitation to join the Epting crew seemed real.

As the 93rd crews climbed into the skies over Alconbury the day before the Pearl Harbor anniversary, Ben and most of the men could only speculate about their destination. The first leg of the journey took them across England to the country's far southwest peninsula. In addition to the combat crews, some of the planes carried a skeleton force of maintenance and administrative specialists. They landed at RAF bases in Portreath and Exeter to refuel and spend the night.

Shortly after daybreak on the morning of December 7, 1942, Ben gazed from one of the waist windows as *Red Ass* climbed into the morning sky and turned to the south. The crews were in a jubilant mood. They were leaving behind the damp chill of England and headed to North Africa's balmy Mediterranean coast.[2]

Timberlake's twenty-four aircraft took off in two groups. Their destination lay more than a thousand miles to the south on a straight line, but their planned route would add several hundred miles to the journey to avoid a possible conflict with the forces of Spanish dictator Francisco Franco, the target of delicate US diplomatic negotiations to keep officially neutral Spain out of the war. Timberlake didn't like the fact that he and his men would reach French Algeria well after dark if they flew the assigned route, so, ignoring orders, he climbed to fourteen thousand feet and led his vanguard of six planes over Spain. Timberlake's group touched down at Tafaraoui Aerodrome, just south of Oran, Algeria, in the late afternoon.

Jake Epting and his *Red Ass* crew were assigned to the second flight, which flew the stipulated route. By the time the second contingent reached the Straits of Gibraltar, dusk was settling over the Mediterranean coast of northwest Africa. As the B-24s flew east through the straits, French antiaircraft gunners opened fire from positions along the coast of Morocco.

The antiaircraft fire and gathering darkness set the 93rd men on edge. By the time the second 93rd flight reached Oran, mist and rain had moved in and visibility was deteriorating. The city and the surrounding area were blacked out. Their destination lay only a few miles south of Oran, but there were mountains around the field, and the personnel at Tafaraoui Aerodrome had done nothing to mark the location for the 93rd crews. Some of the pilots couldn't locate the airfield, and some were "afraid to turn on their purple formation lights, lest they attract enemy fighters," pilot Al Asch recalled. "We started circling where we thought the field was. Finally, extending from a truck's headlights was a string of kerosene-fueled flare pots strung in a single line dimly marking the runway." Colonel Timberlake radioed and told Asch and the others to land on the north side of the flares; the other side was lined with aircraft.[3]

Among the 93rd pilots struggling to find Tafaraoui's poorly lit runway in the dark and rain was a strapping Iowa native named Lieutenant Robert A. Johnson. Better known to his comrades as Ox because of his muscular six-foot, 188-pound frame, the twenty-one-year-old Johnson was a much-loved figure in the group. In the challenging conditions, Johnson's navigator may have forgotten his maps measured the local mountains in meters. In any event, Bob Johnson crashed into one of those mountains, killing all aboard.[4]

The Epting crew avoided that fate and rolled to a stop on Tafaraoui's short runway. With stiff muscles after the long and arduous flight, Ben and his crewmates dropped from the fuselage of *Red Ass* onto African soil.

Ben had never been so close to combat, and the knowledge that he would finally get the chance to prove himself under fire was cause for euphoria and anxiety. But the loss of beloved comrades served as a sobering reminder to Ben and his crewmates: Death would be their ever-present companion as they faced off against Axis fighter planes and flak crews in the battle for North Africa.

Chapter 13

"NOW, I BELONG"

Anticipating a balmy respite from England's chilly autumn weather, the 93rd airmen arrived in Algeria to a cold rain and shabby accommodations. Their new home at Tafaraoui Airfield was a former French naval air cadet training station that had fallen into disrepair. The men were issued mattress covers filled with straw and shown to a low-slung building that would serve as a barracks. The iron beds were so uncomfortable that most of the men spread their mattresses on the clammy concrete floor. When it was discovered that cracks in the walls teemed with bedbugs, some of the men decided to sleep beneath their planes. That option lost its appeal when a steady rain became a sustained downpour, sending the airmen scurrying back to their quarters. After a wet and restless night, many of them awoke with colds.[1]

Daylight brought orders to prepare the 93rd Liberators for a mission, but more rain forced a cancellation a few hours later. The rain didn't relent for three days. With each passing day, the 93rd's new airfield more closely resembled a swamp.

When the skies finally cleared, Twelfth Air Force headquarters ordered Colonel Timberlake to get his men ready for a mission. The 93rd commander protested that the field was too soggy for his heavy bombers to leave the flight line, but he was curtly overruled.

Ben took his position as a gunner in *Red Ass* as B-24 engines around the field roared to life. The first plane to roll out of its parking spot was a Liberator named *Geronimo*. As it sloshed toward the runway, *Geronimo* mired in knee-deep mud. When the pilots tried to coax the aircraft forward by increasing the power, the nosewheel collapsed and the bomber's forward section plopped unceremoniously into the mud. A furious Timberlake ordered his aircraft to hold in place while he reported the mishap to headquarters. With Timberlake's warnings validated at the cost of one of his precious B-24s, his Twelfth Air Force superiors canceled the mission.[2]

The 93rd's North Africa sojourn was off to a shaky start.

THE RAIN RESUMED, BUT WITH AMERICAN and British ground forces facing grave peril amid a German counterattack in Tunisia, the Twelfth Air Force headquarters brusquely ordered Timberlake to get his bombers off the ground on December 13. The 93rd's assigned target was Bizerte, a bustling port critical to German field marshal Albert Kesselring's ongoing efforts to expand the Axis bridgehead in Tunisia. Bizerte was Africa's northernmost city, only 110 miles south of Sardinia and 145 miles southwest of Sicily. From Tafaraoui, Bizerte was a 600-mile one-way flight—a little more than three hours at B-24 cruising speed.

Timberlake finally extricated his bombers from the Tafaraoui mud and got them airborne without mishap. Inside *Red Ass*, Ben settled into his assigned area around the waist windows in the rear third of the fuselage.

From nose to tail, the length of the B-24D aircraft flown by the 93rd at the time was about sixty-five feet. The internal layout effectively compartmentalized the ten crew members individually or into small groups. In the cockpit, command pilot Jake Epting occupied the left seat and copilot Hap Kendall the right seat. Their radio operator sat at a small table just behind them. The nose compartment, located below the cockpit, was occupied by the navigator and bombardier. A forward area between the bomb bay and the cockpit was the duty station for the flight engineer, who monitored the engines and other mechanical systems during flight and doubled as the top turret gunner.

At the other end of the plane, the defense of *Red Ass* from enemy fighters was anchored by one of Ben's new friends, tail gunner Elmer (Bill) Dawley. The nineteen-year-old from East Orange, New Jersey, sat inside a Plexiglas turret that afforded 270-degree coverage of the area behind the aircraft and to either side. Ben and two other men were responsible for machine guns mounted in the two waist windows on either side of the tube-like fuselage and a "tunnel gun" fired through a small Plexiglas bubble in the floor. (Later B-24 models were equipped with a swiveling ball turret rather than a tunnel gun.)

The three-hour flight to Bizerte took the 93rd bombers over a verdant coastal plain of wheat and rice fields, olive orchards, and palm groves. As the aircraft climbed above ten thousand feet, one of the gunners reminded Ben to put on his bulky oxygen mask. Approaching the target area, Ben could see the bomb bay doors of nearby bombers open.

Without warning, bursting antiaircraft shells engulfed the bombers, rocking *Red Ass* with concussion waves. As the B-24s released their bombs on the docks and harbor below, some of the unfortunate souls in harm's way included several hundred Jews from Tunis who had been forced to perform war-related work by German troops.[3]

Lying in wait for the B-24s was a veteran contingent of German fighter pilots—part of a much larger Axis air force than Allied commanders had anticipated in planning Operation TORCH. Intelligence officers had estimated the Germans would be able to muster no more than 515 warplanes in the defense of Tunisia. In fact, the Germans had massed nearly 700 transport planes and more than 850 fighters and bombers.[4] Now, in the skies over Bizerte, Timberlake's B-24s experienced the intensity of the German air resistance.

Seconds after the B-24s released their bombs, Focke-Wulf Fw-190 fighters attacked. A piece of shrapnel from an exploding shell smashed through the *Red Ass* tail turret and into the head of Bill Dawley. As blood poured from Dawley's wound, Ben and the two gunners around him tried to defend the crew from the slashing enemy fighters. The fighters darted in and out of the bomber formation in attacks of dizzying speed. Ben had never experienced such fear. Suddenly, smoke erupted from a B-24 nearby and the bomber dropped from the formation.[5]

Once the B-24s outran the enemy fighters, *Red Ass* copilot Hap Kendall scrambled back to attend to Dawley. He was poised to jab a morphine syrette into the tail gunner's leg when Ben remembered an instructor's admonition during his gunnery training in England: A morphine injection could be fatal for someone with a head wound. Ben frantically gestured and made himself clear to the copilot: No morphine for a head wound.[6]

It wasn't clear whether Dawley would survive the flight back to Tafaraoui, but he did. As *Red Ass* rolled to a stop, an ambulance appeared and the wounded tail gunner was loaded inside and rushed to a nearby hospital.

Two 93rd crews were missing, their fate unknown for the time being.

The stricken B-24 that Ben had watched drop from the formation was piloted by Lieutenant John Roche, a lanky Iowa farm boy who had earned the nickname of Packy. He had named his aircraft *Ambrose*, after St. Ambrose College, which he had attended in Davenport, Iowa. After Ben watched *Ambrose* drop from the formation, Roche lost all four engines. He was attempting a dead-stick landing on a dirt airstrip along the Algeria coast at Bône (now Annaba) when he hit a gully in the middle of the field. The nosewheel snapped, and as *Ambrose* rose on its nose the fuselage snapped and three members of Roche's crew died in the wreckage. Roche and his six surviving crewmen spent a cold night watching over their dead while waiting for help to arrive.[7]

The mission was marred by one final tragedy. Over the target, a B-24 named *Flying Cock* was hit by flak and the crew's bombardier, Lieutenant John T. Sparks, suffered "a horrible head wound," pilot Llewellyn

(Lew) Brown of Malvern, Arkansas, later recalled. It was clear that Sparks wouldn't survive the flight back to Tafaraoui, so Brown made an emergency landing on the nearest Allied fighter strip he could find. The injuries suffered by Sparky, as he was known to comrades, proved fatal. He was buried in the Allied El Alia Cemetery in Algiers.[8]

Ben's first battle left him with conflicting emotions. He felt relief at finally earning membership in the exclusive fraternity of 93rd warriors after "the loneliest and longest year of my life, walking on eggshells, fearful that one wrong move or one incident, right or wrong, would jeopardize my chances to prove my loyalty." Now, "for the first time, I belonged." But the terrifying experience of flying through exploding enemy shells had convinced him that he didn't have long to live. Alone with his thoughts, Ben contemplated fears that he didn't dare share with his comrades. *I'm going to be lucky if I make it through ten missions.*

A DOZEN 93RD BOMBERS BOMBED BIZERTE again the following day, but Jake Epting's crew was among those that got the day off. The two missions flown from Tafaraoui Airfield were enough to convince Colonel Timberlake that his bombers needed a new home with a drier climate and longer runway. Timberlake's bosses at Twelfth Air Force headquarters agreed.

On December 17, the 93rd crews packed their gear and bade good riddance to Tafaraoui. In a nine-hour flight that spanned fifteen hundred miles, the 93rd crews flew eastward to Gambut (now Kambut), Libya, site of a British air force base near the border with Egypt. What was supposed to be a quick ten-day jaunt to North Africa had now become an open-ended adventure for Ben and his comrades.[9]

Chapter 14

GAMBUT

Throughout the night of December 17–18, 1942, Ben and his 93rd comrades flew eastward across North Africa. After losing fourteen men in eleven days since leaving England, disconcerting questions nagged the crews. What would they be asked to do next? How ferociously would the enemy resist their raids? How many more of them would die in the days ahead? The men were left alone with these thoughts as the Liberators droned toward the dawn.

Far below lay the land and sea on which the epic North Africa campaign had unfolded over the past two years. They passed over the current battle-fields of Tunisia, where the failure of the Allied race to Tunis had tipped momentum to the Germans. They crossed Tunisia's east coast and headed out over the Mediterranean, with Ben and other gunners keeping a watchful eye out for enemy night fighters as they skirted Axis-held Libya.

Not quite six weeks earlier, the British had stunned German field mar-shal Erwin Rommel at El Alamein in Egypt. The vaunted Desert Fox had saved the bulk of his army, but only after abandoning seventy-five thou-sand Italian troops to a sacrificial rearguard action. Rommel's survivors had been in an inexorable retreat ever since, ceding territory under ground and air attacks.

The previous week had witnessed more setbacks for Rommel in run-ning battles with British general Bernard Montgomery's Eighth Army. Rommel had been arguing bitterly with Hitler, Reichsmarschall Hermann Göring, and Field Marshal Albert Kesselring over the proper course of action. It was Rommel's view that Libya was lost and that he should con-centrate his forces in Tunisia, but Libya was the last piece of Italian dictator Benito Mussolini's African empire, and Il Duce wasn't ready to accept its loss. In recent days, Mussolini had ordered Rommel to make a stand at El Agheila, a Libyan coastal town notorious as the site of an earlier concentra-tion camp where Italian colonial forces had brutally incarcerated ten thou-sand Bedouin tribesmen. Hitler concurred with Mussolini's latest request, and so Rommel had ordered his men to prepare to meet the British.

What made the futile stand even more bitter for Rommel was Hitler's diversion of reinforcements and supplies from his battered army to Kesselring's Tunisian bridgehead. Rommel was determined not to sacrifice his Panzer Army in a futile last stand, and so when the British attacked his lines around El Agheila, he began withdrawing his forces on the night of December 12. Now, as Timberlake's men marked their seventh hour in the air while flying over the Mediterranean gulf that separated the Libyan provinces of Tripolitania and Cyrenaica, Ben and his comrades passed about ninety miles north of Rommel's dispirited army.

Crossing the gulf's eastern shore near the Libyan city of Benghazi, only recently reclaimed from Rommel's forces, the weary 93rd men once again entered Allied-controlled airspace. Finally, in the morning light of December 18, their new home came into view.

Emerging from the fuselage of *Red Ass*, Ben beheld a stark and treeless landscape. The forlorn airfield had been established by Italian forces in 1939, and it had changed hands four times in the fighting between Axis and Allied forces over the past two years. From this bleak outpost, Ted Timberlake's 93rd airmen were poised to play a crucial role in the quest for victory in North Africa.

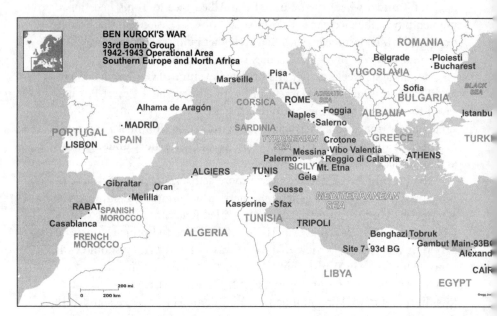

93rd Bomb Group, 1942–1943 operational area, Southern Europe and North Africa

BEN'S NEW BASE, ABOUT THREE MILES FROM the Libyan village of Gambut, was variously known as Gambut Main or LG (Landing Ground) 139. Situated about thirty miles southeast of the Libyan port city of Tobruk, the Italian field had been captured by the British in 1941, and the RAF added several satellite airstrips in the surrounding desert. Axis forces had recaptured Gambut Main on June 17, 1941, following the first battle of Tobruk, and the field had been heavily used by German and Italian air units in Rommel's drive eastward into Egypt. After the recent Axis defeat at the second battle of El Alamein, Gambut Main had been liberated by the New Zealand 4th Infantry Brigade on November 25, 1942.

In the three weeks since the Germans had fled, the same B-24 men who had preceded the 93rd at Fort Myers had used Gambut Main as the staging ground for raids on Axis-held ports in Libya and Tunisia. The men were members of two US B-24 groups now based in the Middle East: the 98th and the spinoff detachment led by Colonel Harry Halverson and now known as the 1st Provisional Bomb Group. Halverson's crews would soon be reconstituted as the 376th Bomb Group and put under the command of Major Keith Compton, the 93rd's operations officer, and the 98th and 376th would also take up residence at Gambut Main and a nearby field.

In their brief stay in Algeria, the 93rd had been attached to Major General James H. Doolittle's Twelfth Air Force. Now they would be assigned to the Ninth Air Force led by fifty-two-year-old General Lewis Brereton, a pioneering aviator of Hap Arnold's vintage, and his IX Bomber Command, led by General Patrick Timberlake, Ted Timberlake's oldest brother.

Patrick Timberlake was among the welcoming party for the 93rd as they touched down at Gambut Main. In the weeks prior, the 98th and the Halverson elements had used Gambut as a staging base for raids on Rommel's supply lines, and the 98th had built a small tent camp at Gambut for bomber crews flying in and out of the base.[1]

The 93rd would join an escalating campaign aimed at destroying Axis shipping and port facilities in Tunisia and Sicily. The missions promised to be long: It was 885 miles to Tunis, slightly more to Bizerte, and slightly less to the Tunisian ports of Sousse and Sfax; 830 miles to Naples on the Italian mainland and 650 miles to the vital Italian ports on either side of the Straits of Messina separating the toe of mainland Italy from Sicily. Through the fall of 1942, the 93rd's new parent outfit, the Ninth Air Force, had flown 1,621 sorties and dropped 2,632 tons of bombs on Rommel's forces and Kesselring's Tunisian bridgehead.[2]

Now the 93rd B-24 crews were poised to add their firepower to the punishing campaign against Axis forces in North Africa.

HAVING PRONOUNCED THE GAMBUT AIRFIELD "perhaps the lonesomest place" following a recent visit, General Brereton had described the B-24 crews who began using the base as living "strange lives in the desert." Brereton's words would prove prophetic as Ben and his comrades settled into their harsh environment.

When the 93rd arrived, the base boasted only one permanent structure—a blockhouse, in Brereton's description. Amid warnings of the strong winds and sandstorms they could expect, the 93rd airmen set to working improving the crude tent settlement established by the 98th crews. The six enlisted men of Jake Epting's *Red Ass* crew, Ben among them, moved into one of the white, slant-walled tents that were pitched in two clusters. Larger green pyramidal tents would be erected as needed.

The crews would learn through hard experience how to weatherize their tents against temperature swings, sandstorms, wind, and occasional rains that afflicted daily life on the Sahara Desert's northern fringe. They learned to tether tents securely, dig ditches for drainage, and arrange piles of sandbags to block the fine grains of windblown sand. They fashioned wind and sand breaks with sheet metal scavenged from the shattered German and Italian aircraft that littered the surrounding landscape. Their living arrangements were "tolerable but rugged," in the dry observation of 93rd historian Cal Stewart.[3]

Among the hardy creatures that shared the space with the 93rd crews were flies, scorpions, and hyenas. The 93rd's flight surgeon, Major Wilmer Paine, drew a cot that "was crawling with bedbugs until I killed them with 100-octane gas from *Teggie Ann*."[4] But the crueler challenge to daily life was the scarcity of water. Their closest water source—a shallow hole dug by British army engineers—was several miles away. On their arrival, the crews were informed that they would receive one canteen of water per day for all their personal needs—drinking, bathing, shaving, and laundry.[5]

Exploring their surroundings, the 93rd men discovered that their closest neighbors were "Bedouins and goats." During his recent visit, General Brereton had watched with bemusement as airmen bartered with the Bedouins for eggs. "It requires an art all its own, especially after the [Bedouins] found out how much the Americans hated [military-issue] dried eggs and how much they'd give for fresh eggs," Brereton observed. "About the only other amusement on off days was souvenir-hunting for items left behind by the Jerries [Germans] and Eyeties [Italians] when they occupied these same fields."[6]

As was the case in England, the weather in North Africa wreaked havoc on operational plans. The 93rd didn't have weather forecasting capabilities at Gambut, so they relied on coded radio messages from higher authorities. The messages were frequently disrupted by atmospheric conditions or enemy jamming efforts. If the forecasts reached Timberlake and his officers at all, they were at least twelve hours old, limiting their usefulness.[7]

After two days of housekeeping and exploration, the 93rd resumed operations on December 21. Their target was the harbor at Sousse, Tunisia. The 93rd was expected to fly a mission nearly every day, and so Timberlake committed about half his force—a dozen or so crews—to each mission.

The Epting crew sat out the December 21 attack on Sousse, but the following day Ben and his crewmates crowded into the intelligence tent for a pre-mission briefing. They were told they would strike the Tunis harbor and docks. With Ben once again assigned to one of the waist guns, Jake Epting and copilot Hap Kendall coaxed *Red Ass* into the air and slipped into their assigned spot in the formation for the 850-mile flight to Tunis. The Liberators reached the target without incident, dropped their bombs, and headed for home. By the time Epting and Kendall landed *Red Ass* at Gambut Main, the crew had been in the air for nine hours and forty-five minutes. Ben was credited with his third mission.

Bad weather over Tunisia grounded the crews for the next seventy-two hours. Some of the men took advantage of the downtime to do more exploring. Others built crude slit-trench bomb shelters or windbreaks, slept, wrote letters, played baseball, or searched for souvenirs.

The officers weren't reticent about exercising their privileges, and some roared off into the desert in jeeps to search for souvenirs or Bedouins from whom they might be able to procure eggs. One group of officers drove to the Mediterranean seashore, six miles to the north.

On Christmas Eve, Doc Paine and pilot Ken Cool were lounging in the tent they shared when they heard an airman playing a cornet off in the distance. Paine tracked the man down and asked if he would provide musical accompaniment for a Christmas Eve service in the tent that served as the 93rd's Officers' Club. A popular 328th Squadron pilot from Racine, Wisconsin, named John L. Jerstad—affectionately known as Jerk—read the story of the birth of Jesus from the Gospel of Luke. After the service, the homesick officers got drunk on bottles of Canadian Club and VO whisky. Christmas arrived with at least one officer in a drunken stupor and others throwing up before collapsing on their cots.[8]

On Christmas morning, there were Protestant and Catholic chapel services for enlisted men and officers. The Christmas meal didn't differ from any other day, except for those men who had received canned turkeys from loved ones back home.[9] Exercising the privileges of his rank, Ted Timberlake celebrated an elegant Christmas in Cairo with his older brother Patrick.

On December 26, with the weather to the west still foul, the 93rd prepared to resume operations. Fifteen crews were assigned to bomb Tunis, and they huddled for a 10:00 a.m. briefing. A crowd of brass, including generals Frank Andrews, Lewis Brereton, Patrick Timberlake, and Jacob Devers, flew in from Cairo to witness the 93rd in action. They landed at 11:45 a.m., in time to watch fifteen Liberators take off for Tunis. The bombers formed up in the skies overhead and were about to set off for the target when the mission was canceled because of weather. After pumping themselves up for combat, the men were "pretty disgusted" by the development.[10]

At 7:00 p.m., six crews were summoned back to the intelligence tent for another briefing. The weather in the Tunis area remained questionable, but higher-ups had decided to attempt a raid by a small group of B-24s flying individually. At 10:00 p.m., a raiding party of six B-24s took off, led by Ken Cool in *Teggie Ann*. Cool missed Tunis in the overcast skies and came under fire from a solitary enemy antiaircraft gun over Bizerte. Blown off course by high winds, he made landfall near Sfax and his bombardier dropped their bombs on the harbor and dock installations before heading for home. They reached Gambut Main at 11:15 a.m. on the morning of December 27 after a long and adventurous night.[11]

By the time that Cool landed *Teggie Ann* at Gambut Main, Ben and the Epting crew were preparing for action. Their mission would mark another milestone for Ben, for Epting had asked him to take over the tail turret. At noon, *Red Ass* was among twelve B-24s led by the 328th Squadron CO Addison Baker that embarked for Tunis. It was a long raid, and the weather forced the crews yet again to divert to an alternate target, but the Epting crew managed to drop their bombs on the Sousse harbor area. It was around 10:30 p.m. when they touched down at Gambut Main.

BACK AT CAMP, THE UNSANITARY conditions and cold desert nights spent shivering under damp blankets were taking a toll on the men. Doc Paine had admitted about fifteen men to the medical tent, some suffering from diarrhea and others with flu-like symptoms.

The men were constantly reminded of the hazards of their work. Around 11:00 p.m. on the night of December 28, Paine was summoned to the airstrip, where a battle-damaged 98th B-24 had made a belly landing. One of the pilots had been killed by a flak burst over Sousse. The surviving pilot had managed to land the damaged bomber without the use of his landing gear.

The raids continued as weather allowed. The 93rd briefed twelve crews on December 29, with Tunis the primary target and Sousse the alternate. The raiders were led by pilot K. K. Compton in *Teggie Ann*, which took four flak hits over Sousse. One member of Compton's crew earned a Purple Heart when a flak splinter pierced his hand. The bombers hit three ships in Sousse harbor, igniting an explosion in one of the vessels. It also damaged the docks and railroad yards.[12]

On December 30, Jake Epting and another pilot flew to Abu Suwir, Egypt, along the Suez Canal, on a supply run. Doc Paine tagged along, ostensibly to pick up medical supplies, but he also got in some shopping and sightseeing. The desert between Gambut Main and the Nile River was littered with what Paine estimated to be sixty to one hundred shattered tanks and countless airplanes.

Paine was mesmerized by the sharp contrast between the desert and the Nile Delta, with its heavily populated adobe towns. "Canals, sailing vessels, cypress trees, orange groves, endless tent camps of British troops," Paine observed. He found the Suez Canal "most interesting." In the city of Ismailia, Paine bought a watch for himself, silk stockings, a silver bracelet, and a bottle of chianti. He checked into a hotel and "had [a] wonderful hot bath and delicious supper."[13] The following day, before heading back to Gambut Main in the afternoon, Epting and his wingman treated themselves and their passengers to an aerial tour of the Nile Delta area, making two passes around the Sphinx and the Great Pyramids before turning west for their home base.

On New Year's Eve, the 93rd dispatched twelve Liberators to bomb Sfax. All landed safely by 10:00 p.m. While waiting for their comrades to return, several pilots packed into the Doc Paine–Ken Cool tent to finish off their last quart of rum. At the stroke of midnight, the camp erupted in celebratory pistol fire and the *pop-pop-pop* of crude firecrackers fashioned by extracting gunpowder from shells.

Ben and his comrades on the Epting crew had finished the year with a four-day break from combat. In the twenty-four days since earning a spot on the crew, Ben had logged four missions and he had earned the trust of his comrades under fire. He had achieved his goal of proving himself in combat, but the missions were taking their toll on all the men.

Over the past week, Doc Paine had expressed deepening concern with the impact of combat stress on the 93rd airmen. One of the men whose mental state especially worried him was a twenty-one-year-old pilot from San Diego named George E. Piburn. In his journal that week, Paine observed, "Piburn needs a rest."

Since the move to Gambut, Paine had twice spoken to Colonel Timberlake about his concerns over the "strain the men are under." Paine had also observed worrisome signs within the crew commanded by Arkansan Lew Brown, whose bombardier, Lieutenant John Sparks, had suffered a fatal flak wound in their first raid in Africa. Brown's copilot, Robert J. Quinlivan, had been badly shaken by the tragedy, and other members of the crew weren't doing well. "Lew Brown's crew needs rest—cracking after Lt. Sparks died of flak in frontal lobe left. Advised Col. Ted," Paine recorded in his journal on December 28. Later that same day, Timberlake convened a meeting with Paine and other senior officers to discuss "flying fatigue," as the flight surgeon called it.[14]

There were no easy answers—Timberlake was under pressure from higher-ups to keep his crews flying as the campaign in North Africa hurtled to a climax. Yet the concern about men breaking under the strain was also a subject of urgent discussion among senior US air commanders and medical personnel in England. How long could men like Ben withstand the unique physical and psychological demands of aerial combat? The American air commanders could only speculate, but the New Year would reveal some worrisome answers.

Chapter 15

BROTHERS IN ARMS

Never in his wildest dreams could Ben have imagined that on the first morning of 1943 he would awaken in a tent in North Africa's Sahara Desert. Yet here he was. In his twelve months in the US Army Air Forces, he had encountered more bigotry than he had experienced in his entire prewar life. But he had remained unbowed, and now he could proudly call himself a combat veteran. He had made his combat debut with Jake Epting's crew as a waist gunner on December 13, and on his fourth and final mission of 1942 he had been entrusted with the even more demanding and solitary assignment of tail gunner—the role he carried into the New Year.

At first glance, Jake Epting was an improbable champion of the Japanese American farm boy he had now entrusted to watching his back. Epting was born on January 14, 1921, in the racially segregated town of Tupelo, Mississippi. He was the only child of a postal clerk and a homemaker who later found work as a saleslady in a local dry goods store. Jake Sr.'s job with the post office spared the Epting family the worst privations of the Depression years. The family wasn't wealthy, but they didn't want for much, and so young Jake's childhood was stable and largely devoid of hardship or heartache. Life revolved around family, church, school, and sports. Upon graduating from high school in Tupelo in 1938, Jake Jr. entered Mississippi State College in Starkville. He studied business, pledged a fraternity, and joined the campus Reserve Officers Training Corps, serving in one of the regiment's two infantry battalions. An article in the Jackson *Clarion-Ledger* newspaper in his freshman year listed J. B. Epting as one of eleven young men inducted into the Phi Kappa Tau social fraternity. A year-and-a-half later, the 1940 Mississippi State yearbook listed Epting with an even more prestigious affiliation: Signa Alpha Epsilon, a fraternity founded in Alabama in the 1850s as a paragon of the antebellum South's notions of virtuous manhood.

Jake Epting was about to begin his sophomore year at Mississippi State when Hitler invaded Poland, and by the early weeks of his junior year America had initiated the first peacetime draft in the nation's history. Epting had just finished his junior year when he enlisted in the Army Air Corps on May 31, 1941.

Epting quickly found himself on a track to earn his pilot's wings. He was slight of build for a pilot—enlistment records listed him as five-foot-eight and 133 pounds—but he had a natural flair for flying. He cruised through two phases of training in Texas and was progressing through the advanced course at Brooks Field in San Antonio when the Japanese attacked Pearl Harbor. One week later, with America now at war with not only the militaristic government of Japan but also Nazi Germany and Fascist Italy, Epting proposed marriage to his girlfriend—a smart and socially prominent young woman from Chattanooga, Tennessee, and on January 8, 1942, he earned his pilot's wings at Brooks Field. The following day he married Nancy Roddey at St. Mark's Episcopal Church in San Antonio, and after a brief honeymoon, Epting entered four-engine bomber training. Two months later, he was assigned to the 93rd Bomb Group at Barksdale Field, Louisiana.

In the cockpit of a B-24 Liberator, Epting's deft feel for flying was tested by his size. He had to scoot his pilot's seat all the way forward so his feet could work the rudder pedals. His nickname was Baby Jake, one senior 93rd officer recalled. Yet Epting's skills as a pilot weren't in question. As an aircraft commander responsible for an expensive four-engine bomber and the lives of nine men, Epting adopted a stern by-the-book leadership style. He wasn't humorless, but he ran a tight ship. The enlisted men on the crew were glad that their other three officers took a much more lenient approach to military discipline and protocol.

Epting's cockpit partner was a copilot who shared his flair for flying, but not his stern style of command. Born in central Iowa on July 19, 1917, Harold (Hap) Kendall grew up in Chariton, a small town about forty miles south of Des Moines. He was four years older than Epting. His laid-back approach toward the men of his crew wasn't the only contrast he struck alongside Epting. Kendall had played college basketball, and, at six-foot-two and 170 pounds, with brown hair and blue eyes, he was physically imposing. Kendall had been a star basketball player at Grinnell College in Iowa and excelled at track. He was a cool hand in the cockpit, and Kendall and Epting formed a formidable team.

When gunner George Ingle received his orders detaching him from the crew on Thanksgiving Day, Epting had done his due diligence in his search for a replacement. Ben Kuroki had come highly recommended from several sources, including Chaplain Burris and fellow 409th Squadron pilot Dick Wilkinson. In his brief association with Epting and the rest of the crew, Ben had acquitted himself well. He knew how to handle the .50-caliber machine guns, didn't panic under fire, didn't drink to excess, and got along well with others. From Epting's vantage point, Ben Kuroki was worthy of his trust.

LIKE MOST BOMBER CREWS, JAKE EPTING and his nine men were a diverse group in terms of geography, education, and socioeconomic status. They were an American cross section to an extent, with the notable exception that no Black Americans were assigned to bomber units at that point. Epting and his men had roots in big cities, small towns, and farming communities. Some had grown up in comfort, while others, like Ben, had known hard times. Five of the men had attended some college. Five of them, Ben included, hadn't progressed beyond high school.

The Epting crew was divided into two groups by military rank. At the top of the hierarchy were the crew's four commissioned officers, all bearing the rank of first or second lieutenant. As the aircraft commander, Epting was senior in rank to Harold Kendall, bombardier Al Naum, and navigator Edward Weir. Below the commissioned officers were the crew's six enlisted men, all of whom had entered the army as privates and now held the rank of technical sergeant or staff sergeant. None of the enlisted men could expect to rise any higher unless they received a battlefield commission or some other special dispensation. That had recently happened to gunner George Ingle, who made the Atlantic crossing with Epting and flew three missions with the crew before receiving permission to enter pilot's training back in the US.

In a heavy bomber squadron, pilots tended to congregate in their own informal groups within the larger body of commissioned officers, and such was the case with the Epting crew. Navigators and bombardiers, many of whom had "washed out" of pilot's training before receiving orders to attend another Army Air Forces specialty school, formed their own social groups. Army fraternization rules discouraged close personal relationships between commissioned officers and enlisted men, but Naum and Weir horsed around with Epting's enlisted contingent to an extent that was atypical on most crews—a fact that sometimes irritated Epting, but endeared Naum and Weir to Ben and the other enlisted men.

Ben forged his deepest bonds with the five other enlisted men on the crew: radio operator Dell Kettering; engineer and top turret gunner Alexander Halbridge; and gunners James Holliday, Richard Ryan, and Ples Norwood. Oldest among them was Kettering, who had just turned twenty-six, followed by Ben at twenty-five, Halbridge and Ryan at twenty-four, and the twenty-one-year-old Norwood. Kettering and Ryan were both married—Kettering had exchanged vows with his hometown sweetheart in Manchester, New Hampshire, as the Epting crew picked up their new B-24 and prepared to depart for England, while Ryan had married in 1938 and had a three-year-old daughter back home in Massachusetts.

At five-feet-ten-and-a-half-inches and 170 pounds, Ryan was one of the most physically imposing men on the crew, with brown hair and brown eyes. He grew up in a large Irish-Catholic family in the Boston area. His father was a salesman and his mother a hairdresser. Ryan had married an Irish Catholic girl whose parents worked in shoe factories in the Boston suburb of Lynn, where Ryan and his family were living. Before the war, Ryan held a good job as a lab assistant for a chemical company in Cambridge.

Kettering, who would become Ben's closest friend on the crew, hailed from Monmouth, Illinois, near the Mississippi River in the west-central part of the state. When the federal census was taken in the spring of 1940, Kettering was living with his parents and younger sister in Monmouth and working as a salesman. Not long afterward, he moved to Southern California. At five-foot-eight, 152 pounds, Red Kettering, as he was widely known, had a more compact build that was common among the men serving on bomber crews. He had a ruddy complexion, hazel eyes, and a head of red hair that inspired his nickname.

Ben was also especially fond of Alex Halbridge, the Brooklyn-born-and-raised son of Russian Jews who had immigrated to America's East Coast not long after Ben's parents had arrived on the West Coast. Halbridge was tall and lanky at six-foot-one and 174 pounds, with blond hair and brown eyes. He was the youngest of three children in a home where Yiddish was the first language. His mother took care of the children and managed the household while his father worked in a Brooklyn hat factory, crafting the wooden blocks used to mold hats into specific shapes and sizes. Halbridge had another distinction among Epting's enlisted men: He had attended college for a year before going to work as a clerk at a Brooklyn industrial firm that manufactured screws and other metal products.

The most experienced and poised gunner on the Epting crew at this point was James Holliday. He was the youngest of five children born to a bricklayer and a homemaker in Canton, Ohio, but Holliday's mother had died when he was five. He was raised by three older sisters and his paternal grandparents, who had emigrated from England. At the time of his enlistment in April 1941, Holliday was working as a stock boy at a Canton business. Ten days before the Japanese attack on Pearl Harbor, he entered the Army Air Forces. He was five-foot-seven and 158 pounds, with a ruddy complexion, brown hair, and blue eyes. He projected an air of coolness under fire that played well with his peers on the crew.

The youngest member of Ben's group was Ples Norwood. He had followed a path to the Epting crew that was similar to Ben's. Norwood had been a ground crew member with the 93rd in England when he had talked his way into gunnery school and a combat assignment. Back home in eastern Tennessee, Norwood was the oldest of three boys. He grew up in a rural area on the western edge of the Great Smoky Mountains, outside Knoxville, Tennessee, where his father was a manual laborer in a marble mill. Norwood was close to Ben in size at five-foot-eight and 144 pounds, with brown hair, brown eyes, and a ruddy complexion. Economic necessity had been a factor in Norwood's decision to enlist: When the draft got underway in the fall of 1940, he was jobless and single, and thus a prime candidate for conscription. Rather than wait to be drafted and lose his freedom of choice as to branch of service, he had traveled to Atlanta after Christmas and enlisted in the Air Corps on January 4, 1941.

These were the men with whom Ben now spent every waking hour as the crews adjusted to their primitive desert life and prepared to ramp up the air war against Axis supply lines. Epting had already seen two gunners leave his crew—one who was still recovering from severe frostbite in his fingers suffered on the crew's first raid and the other to pursue pilot's training. In the months ahead, as combat took its inevitable toll, the Epting crew would see more turnover.

BEN AND HIS COMRADES AWAKENED TO A cool morning in their desert camp on January 1, 1943. The 93rd had been informed that they would have the day off from flying—their comrades of the 98th were scheduled to bomb the Tunis harbor later in the day—and so a leisurely day was on tap for Ted Timberlake's men. There would be time for naps, writing letters, chewing the fat, searching for souvenirs, and a pickup baseball game.

Flight surgeon Wilmer Paine awakened at ten minutes past seven, lit the oil heater he and Ken Cool had procured for their tent, and washed his face and hands in a meager ration of water that filled the bottom quarter of his steel pot helmet. After getting dressed and eating breakfast, Paine held sick call for men complaining of assorted ailments. When that was done, he caught up on his paperwork, filling out certificates for twelve men who had earned the Purple Heart for injuries received in the December 13 raid on Bizerte and the December 29 raid on Sousse.

That still left time for the bearded flight surgeon to convene with Colonel Timberlake and three other officers to welcome the New Year with a warm-up drinking session before lunch. Between the five of them they polished off a half bottle of Canadian Club whisky and three bottles of Palestinian wine while they read poems from a new anthology. After lunch,

Paine and Jake Epting hopped into a jeep with a supply of tea, sugar, cigarettes, and whiskey and spent the afternoon driving from one Bedouin
camp to another in hopes of trading for a German officer's Luger pistol.
They returned to camp empty-handed.[1]

The day ended with some excitement when British antiaircraft guns
opened up nearby and the men braced for an attack. German aircraft had
apparently picked up the trail of the 98th raiding party of fifteen Liberators
as they returned from bombing Tunis, and they tracked the Liberators back
to the 98th's new home at one of Gambut's nearby satellite fields, LG 159.
A Luftwaffe Ju-88 shot up one 98th B-24 as it landed, wounding three men.
Another 98th crew missed the airstrip and bailed out over the desert. Several bombs fell harmlessly around the airstrip and the 98th camp, and the
guns fell silent.

The first night of the New Year held more unpleasant surprises for the
men. Rain began to fall, and the wind stiffened, and around 2:00 a.m. a dust
storm hit the camp. The wind howled and dust and sand scoured the camp
all night, and when the men awakened bleary-eyed on the morning of January 2 it was still blowing strong. It was a lost day as the dreaded *khamsin*, as
the Sahara dust storms were known, lashed the camp without respite. The
mess tent blew down, and so the enlisted men huddled in their tents, picking at canned C-rations, writing letters, playing cards, and sleeping. Part of
the 93rd's headquarters tent collapsed, and the day ended with the men still
hunkered down, waiting for the storm to blow itself out.

The wind and dust finally eased on Sunday, January 3, but the rain
returned. The 93rd had been scheduled to send twelve aircraft to bomb Bizerte. The crews were briefed and the gunners climbed aboard their ships
with their .50-caliber weapons and ammunition, waiting to take off, only
to be told to stand down because of the foul weather.

Another wasted day, leaving the men of the 93rd and their officers discouraged. The chilly, damp weather in England had gotten old in a hurry,
but life in the desert was even more dispiriting. "We left Alconbury four
weeks ago this morning," Doc Paine scribbled in his diary. "Wish the devil
we were back there now."

Chapter 16

ON TO ITALY

While Ben and his B-24 comrades waited for the storms to subside, events in Tunisia had taken another unhappy turn for the Allies. An early December debacle had decimated American armored units, and now the Allies were making a final attempt to sever Rommel's lifeline to Italy by seizing Tunis.

As a prelude to the push through the Medjerda River valley, Anglo-American forces sought to secure a strategic patch of high ground that had fallen into German hands. The Coldstream Guards drew the assignment to seize what the cricket-loving British had christened Longstop Hill. The eight-hundred-foot hill was two miles long and sprawled to within a few hundred yards of the Medjerda River, posing a threat to any Allied advance through the valley.

The Coldstream Guards seized the hill as planned on the night of December 22, and at 4:30 a.m. on December 23, began abandoning their positions for soldiers of the US Army's 18th Infantry Regiment, part of Major General Terry Allen's Big Red One Division. In the dark and rain, eight hundred US infantrymen ended up scattered around the hill. But the Coldstream Guards had abandoned several forward positions before the Americans were in place, allowing the Germans to promptly reclaim the ground. Even worse, the British had somehow failed to notice that Longstop Hill actually was two hills, one of which was nominally in American hands and the other of which was still in German hands.[1]

The Germans quickly took advantage of the Allied mistakes. Under fierce attack by German Panzergrenadiers, the Americans called for help and the weary Coldstream Guards slogged back to Longstop to stave off an Allied disaster. The Coldstream Guards counterattacked on the afternoon of December 24, and by nightfall the British soldiers with some help from American forces had reclaimed the positions they had vacated the previous day and even gained a tenuous toehold on the second hill. In a Christmas Eve message to the British high command, General Vyvyan Evelegh confidently predicted imminent victory.[2]

Once again, enemy forces struck first. At 7:00 a.m. on Christmas morning, the Germans launched a fierce counterattack that shattered Allied positions around Longstop. With his forces in danger of being cut off, General Evelegh ordered a retreat. The American and British survivors withdrew in a pouring rain, leaving the Germans to celebrate their victory atop the newly rechristened Christmas Hill.[3]

With Allied designs on Tunis now in tatters, recriminations rattled through American and British senior ranks. The Americans were "our Italians," sniffed some British officers. A British after-action report denigrated Terry Allen's troops as "unfitted and unprepared for the task they were asked to perform, which would, in fact, have been difficult for any battalion."[4] Incensed by the sniping from comrades-in-arms, Allen confronted his British counterpart with an American report that accused the British of having "completely misused" his 18th Infantry soldiers.[5]

With the early promise of the Operation TORCH offensive now a distant memory, General Eisenhower braced for a hard fight ahead. In a December 26 cable to the combined Anglo-American chiefs of staff, Eisenhower confessed that the abandonment of the drive on Tunis "has been the severest disappointment I have suffered to date."[6]

His original orders had envisioned TORCH forces driving eastward across North Africa to trap Rommel's army in an Allied vise in the Libyan desert. Now such a spectacular victory seemed unlikely, and in its place loomed the prospect of a bloody slugfest pitting two Allied armies against two Axis armies within the rugged confines of Tunisia.

Under unprecedented pressure, his patience wearing thin, Eisenhower had recently snapped at his handpicked air chief when Major General James H. Doolittle tried to explain why the Luftwaffe still dominated the skies over Tunisia. "Those are your troubles," Eisenhower barked. "Go and cure them."[7] In the monumental campaign that now confronted Eisenhower, Axis fortunes hinged on continued control of the air and the preservation of vulnerable supply lines. The American B-24 Liberators grounded by weather in the Libyan desert had emerged as a potentially decisive chip in the high-stakes poker game underway in North Africa.

THE INHOSPITABLE WINDS THAT SCOURED the eastern Sahara resumed on January 4, and Ben and his 93rd comrades spent another long day huddled in their tents as dust and sand penetrated every crevice, covering their cots and mess kits and everything else inside the tents. The enlisted men had limited options for coping with the tedium of being cooped in their tents. They could sleep, write letters, play cards, or reminisce about their homes and families or dream about their hopes for the future. The 93rd officers, on the other hand, tapped liquor stashes to help pass the hours.

As the winds screeched, Timberlake joined 328th Squadron leader Addison Baker in a drinking session in the tent shared by Doc Paine and Ken Cool. Between the four of them, they polished off a quart of Canadian Club whisky while awaiting the supper hour. An inebriated Paine regaled the others with stories about Meadow Creek Farm, his Blue Ridge homestead outside Charlottesville, Virginia, where he raised sheep and lived the life of a gentleman farmer.

The weather wasn't the only concern for the generals leading the air campaign in North Africa. The secret discussions about combat fatigue that had become a sudden preoccupation of senior Eighth Air Force officers as the 93rd departed England in early December now vexed the brass of the 93rd's new parent outfit.

Riding out the storm at his Cairo headquarters, the Ninth Air Force commander, General Lewis Brereton, fretted about this insidious new threat to the combat efficiency of his bomber crews. "Operational fatigue is evident among our combat crews," Brereton acknowledged in his diary on January 4. But the awareness of combat stress disorders was still embryonic, and Brereton held the prevailing view of his peers that the condition wasn't so much a medical one as it was a lapse in leadership. He said as much in conversations with Ted Timberlake and the commanders of the 98th and 376th bomb groups. In Brereton's recollection, "I emphasized to the Group Commands that there was no such thing as a poor organization—that (to paraphrase Napoleon) 'there are only poor leaders.'"[8]

In other words, the fatigued airmen were expected to fight through their dark thoughts.

THE WEATHER FINALLY BROKE ON JANUARY 5, and the 93rd crews were briefed and climbed into their aircraft for takeoff. For the Epting crew, it would be their first combat mission in nine days. Their target was the port area of Tunis, but weather forced a diversion to their alternate target, the port of Sousse, seventy-five miles south of Tunis, on Tunisia's east coast. Ben spent ten-and-a-half hours in the air, much of that seated in the cold and cramped tail turret of *Red Ass*, keeping an eye out for prowling enemy fighters. The mission was otherwise uneventful, and when Ben emerged from the belly of *Red Ass*, he had earned his first combat award: the Air Medal, bestowed on an airman for every five combat missions completed.

As if the commanders of the bomb groups didn't have enough worries with the weather and the combat fatigue among their men, the condition of their aircraft now loomed as an issue. The sandstorms had begun to take a toll on the Liberators, and this became apparent during missions. The 328th Squadron commander, a 1941 West Point graduate named Joe Tate, didn't even attempt a takeoff on the January 5 mission because of aircraft performance issues. The pilot of *Hot Freight* had turned back because his number three engine kept cutting out.

The sun had emerged in the aftermath of the latest storms, but the weather had turned cold. January 6 was an off day for the airmen, and it happened to be one of the nicest days since their arrival at Gambut. The sun shone and temperatures warmed to the point that Doc Paine and others stripped down to cut-off khaki shorts to soak up some rays. Several of the men organized a raucous softball game. When Ben muffed an attempt to catch a fly ball, one of his crewmates expressed mock outrage and called on the Japanese American gunner to "commit hara kiri" to atone for his miscue. The officers watching the game laughed and Ben played along.[9]

The 93rd was back in action the following day, January 7, and their target marked a new milestone: They were to attack Italy for the first time, striking Palermo, the largest city on the island of Sicily and the port of origin for many of the ships now funneling supplies to the two Axis armies in North Africa. Palermo was a 750-mile flight from Gambut for the 93rd bombers.

Jake Epting and his men were among the 93rd crews selected to fly the raid. They were briefed at 9:00 a.m. and took off at noon. The mission called for twelve 93rd aircraft to rendezvous with another twelve B-24s from the 98th and the 376th. The plan quickly unraveled when two 93rd aircraft aborted en route to the target because of mechanical problems and the dozen 98th and 376th bombers returned to Gambut Main because of bad weather. The 93rd's remaining ten aircraft, Epting's *Red Ass* among them, pressed on in the gathering twilight.

Arriving over Palermo harbor, *Red Ass* bombardier Al Naum dropped his bombs without incident and navigator Edward Weir set a course for Gambut Main. Ten hours after departure, Epting and copilot Hap Kendall landed at Gambut Main. It was a triumph for Ben and his crewmates and the other 93rd men who carried out the mission; they had taken the war to the Italian enemy's homeland for the first time, and they had done so without a single casualty.

No mission was scheduled for January 8, which allowed the men to spend a leisurely day lolling around the camp. Shortly after nightfall, air-raid sirens wailed and the men scanned the skies for signs of enemy marauders. Flares suddenly lit the night sky to the north and antiaircraft guns boomed. The target was an Allied convoy steaming just offshore the Libyan coast, and the antiaircraft guns were aboard the ships. The attack ended, the flares faded, and silence settled over the 93rd's desert camp.

January 9 marked another day of soothing sunshine. The wind kicked up a bit, but nothing like the previous week. In addition to his duties as flight surgeon, Doc Paine had become the 93rd's expert on the roving bands of Bedouins, and he had made a game of sorts out of negotiating bigger and better transactions with the locals. He headed off into the desert in a jeep with tins of tea and eight pounds of sugar he had finagled from 93rd mess sergeants for several boxes of cigarettes. In his biggest deal to date, Paine returned to camp with two dozen eggs for him and his tentmate and invited guests. While the enlisted men dined on C-rations, Paine and Ken Cool whipped up a lunchtime spread of scrambled eggs, hash, fried sweet potatoes, and canned peaches, washed down with canned tomato juice and coffee.

After two weeks of close-quarters living in the desert camp, sanitary conditions had deteriorated. There were no latrines or privies, so the men performed their excretory functions by digging a hole and covering it with sand when they finished. This became a problem when the relentless winds began to uncover some of the holes. An army medical inspector visited the 93rd camp on the afternoon of January 9 and was appalled by the filthy conditions, including "crapping paper being blown all over [the] camp," Doc Paine recorded in his diary. Plans were made to construct latrines before an outbreak of dysentery or other illnesses.

A mission to Bizerte was briefed during the daylight hours of January 9, but it was canceled before takeoff because of weather in the target area.

In the month since their arrival in North Africa, Ted Timberlake's crews had flown nine missions. They had lost eighteen men in their first week, including fourteen in the crash involving Ox Johnson and his crew. Since the December 13 raid on Bizerte, the 93rd had gone twenty-seven days without any deaths or serious injuries. Most of the raids were carried out in darkness, exploiting the dearth of enemy night fighters in North Africa and Italy. The raids were far longer than what the 93rd crews had experienced flying out of Alconbury, but enemy resistance seemed markedly weaker.

Ben's initial shock after his first raid on December 13, marked by the traumas of experiencing an antiaircraft barrage and witnessing the wounding of a comrade for the first time, had caused him to doubt whether he would live to see ten missions. Now, with six missions to his credit and four weeks without a casualty, Ben's odds of survival had seemingly improved. But a tragic ten-day stretch ahead shattered that thinking and impressed upon Ben and his comrades the grim reality of their situation: Death would be a constant and capricious companion any time they took off for a mission.

Chapter 17

BIG DEALER

Around midmorning on January 10, 1943, a 93rd Bomb Group B-24 rumbled down the Gambut Main runway in a stiff breeze and climbed into a sunny winter sky. At the controls was a big, bearlike man, twenty-eight-year-old Major William Barksdale Musselwhite.

A former starting tackle on the Mississippi State College football team at Starkville, the easygoing native of Jackson, Mississippi, had written his name in the history books the previous August by piloting one of a dozen B-17 Flying Fortresses on the first Eighth Air Force raid of the war. In fact, Musselwhite's *Peggy D* had dropped the first Eighth Air Force bomb of the daylight campaign against a German target. Newspapers across America had published photos of the brawny Musselwhite with his crew both before and after the raid on Rouen, France. Later in the fall, Musselwhite had been transferred to the 93rd Bomb Group's 409th Squadron to fly B-24 Liberators. He was leading today's raid.

One of the pilots that formed up on Musselwhite's lead in the clear skies over the eastern Sahara was Jake Epting. While Epting and Hap Kendall guided *Red Ass* into its assigned spot in the formation, Ben chatted with his fellow gunners in the back until it was time to climb into his tail turret for another day at work.

Their target was a key link in the Axis supply pipeline in Tunisia: La Goulette, the portside complex of warehouses and docks built on a sandbar that separated the brackish Lake Tunis from the Mediterranean gulf. The weather forecast for the target area wasn't good, but General Brereton had stressed the need to keep the pressure on. Sketchy weather or not, the B-24s would take a shot at crippling the taproot of the Axis armies in North Africa.

It was nearly nine hundred miles to the target, a distance Musselwhite and the other 93rd bombers covered in about five hours, most of which was spent over the Mediterranean. Approaching Tunis from the sea, the pilots found the weather better than feared. The bombers began their final sprint to the target.

In the late afternoon light, the B-24s toggled their bombs on the bustling port facilities of La Goulette. In less than ten minutes, Musselwhite and his raiders were in and out of the target area, and the crews settled in for the long flight back to Gambut Main.

With night falling and the risk of a midair collision rising, Musselwhite gave the order for the bombers to transition from an attack formation to a staggered file of solo flights. Every bomber was now on its own.

Back at the Gambut camp, Doc Paine had kept several of the enlisted men who weren't flying today busy on a project triggered by the previous day's health inspection. Their mission was to install a barrel-latrine system. Under Paine's supervision, the men cut both ends out of several oil drums, buried two-thirds of each in the sand, and covered each with a wooden lid. The work was done by lunch.

The hours passed slowly when the men were away on a mission, and such was the case for Paine on this day. After lunch and a nap, he read for an hour or two, choosing a selection from the Jeeves series penned by English novelist P. G. Wodehouse. Around four, Paine checked out a jeep and drove to a nearby RAF medical reception station to chat with his British counterparts. He returned to the Gambut camp in time for dinner, and then spent the early evening waiting for word that the bombers were nearing the field.

Around nine o'clock, the lead 93rd aircraft alerted the Gambut Main tower of their approach. At 9:06 p.m., Paine headed to the control tower with his tentmate Ken Cool to watch the bombers land.[1]

One of the La Goulette raiders winging eastward through the evening of January 10 was a 330th Squadron Liberator named *Big Dealer*. The pilot was a twenty-three-year-old first lieutenant named Owen Kunze, one of the 93rd's rising stars.

A wiry six-footer with a genial demeanor, blue eyes, and brown hair, Kunze grew up on a farm in east-central South Dakota, about 250 miles north of Ben's Nebraska home. The area was known for farming and pheasant hunting. Farm families grew corn and other grains and raised hogs and cattle, both dairy and beef. Kunze was the youngest of four children born to George and Maude Kunze, and his grandparents on both sides of the family were immigrants—from Germany on his father's side and England on his mother's.

Young Owen distinguished himself as a schoolboy in spelling bees, essay-writing contests, Boy Scouts, and sports. He hunted pheasants and ducks in the fall, fished in the summer, and played baseball and basketball in season. After high school in the small town of Alpena, Kunze entered the South Dakota School of Mines in Rapid City. He studied to be a mining engineer while playing guard and forward on the school's Hardrockers basketball team. In mid-September 1940, the same week the first peacetime draft in American history got underway, Kunze was one of ten students selected for the third flight-training class conducted by the School of Mines. Kunze successfully completed the course in early December 1940 and earned his civilian pilot's license in early January. Seven months later, on July 20, 1941, after two years of college, Kunze entered the Army Air Forces.

On the day he reported for his Army physical that summer of 1941, Kunze met two other aspiring military pilots, Iowans John "Packy" Roche and Robert "Shine" Shannon. The three passed their army physicals and became inseparable over the ensuing months of pilot's training. All three earned their wings in early 1942 and were assigned to Ted Timberlake's fledgling B-24 group at Barksdale Field that spring. Their close friendship, prowess as pilots, and penchant for practical jokes earned them a mock-serious sobriquet. They became known as the 93rd's "Terrible Three."[2]

Kunze wore his officer's peaked cap at a jaunty angle, and he brought a reassuring can-do style to his command of the *Big Dealer* crew. He was one of twenty 93rd pilots who had flown the October 9, 1942, debut raid on Lille, and two of Kunze's gunners were credited with shooting down enemy fighters on the mission. Recounting how *Big Dealer* got shot up over enemy territory without any of his crew suffering so much as a scratch, Kunze quipped to a news correspondent, "I think we must have had a rabbit['s] foot along."[3]

Kunze again caught the attention of American war correspondents a few weeks later after tangling with German fighters on an anti-submarine patrol over the Bay of Biscay. In a shoot-out with three twin-engine Messerschmitt Me-110 fighters on the November 9 patrol, Kunze's men shot down two enemy aircraft and drove off the third.[4]

Fortune continued to favor Kunze and his crew in North Africa. On the 93rd's first mission, the December 13 raid on Bizerte, *Big Dealer* had taken multiple hits from enemy fire without any injuries, and Kunze and his copilot, Lieutenant John "Babe" Emmons, another Iowan, had safely landed the aircraft. Kunze had mentioned the incident in a letter that had just reached his parents in South Dakota in early January. "A funny thing happened the other day. 'Big Dealer' was fairly well riddled and looked like a sieve but is all repaired and ready to go again. Believe me, Jerry is really going to pay for that. Tell [cousin] Kenneth that I dropped a bomb with his name on it. Not only that, it hit smack on the target too."[5]

Now Kunze and his *Big Dealer* crew were among the broken line of

93rd B-24s closing on Gambut Main in the darkness. Between 9:00 and 10:00 p.m., eleven Liberators landed safely and taxied to their assigned parking spots. As silence settled over the blacked-out field, a quick check revealed one missing aircraft: *Big Dealer.*

Several men waited at the field, straining to hear the sound of approaching aircraft engines. But there was only silence. Doc Paine and Ken Cool finally left the control tower and returned to their tent. They stayed up reading and hoping to hear good news about *Big Dealer*, but finally gave up at midnight and extinguished their oil lamps.

The rest of the 93rd camp awoke on January 11 to the disconcerting news that Owen Kunze and his crew hadn't made it back. Throughout that day and the next, word of *Big Dealer's* fate trickled in. Her navigator had erred in his calculations and Kunze missed Gambut Main in the darkness. Flying over the desert of central Egypt, about one hundred miles southeast of Gambut Main, *Big Dealer* neared the point of fuel exhaustion. Kunze ordered his men to abandon ship. Five of them, including copilot Babe Emmons, parachuted to safety. Kunze remained at the controls to the end, and when his final engine quit, he attempted a dead-stick belly-landing east of Bir el Khamsa, Egypt. *Big Dealer* broke apart on impact and exploded in flames. The bodies of Owen Kunze and three men who had stayed with the ship for reasons unknown were pulled from the wreckage.[6]

THE LOSS OF THE INDEFATIGABLE OWEN KUNZE and three of his men sent shock waves through the 93rd, but their comrades kept flying. Four of Kunze's closest friends, including Packy Roche, were so upset that Doc Paine gave them a sedative so they could get some sleep. With the losses mounting and the 93rd now down to nineteen battle-fit aircraft, there would be fewer days off for the remaining bombers and crews.

Midday of January 13 found Ben in the rear compartment of *Red Ass* with his fellow gunners as Jake Epting and Hap Kendall coaxed their B-24 into the sky and into the formation of a dozen Liberators heading east to bomb the port of Tunis. Still coping with the loss of his friend, Packy Roche was assigned to fly as copilot with the mission leader, Ramsay Potts, a basketball and tennis star at the University of North Carolina who had grown up in Memphis, Tennessee. The weather over Tunis was bad so Potts diverted the formation down the Tunisian coast to their alternate target, the port of Sousse. Bombs were dropped and the pilots and navigators began the long nighttime flight back to Gambut Main—acutely aware of the consequences of even the simplest navigational error.

For the men who had the day off or officers assigned to ground duties, the routine around the desert camp had become drearily familiar. After a long day marked by the conspicuous absence of so many comrades, they would head out to the airfield around 9:00 p.m. to await the return of the bombers. The question on everyone's mind was whether tragedy had once again struck their close-knit group. On this night, Doc Paine was given the honor of firing the flares to guide the bombers to the darkened LG 139 on their final approach. When the parade of returning bombers ended and the tally was taken, once again it was discovered that one bomber was missing. Timberlake and several other officers waited at the airfield until midnight before returning to camp to await further news. After another anxious night, the morning of January 14 brought good news: The missing 93rd crew had made an emergency landing on the British island fortress of Malta, and all were safe.

For Doc Paine, the good news was tempered by the solemn duties that awaited him in his role as the 93rd's chief medical officer. The previous day he had filled out casualty reports on Owen Kunze and sergeants James Anderson, Byron W. Smith, and Robert E. Woody. Now Paine boarded a B-24 flown by a pilot who was taking a break from combat duties because of his deteriorating mental health. They took off and headed east to Egypt, where Paine was to represent the 93rd at the funeral services for Owen Kunze and his three men.

Before burying the four, Paine carried out the gruesome task of identifying the remains of each man. At graveside services in the British military cemetery at Mersa Matruh, he read the opening verses of the fourteenth chapter of the Gospel of St. John: "Do not let your hearts be troubled. You believe in God; believe also in me. My Father's house has many rooms; if that were not so, would I have told you that I am going there to prepare a place for you? And if I go and prepare a place for you, I will come back and take you to be with me that you also may be where I am."[7]

At the conclusion of the service, Paine tossed dirt onto the coffins of Owen Kunze and his three men. Back at the 93rd's desert camp later that afternoon, Paine tried to drown his sorrow in a bottle of Johnnie Walker whisky.

Chapter 18

DOUBLE TROUBLE

Friday, January 15, brought more bad news, and this time the anguish was centered in Ben's 409th Squadron. Twelve 93rd crews were dispatched to bomb Tripoli, Field Marshal Rommel's final Libyan stronghold. The Liberators encountered heavy flak and a handful of fighters in the target area. The 409th Squadron bomber *Flying Cock*, commanded by First Lieutenant Lew Brown, had dropped its bombs and was nearly clear of the target area when it took a direct hit. The number three engine burst into flames. Brown tried to feather the prop on the burning engine but the mechanism wouldn't work. Brown alerted his men to be ready for an abandon-ship order.

Four gunners in the rear of *Flying Cock* either misunderstand the warning or decided the ship was doomed and didn't see the point in waiting for Brown to tell them as much. Two of the men helped wounded comrades snap on their chest parachutes and pushed them out of one of the waist windows, then followed. *Flying Cock* was flying over the Mediterranean at fourteen thousand feet, about thirty miles south of Tripoli, when the four men left the aircraft.

In the cockpit, Brown and copilot Robert Quinlivan battled to save *Flying Cock*. With one engine afire and enemy fighters attacking, the two of them managed a rapid descent to six thousand feet. Suddenly, the engine fire went out and the crisis eased. The last the other crews saw, Brown was flying under control and headed eastward into the night.

After another long night at the desert camp, the 93rd men once again awakened to good news: Brown had somehow managed to land *Flying Cock* at an airfield on the outskirts of the Libyan city of Benghazi. But the rest of the story was painful: The four *Flying Cock* crew members who bailed out over the Mediterranean were missing. Doc Paine said a prayer for the men as he recorded their plight in his diary: "No report of the 4 poor devils who bailed out over enemy waters." The four missing airmen—sergeants Ernest J. Kish, Arthur Batson, Harold M. Sena, and Charles O. Starcher—were never found. Batson was a ground crewman who had volunteered to fly with Brown as a replacement gunner for that one raid.[1]

THE GROUP WAS LOSING MEN AND PLANES at an accelerating pace, but the demands of higher authorities took precedence. On January 19, after a single day's respite, Timberlake's dwindling force—Ben and the Epting crew included—was back in action. Their target for the second time in a week was the port of Sousse. German hopes for victory in North Africa hinged on keeping the Tunisian ports open, and so they had continued to bolster antiaircraft defenses. That much was clear to the men of the 93rd, who were on the receiving end of the enemy flak.

The 93rd's lead aircraft for the mission was a 328th Squadron bomber named *Shoot Luke*, and the crew members found themselves fighting for their lives over the target. An enemy shell smashed into the nose compartment, passing between the heads of *Shoot Luke*'s navigator and bombardier. Fighters swooped in and the crew's top turret gunner was hit in both ankles and knocked from his perch. Ignoring his injuries, Sergeant Arvle D. Sirmans of Shreveport, Louisiana, climbed back into his turret and resumed fire against the enemy fighters. Sirmans would receive the Silver Star valor award for his actions.

It was the nineteenth birthday of the crew's radio operator, Sergeant William Mercer of Zanesville, Ohio, and he went down with a serious thigh wound. Pilot John Murphy threaded the gauntlet of enemy fire and landed his mangled aircraft at Malta with two good engines and a fire crackling in one of his wings. The crew counted six hundred holes in their aircraft; *Shoot Luke* would be back in action in two weeks' time.[2]

The B-24 *Double Trouble*, piloted by Captain Benjamin Riggs, wasn't as fortunate. Enemy antiaircraft fire knocked out the two port-side engines and *Double Trouble* fell into a flat spin. The radio operator of a nearby ship, *Jerk's Natural*, counted six parachutes as *Double Trouble* descended in its death spiral. Two of the four men who managed to bail out were plucked unconscious from the Mediterranean by local fishermen. The fishermen handed them over to the Germans, and the two men ended up in a prisoner of war camp.[3] Riggs and seven other crew members joined the growing list of 93rd men killed in action.

ON JANUARY 21, 1943, BEN COMPLETED his tenth mission with the Epting crew. Their target was Tripoli, the Libyan city that had served as Rommel's main supply base during the early stages of his retreat. The raid helped pave the way for one of the greatest Allied triumphs of the war to that point when British Field Marshal Bernard Montgomery's Eighth Army claimed Tripoli for the Allies two days later. For Montgomery and his seasoned army, the triumph marked the culmination of a fourteen-hundred-mile advance following their spectacular defeat of Rommel at the second battle of El Alamein three months earlier.[4]

Ben and his 93rd comrades had played an integral role in the rising Allied fortunes in North Africa in the first weeks of 1943, but it had come at a dear cost. Thirty-four comrades had died or were lost forever in six weeks of raids, on what was supposed to have been a ten-day temporary assignment. Now, orders were being drawn up for the 93rd to begin a new phase of what was becoming increasingly deadly duty.

Chapter 19

NO END IN SIGHT

The capture of Tripoli on January 23 took a prime target off the table for Hap Arnold's heavy bombers in North Africa. General Doolittle's Algeria-based B-17s now assumed primary responsibility for bombing the Tunisian ports of Tunis, Bizerte, Sfax, and Sousse, while the desert-based B-24s turned their sights on a set of crucial targets in southern Italy.

In the supply chain that now sustained Axis forces in North Africa, three Italian ports had emerged as chokepoints: Naples, 110 miles south of Rome and the primary port of origin for Axis supply ships destined for Tunisia; Messina, the terminus for six specially constructed ferry vessels that transported railcars from Reggio di Calabria and San Giovanni on the Italian mainland to the island of Sicily; and the Sicilian port of Palermo, which, as a result of the massive train-ferries arriving on the island via Messina, had emerged as an even closer point of origin for Axis transports attempting the increasingly perilous run to Tunisia.[1]

Severing these links in the enemy lifeline became the objective of Ben and his comrades.

As had so often been the case in the 93rd's five months of fitful combat, weather complicated the well-laid plans. Missions scheduled for January 24 and 25 were scrubbed by rainy weather that enveloped much of the eastern Mediterranean region. After two days of delays, the 93rd crews got airborne around midday on January 26. Their target was the Naples port area, which was bustling with transports bound for Axis forces in Tunisia.

The *Red Ass* crew earned the honor of leading twelve 93rd aircraft to the target, but with one notable change: Colonel Keith K. Compton, the 93rd's operations officer, occupied the pilot's seat. A strapping twenty-seven-year-old from St. Joseph, Missouri, Compton had joined the Army Air Corps after graduating from Westminster College in 1938, and was now one of the 93rd's most experienced pilots. He had originally joined the group in Louisiana as the 409th Squadron commander, and he had quickly risen to become Timberlake's trusted operations officer at 93rd headquarters. With Compton in the left seat, Jake Epting took the copilot's seat.

After crossing the Mediterranean and heading up Italy's west coast, the bombers arrived at Naples to find the port area obscured by darkness. Rather than bomb blindly, Compton turned the 93rd force south to Sicily. Messina was the alternate target, and visibility over the busy Sicilian port was good enough for bombing. It also was good enough for enemy gunners on the ground to pepper the 93rd Liberators with bursts of flak. Al Naum locked his bombsight on the distinctive curved building that housed the massive machinery where train cars were lowered onto rails as they arrived from the mainland on the customized ferries. With the push of a button, Naum released five 1,000-pound bombs on the Messina harbor area.[2]

With Compton leading the way, the dozen 93rd bombers set a southeasterly course, dissolved their formation, and proceeded individually across the moonlit Mediterranean. At 9:45 p.m., the 330th Squadron leader, Ken Cool, awakened his tentmate, Doc Paine, to let him know that K. K. Compton and the boys were preparing to land. By the time that *Red Ass* rolled to a stop, the crew had been airborne for nine hours. Ben had survived his eleventh mission.

The B-24s perfected a routine to keep the enemy guessing as they replicated their attacks on the three Italian ports. The Liberators would take off from Gambut in the late morning or early afternoon, assemble over the desert, then angle northwest over the Libyan coast to begin the Mediterranean crossing. The bombers would obscure their intentions as long as possible, making landfall on the sole of the Italian boot, in the vicinity of Catanzaro, a blind spot in enemy radar coverage. They would continue on a westerly vector to a point over the Tyrrhenian Sea, off Italy's west coast, that was equidistant from the three targets. Only then would the bombers home in on their destination. The B-24s took other precautions, such as bombing at last light and then sprinting seaward, a tactic adopted after crews observed that enemy fighters "were noticeably less aggressive over the water."[3] In the gathering twilight, the bomber formations would dissolve and the B-24s would undertake the long flight home in solitude.

The tragedy that culminated with the deaths of four members of the crew of *Big Dealer* earlier in January had underscored the perils of a nighttime return to the darkened desert airstrips, particularly with the Germans intent on blocking radio transmissions. The shoreline was rarely visible to the returning bombers, and the Gambut runways were marked by only a single row of lights and a low-frequency radio beacon with a range of only a few miles.[4]

The B-24 raids on Naples, Messina, and Palermo were an integral piece in the unfolding Allied plan to defeat the last stand in Tunisia by the combined Axis forces of Field Marshal Erwin Rommel and General

Hans-Jürgen von Arnim. Far removed from the strategic debates of the commanding generals, Ben and his comrades derived a special satisfaction from their raids on the Italian ports. They were taking the war to the Axis homeland.

THE NEWS OF TRIPOLI'S CAPTURE BY British forces dominated newspaper front pages across America on Sunday, January 24, with banner headlines like the one in western Nebraska's *Scottsbluff Star-Herald*: "Tripoli Falls to British, Rommel Speeds Up Dash in Tunisia." Many newspapers also ran another story on their front page that Sunday—a London-datelined scoop by Joe Alex Morris, the United Press foreign editor. Military censors had cut seventeen words from the opening paragraphs, but enough remained to hint at a major development brewing in Allied circles. "Transatlantic negotiations between Britain and the United States tonight were expected to result in imminent announcement of important decisions," the dispatch began.

In fact, by the time many Americans read their Sunday papers, twenty-seven reporters and about two dozen photographers were pounding out stories from an extraordinary joint press conference conducted by President Franklin Roosevelt and British Prime Minister Winston Churchill in Casablanca, French Morocco. Roosevelt explained to the astonished reporters that the Allies had just completed a war conference "unprecedented in history." Although the details would have to remain secret, Roosevelt told the reporters, there was one takeaway he wanted the reporters to convey to the Axis powers and the world.[5]

"I think we have all had it in our hearts and heads before, but I don't think that it has ever been put down on paper by the prime minister and myself, and that is the determination that peace can come to the world only by the total elimination of German and Japanese war power," Roosevelt began. And that could only happen if Germany, Italy, and Japan were forced to surrender unconditionally to the Allies. "It does not mean the destruction of the population of Germany, Italy, or Japan, but it does mean the destruction of the philosophies in those countries which are based on conquest and subjugation of other people," Roosevelt added. And then, in a comment calculated to shape news coverage of the event, Roosevelt suggested that the reporters might want to call the conference the "unconditional surrender meeting."[6] Churchill concurred, and the reporters obliged with one hundred thousand words collectively filed from Casablanca in the hours that followed.

Although Churchill and Roosevelt couldn't reveal it publicly, the Casablanca Conference had produced two important strategic decisions: The cross-channel invasion of France advocated by the Americans had been pushed beyond 1943 in favor of the British Mediterranean strategy aimed at knocking Italy from the war; and the American heavy bombers based in England would continue their daylight campaign against Nazi Germany rather than join the RAF nighttime raids, as Churchill had suggested at the outset of the conference.

Upon learning of Churchill's desire to end the American daylight bombing campaign, Hap Arnold had personally lobbied the British prime minister at Casablanca. He had also urgently summoned his Eighth Air Force commander, General Ira Eaker, from England to make the case to Churchill. Having earned a reprieve for the daylight campaign, Arnold and his small traveling party had slipped away from Casablanca in an Army Air Forces B-17.

After a day of discussions with his senior air chiefs in North Africa, Arnold devoted Monday, January 25 to a whirlwind tour of American air outfits in northwest Africa. He listened in thrall to stories about combat heroics and the miraculous escapes of men who had been shot down over the desert or over water. As his aircraft approached Biskra, his last stop in Algeria before heading to Egypt, Arnold experienced one of the sandstorms that was bedeviling Allied air operations across North Africa and the Middle East.

Later that evening, Arnold's flight across North Africa in a B-17 gave him another taste of the challenging winter weather. Arnold shared the 10:00 p.m. to 2:00 a.m. watch with one of his fellow passengers while two senior aides slept. When he finished his watch, Arnold curled up in a sleeping bag "with a strong draft blowing on my head from the opening around the ball turret." He awoke several hours later "with the sun shining on my face" as his aircraft prepared to land at Cairo.[7]

On Wednesday, January 27, after a day of briefings and discussions with British and American commanders in Cairo, Arnold flew 380 miles to the west, to Tobruk, Libya. He was driven forty miles into the desert to Gambut Main to have lunch and a chat with the astonished men of the 93rd Bomb Group.

For the 93rd, the day had already been a memorable one, thanks to the efforts of Doc Paine. The flight surgeon had just returned from several days of leave in Egypt, and among his many purchases had been an American flag procured in Alexandria. At 10:30 a.m., Paine staged an official flag-raising ceremony attended by Colonel Timberlake, a cornetist, and about thirty other officers and men. As if on cue, the desert breeze unfurled the Stars and Stripes as Ken Cool snapped away with his camera.

Hap Arnold had rolled into the camp a little more than an hour later, accompanied by generals Lewis Brereton and Pat Timberlake. Arnold had been briefed on the circumstances of the 93rd's North Africa sojourn, including the fact that they had been dispatched from England without ground crews for what was supposed to have been a ten-day assignment, and they were "still here after two months." In freewheeling conversations with officers and men, Arnold demonstrated keen interest in the men's work. He asked about their oxygen equipment, guns, bombsights, and overall aircraft performance. "How do you like the B-24?" he pressed. At Gambut Main and two other nearby fields, Arnold regaled the men with talk about new planes, bombs, and guns under development. And he candidly acknowledged problems that had forced the men to deal with equipment shortages and substandard equipment.[8]

In his discussions with the 93rd men, Arnold said nothing of the decisions that had been made at Casablanca. One of these decisions—the approval of a raid to bomb the Romanian oilfields at Ploiesti—would result in thirteen hours of unparalleled valor and loss for the 93rd before the summer was out.

One issue came up repeatedly in Arnold's discussions with the 93rd men: the lack of replacement crews, and the resulting sense of doom that had begun to haunt some of the men.

ARNOLD'S RESPONSE TO THAT QUESTION has been lost to history, but the truth—if that's what he shared with the men—couldn't have been reassuring.

Given all the demands that Arnold faced from American commanders around the globe, there simply weren't enough aircraft or replacement crews to go around, and there wouldn't be enough for months to come. Arnold couldn't be expected to be so blunt with his boys, but a hard reality awaited the weary 93rd men: Unless they were killed or disabled, became prisoners of war, or broke under the stress and quit flying, Ben and the others would keep grinding out missions, with no end in sight.

Chapter 20

RETURN TO ENGLAND

Hap Arnold's visit briefly boosted morale in the 93rd camp, but feelings of hopelessness bred by the existing policy of open-ended combat tours had pushed a growing number of men to the breaking point. The concerns raised by Doc Paine and others about debilitating combat stress had come to fruition by early February. Over the span of several days, Paine sent five men to Cairo for treatment of combat stress and none resumed their 93rd duties.[1] Perhaps most disturbing of all, some men were beginning to demonstrate erratic or even dangerous behavior during missions. One gunner had to be restrained by his crewmates during a raid.

On his return to Gambut Main from some rest and relaxation in Egypt in late January, Paine had a disconcerting conversation with pilot George Piburn. A handsome Southern Californian with an angular face and a solid five-foot-ten frame, Piburn had first exhibited worrisome symptoms in late December, and his mental state had deteriorated since. After speaking to the pilot on January 26, on the eve of Piburn's twenty-second birthday, Paine concluded Piburn "has 'thrown in the towel.'" Days later, with fourteen missions to his credit, Piburn made it official and took himself off combat duty. He would leave the 93rd and be assigned to a training command back in the United Kingdom.

Piburn was hardly alone in his struggles. Paine suspected that another pilot who had recently checked into a military hospital complaining of shoulder pain was also suffering from combat stress. "Think he is cracking," Paine confided to his diary.[2]

Another source of concern for Paine was First Lieutenant Robert A. Quinlivan, a twenty-one-year-old pilot from Jersey City, New Jersey. Quinlivan had already survived two traumatic combat experiences as the copilot of *Flying Cock*. On the group's first raid in North Africa, the December 13 strike on Bizerte, a piece of flak smashed into *Flying Cock*'s nose compartment and inflicted a fatal head wound on the crew's bombardier as he sat at his station below Quinlivan's feet. More recently, during the January 15 raid on Tripoli, Quinlivan narrowly escaped death when an enemy flak burst spattered his helmet with steel splinters. Quinlivan confided to Doc Paine that he "couldn't stand the idea of flying into flak again."³ Although he had proven his courage by completing at least ten missions, earning an Air Medal with an Oak Leaf Cluster, Quinlivan was finished as a combat pilot.

How many more good men would break in the days ahead? As February 1943 arrived, that question preoccupied the 93rd's senior commanders and medical personnel.

WET AND FRIGID WEATHER FOLLOWED ON the heels of Arnold's visit, postponing any reckoning for the battle-weary men of the 93rd. To pass the time, Doc Paine spent three hours on January 29 mending tears in his wind-whipped Stars and Stripes, using scraps of bandages to patch the holes. The patches didn't hold in the fierce winds, and Paine would start using canvas threads to mend his beloved—and increasingly tattered—flag.

Paine was scheduled to join the welcoming party for a visit by Arnold's new air chief for North Africa, General Carl "Tooey" Spaatz, but the visit was canceled because of poor flying conditions. Instead, the doctor spent part of the afternoon patching up the mangled toe of a pilot who'd accidentally shot himself while cleaning his pistol.

Despite more rain and cold winds on January 30, the 93rd managed to launch a dozen planes for a raid on Messina. The bombing was deemed a "great success" and was cause for celebration by senior officers who knocked back shots of VO Canadian whisky.

On Sunday, January 31, the weather finally cleared and the stir-crazy 93rd men emerged from their tents to exercise and perform chores. A series of air-raid alarms over recent days motivated Doc Paine to undertake an ambitious project to transform his foxhole into a bomb shelter. He procured two halves of fifty-five-gallon oil drums and sheets of canvas as cover and arranged them over his foxhole. He piled eight inches of dirt on top of the hardened shell before adding a final inspired touch: He planted desert flowers in the layer of dirt "to make the best and prettiest bomb shelter I've seen anywhere."⁴

As satisfying as the men found the weather, even more welcome was a rumor that began making the rounds: The 93rd was finally returning to England. The news wasn't official yet, but Ted Timberlake had been alerted to stand by for orders. To celebrate the long-awaited news, Doc Paine broke out a bottle of Scotch that he shared with comrades.

The timing of the rumors wasn't a coincidence.

After persuading Prime Minister Churchill at the recently concluded Casablanca Conference to drop his opposition to the American daylight bombing campaign, Hap Arnold was determined to deliver on his promises. One of Churchill's criticisms of the American campaign had been the modest achievements of Arnold's forces, including the American failure to drop a single bomb on the German homeland after five months of raids. The RAF, by contrast, was already mounting thousand-plane raids on Berlin.

With a nudge from Arnold, Eaker wasted no time in addressing Churchill's criticism.

On the same day that Arnold was mingling with the 93rd men at Gambut Main, Eaker dispatched ninety-one B-17 and B-24 bombers to attack the U-boat yards at Wilhelmshaven, Germany. Only fifty-three aircraft reached the target, but the message had been emphatically delivered—to the Germans and to Churchill. After months of tiptoeing around the fringes of the Third Reich, the Americans had finally hit the Nazi homeland, and they had lost only three bombers doing it.

As it turned out, the light losses had been a stroke of luck for the Americans. In fact, Eaker's sudden willingness to roll the dice on an unescorted strike on German territory had caught the Luftwaffe by surprise. Unfortunately for the Americans, it wouldn't happen again.

To meet Hap Arnold's unreasonable expectations for the largely aspirational daylight bombing campaign, Eaker badly needed Ted Timberlake's 93rd crews to fill holes in his depleted ranks. For the 93rd men, accustomed to the half-hearted enemy fighter resistance around the Mediterranean, the lion's den beckoned.

Doc Paine's Scotch-soaked celebration of the 93rd's return to England proved premature.

The first week of February came and went without the anticipated orders for the move. Another week passed without orders or further word. And then another.

The pace of raids on the Italian ports tailed off because of poor weather and overworked aircraft and crews. The 93rd was down to nineteen aircraft, and the Liberators still flying had gone without proper maintenance for more than two months. Sand-scoured engines failed more frequently, and that put crews in peril during missions and made it increasingly difficult for the airmen and their handful of mechanics and technicians to keep the B-24s battle ready.

The 93rd logged its first mission of the month on February 3. Ben and his crewmates didn't see action until bombing Naples on February 7 and Palermo on February 10. They were Ben's twelfth and thirteenth missions.

The men of the Epting crew could count themselves more fortunate than most of their comrades. Only two members of the crew—Ed Bates and Bill Dawley—had been injured thus far, and both Bates (frozen fingers) and Dawley (flak wound) had recovered and were flying again with the 93rd's 329th Squadron back in England. Furthermore, Jake Epting and his men had avoided the ravages of combat stress that were creating holes in some crews.

The 93rd made it through the first two weeks of February without the loss of an aircraft or a single fatality. But the mounting losses of their new 98th and 376th Bomb Group neighbors at Gambut Main served as unnerving reminders to Ben and his comrades.

On February 4, generals Brereton and Patrick Timberlake flew in from Cairo for an awards ceremony for the 93rd men. They pinned various valor awards—the Distinguished Flying Cross for a few officers, the Purple Heart for several enlisted men who had sustained combat wounds, and the Air Medal for those who had completed five missions or Air Medal with Oak Leaf Cluster for those who had passed the ten-mission milestone. Among those honored and photographed were the combat-stressed pilots George Piburn and Robert Quinlivan.

More festivities followed on February 5 when the entire 93rd contingent assembled for a rousing review and retreat parade in honor of their operations officer, Major K. K. Compton, who had been tapped to take command of their Gambut Main neighbors, the 376th Bomb Group. The 93rd men were anxious to get back to England, but Compton would be making his home in the inhospitable North Africa desert for the foreseeable future.

THE RAINS OF LATE JANUARY AND EARLY February had complicated daily life for the men of the 93rd, but there was one delightful benefit: The wadis and escarpments around Gambut Main erupted with desert flowers. By Doc Paine's count, there were no fewer than twenty-two varieties of flowers blooming in the area. Paine was among the men who marveled at the welcome burst of color on their target-shooting forays, which had become a favorite pastime of those officers who had procured German Luger pistols and Mauser rifles from Bedouin tribesmen.

The 376th had a recurrence of bad luck on February 7, when the groups at Gambut Main combined forces for a raid on Naples. Twelve 93rd crews, including Jake Epting's *Red Ass* lads, were dispatched and returned safely; three 93rd men returned with mild cases of frostbite, and one officer had been wounded in the thigh with a piece of flak, which Doc Paine removed and sewed up. That was the extent of the group's casualties. The 376th, on the other hand, had ten men killed in action when one of their bombers was shot down in the target area.

Despite the losses, Ken Cool was ecstatic. The raid's exceptional accuracy would have justified the loss of all twenty bombers that reached the target, Cool enthused. BBC News echoed that view in a shortwave radio broadcast monitored at Gambut Main the following evening. It declared the strike "the best raid put on by any American bomber in the war."[5]

On February 10, during their raid on Palermo, Ben and his crewmates experienced some anxious moments with the failure of one of their super-chargers, the device that compensated for the loss of engine power at higher altitudes. Adding insult to injury, poor visibility forced the B-24s to drop their bombs in the sea rather than risk excessive civilian casualties, so the raid had been a waste. The Epting crew sweated out their solitary return flight to Gambut Main in the dark. They landed after seven hours and forty minutes of flight with the knowledge that the seemingly indestructible *Red Ass* was beginning to show the effects of two months of desert duty.

The men of the 93rd were also showing the effects. They had learned to live on little water and monotonously bland C-rations, and their uniforms, flying gear, and shoes were falling apart.[6] The men had learned to supple-ment their diet by bartering with the locals for tangerines, lemons, oranges, and fresh eggs, but with those transactions came exposure to illnesses that were endemic in the Bedouin encampments and local villages.

With the passage of time, some of the men had become dangerously inured to the fact that they were living in the middle of a vast battlefield littered with unexploded ordnance and other hazards. Some bored air-men invented games with captured German ordnance by repurposing the explosives from antiaircraft shells for use in improvised fireworks displays.[7] Around eleven in the morning on February 13, Doc Paine was in his tent reading a British spy novel when an explosion jolted him from his cot. He heard shouts and screams and emerged to witness a horrifying scene. Afterward, Paine distilled the mishap in a caustic diary entry: "Six dumb guys put an 88mm shell in a hole and threw rocks in on top to set it off and blow the hole deep enough for a latrine. It did. We hauled 4 to [a nearby] hospital in [an] ambulance. One lost his left eye and several were in foul shape from flak wounds."[8]

AMID THE FRUSTRATING UNCERTAINTY about the group's rumored return to England, the men mounted another mission on Monday, February 15. The target was Naples. It was the 93rd's first mission in five days, and only the fourth of the month. Twelve crews were briefed at 10:00 a.m. and took off at 12:15 p.m. They were joined by nine B-24s of the 376th. Flying in formation, the two groups wheeled to the north for the Mediterranean crossing.

Problems arose soon after takeoff. Six of the twenty-one aircraft—two from the 93rd and four from the 376th—turned back with mechanical problems. The remaining bombers arrived over Naples at dusk, and were greeted by heavy flak and twelve to fifteen enemy fighters.

In the darkness and chaotic interplay of American bombers and German fighters, a 93rd B-24 named *Cephalopod* disappeared. Piloting the aircraft was a twenty-two-year-old Oklahoman, Lieutenant Charles T. Moore, affectionately known to his friends and fellow officers as Chub. When the last of the American bombers landed at Gambut Main around 11:00 p.m., Moore's crew wasn't among them. "He failed to return, but we hope he is in at Malta," Doc Paine wrote after returning from the airfield.[9]

Overnight a radio message from Malta arrived: Charley Moore wasn't there. The mood among the 93rd officers was already grim over Chub Moore's disappearance when Ted Timberlake arrived from Cairo at noon with the latest from Ninth Air Force headquarters on the group's fate. There were still "no orders to return us to England due to brass hats being void between the ears," as Doc Paine paraphrased Timberlake's report.[10]

Heartbroken over Chub Moore's disappearance and incensed by headquarters indecision over the 93rd's status, Doc Paine, Ken Cool, and Packy Roche tried to drown their sorrows in a bottle of Canadian Club whisky. Late in the afternoon, in what seemed like a feeble attempt to bolster 93rd morale, Pat Timberlake flew in to present medals to about thirty men. Doc Paine and Ken Cool were fed up. Each took a sedative from Paine's dispensary and collapsed onto their cots at 7:30 p.m. for a long night's sleep.

As the dispiriting week wore on, hopes for the return of Chub Moore and his men faded. "The general morale is at a low ebb due chiefly to the fact that no one knows what the score is," Doc Paine groused. "Col. Ted has made no statement and all the men get is via damn rumor—which is bad."[11]

At 11:00 a.m. on Thursday, February 18, the 93rd men made their way to the 376th encampment for another medal ceremony, this one presided over by General Brereton. Ken Cool and Packy Roche, among others, received the Distinguished Flying Cross, but the men couldn't help but think about Chub Moore and his missing crew. Only a few days earlier, Moore had stood at attention at one of these ceremonies as he was decorated with an Oak Leaf Cluster added to his previous Air Medal. Standing to Moore's left had been the pilot George Piburn. Now, Moore was dead, along with his entire crew—shot down near the target, the 93rd men would later learn—and Piburn was an emotional wreck who would never fly another combat mission.[12]

Afterward, Doc Paine overheard one of Brereton's aides tell Timberlake that he was carrying orders that would send the 93rd back to England after one final mission. It was finally happening.

Thrilled by the news, Doc Paine joined the group's pickup baseball game after lunch and for two hours ran around the field like a teenager rather than a slightly paunchy thirty-eight-year-old gentleman on the precipice of middle age. Still fired up that evening, he drank and sang into the wee hours. He would awaken in the morning with aching muscles, strained vocal cords, and a pounding head, yet still overjoyed at the knowledge that the 93rd's time in this godforsaken station was coming to an end. No one in the 93rd would be happier to bid farewell to the desert than the gentleman doctor from Virginia.

By MID-FEBRUARY, THE GROUND WAR in North Africa was centered in the rugged hills and valleys of central Tunisia. In January, the Americans and British had pushed eastward through the Grand Dorsal system of the Atlas Mountains, establishing a line that was only about sixty miles from Tunisia's east coast in places. Faced with the threat of the Allies splitting his Tunisian bridgehead in half, Field Marshal Rommel attacked in early February. By the middle of the month, Rommel was poised to unleash the next phase of his long-shot attempt to conjure a victory over the Allies in Tunisia.

General von Arnim's forces dislodged elements of the US 1st Armored Division in attacks that began February 14, and Rommel followed with attacks of his own that drove American troops back to the Western Dorsal, one of two roughly parallel mountain ranges that dominated the topography of central Tunisia. On February 19, Rommel and von Arnim combined their forces in an attempt to cripple the Americans at Kasserine Pass.

In the initial stages of the battle, the Americans retreated in disarray, falling back as far as fifty miles in places. Finally, on February 22, troops of the US Army's II Corps, supplemented by British reinforcements, halted the German advance. Battered by heavy artillery and air attacks, Rommel abruptly ended the offensive. By February 24, after more US air strikes, Allied troops had reclaimed Kasserine Pass and regained the momentum in Tunisia.[13]

As the battle in the Kasserine Pass raged, weather grounded the 93rd crews. On Friday, February 19, the crews were briefed to bomb Naples, but the mission was canceled before takeoff because of poor weather in the target area. After lunch, the group ordnance officer was "tinkering with a M103 bomb fuse" when it exploded in his face, injuring his fingers and sending a steel splinter into his right eyeball.

The crews were briefed again and cleared for takeoff on Saturday, February 20. Their target again was Naples. En route to Italy, the crews received orders to turn east to their alternate target and dropped their bombs on a chemical factory in Crotone, along southern Italy's Calabrian coast. It was another long mission—nine hours and thirty-five minutes for the Epting crew—but, most important of all, the 93rd returned with all its crews and without a single casualty. Ben would be returning to England with fourteen missions to his credit.

As Ben and his comrades celebrated their final mission in North Africa, American forces were fleeing westward from Kasserine Pass. Unknown to the men of the 93rd, their fate was tied to that of the retreating American ground forces. If the Axis forces continued to advance, the 93rd would have to remain in North Africa to help swing the tide of battle. But the crisis passed when Rommel withdrew his forces from Kasserine Pass. With the situation in Tunisia under control once more, generals Eisenhower and Spaatz released the 93rd from its temporary duty in North Africa. Orders were cut for Ted Timberlake and his men to return to England.

At one o'clock on the morning of February 24, 1943, Ken Cool guided *Hot Freight* down the Gambut Main runway for the final time and led the first flight of five 93rd bombers into the night sky. Doc Paine was among the passengers joining Cool on the flight. Their destination was Tafaraoui, Algeria, outside Oran, the soggy spot where the 93rd had briefly stopped before inclement weather drove them into the Libyan desert.

In the hour after Cool led his flight of B-24s away from Gambut Main, Jake Epting coaxed *Red Ass* into the sky for the first leg of the journey back to England. Nothing about Ben Kuroki's military career had come easily, and so it would be with what was supposed to be a routine transit flight. As the long and harrowing night unfolded, Ben and his brothers-in-arms would wonder whether they would ever see another dawn.

Chapter 21

MISSING IN ACTION

Heading away from Gambut Main, Jake Epting joined the long train of B-24s tracking westward across North Africa on an all-night flight. Their briefing called for a refueling stop at Tafaraoui and then the final leg home. If everything went according to plan, Ben and his crewmates would take their breakfast in Algeria and dinner in England.

But nothing about the journey went according to plan.

At the head of the column, *Hot Freight* ran into overcast soon after takeoff. When celestial navigation became impossible, pilot Ken Cool switched to instruments. Dawn revealed zero-visibility flying conditions, and by the time the bombers neared Tafaraoui clouds and fog obscured the ground. Ted Timberlake radioed the trailing aircraft to reduce altitude and search for a hole in the clouds, but the only openings were too small or too fleeting to risk entering.

Cool caught a glimpse of the airfield, but before he could get his landing gear down the fog sealed the opening. He tried to wait out the weather, but after ninety minutes of circling the area, visibility was even worse. Critically low on fuel, Cool landed *Hot Freight* at an airstrip forty miles east of Tafaraoui.

In the pilot's seat of *Teggie Ann*, Colonel Timberlake feared that his entire force might exhaust their fuel and fall from the sky. Timberlake saw two options: They could gamble on better weather at Gibraltar or roll the dice on the fog lifting over Tafaraoui. Either way, they were going to be cutting it close. The pilots switched to low power settings to conserve fuel, and some tried to reduce their fuel consumption by lightening their load. Timberlake had his men toss out some of their heaviest nonessential items, including their waist guns and a stash of fresh eggs bartered from Bedouins. Timberlake glimpsed flashes of runway through the fog, but deemed it too risky to attempt a landing without a beacon to guide his ships. Some pilots dropped down to as low as fifty feet in their desperate search for the runway.[1]

One Liberator had already lost an engine to fuel exhaustion when the ragged holes in the fog revealed enough runway to attempt a landing.

Another of Timberlake's pilots spotted the smoke from a locomotive and asked the Tafaraoui control tower for a heading from the train to the runway. Emerging from the fog at treetop level, the pilot guided the B-24 to a safe landing, barely avoiding a collision with a Liberator approaching from the other direction.

Several courageous C-47 pilots from a nearby field heard the appeals from Timberlake's men and climbed into the clouds to search for the lost Liberators. The selfless transport pilots found the Liberators and led them back to their field. Miraculously, thirteen bombers landed safely at Tafaraoui and nearby fields—some with less than five minutes of fuel in their tanks.

Safely on the ground, Ted Timberlake pieced together a status report on his boys. One 93rd aircraft was missing: Jake Epting's *Red Ass*.

THE DIMINUTIVE EPTING AND LANKY Hap Kendall had guided their battle-scarred B-24 into the night sky above Libya with four passengers joining the crew for the ride home. The intelligence briefing had suggested the 93rd Liberators faced an uneventful first leg. Luftwaffe air capabilities in North Africa had been decimated by nearly three years of nonstop combat, and the remaining Axis fighters in the area were limited to airfields in northern Tunisia and nearby Sicily. Given the remote odds of encountering enemy night fighters on their flight to Algeria, most of the crew and passengers curled up in the back to catch some sleep. Some four hours into the flight, Epting and Kendall entered Tunisian airspace. The pilots alerted Ben and the other gunners to be on the lookout for prowling enemy fighters, but there was no sign of the Luftwaffe in the hour it took to cross Tunisia.

They were home free—or so it seemed.

Dawn was approaching, but the farther west the Liberators flew the worse visibility became. Sitting in his Plexiglas-encased nose compartment, navigator Edward Weir had been unable to use celestial navigation for hours. With the moon and stars obscured, Weir attempted dead-reckoning navigation techniques, an imprecise method using the last-known location as a baseline and factoring in airspeed, wind, and estimated drift to calculate the current location. It soon became clear to Epting and Kendall that their navigator didn't have a clue where they were.

Epting eased the bomber down through the clouds in search of clear skies, but none were to be found. Ben's friend Red Kettering checked various radio frequencies, trying to get a fix on the Tafaraoui airfield, without success. Epting found the coastline, but he couldn't find the airfield in the fog. He weighed whether to attempt a landing in the water or on a beach, or whether to press on. The debate took on even greater urgency as their fuel gauges dipped into the red. What was supposed to be a routine flight had suddenly become a life-and-death emergency.

The thought wasn't lost on some of the men that the 93rd might end its seventy-nine-day Africa sojourn the same way it began: with the loss of fourteen men in a crash. It was the beloved Iowan Ox Johnson who had collided with a mountain while trying to find the Tafaraoui airfield in similar weather on December 13. Now Jake Epting and his crew and passengers were reliving that doomed flight. In the nose, navigator Edward Weir prepared to die. "We figured we were going to crash any minute," Ben later recalled.[2]

Suddenly, Epting spotted a small hole in the clouds. He reacted instinctively, threading the B-24 down through the ragged portal. In the gray half-light beneath the fog, mountains loomed on three sides, but Epting spotted a sliver of flat terrain tucked into the hills. He lowered the landing gear and ordered the men to brace for a rough landing. A wheat field rushed up to meet them, and the wheels gently touched the stalks then found solid ground. Epting eased the bomber to a stop as perfectly as if the wheat field had been a paved runway.

They had overshot Oran by more than one hundred miles and had flown into the Atlas Mountains. The break in the clouds had led them to an improbable safe haven surrounded by hills and peaks that soared to seven thousand feet. Jake Epting's stellar flying had saved Ben and his comrades—but not for long.

SHAKEN BY THEIR BRUSH WITH DEATH, and exhilarated by their escape, several of the fourteen men aboard *Red Ass* exited the B-24 to survey their surroundings. The shard of flat terrain that had proven their salvation was surrounded by craggy hills and mountains. Exactly where they were in relation to the coast and Oran wasn't clear. The men were still pondering that conundrum when they heard hoofbeats. Suddenly, a hundred or so men armed with antiquated rifles and clubs converged on the aircraft—some on horses, some on camels, some on foot. It was like a scene out of *Revolt in the Desert*, the bestselling memoir of British Army colonel T. E. Lawrence that many of the men had read as boys.

The horsemen were probably ethnic Berbers known as Riffians, a tribe that had waged a bloody insurgency fifteen years earlier against European colonial rule. They didn't speak English, but they made themselves understood: They wanted everything.

The marauders swarmed through the plane, grabbing mess kits, canteens, goggles, shaving gear, and anything else they could find. They roughly relieved the men of their wallets and other personal possessions. Some of the intruders made their way to the flight deck and grabbed Epting's flight manual. Bombardier Al Naum tried to smash his bombsight with his boot before he was forced from the nose compartment. One of the crew's waist gunners had remained at his weapon to protect the men if needed, with instructions to fire only on Epting's order. When it became clear that resistance would provoke a slaughter, the gunner was told to stand down. "We thought we were gonna be killed by those people," Edward Weir later recalled.[3]

The gunmen had begun to herd the Americans away from the plane when suddenly another group of horsemen approached. The looters disappeared as suddenly as they had arrived. Several men in uniforms cantered up to the bewildered Americans. An officer addressed them in Spanish. They had landed in Spanish Morocco, a possession of neutral Spain.[4]

The Spanish officer and his men led the Americans to a nearby town and ushered them into a holding pen outside the courthouse. While Spanish soldiers served the Americans wine, hot tea, and cookies, an English-speaking officer began interrogating the airmen, one by one. When the questioning ended, the officer informed the Americans that they wouldn't be leaving anytime soon. Spain was a neutral country, he explained, and the laws of war required them to hold soldiers of a belligerent nation.

Ben and his comrades had avoided the Germans and Italians, but not the snares of international law. Legally they were internees, not prisoners of war, but they weren't free to go.

THE AMERICANS WERE DAZZLED BY THE hospitality of their hosts. They were given haircuts and shaves, clean beds, and blankets. They were allowed to roam freely around the town. Jake Epting and the other commissioned officers ate in the mess hall with the Spanish officers, while the enlisted men ate with their Spanish counterparts. They adopted Spanish habits, eating a light breakfast, followed by a more robust breakfast a few hours later, then lunch, and a sumptuous evening meal. After subsisting on canned C-rations for three months, the Americans were awed by the dinner menu: shrimp cocktail, olives, soup, egg omelet, fish, beans, beefsteak, coffee, bananas, bread, and cakes, washed down with Spanish wine.[5]

Ben and his comrades didn't know what to make of the hospitality.

Ben was more than wary. He had enlisted to fight America's Axis enemies. It had taken him a year to get an opportunity to prove himself in combat, and now the Spanish officers were saying they would be interned in Spain for the rest of the war. Ben was being offered an opportunity to sit out the war in style, but he wouldn't hear of it. The war was his opportunity to prove his patriotism, and he *had* to get back to it. Ben pulled Jake Epting aside and asked for permission to attempt an escape. Epting gave his blessing.

In early March, Ben made his break.

BEN HAD SEEN ENOUGH OF HIS SURROUNDINGS to be convinced that he could pass himself off as a local. He fashioned a turban from a T-shirt and turned his raincoat inside-out and splattered it with mud, then waited until nightfall and set out in the rain. As he tried to slip out of the enclosure where they were being held, Ben grabbed the wire of a fence. It was electrified. "It scared the hell out of me," he later recalled.[6]

He slipped under the fence and set off walking. He passed through two villages. Around dawn, he was nearing the crest of a hill when he encountered a soldier who started yelling at him. Ben bolted. The sentry fired some shots and other security personnel joined the chase. Ben stopped and held up his hands in surrender.

He was marched at gunpoint to a nearby town and thrown into a cage with a dozen or so unkempt prisoners. An English-speaking military officer arrived. When he discovered that the prisoner was one of the American airmen who had been taken into custody the previous week, the officer wanted to know why Ben had tried to escape. Ben tried to explain to the officer the backlash against Japanese Americans back home. "I'm trying to prove my loyalty," Ben said.

Ben's stay in the rural jail was short. The officer led his prisoner to a waiting vehicle and Ben was driven north to the port city of Melilla. At the seaside air base, he was reunited with the other members of the Epting crew and their passengers from Gambut Main.

Within a few hours, Spanish Air Force officers ushered the Americans aboard a Junkers-52 transport, a gift of Nazi Germany during the Spanish Civil War. Jake Epting and several of the men briefly discussed whether they should try to overpower the Spanish crew and fly to nearby Allied territory, but "thought better of it," Weir said.[7]

As the engines throbbed, the Spanish pilot pushed the throttles forward for takeoff and, to the consternation of the American captives, crossed himself as any good Catholic might. The pilot got the plane airborne and turned north toward their unknown destination in Spain.

Chapter 22

PRISONERS IN A GILDED CAGE

As the Junkers transport bearing Ben and his fellow detainees flew north-ward across the Mediterranean to an unknown destination, Spain was a smoldering preoccupation of US president Franklin Roosevelt. Since 1939, the country had been ruled by Francisco Franco, the military strongman who led Nationalist forces to victory in a four-year civil war that over-threw the elected Republican government. Hitler and Mussolini had forged close ties with Franco, providing men and materiel to his army through-out the civil war. In the spring of 1940, when Germany stood poised to defeat Britain and France in Hitler's broader European war, the Nazi dic-tator had assumed that Franco would join the Axis cause, but Franco had demurred—much to Hitler's annoyance.

Franco needed a source of oil and other economic aid that exceeded the means of the Axis powers, and so, while assuring Hitler of his ideological sympathies, the Spanish *caudillo* staked out an official policy of neutrality. Increasingly frustrated by Franco's reticence, Hitler secretly drew up plans to invade Spain, which the German leader viewed as a steppingstone to the conquest of Gibraltar, Britain's Mediterranean stronghold at the southern tip of the Iberian Peninsula. Twice in the eighteen months prior to Amer-ica's entry into the war, Hitler considered overrunning Spain, but both times stopped short.[1]

Spain's status took on even greater urgency for President Roosevelt after the Japanese attack on Pearl Harbor triggered an Axis declaration of war on the United States. Roosevelt now made keeping Spain out of the war a diplomatic priority. In March 1942, Roosevelt set in motion his plan to achieve this goal by carefully handpicking his ambassador to Madrid.

The envoy was Carlton Joseph Huntley Hayes, a fifty-nine-year-old Columbia University historian. Born and raised in upstate New York, Hayes had majored in history at Columbia at the turn of the century. In 1904, around the time of his graduation, Hayes broke with his Bap-tist upbringing to convert to Catholicism. In the years that followed, his Catholic faith became a bedrock of his scholarly life. Hayes made a name for himself as an expert on modern European history and nationalism. He concluded that the senseless slaughter of the First World War had been an outgrowth of three destructive threads of modern life: nationalism, militarism, and imperialism. In the great global ideological struggle between left and right that followed the war, Hayes ardently denounced totalitarianism and American isolationism.

The Spanish Civil War of the late 1930s created deep fault lines in American and British political, cultural, and academic life. The cause of Spain's beleaguered Republican government was championed by the political left in the United States and the United Kingdom. Some twenty-eight hundred Americans fought for the Republican cause with the Abraham Lincoln Brigade, and 681 died from battle injuries or illness. Throughout the conflict, Roosevelt maintained ties with both the Republican government and Franco's Nationalist rebels. When Franco entered Madrid and declared victory on April 1, 1939, Roosevelt ignored pressure from the American left to cut diplomatic relations with the new Nationalist government.

In the aftermath of America's entry into Hitler's war, Roosevelt's appointment of Hayes as ambassador to Spain was a shrewd political stroke. By appointing a Catholic of moderate political views, Roosevelt had signaled to Franco his desire for closer relations with Spain. Hayes was no closet fascist, but rather he viewed Franco through a lens of pragmatism: The Spanish leader was an authoritarian, but not a totalitarian in the vein of Adolf Hitler or Benito Mussolini, Hayes concluded. In his view, America could do business with Franco.

Arriving in Madrid in the late spring of 1942, Hayes set to work shoring up America's relationship with Spain. He built relationships with Franco and his foreign minister. To win the sympathies of the Spanish elite, he hosted cultural programs that stressed the shared values of the two countries. Balding and bespectacled, with a large nose and stern face, Hayes proved to be a warm and gracious host. One of the most popular events he hosted was a screening of the Hollywood film *Gone with the Wind*. High government officials and even members of Spain's Catholic hierarchy turned out for the event.[2]

Hayes found common ground with Franco in other areas. A trickle of Europeans fleeing Hitler's depredations had found safe haven in Spain early in the war. After Hayes arrived, the trickle became a torrent. Jews and other displaced people as well as downed Allied airmen made their way from Vichy France through the Pyrenees mountains into Spain and on to safety in Allied-occupied North Africa. By war's end, Hayes—with Franco's acquiescence—had aided the escape of forty thousand refugees.

A more urgent concern for Roosevelt was the question of Franco's

104 • Gregg Jones

commitment to military neutrality—an issue that loomed ever larger as 1943 began. Based on months of conversations with Franco and Foreign Ministry officials in Madrid, Hayes communicated to Washington his optimism that Franco intended to remain on the sidelines. But he was far less convinced Hitler would respect Spain's continued neutrality. In a January 15, 1943, cable to Secretary of State Cordell Hull, Hayes reported steady improvement in US relations with Spain following the Operation TORCH landings in North Africa, and he urged the US to offer "military assistance to Spain in the event of German aggression." Furthermore, he suggested a German invasion might occur "between the latter part of February and May."[3]

As part of Roosevelt's intensifying efforts to keep Franco out of the war, the powerful Catholic archbishop of New York, Francis Spellman, arrived in Madrid in early February 1943. During his week in Spain, Spellman met privately with Franco and reported to Roosevelt that the Spanish strongman did indeed appear committed to neutrality.

Despite the encouraging cables arriving in Washington from Hayes and his top diplomats in Madrid, Spain remained a potentially game-changing wild card in the European war. If Franco cast his lot with Hitler and attacked the British stronghold at Gibraltar, or allowed Hitler to invade Spain and control access to the Mediterranean, the Allied summer plans to invade Sicily would be jeopardized.

It was against this backdrop of high-stakes Allied and Axis intrigue that Ben and thirteen 93rd Bomb Group comrades arrived in Spain in early March 1943.

BEN AND THE OTHER AMERICANS EMERGED from the Junkers into the sunlight of Zaragoza, a provincial capital in Spain's northeast Aragon region. They were herded aboard a bus and driven southwest into the mountains. After a journey of about ninety minutes, the bus stopped and the Americans were ushered into a luxury hotel in the spa town of Alhama de Aragon.

The past year of war had seen the town play host to a small colony of about twenty-five interned Allied air personnel from the United States, Australia, Britain, Canada, New Zealand, Palestine, and South Africa. Confined to hotels paid for by their governments, the Americans were among more than one hundred US military personnel interned by Spain at that point in the war.

Ben's place of "confinement" was the Hotel Termas de Pallares, a popular spa and casino opened in 1863. The four-story brick structure had been constructed in the Romanesque Mudéjar style popular in Aragon, blending Moorish tastes with traditional Roman and Christian architecture. Marble statues adorned the entrance and a tiled patio overlooked lush gardens with strutting peacocks and a thermal lake where guests could bathe or sun themselves while lying in lounge chairs on a sandy beach.

Beyond the cavernous marble-tiled lobby lay a genteel world of dark-paneled salons, chandeliers, and high-ceilinged hallways. The main dining room could seat two hundred guests, and an al fresco dining area decorated with Moorish tile mosaic a hundred more. Guests could soak in soothing mineral waters in the hotel's communal spa in the basement or in claw-footed porcelain tubs in the privacy of their elegant rooms. The Americans were technically prisoners, yet they had the privileges of a paying guest. For Ben and the other internees of modest origins, the Termas de Pallares transported them into a world of Gatsby-like luxury and excess.

Each day for the internees began with a knock at the door and breakfast served in bed. From 8:00 to 10:00 a.m., the men swam and bathed in the clear thermal lake a short walk from the hotel building. At 1300 hours, they gathered in the dining room for a hearty lunch of meat, potatoes, peas, salad, red wine, and bread made from flour supplied by the US Embassy. Afterward, the men adjourned to a large salon to gaze out on the National Highway and the well-manicured park beyond. Games of bridge (sometimes joined by an English-speaking Spanish gentleman), chess, checkers, and Ping-Pong ensued. The activities paused for a midafternoon snack of tea, coffee, and olives, followed by another two hours at the lake.

Back at the hotel, the airmen gathered around a shortwave radio in the lobby to catch the evening BBC news broadcast from London. They spent much time at the bar, drinking wine and nibbling shrimp. They attended evening dances in the casino and screenings of French, Italian, German, and American films. The hotel's daily activities culminated with a late dinner.[4]

As Ben and the others soon discovered, Alhama de Aragon was a compact town of about a thousand inhabitants, tucked into a limestone gorge carved by the ribbon-like Rio Jalón as it threaded its way northeast through the mountains. Some of the most prominent buildings, including the town hall, echoed Aragon's Moorish influence.

Representatives of the US Embassy in Madrid, 110 miles to the southwest, regularly made the drive up the National Road to visit the American airmen. The embassy air attaché brought mail, sweaters, chocolates, cigarettes, and a stipend paid in pesetas on his weekly visits. The airmen were allowed to wear their uniforms around the hotel, but not outside, so the embassy's first secretary brought Ben and his comrades civilian clothes and a skilled tailor to take their measurements. Within a matter of days, the

Americans upgraded their desert wardrobes to include business suits and ties. Ben took to wearing a fedora.

Their circle of friends included a colorful cast of airmen who had been shot down over France and found refuge in Spain with the courageous assistance of the French underground. Among them were a half-dozen British airmen, a US P-38 pilot, and an Australian flier who had reached Spain on his second escape attempt after thirty months as a German prisoner of war.

On festival days, the streets of Alhama de Aragon teemed with local residents dancing the *jota*, a traditional Aragonese dance—men in knee breeches, white stockings, and broad-brimmed hats; women in red skirts, embroidered white blouses, and red roses pinned to their hair. Young women with long black hair, brown eyes, and delicate features began to frequent the hotel to catch a glimpse of the Americans, but they were good Catholic girls who shyly deflected the amorous advances of the sex-starved airmen. A Spanish girl gave one American enlisted man a silver band that he wore on his little finger, yet he grumbled to his comrades, "She won't even let me hold her hand."[5]

The Spanish Air Force officers responsible for the internees imposed few rules, aside from punctuality for meals and mandatory room check and roll call at 2300 each evening. For the most part, the Americans behaved themselves. Epting and his officers had befriended their Spanish counterparts, and so the occasional infraction went unpunished.

The presence of mysterious German-speaking visitors who claimed to be businessmen or tourists added an air of intrigue to their stay. The visitors were suspected to be agents of the Abwehr, the German military intelligence branch, and so the Americans steered clear of them.

It was the most civilized captivity imaginable, yet the passing days weighed on Ben. He didn't have to be reminded that his comrades were back in England, fighting and dying in raids against Nazi Germany. Every time a new airman shot down in France arrived in Alhama de Aragon, the Americans were reminded of their 93rd brothers.

But what could they do about it? The men began to discuss their options.

Unbeknownst to Ben and his comrades, diplomatic negotiations to secure their release had taken on added urgency by mid-March. Cables from the US State Department marked "TOP SECRET" were arriving daily at the US Embassy in Madrid, warning that five hundred Nazi troop trains were supposedly headed toward the border with France.[6]

Hitler, the cables advised, was poised to invade Spain. If the Americans were still there when the Germans arrived, they could expect a harsh conclusion to their gilded captivity.

AS FEARS OF A GERMAN INVASION HUNG over the secret negotiations, a deal was struck to release the Americans in small groups to avoid the attention of German spies. The military attaché from the US Embassy in Madrid gave the men passports that had been so hastily prepared that they bore little relation to the men's actual personal details.[7]

On March 22, 1943, an automobile pulled up to the Termas de Pallares to begin the first transfer. Six Americans—pilots Jake Epting, Hap Kendall, and Homer Moran, bombardier Al Naum, and ground crew chiefs George Metcalf and Lyman L. Dulin—climbed inside. The men were driven to the local train station for the first leg of their journey back to England.

Later that day, Ben and the remaining eight Americans interned as a result of the *Red Ass* mishap and six British and French internees posed for a photo outside their hotel. They looked like college boys in their civilian attire. Ben knelt in the front row, his fedora atop his head, and the right arm of one of his new friends draped around his neck.

The departure of the first group raised Ben's hopes that his freedom would soon follow. Another month passed before he and three other men were whisked away from the Termas de Pallares in a car driven by a US diplomat. From Gibraltar, Ben flew to London.

As if the Spanish sojourn had not been surreal enough, Ben and his three comrades were driven to the London flat of two expatriate American film stars and quartered there until they could be debriefed by US intelligence officers. Ben Lyon and his wife, Bebe Daniels, had starred in Hollywood silent films and "talkies" in the 1920s and 1930s. One of the highlights of Lyon's career had been playing a heroic World War I aviator in the 1930 film *Hell's Angels*, starring Jean Harlow. In the film's aftermath, Lyon had served as a pilot with the US Army Air Corps 322nd Pursuit Squadron in the southwest US.

In 1936, the couple moved to London following a kidnapping scare involving their daughter and Daniels's repeated encounters with a mentally ill stalker. In 1940, the former Hollywood power couple launched a hugely popular BBC Radio comedy series. Now they produced and hosted a radio interview show called *Stars and Stripes in Britain*, in which the couple took turns interviewing US military personnel in England. It had become a big hit in America in recent months by featuring the stories of Eighth Air Force bomber boys.

Lyon and Daniels were moved by Ben Kuroki's saga of overcoming bigotry to prove himself in combat with a B-24 bomber crew, and they asked if they could interview him for their show. He agreed. Under Lyon's gentle questioning, the soft-spoken Nebraska farm boy recalled the prejudice he had encountered in his quest to fight for his country, his months of combat, and his Spanish captivity. Ben's story was beamed across America.

As thrilling as the interview was for Ben, he was ready to rejoin his comrades. His debriefing finally complete, he and his three companions bade farewell to their gracious London hosts and boarded a train to the east of England. As luck would have it, Ben's return to the 93rd came at an especially fraught moment in the escalating air war against Nazi Germany.

Chapter 23

TUPELO LASS

Shortly after Ben and his comrades left for North Africa the previous December, the 93rd had departed Alconbury for another base to the east. The group was now flying out of US Army Air Forces Station 104, a triangle of runways and Nissen huts wedged amid the fields and pastures of East Anglia. In the nine-hundred-year-old market city of Norwich, eighteen miles inland from the English Channel, Ben and his three traveling companions exited the train station and boarded an army truck. Soon, the truck was rumbling along country lanes flanked by lush hedgerows. After a few minutes, the men could hear the sounds of aircraft engines. They turned off a road, passed a guard post, and rolled to a stop in front of a low-slung brick building.

The base had been carved from farms and pastures on the eastern fringe of the village of Hardwick, twelve miles due south of Norwich. Originally a temporary aerodrome, the facility had been upgraded to a fully equipped base and turned over to the Eighth Air Force in 1942. In addition to hangars, workshops, mess halls, and barracks, there were three runways laid out in a crisscross pattern that covered the points of the compass. The main runway stretched six thousand feet on a north-south axis. Two alternate runways were forty-two hundred feet in length. Farms, pastures, and patches of woods lay all around them. The setting seemed so pastoral that it was hard to imagine this as a war zone. Place names around the base added to the quaint ambiance: Topcroft Street, Spring Wood, Misery Corner, Hangman's Hill, Websdill Wood, Castle Hill.

A road bisected the base, with the runways, hardstands, hangars, and technical shops to the west and the headquarters, mess halls, barracks, sick quarters, and recreational facilities to the east. After an official welcome, Ben was directed to the corrugated steel Nissen huts east of the headquarters that were home to the 409th Squadron. Officers lived separately from enlisted men, with two crews (eight officers or twelve enlisted men) sharing each half-moon-shaped hut. The men slept on iron cots, with mattresses stuffed with wood shavings. Each hut was heated by a "tortoise," an English potbelly stove that sat in the middle of the room.

With more than thirteen miles of roadways, two hundred buildings, and two thousand men on the station, it took Ben a few days to get his bearings. West of the road lay the business end of the base: the control tower, three hangars, fire stations, the communications building, and a bomb dump. When they weren't undergoing maintenance or repairs, the group's B-24 Liberators were parked on fifty hardstands that fed into taxiways looped around the runways.

Ben was shocked by the sea of new faces. In his absence, the Eighth Air Force had set twenty-five missions as the duration of a combat tour. Some of his comrades had completed that number and moved on to other assignments in the United Kingdom, and the US replacements had begun to trickle in. The new guys were easy to spot.

Many of the veterans who had just completed their tours—and those who were nearing twenty-five missions—suffered from combat stress. Throughout the late winter and early spring, hopelessness had begun to permeate the ranks of the Eighth Air Force as losses rose. Medical officers documented the signs of depression and combat fatigue that became common in the spring of 1943. There was at least one suicide. Binge-drinking had emerged as another outlet for some combat-stressed men. "Our tactical units have been worn down about to the vanishing point, and their morale has reached a critical low," General Ira Eaker's aide-de-camp, James Parton, observed in March.[1]

About two weeks before Ben's return to the 93rd, on April 16, the 93rd had experienced one of its most devastating days of the war. In a raid on the port of Brest, France, the 93rd lost thirty men on four crews, including nineteen killed in action or missing and never found, and eleven captured. There was an uneasiness in the air as Ben rejoined the 93rd.

BEN ALSO HAD A NEW AIRCRAFT TO GET used to. His beloved *Red Ass* was last seen taking off from Melilla, Spanish Morocco, a Spanish air force pilot at the controls as the battle-scarred bomber disappeared over the Mediterranean horizon. By the time Ben returned to the 93rd, Epting had broken in a new aircraft with a more elegant name: *Tupelo Lass*.

Ben flew his first mission in *Tupelo Lass* on May 17. Fifteen 93rd bombers joined with nineteen B-24s from the 44th Bomb Group to undertake the first all-Liberator raid by the Eighth Air Force: a raid on the French port city of Bordeaux. It was Ben's fifteenth mission.

On May 29, after a twelve-day lull, the Epting crew was among the 93rd men assigned to bomb the German submarine pens in La Pallice harbor, on the Atlantic coast of France.

Ben was in his tail turret when disaster struck *Tupelo Lass* as they were approaching La Pallice at twenty-three thousand feet. The propeller blades on two engines began to windmill wildly, then all four engines stopped. *Tupelo Lass* fell into a sickening descent toward the sea. Epting sounded the alarm to prepare to abandon ship. Bombardier Al Naum dumped his bombs while Epting frantically tried to get the engines restarted. "This is it!" Epting shouted over the intercom. They were down to two thousand feet, only seconds from smashing into the Bay of Biscay, when the engines coughed to life. In a few seconds, Epting got *Tupelo Lass* under control and leveled off.[2]

Back on the ground, the men of the Epting crew tried to joke about their close call, but they were badly shaken. In their post-mission debriefing, the intelligence officer scribbled a note on the crew's sortie report: "10 nervous wrecks. Candidates for rest home."[3]

THE LA PALLICE RAID WAS THE FINAL mission for several 93rd men, and their departure only increased the sense of isolation for Ben and others who had arrived in England with the group the previous September. Ben was now at sixteen missions, and the sporadic rate of action in the 93rd meant that he probably wouldn't reach twenty-five until the fall.

In the bigger picture, May had been a better month for Ira Eaker's Eighth Air Force heavy bombers than April, when weather and casualties had limited his B-17s and B-24s to only four missions during the entire month, and only one raid to Germany—all while losing another twenty-eight aircraft. In May, the 93rd had logged nine missions, including four into Germany. As had been the case with the La Pallice raid, the group's primary focus had been German submarine pens and construction yards, part of a larger effort to stem the loss of Allied shipping to German U-boats in the North Atlantic.

Another bright spot for Eaker and the Eighth Air Force during the month was the surge in replacement crews and aircraft arriving from the United States. Four new B-17 heavy bombardment groups had joined the Eighth in May, along with groups of replacement crews that were being sent to depleted units in the English countryside.

Ira Eaker had been losing men and crews at an accelerating pace because of rising casualties and the twenty-five-mission policy, but he was finally getting the infusion of new blood he had sought for months. The reinforcements were arriving just in time for the planned summer air offensive against Nazi Germany.

THE 93RD HAD HOSTED ANOTHER important visitor during May. Forty-seven-year-old Robert Abercrombie Lovett was a former Wall Street banker now serving as assistant secretary of war for air, and during a spring tour he had shared meals and cigars with commanders at B-17 and B-24 bases throughout England. He spent two days at Hardwick, quizzing Colonel Ted Timberlake and other 93rd officers and men about their eight months of combat against the Germans in three theaters. Lovett had already concluded that German fighter attacks revealed a potentially devastating vulnerability for the Eighth Air Force bombers and crews.

Lovett had been lured to the War Department in 1940 as a high-level troubleshooter and a minder of sorts to keep the volatile Hap Arnold out of trouble. A polished and charming patrician, Lovett was masterful at his work. By the spring of 1943, he was intimately familiar with Arnold's foibles, and one blind spot in particular: Arnold's stubborn belief that American B-17 and B-24 bombers could attack Nazi Germany without long-range escorts.

As Lovett gathered information from bomber crews and air commanders, Arnold was recuperating from his second heart attack since visiting with the men of the 93rd at Gambut Main in February. He had spent most of May resting and fishing in the Pacific Northwest. He had missed the ten-day TRIDENT war conference in Washington, DC, during which major decisions had been made about the summer priorities for the air campaign against Germany.

On his return to Washington on May 27, Arnold was briefed on all that had transpired in his absence. The news of a more productive month by Eaker's bombers was encouraging, but the rising losses from German fighter attacks were a concern. Robert Lovett was due back in Washington in early June, and Arnold expected to learn much more about the state of affairs with the Eighth Air Force. Lovett had yet to put his thoughts to paper, but by the end of May, Hap Arnold's troubleshooter had heard enough to conclude that the young airmen he had met during his tour of bomber bases in East Anglia faced a grim reckoning in the months ahead.

Chapter 24

SPECIAL ORDERS NUMBER 174

As the month of June 1943 began, the 93rd crews waited anxiously each day for the alert that would signal their next combat mission. Days passed and the alert didn't come. Instead, the crews began treetop-level practice flights over the East Anglian countryside. "Buzzing," as the low-altitude flights were known to fliers, had been strictly forbidden during their stateside training. Now they were buzzing the English countryside under orders. They would take off from Hardwick, form up wingtip-to-wingtip with other aircraft, and then swoop back and forth over the farms and pastures. It was a strange turn of events that no one could explain.

Some of the men found the training exhilarating because of its previously forbidden nature. Others found it excruciating because of motion sickness, a malady exacerbated by the choppy air of low-altitude flight. The drills also irritated local farmers, who complained to the Americans about a litany of disruptions to their livelihoods: cows that suddenly wouldn't produce milk, plow horses that became skittish, and bees that ceased to make honey.[1]

The odd low-level training was a welcome change of pace for those men who were battling homesickness and combat anxiety. One morose gunner seemed to take perverse pleasure in chronicling the misery of airsick comrades and frightened livestock. "Flew formation all afternoon. Guy got sick as hell," the gunner wrote in one diary entry. "Buzzed everyone for miles," read another. "Did some low-altitude bombing practice. Scared every cow and horse in England." And, "More low-altitude bombing. Two guys got sick as hell."[2]

Laughs aside, no one doubted that the unconventional training foreshadowed a mission of great importance—one that would likely claim at least some of their lives. Imaginations ran wild. Some of the men coined a name for the mystery mission: The Big One.

While B-17 groups in the area continued to fly combat missions, the 93rd focused solely on the low-level flights. Some of the 93rd old-timers like Ben missed their lives in Alconbury, with its proximity to Cambridge and

London. But Hardwick had its bucolic charms, and, with its patchwork of farms, lanes, and villages, it reminded Ben of home.

On the morning of June 14, the crews were briefed for a mock mission that would be flown at treetop level. The men were assigned to aircraft, climbed into the sky, and staged a low-level "attack" on the Hardwick base. Renewed speculation swirled about the target that beckoned from some distant land: Germany? Russia? Norway? North Africa? Nobody knew for sure.

With each passing week, Ben and those members of the 93rd who had yet to finish their tours felt more alone than ever. Radio operator William L. Gros of the 328th Squadron finished his twenty-five missions with the raid on La Pallice, only days after his twentieth birthday, and then spent two weeks relaxing in a convalescent home with a wounded comrade. On his return to Hardwick in mid-June to train new radio operators for action, Gros and one of his few remaining friends in the group walked into the combat sergeants' mess hall, looked around, and stopped dead in their tracks. They didn't recognize a soul. The two 93rd veterans turned around and walked out. "We sat down on the steps of the mess hall and cried like babies," Gros said. "I think it was the first time that either one of us ever stopped to think of what had happened to us and the guys we were with."[3]

WHILE THE 93RD AND TWO OTHER B-24 groups practiced low-level flights for a secret mission yet to be revealed, Ira Eaker unleashed a flurry of June raids that he hoped would silence Hap Arnold's sniping about Eighth Air Force inactivity. The American bombers were greeted by the most ferocious Luftwaffe fighter resistance yet encountered. During the period of June 11 to 22, Eaker lost fifty bombers to enemy fire and had another two-hundred-plus damaged.

It was against the backdrop of these losses that Robert Lovett on June 18 crafted a memo to Arnold that incorporated the conclusions of his recent fact-finding trip to England. There was an "immediate need for long range fighters," Lovett wrote. "Fighter escort will have to be provided for B-17s on as many missions as possible in order particularly to get them through the first wave of the German fighter defense, which is now put up in depth so that the B-17s are forced to run the gauntlet both in to the target and out from it."[4]

Three days passed without action by Arnold. On the fourth day, June 22, word of another costly raid arrived from England. More than 200 B-17s had been dispatched to hit the chemical works and synthetic rubber plant at Hüls, in the Ruhr Valley. Of 183 bombers that reached the target, 16 were shot down and 75 damaged. The day's official casualty numbers for the Eighth Air Force were 2 killed in action, 16 wounded, and 151 missing.

At this rate, Eaker's recent reinforcements would be wiped out by summer's end.

On June 22, Arnold issued a terse directive to his trusted deputy, General Barney Giles. "Within this next six months, you have got to get a fighter to protect our bombers," Arnold decreed. "Whether you use an existing type or have to start from scratch is your problem."[5]

In the meantime, without the protection of long-range escorts, more than one thousand Eighth Air Force bomber boys would pay the ultimate price for Hap Arnold's delay. Ben would be trying to finish his twenty-five missions during some of the darkest days of the American bombing campaign against Nazi Germany.

On Thursday, June 24, the 93rd's carefree days of buzzing the English countryside ended abruptly. The men were ordered to assemble for an inspection. Soon, a staff car rolled through the gates at AAF 104, and the guest of honor emerged. It was General Jacob Devers, who, a few weeks earlier, had become commander of US forces in the European Theater of Operations, replacing Frank Andrews, killed in the crash of a 93rd aircraft that was ferrying him to Washington for important meetings. Devers congratulated the 93rd veterans for their work of the previous months and welcomed the new arrivals. He exhorted the crews to carry on under their new group commander, Addison Baker, as they had under the recently promoted Ted Timberlake. Devers then climbed into his staff car and roared off.

No sooner had Devers departed than Special Orders Number 174 set in motion another temporary deployment. Combat crews packed their gear for departure the following day, destination still unknown.

On Friday morning, June 25, the men were briefed on the first leg of their journey. With puffs of smoke and a rising roar, engines coughed to life. At two o'clock, the first 328th Squadron aircraft rumbled down the Hardwick runway and lifted into the English sky. The lead contingent climbed to their designated altitude, formed up, and set off on a southwest heading.

For Jake Epting, Special Orders 174 marked a new chapter in his combat tour. Epting had just been promoted to the rank of captain and he was a half-dozen missions shy of completing his tour. His trusted copilot, Hap Kendall, had his own crew now, so Epting had taken on a new copilot, Flight Officer Charles S. Young, who had joined the 93rd in April after serving with the Royal Canadian Air Force in England. Bombardier Al Naum had flown his twenty-fifth mission to La Pallice on May 29, but he was still with the crew, awaiting further orders. Lieutenant Edward Weir, who had been among the last Americans released from Spanish captivity, was also in his usual spot at the navigator's table in the nose.

Ben's world in the back of the plane had seen dramatic changes. Of the six enlisted men who had accompanied Epting to Africa in December, only Ben and his close friend, radio operator Red Kettering, remained. With four gunnery slots open on his crew, Epting had added a mix of familiar faces and new arrivals. The familiar face was Sergeant Harold E. Dafoe, a tough, twenty-one-year-old fur trapper from Canton, New York, near the Canadian border. The three new faces among Epting's gunners stood out because of their impressive heights: Sergeant David L. Wightman, a twenty-year-old auto mechanic from Los Angeles, who stood a lanky five-foot-eleven; Sergeant James Wisniewski, a twenty-year-old from Detroit, Michigan, who topped out at just under six feet; and Staff Sergeant Robert N. Daves, a twenty-one-year-old from Englewood, New Jersey, who found it challenging to navigate the tight confines of *Tupelo Lass* with his gangly six-foot-four frame.

In Epting's steady hands, *Tupelo Lass* rose into the skies over East Anglia and banked west. The B-24 passed over London after about half an hour, and the Cornwall peninsula loomed ahead. As the lead Liberators began their descent, the Cornish moorland and craggy coast flashed beneath them. The vanguard landed at an RAF base in the village of St. Eval. The trailing crews landed down the coast in the seaside village of Portreath, and at other Cornwall bases.

After a night of heavy drinking, the predawn Reveille in the 328th Squadron dormitory at RAF St. Eval revealed a sorry sight on Saturday morning, June 26, 1943. "We were all up early, but not feeling very bright," one 328th scribe reported.[6] At 8:00 a.m., up and down the Cornwall peninsula, B-24 Liberators rose into the morning sky, maneuvered into formation, and headed to sea, past Land's End, at the southwest tip of Cornwall, and the Isles of Scilly beyond.

Flying south, the Liberators crossed the Celtic Sea, skirted the Brest peninsula of occupied France, and then cut across the Bay of Biscay. Around midafternoon, off the southwest coast of Portugal, the B-24s turned east for the final five-hundred-mile leg. Roaring eastward through the Straits of Gibraltar, the bombers hugged the coastline of North Africa. Nine-and-a-half hours after leaving England, the vanguard touched down at the French aerodrome of La Sénia, five miles south of a city etched in Ben's memory: Oran, Algeria. Stiff from the long flight, the crews stepped onto African soil in the muggy afternoon heat.

Nearly four months after departing the continent in Spanish custody, Ben was back in Africa for reasons that remained a closely held secret.

Chapter 25

THE BIG ONE

On Sunday morning, June 27, Ben and the other 93rd men awoke to the strains of "the best bugler any of us ever heard," as one diarist wrote.[1] Sand and dust whipped off the Sahara as the men arrived at La Sénia airfield and loaded their aircraft. At 9:30 a.m., the lead elements of the 328th Squadron rose into the blue Mediterranean sky. They formed up at three thousand feet, turned east into the morning sun, and began climbing.

Beyond the battlefields of Tunisia, where the remnants of Rommel's shattered army had surrendered on May 13, the 93rd bombers retraced the long route of the Axis retreat across North Africa. Off to their left, Allied convoys plied the shimmering blue waters of the Mediterranean. To their right loomed the vastness of the Sahara Desert. They crossed into Libyan airspace and passed the city of Tripoli. In the late afternoon, the lead aircraft began their descent into a desert airstrip outside Benghazi, a battered former Italian colonial outpost that had changed hands five times since February 1941.

The 93rd had been assigned to a field designated Site Number 7, in a stretch of flat desert eighteen miles south of the city, near the Mediterranean coast. Ben and his comrades stepped into stifling heat and choking dust. Their welcoming committee included sun-bronzed British troops, wearing pith helmets and khaki shorts, and swarms of desert locusts. "It didn't look any too pleasant to us," one 93rd gunner wrote.[2]

Ben and the dwindling fraternity of 93rd veterans had seen it all before during their time at Gambut Main.

Trucks arrived and the men climbed aboard with their sleeping bags and gear and were driven a short distance to their new campsite, which consisted of two Nissen huts and a tent. The men retrieved their mess kits from their packs and lined up for their first meal at their al fresco mess hall. Flies descended as the men shoveled down Spam speckled with grains of desert sand.

After dinner, the men were issued cots and tents and set to work making camp. They were like a rowdy bunch of teenagers on a campout, hooting at those among them who struggled to secure their tents in the stiff breeze. Some of the men who had gotten their tents squared away commandeered a truck and drove to a nearby beach for a twilight swim. Nightfall brought a cool breeze, and the weary crews collapsed onto their cots for their first night in the Libyan desert.

As Ben and his comrades would discover in the days ahead, the low-level raid that had been the subject of so much speculation wouldn't be their first order of business.

ON THE FIRST MORNING IN THEIR DESERT bivouac, the men of the 93rd awakened to the warble of desert larks exulting in the cool morning air. After a breakfast of oatmeal, powdered scrambled eggs, and coffee, the crews were trucked to their planes to unload gear and supplies. By the time they returned to camp at midmorning, a sandstorm blotted out the blazing sun.

To cope with the oppressive daytime heat, the men cut their hair short and lopped off khaki trousers above the knees. But there was nothing to be done about the swarming flies and locusts, and at every opportunity the men sought escape at the nearby beach. Officers and enlisted men alike stripped naked and splashed like children in the cool waters. "The sand is pure white and the water clear as crystal," observed intelligence officer Brutus Hamilton.[3]

Nightfall brought a soothing breeze and pleasant temperatures, and as the men settled into their tents the desert came alive. Kangaroo rats and mice prowled about, scavenging for food in and around the tents. The local fauna also included side-winding desert vipers and scorpions. The men quickly learned to begin each day by shaking out their shoes and uniforms to avoid a painful sting by a scorpion that had taken up residence during the night.

More urgent concerns greeted the crews. In the week before their arrival, Italian commandos had struck their old friends of the 98th Bombardment Group, the Ninth Air Force B-24 outfit they had come to know at Gambut Main, now based at Benghazi's main airport, less than ten miles from the 93rd's camp. The enemy commandos killed two 98th men and blew up three aircraft before disappearing into the darkness.

The commandos had been captured a few days before the 93rd's arrival, but the Allied air forces in the area braced for more sabotage and perhaps even a full-blown Italian invasion. The 93rd men joked about getting shot on nighttime trips to the latrine, but it was no laughing matter. Many of the 93rd officers kept revolvers or knives close at hand. One gunner who got lost while trying to find his tent in the dark fearfully crept through the camp before finding his way.

AFTER THREE RAIDS WERE ABORTED DUE TO bad weather over Italy, Ben returned to action with the Epting crew on July 2. The target was a German airfield at San Pancrazio, Italy, along the southeastern coast of the Italian mainland. It was Ben's seventeenth mission and his first since the Epting crew's near crash en route to La Pallice on May 29.

Weather caused another pause in the bombing, and it was July 7 before Ben flew again. His command pilot for this mission was the 409th Squadron commander, Major K. O. (Kayo) Dessert. Their target was a German airfield on Sicily known as Gerbini #6, part of a complex of Luftwaffe fighter bases scattered through the flat farm fields south and west of Mount Etna. One of the highlights of the raid for the crews was a spectacular view of the volcano.

On July 9, Ben notched his nineteenth mission. The target was another German airfield on Sicily, this one at Ponte Olivo, a mile inland from Gela Beach. The crews spotted a massive Allied convoy headed toward Sicily during the raid. What they didn't know was that Gela Beach was the destination of the American soldiers aboard the troop transports.

Casualties had been exceptionally light on the Italian raids, and the reason was clear to Ben and other veterans of earlier raids in North Africa and Europe. Enemy fighter defenses had nearly collapsed. For more than three years, German and Italian fighter pilots had been locked in nonstop combat in North Africa and the Mediterranean rim, and scores had been killed in action. The survivors were increasingly unwilling to challenge the machine-gun fire of massed bombers.

The peril of fighter attacks had plummeted, but the 93rd men still faced mortal danger. Returning in the evening from the July 7 raid on Sicily, the crews were forced to circle while awaiting their turn to land on the lone lighted runway. A new crew flying a B-24 named *El Lobo* ran out of fuel and crashed within sight of the runway, killing four of the ten men. Two days later, a crew failed to find the 93rd's airstrip in the darkness and flew three hundred miles into the desert before running out of fuel; the entire crew bailed out, but the pilot and three other men disappeared in the desert and were never seen again.

For the new crews, the mishaps were a shock. For Ben and other hardened veterans, they were a reminder that even if their Axis enemies were losing strength, death was never distant.

———————

AT 4:00 A.M. ON THE MORNING OF July 10, General Patton's Seventh Army soldiers stormed ashore at Gela Beach, and the thirty-eight-day battle for Sicily was on. Patton's troops pushed inland along Sicily's south shore while the British Eighth Army, commanded by General Bernard Montgomery, seized the island's southeastern extremes.

The Sicily beachheads had been secured when the 93rd Liberators returned to action on July 12. Over an eight-day period, Ben logged another four missions as the 93rd bombed airfields and other targets on mainland Italy to suppress enemy air attacks and resupply efforts aimed at swaying the battle for Sicily.

The raids were lightly contested by the collapsing Axis air defenses, but they were occasions for mourning for Ben and his 409th comrades. During the July 12 attack on train ferries and railroad yards around San Giovanni, the squadron lost one of its best bombardiers. A piece of flak pierced the nose of the lead aircraft and mortally wounded Lieutenant Clinton P. Sipe, a twenty-eight-year-old Pennsylvanian who had been with the group from the beginning. On a July 13 mission to the Vibo Valentia Aerodrome in southern Italy, one of the 409th's new crews crashed just after takeoff, killing all ten men in a fiery explosion.

The flurry of raids culminated on July 19 with the biggest American strike to that point in the war, a five-hundred-plane attack led by the celebrated General James (Jimmy) Doolittle on rail chokepoints and airfields around Rome. The 93rd contributed twenty-five planes to the effort, striking a vital cluster of tracks and sidings that formed the freight gateway to Rome's northern fringe.

En route to the target, *Tupelo Lass* and the other 93rd bombers crossed Sicily and traversed the Tyrrhenian Sea to a point some thirty miles northwest of Rome before wheeling to the east. As the Americans crossed the coast, the sky blossomed with black puffs of fire from enemy antiaircraft batteries. The 93rd bombers streaked eastward across a pastoral landscape of dormant volcanoes and crater lakes ringed by medieval castles and villages. The blue waters of Lago di Bracciano glittered below, and then the smaller Lago di Martignano. The bombers pivoted again, angling south-southeast on a 148-degree heading over a picturesque landscape of castles, villages, and farms threaded by ancient Roman roads. Five miles out, the bombers drew a bead on the Littorio rail yards.

As the 93rd crews began their bomb run, antiaircraft shells pocked the sky. The aim of the Italian gunners was poor and did little damage. Some crews would describe the enemy barrage as "white flak bursts breaking like silver hail, sleet, pieces of white paper or confetti."[4] At 12:18 p.m. (10:18 a.m. GMT), from an altitude of 21,500 feet, each of the 93rd bombardiers unleashed nine 500-pound bombs on the Littorio marshaling yards. As they pulled away from the target, members of the crew observed the rail yards erupting in flames and explosions that engulfed trains and track. The 93rd Liberators roared past the eastern fringe of Rome on a southeast vector, stalked by cautious German and Italian fighters, then turned to the west. They passed over the town of Castel Gandolfo, on Lago Albano, the summer residence of the Pope during more peaceful times, then encountered a parting flurry of antiaircraft fire as they crossed the coast. A few miles out to sea, the Liberators set a southward course for Benghazi.

The damage to Rome's rail yards and airfields was extensive. More problematic for the Americans was the destruction of part of the seven-hundred-year-old papal Basilica of San Lorenzo, which had been overlooked in the mission planning because of its location well outside the Vatican walls. Other bombs damaged an area known as University City, where the German Air Force had its headquarters. Civilian casualties were officially reported at 717 killed and 1,599 wounded. On Rome's southern outskirts, the Ciampino military airport was rendered unusable and about two hundred planes on the ground were destroyed.[5]

Out of more than five hundred aircraft participating in the raid, only two were shot down: one B-25 and one B-26, both lost in the attack on the Ciampino military airfield. Not a single B-17 or B-24 was lost. Seven 93rd bombers had sustained minor flak damage, with only two gunners scratched.

The only 93rd death was a New York City native whose parents had immigrated from Sicily. Sergeant Gelorme Musco's B-24, *Blasted Event*, had come under attack by enemy fighters during the outbound flight after his pilot dropped out of the formation because of engine problems over Mount Etna. An enemy cannon shell exploded near Musco's tail turret, mortally wounding the *Blasted Event* gunner. Pilot Raymond A. Walker of New Haven, Connecticut, landed at a recently liberated airfield eight miles south of Catania, Sicily, so his beloved tail gunner could be buried in his ancestral soil.[6]

Ben and his comrades had written another notable chapter in history's most terrible war. They had flown eight hundred miles into enemy territory and bombed an Axis capital in Europe—the first Americans to do so during the war. And they had done it with ease.

For Ben, Rome was mission number 23.

FOLLOWING THE ROME RAID, THE 93RD crews resumed the low-level practice missions that had stoked so much speculation before their departure from England. The target remained a mystery to all but a few senior officers.

To keep their minds off the rumors, men swam in the sea, wrote letters, played poker, and watched movies and live shows under the stars. The officers had the additional diversion of a casino built by one enterprising pilot in a spacious military tent.

On the afternoon of July 24, Jake Epting and the other commissioned officers were summoned to a briefing where they were finally informed of their target: the massive complex of oil refineries around Ploiesti, Romania, a primary source of Hitler's oil. The officers were shown a photograph that mapped their route to the target, two thousand miles out and back, reachable only by installing auxiliary fuel tanks in the bomb bay of each B-24. "I watched the men carefully as the target was announced," intelligence officer Brutus Hamilton recorded. "No one flickered."[7]

To shore up morale, a USO troupe was trucked out from Benghazi on July 24 to entertain the 93rd. The performers sang and danced and cracked jokes on a stage built of sandbags and marble slabs. Later in the evening, an air raid warning was issued, but no attack ever came.

Bored with their desolate surroundings and bland diet, the 93rd veterans drew on their Gambut Main experience and befriended Bedouin peddlers who lived in a tent settlement near the American camp. Riding donkeys, camels, and the occasional bicycle, the Bedouins struck up a brisk trade in fresh eggs, grapes, and melons, which they sold or traded for American cigarettes. The 93rd men welcomed the addition of real scrambled eggs and fresh fruit to their diet, until bouts of dysentery and diarrhea swept the camp.

On July 25, 93rd intelligence officers set up a carefully guarded tent with Ploiesti target folders and maps for the pilots and navigators to peruse. The crews continued to fly low-level practice missions, but the enlisted men remained oblivious. Finally, on Thursday, July 29, Ben and the other gunners and radio operators were briefed and shown photographs and models of their respective targets. A flurry of briefings and pep talks followed.

Saturday, July 31, was consumed by final preparations. Mission commanders scrambled to replace ill officers and enlisted men too weak to fly. The commander of the Ninth Air Force, General Lewis Brereton, and General Uzal Ent, commander of the Ninth Bomber Command, arrived from Cairo to deliver a final pep talk. After lunch, Ben was among the throng of men who gathered for another review of the plan conducted by their group commander, Lieutenant Colonel Addison Baker. The men were paid and given the rest of the day off.

As evening fell, some wrote final letters and jotted their hopes and fears in diaries. "We take off in [the] morning early to bomb Rumanian oil fields from low level," scribbled one 93rd gunner. "Everyone all keyed up about it. Very big."[8]

Chapter 26

TIDAL WAVE

It had been a sleepless night for many of the 93rd men when whistles and horns sounded across the desert camp at 0200 Greenwich Mean Time on Sunday morning, August 1, 1943. It was 4:00 a.m. local time. In the predawn darkness bleary-eyed airmen dressed and made their way to the mess tent to sip coffee and pick at powdered eggs and pancakes. After two months of preparation and speculation, the mystery mission was a go.

A flurry of last-minute activity had swept the camp over the previous twelve hours. Urgent cables from Washington and Cairo grounded several senior officers who had planned to fly today's raid. These and other scratches from the mission manifest due to illness now set off a last-minute scramble to finalize crew assignments.

In one of the previous day's briefings, General Brereton, the Ninth Air Force commander, had characterized the low-level raid as the most important air mission to this point in the war. A successful strike on Hitler's vital Romanian oil refineries could end the war by Christmas, he said. But casualties could run as high as 50 percent. Even if that proved true, the damage to the Axis cause would be worth it, Brereton declared.

In the coolness of the desert morning, the men were spared the scourge of swarming flies that tormented their daylight hours. They finished their coffee and what breakfast they could eat before shuffling off to the final briefing. The veil of mystery gone, the men now quietly pondered what they were being asked to do. Whether it was a brilliant stroke or a suicide mission would be revealed in the hours ahead.

The plan called for 180 aircraft from five B-24 groups scattered around the desert airfields outside Benghazi to cross the Mediterranean and Ionian seas to the north and the mountainous Balkans of southeastern Europe before converging at Ploiesti. The 93rd would contribute thirty-seven bombers in two attack groups. The Epting crew would be among twenty-two planes led by the 93rd group commander, Addison Baker. A second fifteen-plane force of 93rd bombers would be commanded by Major Ramsay Potts.

The 93rd bombers would proceed to their final checkpoint thirteen miles northwest of Ploiesti, then wheel to the southeast for the sprint to their target: the Concordia Vega Refinery, third largest of Ploiesti's refineries, designated by mission planners as White 2. Each refinery complex featured a cluster of buildings where crude oil was refined into various products, including high-octane aviation fuel and engine lubricants devoured by Axis military vehicles and aircraft. In addition to the smokestack-level final approach, the attack would be distinguished by another unusual tactic: The B-24s would form into waves, six to twelve bombers abreast, and sweep across the enemy refineries like an old-style cavalry charge.

With the briefing complete, the men climbed into trucks for the short ride to their parked aircraft. Ben and his crewmates arrived at *Tupelo Lass* to find their lineup still in flux. Major K. O. Dessert had exercised his privilege as 409th Squadron commander by assigning himself to pilot *Tupelo Lass*; Dessert had originally picked Colonel Jacob Smart, a top Arnold aide, to occupy the copilot's seat, relegating Jake Epting to the role of a spare pilot. But orders from Washington had grounded Smart, whose vast knowledge of secrets included the Manhattan Project. Epting took the copilot's seat and Charles Young, the Texan that Epting had taken on as copilot after Hap Kendall got his own crew, would serve as a waist gunner and spare pilot.

Charles Stenius Young—Bubba to family and friends back home in Liberty County, Texas, in the Lonestar State's southeastern swamps—had been studying medicine at the University of Texas in the fall of 1941 when Britain's brave stand against Hitler inspired him to join the Royal Canadian Air Force. After earning his pilot's wings, Young had notched six months of combat with the RAF in England before transferring to the 93rd in April 1943. Since joining Ted's Travelling Circus, Young had earned a new nickname: Five-by-Five, a reference to his stature—five-feet-five-inches, or a half inch shy of that, as some military records indicated. Young was slight of stature, but he was built like a football fullback, with a muscular 160 pounds packed onto his sixty-five-inch frame.[1]

Young had forged a close friendship with another Texan new to the 93rd. Ivan Canfield had dropped out of Brackenridge High School in San Antonio and, with the blessing of his mother and stepfather, an army sergeant, had enlisted in the Army Air Forces. Canfield had fudged his age to enter pilot training, and he had been among the youngest graduates in the Gulf Coast Training Center's Class 43-A, earning his wings on January 14, 1943, in ceremonies at Ellington Field, on the outskirts of Houston—forty miles from Five-by-Five Young's hometown.[2]

Canfield had been assigned to the 409th Squadron in June as copilot on a crew commanded by another newcomer, Nicholas Stampolis, the twenty-one-year-old son of Greek immigrants from Kalamazoo, Michigan. With his infectious gap-toothed grin and youthful appearance, Canfield was christened Junior by his 93rd comrades. Junior and Nick Stampolis had made their combat debut after the group's reassignment to the Libyan desert, and the pair had logged eight missions together, including the Rome raid, at the controls of a bomber named *Jose Carioca*, after the dapper Brazilian parrot in a recent Disney film. Now, with Junior Canfield and Nick Stampolis assigned to Addison Baker's third wave for the attack on White 2, Bubba Young would be able to keep an eye on his young friends from the right waist window of *Tupelo Lass*.

There was one more new addition to the Epting crew for the mission—a familiar face, just not in a combat role. As the officers and men of *Tupelo Lass* were heading out to the flight line, their chief mechanic, Master Sergeant Raymond Wierciszowski, had stopped the squadron commander. "Major Dessert, do you mind if I go with you?" he had asked. It was an unusual request, but no one knew *Tupelo Lass* and its engines better than Sergeant Wier, as everyone called him. "I'd love to have you, Sergeant Wier," Dessert replied. And so, Ray Wierciszowski posed alongside the flying members of *Tupelo Lass* as someone used Sergeant Wier's Kodak Brownie camera to snap a final photograph of the crew in the dawn light.

At 0400 GMT, Addison Baker guided *Hell's Wench* down the Site 7 airstrip and into the brightening skies. A few minutes later, with K. O. Dessert at the controls and Jake Epting assisting from the copilot's seat, *Tupelo Lass* lumbered down the runway. With more than four thousand pounds of bombs and 3,100 gallons of hundred-octane fuel, including four hundred gallons in a pair of auxiliary tanks bolted in the bomb bay, getting airborne this morning was the first of many perilous challenges the pilots faced. As Sergeant Wier stood behind the pilots and Ben lounged a few feet farther back, Dessert and Epting got their overloaded Liberator airborne. *Tupelo Lass* slowly climbed into the Mediterranean dawn.

It was 0435 Greenwich Mean Time (GMT)—7:35 a.m. local time. TIDAL WAVE, as the low-level raid on Ploiesti had been recently code-named, was underway.

THE 93RD'S THIRTY-SEVEN LIBERATORS got airborne without incident, but the spectacular split-screen of shimmering desert and sparkling sea that spread beneath Ben and his crewmates in the rising morning light revealed the smoldering fires of the day's first casualties. The 93rd had contributed a spare crew, newly arrived from England, to their friends of the 98th Bomb Group. Those men had boarded a B-24 named *Kickapoo* and had taken off from an airfield about six miles east of Benghazi. The pilot was Lieutenant Robert Nespor, and, like many of the men assigned to the Ploiesti mission, he had completed his twenty-five-mission tour and was flying The Big One out of a sense of history and duty. Shortly after takeoff, three of *Kickapoo*'s engines cut out. Nespor's bombardier dumped their bombs in the sea and the pilot circled back to their airfield for an emergency landing. As Nespor and copilot Lieutenant John Riley attempted to land, one wing clipped a concrete power pole. *Kickapoo* slammed into the ground and burst into flames. There were two survivors, both badly burned: Lieutenant Russell Polivka, the Wisconsin-born navigator, and Staff Sergeant Eugene Garner, a gunner.[3]

It took nearly an hour for the armada to get airborne and formed for the outbound flight, but finally the 376th Bomb Group aircraft wheeled to the north, followed by the aircraft of the 93rd, 98th, and 44th groups. Bringing up the rear was the 389th, which had only recently arrived in England as the third B-24 group assigned to the Eighth Air Force.

Heading north across the Mediterranean, the groups began to gain altitude. About forty minutes from the Albanian coast, a 376th bomber named *Wongo Wongo* suddenly dropped from the lead group, fell sharply to the left, leveled out briefly, then corkscrewed downward, smoke streaming from one of its starboard engines, before smashing into the sea and exploding. Trailing behind, the 93rd Bombers witnessed the horrifying spectacle. Standing behind K. O. Dessert and Jake Epting on the flight deck of *Tupelo Lass*, Ray Wier snapped a photograph of the column of smoke rising from the spot where *Wongo Wongo* had disappeared beneath the waves. "Kind of a bad omen in a way to see something like that happen," Ben later recalled.[4]

During the Mediterranean crossing, four 93rd aircraft dropped from the formation with mechanical problems and turned back to Benghazi. Around 0900, the 93rd passed over the Greek island of Corfu, and about five minutes later they crossed the Albanian coast. They climbed to ten thousand feet to clear the Pindus Mountains of southern Albania and the Balkan Mountains beyond, only to find an even more formidable obstacle in their path: a wall of cumulus clouds that rose to fifteen thousand feet. Addison Baker now faced a hard choice. He could burn fuel skirting the clouds, or plunge ahead and risk a midair collision. "A cold chill went down my spine," 409th Squadron pilot Edwin Baker later wrote. "It was obvious that we were going to have to fly through."[5]

Addison Baker made the command decision to forge ahead in a gradual ascent rather than waste precious fuel skirting the clouds. With the group maintaining strict radio silence, signals were flashed to the other 93rd aircraft to inform them of the plan. The formation loosened up and the men slipped on oxygen masks as they disappeared into the clouds. For several minutes, the bombers droned on in perilous solitude, with some men offering silent prayers that they would avoid a collision in the clouds. Finally, at fifteen thousand feet, flying over the mountainous border of Serbia and Bulgaria, Addison Baker and his crews broke through the clouds. The 93rd bombers leveled off and re-formed into three-plane Vs.

The bombers finally cleared the mountains about forty miles northwest of the Bulgarian capital of Sofia. Beneath them lay the Danube Basin and the Wallachian Plain. They had descended to fifteen hundred feet when they crossed the Danube River at a point about 130 miles southwest of Ploiesti and dropped to treetop level. As they crossed the great European river they had read about since they were schoolboys, Dessert and his men broke into a spirited vocal rendition of Johann Strauss's "Blue Danube" waltz. "We thought that was the greatest thing to get everybody's spirits up again," Dessert later recalled. As *Tupelo Lass* flashed over the Danube, Ben cracked, "Hey, that river's not blue—it's dirty brown!"[6]

Beyond the river, they dropped to 150 feet. After a month in the desert, the men marveled at the colorful mosaic of cross-hatched fields of ripening corn, wheat, and alfalfa, and copses of trees stitched with meandering streams and rivers. Scenes of bucolic rural life flashed beneath their feet like a film in fast-forward: girls bathing in a stream; wagonloads of hay rumbling along roads; villagers in their Sunday best peering up at the huge machines roaring overhead; women in colorful dresses smiling and waving handkerchiefs. "We could almost reach out and touch these people because we were flying low enough," Ben said.

They roared across the Wallachian Plain at 240 miles an hour, hugging the terrain, desperately trying to avoid German radar. They needn't have bothered. Enemy spotters had been tracking them for more than two hours, from the moment they crossed Albania's coast. Hundreds of German and Romanian antiaircraft gunners and fighter pilots waited in ambush.

At Pitesti, in the foothills of the Southern Carpathian Mountains fifty-five miles west of Ploiesti, the 93rd bombers reached the first of three checkpoints leading to the final sprint to the target. About nine minutes later, they spotted the second checkpoint: the town of Targoviste. The pilots and navigators peered intently at the ground flashing beneath their feet, searching for a long railroad bridge, a road, and then a town—Floresti—which would be their cue to make a hard-right turn for Ploiesti. In the lead 376th Liberator, passing over Targoviste, the pilots saw a long railroad bridge, a power station, and a road, and began the turn—twenty miles too soon.

In many of the 93rd bombers, the error was immediately obvious. Pilots and navigators shouted in dismay over their internal intercom: "Not here!" "Too soon!" "Mistake! Mistake!"[7] But they were under strict orders to maintain radio silence to preserve the element of surprise—unaware that they had been tracked for hours. At the vanguard of the 93rd formation, Addison Baker followed the lead of the 376th bombers and turned to the right rather than forge on alone.

A sinking feeling swept the 93rd men. Instead of Ploiesti, they were now closing on the Romanian capital of Bucharest.

As ADDISON BAKER PONDERED HIS unpalatable choices, the 93rd Liberators fanned out into their two attack forces, wingtip-to-wingtip: four waves in Baker's group, and two waves in the smaller group led by Ramsay Potts. *Tupelo Lass* occupied the lead position in the fourth wave, with Ben's old friend Dick Wilkinson and his copilot Edwin Baker off their left wing and Hap Kendall off their right. Edwin Baker peered out of his right window at Dessert to see if the 409th Squadron command could signal some explanation for the change of plans. Dessert looked back at Edwin Baker, shrugged, and threw up his hands.

Six minutes into the wrong turn, some of the 93rd men spotted smokestacks and a large town visible through the summer haze off to their left. It was Ploiesti, fifteen miles distant. As if on cue, Addison Baker smoothly executed a ninety-degree turn to the north. The other 93rd pilots had been waiting for just such a move, and they pivoted as if they had rehearsed it. The 376th was nearing the outskirts of Bucharest, a target with little military significance, but at least Addison Baker had the 93rd headed in the right direction.

In reality, all the hours spent studying maps and scale models had been for nothing. The 93rd crews would be attacking Ploiesti from the opposite direction to the one they'd practiced, flying headlong into some of the most diabolical air defenses ever devised. Earlier that morning, Addison Baker had promised his men that he would get them to the target, whatever it took. Now the target that had been the subject of so much speculation and secrecy lay four minutes ahead.

Those who survived would forever remember these as the most terrifying minutes of their lives. For many, the terror would culminate in a horrific death.

Chapter 27

A HELLHOLE OF FIRE, FLAME, AND SMOKE

Peering ahead through the Plexiglas top turret of *Tupelo Lass*, Ben clutched the hand controller of his twin .50-caliber machine guns as Ploiesti's smokestacks took shape through the summer haze. More than a minute had passed since K. O. Dessert had followed the three waves of 93rd bombers ahead of him into the corrective left turn executed by Addison Baker, and yet there was still no sign of the formidable enemy defenses that supposedly awaited them.

Ben had sensed that the raid was going to be one of the biggest moments of his life, but his eagerness to make history had been tempered by his doubts about the low-level plan. In the forty-eight hours before takeoff, a couple of his buddies had asked British antiaircraft gunners protecting their desert airfield what they thought about the American strategy. The Tommies thought it was daft. "They said it would be just suicide to go in that [low]," Ben said. "That the smaller guns would really get you."[1] Now, as the American bombers closed within five minutes of Hitler's prized oil refineries without encountering a single enemy gun or fighter plane, some of the 93rd men wondered whether the low-level plan had been a masterstroke after all.

And then, "all hell was breaking loose everywhere," Ben recalled.

In an instant, the 93rd bombers found themselves trapped in a gauntlet of guns—an array of conventional ground emplacements, rooftop positions, and towers. Harmless-looking haystacks and railroad boxcars collapsed to reveal more guns. Now everything in the Ploiesti air defense arsenal—from machine guns and nimble 37-millimeter antiaircraft weapons to hulking 88-millimeter aircraft-killers that fired fifteen or more twenty-pound shells a minute—blasted away at the four-engine American bombers streaking past. Ben watched in fascination and horror as the landscape was suddenly transformed into a sea of pulsating lights.

In the cockpit, K. O. Dessert struggled to keep *Tupelo Lass* steady as prop wash from other B-24s and shell bursts made it feel like he was at the tiller of a small boat in a raging sea. Beside him, Jake Epting made himself useful by shouting out the location of enemy guns: "Eight o'clock! Twelve o'clock! Three o'clock!" And then: "Shoot all over!"[2] As Dessert tried to keep *Tupelo Lass* low to the ground without clipping a smokestack or refinery building, a new threat emerged: bus-size balloons bobbing from steel cables strung with contact explosives.

Inside the bombers, the noise was deafening: the clatter of machine guns, roaring engines, exploding shells, and the sound of shrapnel and enemy bullets spattering and piercing the thin aluminum skin of the B-24s. Clouds of shell fragments and shards of metal sheared from bombers by enemy fire fluttered in the prop-churned air. Sensory overload and fear overwhelmed some of the Americans. In a scene repeated in several bombers, a sobbing 328th Squadron gunner sank to the floor beneath his waist gun.[3]

As terrifying as it was being shot at from point-blank range, some of the 93rd men found they liked being able to see the faces of the gunners who were trying to kill them. For Ben, blasting away from the top turret, the free-for-all bore a vague resemblance to a Nebraska pheasant hunt: Spot a target, fire, spot a target, fire, spot, fire. The frenzied speed of the action gave the battle a surreal air. Jake Epting saw two enemy gunners fall at their weapons, only to be instantly shoved aside by two comrades who took their place and resumed firing.[4]

By now, Dessert had dropped *Tupelo Lass* below fifty feet to avoid the murderous enemy fire; Epting would later say they were even lower, crossing the target at twenty feet. All around them shells and bullets ripped into B-24s and flames streamed from crippled aircraft.

Ben's vantage point in the final wave of the 93rd's main force afforded him a commanding view of the horrific tableau. Dead ahead an 88-millimeter round exploded in the nose of Addison Baker's *Hell's Wench*, followed by other rounds that smashed into the wing and cockpit. Within seconds, the 93rd commander's ship looked like a flying torch. Rather than attempt an emergency landing to save himself and his crew, Baker made good on his promise to lead his men to the target—even if it was an improvised target he had picked out of the haze.

To keep airborne as long as possible, the group commander dumped his bombs and flew on, a stream of flaming gasoline spanning the length of his ship. The flames became too much for one of Addison Baker's men, and he leapt from the nose wheel hatch and tumbled through the air, "so close we could see his burned legs," one pilot recalled.[5] Another shell slammed into *Hell's Wench* and Baker's right wing sagged.

The cockpit of *Hell's Wench* was now consumed by flames, yet Addison Baker and John Jerstad somehow remained in control of their aircraft. In one final act of extraordinary heroism, Baker and Jerstad willed *Hell's Wench* to three hundred feet in a desperate attempt to allow their men to attempt a crazy-low parachute escape. Three or four men jumped from the waist windows only seconds before *Hell's Wench* crashed into a field just beyond the refineries. None of the *Hell's Wench* crew survived; Baker and Jerstad were posthumously awarded the Medal of Honor.

With *Hell's Wench* gone and several sister ships in flames, *Tupelo Lass* roared up a Ploiesti boulevard at treetop level. Ben watched as the wing of a nearby 93rd aircraft struck a smokestack and the aircraft "plummeted to the ground [and] absolutely disintegrated in a terrible explosion." As other Liberators burst into flames or crashed, one of Ben's crewmates broke down and had to be restrained. Ben watched another burning B-24 to his right sink to the ground and explode "into a million pieces."[6]

Ben thought *Tupelo Lass* was doomed when a gasoline storage tank exploded in their path and the tank's metal shell shot skyward like a tin can. But at the last second Dessert deftly turned *Tupelo Lass* nearly upright on one wing and somehow avoided the inferno. As they roared past the pillar of fire, Ben felt the intense heat as if a giant oven door had been opened.

Amid the carnage and chaos, K. O. Dessert kept his cool. Shells that seemed headed for his cockpit somehow kept missing on either side. Al Naum released his bombs on a refinery, and Dessert poured on the power to escape the enemy fire.

All around *Tupelo Lass*, other crews fought for their lives. To the left, Dick Wilkinson and Edwin Baker were flying low and fast in *Little Lady*, their gunners firing nearly nonstop at the enemy gunners trying to bring them down. Over the town, a church steeple suddenly loomed as the bombardier was about to release his bombs. Wilkie coolly raised his left wing and cleared the steeple. The time on the clock tower showed five minutes before three o'clock local time (1155 GMT). Without warning, a flurry of antiaircraft shells whooshed past them, unleashed by guns concealed in a row of eucalyptus trees ahead. Another shell hit the number three engine and still another slammed into their belly. *Little Lady* shuddered and momentarily felt like it "stopped cold in midair," Edwin Baker said. Their number three engine was on fire and gasoline gushed from holes in an auxiliary tank. Baker and the crew's spare pilot pulled the fire extinguisher on the flaming engine and feathered the prop, averting one crisis.

Little Lady's navigator yelled "bombs away" and three thousand pounds of ordnance tumbled from the ravaged aircraft. A few seconds later, when K. O. Dessert turned *Tupelo Lass* on one wing to avoid the ruptured storage tank, Dick Wilkinson followed close behind, praying that the raw gas and fumes that now filled his bomb bay wouldn't explode. They didn't. "As we passed the heart of the explosions, it felt like passing a hot iron close to your face," Edwin Baker recalled. "Suddenly we popped out of the hellhole of fire, flame, and smoke into the clear sky and green fields beyond. Wilkie and I looked at each other and smiled."[7]

Off the right wing of *Tupelo Lass*, Hap Kendall had his own troubles in a B-24 named *Lucky*. He dodged the storage tank explosion and barely cleared a smokestack with his right wing, but the abrupt maneuvers forced the bombardier to hold their bombs. Kendall streaked across the city in search of another target, found another refinery, and the bombardier unleashed their ordnance. As Kendall steered his crew out of the fire, *Lucky* was barely airworthy: control wires severed, hydraulic lines ruptured, and at least one fuel tank riddled with shell holes, leaking gasoline. Kendall alerted his men to prepare to abandon ship.

One of the last B-24s to cross Ploiesti in Dessert's fourth wave was *Honky Tonk Gal*, piloted by a lanky Texan, twenty-two-year-old Second Lieutenant Hubert Womble. By the time Womble emerged from Ploiesti's deadly ring of fire, he had lost three engines to enemy fire and had been wounded when a shell exploded in the control pedestal beside him. His copilot had taken the controls and was struggling to remain airborne. Spotting a lush cornfield, Second Lieutenant Lawrence Lancashire executed an emergency landing that would have been perfect if not for a ditch on the far side. When *Honky Tonk Gal* hit the ditch, the landing gear collapsed and the B-24 came to a lurching halt. Womble tried to rise from his seat, only to discover that his left foot had been severed. "It was still in my boot near the rudder pedals," he later recalled.[8] Womble's men helped him exit *Honky Tonk Gal* through the top hatch and tended to his wounds as they awaited the Romanian troops who would take them into custody.

Emerging from the enemy kill zone around Ploiesti, K. O. Dessert and Jake Epting proceeded to the prearranged rendezvous point to search for comrades with whom they could share the long journey back to Benghazi. Finding no other friendly aircraft, navigator Edward Weir set a course for the Greek coast, and *Tupelo Lass* set off alone. "It was the strangest feeling because we couldn't see any of the planes we were supposed to be flying with," Ben said. "We were all alone."[9]

OF THE THIRTY-THREE 93RD BOMBERS that had reached the target area, six had been shot down and several others were in bad shape. As the four groups of B-24s that now trailed the 93rd approached Ploiesti, enemy fighters scoured the skies around the city to pick off crippled planes that had managed to survive the gauntlet of antiaircraft fire. Those that eluded the guns and the fighters headed south in search of refuge.

It was clear to Dick Wilkinson and Hap Kendall that their battered aircraft would never make it back to Benghazi. Turkey was the closest place of refuge—a neutral country where American airmen would hold the preferred legal status of internees rather than prisoners of war. In *Tupelo Lass*, K. O. Dessert and Jake Epting were amazed by their good fortune—their aircraft didn't appear to have been hit, and so they were flying under full power and control. But navigator Edward Weir had prepared for all contingencies, and he had marked on his maps the location of airfields in Turkey, Crete, and Sicily that could be used in an emergency. For now, the goal was to get as far away from Ploiesti as possible and to get back over the mountains of Yugoslavia and Albania to more familiar territory.

The return trip was proceeding smoothly when *Tupelo Lass* encountered clouds over Yugoslavia. Dessert and Epting were skilled in the art of flying by instrument, and so the transition presented nothing they couldn't handle. A few minutes ahead of *Tupelo Lass*, a cluster of 93rd aircraft from the first waves of Addison Baker's force had encountered the same clouds, with tragic results.

Three B-24s had formed up in a protective *V* for the return journey: *Exterminator*, piloted by Hugh Roper; *Let 'Er Rip*, piloted by Victor Olliffe; and *Thundermug*, piloted by Russel Longnecker. Roper and Olliffe were best friends since the early days of the 93rd, and they were at the end of their combat tours. Roper had six men aboard *Exterminator* who were flying their final mission, as well as another veteran 93rd officer, Captain Jack Jones, who had flown the mission as a spare pilot and observer. Longnecker had been among a group of Americans who had joined the Royal Canadian Air Force before America entered the war and had transferred into the Eighth Air Force in England only in April.

As they flew south from Ploiesti, the lead 93rd aircraft encountered clouds along the mountainous border between Bulgaria and Yugoslavia. Within each three-plane element, the pilots executed a standard maneuver to provide some distance from one another whenever flying into clouds. They would tighten up their formation when they emerged and found each other.

Entering a cloud, Longnecker executed the maneuver and distanced himself from Roper and Olliffe. When he emerged, Olliffe and Roper were gone. Their remains were recovered in Yugoslavia after the war, and the two friends were buried with their crewmates in group graves only a few feet from each other at Jefferson Barracks National Cemetery in St. Louis. Olliffe and Roper prided themselves on the tight formations they flew, and they had collided in a cloud and fallen to their deaths. Nineteen souls aboard the two aircraft were killed: all eleven men aboard Roper's *Exterminator*, and Olliffe and seven others aboard *Let 'Er Rip*. Three gunners toward the rear of Olliffe's B-24 managed to unfurl their parachutes and landed in Bulgaria, where they were captured by Axis forces.

Flying alone through the mountains, *Tupelo Lass* avoided such perils. Reaching the Ionian coast near the Greek island of Corfu, Dessert and Epting made their final decision of the day: Their fuel situation seemed to be good and their aircraft was flying well; they would push on to their home field outside Benghazi, some 525 miles due south.

After the day's trials, the flight across the Mediterranean was uneventful. The men were left alone with their thoughts and visions of the terrible things they had witnessed. Dusk was falling when they lined up the runway at Site 7 and landed. The time was 1740 GMT or 8:40 p.m. local time. They had been in the air thirteen hours and five minutes. It was Ben's twenty-fourth mission, and the longest and bloodiest he would ever fly.

As Dessert taxied to the designated parking stand for *Tupelo Lass*, the men inside were struck by what they saw. The 409th Squadron parking spots that had been filled that morning when they taxied away for takeoff were now empty. The implication hit Ben: *My God, they must not have made it.*[10] Only one more 409th Squadron aircraft would land that evening.

Climbing stiffly from *Tupelo Lass*, Ben and the others gave their aircraft a careful inspection. They were amazed: *Tupelo Lass* didn't have a single bullet hole or shrapnel mark.

Among the men who turned out to welcome the first 409th Squadron crew home from Ploiesti was Colonel Jacob Smart, the Hap Arnold aide who had intended to sit in the copilot's seat alongside K. O. Dessert before his last-minute grounding. Tears streamed down Smart's face as he greeted Dessert. Smart knew a lot of men wouldn't make it back, and, as architect of the low-level plan, he had wanted to put himself in harm's way as an act of solidarity with those who were destined to die. It was already clear to Smart that his fears of heavy losses had been realized. Good men had been lost trying to execute his plan, and the least he could have done was share that danger with them. He would have to live with that haunting knowledge for the rest of his life. "He wanted so badly to go on that raid," Dessert later said.[11]

Dessert walked away from *Tupelo Lass* alongside Ben and Sergeant Raymond Wierciszowski, the courageous mechanic who had risked his life to document many of the raid's heartbreaking moments with his Kodak camera. Sergeant Wier summoned the nerve to ask a question that had nagged him during the flight back.

"Major Dessert, was that a rough raid?" Wier asked uncertainly.

"Sergeant Wier," Dessert solemnly replied, "that's the toughest raid you'll ever be on in your life."[12]

Chapter 28

THE LONGEST NIGHT

Numbed by the day's horrors, Ben and his crewmates made their way to their tent in the gathering darkness. Behind them, smudge pots flickered along the 93rd's desert airstrip to light the way for late arrivals. Few words were exchanged—the men struggled to process all they had seen and heard. Navigator Edward Weir had suffered stress headaches throughout the Epting crew's months of combat, but nothing as severe as those of the past hours.[1]

The men who hadn't flown the mission pressed the survivors with unwelcome questions. "Are you sure you went over the target?" a few curious onlookers asked after seeing the condition of *Tupelo Lass*. The men on the ground were oblivious to the anguish felt by the survivors. Ben and his crewmates weren't in the mood for conversation. They were struck by how quiet and empty the camp felt. As they passed the tents of comrades who hadn't made it back, some quietly called out their names—the first roll call of the dead or missing.

A shocking number still hadn't made it back at that hour. By late evening at least seventeen 93rd bombers remained missing. That meant that nearly two hundred men from the 93rd alone were unaccounted for, including several of Ben's best friends and longest acquaintances in the 409th Squadron. As midnight approached, hopes for a miracle faded. On some level Ben and the others fantasized that "somebody might stagger back." But, in reality, "you knew they weren't going to make it back at that late an hour because they didn't have that much fuel," Ben said.[2]

In the officers' bivouac, Brutus Hamilton captured the sorrowful mood in a long diary entry. "This is written late at night and with a heavy heart and a bewildered, laggard pen," he began. "It's been the saddest day in the history of the 93rd Bomb Gp."[3] Hamilton listed the crews still missing at that hour and briefly noted what little he had learned about their disappearance.

The early pronouncements from headquarters had declared the raid a crippling blow to Hitler and the Axis war effort, but that was wishful thinking. Still, in this moment of shock and anguish, it helped men to imagine that the mission had been worth the terrible cost.

For survivors of the day's ordeal, nothing could ease their pain. Too upset to sleep, Ben tossed and turned on his cot all night. A few times he heard the sound of airplane engines in the distance and his heart leapt with hope. *Oh God, they're coming back to base,* he imagined, if only briefly. "But they never did," Ben said. As the sound of some lone aircraft faded in the distance, a haunting silence again settled over the camp.

Many of the men lay awake reliving the day's terrors, their mind's eye a horror film running in an endless loop. "I don't think anybody slept," K. O. Dessert later recalled. "Everybody's tent had somebody missing in it, or right next to your tent a guy was gone or something." Those sleepless hours of August 1–2, 1943, would be forever remembered by Dessert and other Ploiesti survivors as "probably the longest night of our lives."[4]

DAWN OF MONDAY MORNING, AUGUST 2, brought no relief. Ben was still in his tent when a familiar voice shattered the stillness. "Junior!" the voice plaintively wailed. "Junior! Junior!"

It was Ben's copilot, Charles Young, searching for his friend Junior Canfield. From his turret, Ben had witnessed Junior's final moments as copilot of *Jose Carioca*. Five-by-Five Young had a similar vantage point from the right waist window, where he had taken over gunnery duties for the day's mission. There was no doubting Junior was gone—no one could have survived the fiery crash that consumed *Jose Carioca* and the Stampolis crew. But the twenty-three-year-old Young couldn't accept the fact that his best friend was gone forever at the age of nineteen, and so he continued to search the desert camp and the nearby flight line.

The log of missing crews had grown overnight. In addition to the spectacular end of the Stampolis crew, nearly everyone had watched the final seconds of Addison Baker and his crew in *Hell's Wench*. But the fate of other comrades remained murky. Several aircraft had taken hits and fallen behind the rest of the group, and so hopes of their eventual return lingered.

Such was the case with the pair of 409th Squadron Liberators flying off either wing of *Tupelo Lass* as they approached Ploiesti. One was piloted by Dick Wilkinson, the other by Hap Kendall. Now both were missing.

Also missing was the 409th Squadron pilot Lew Brown, the courageous Arkansan who had nearly been shot down twice during the previous months and had lost six men along the way. Through all that, Lew Brown had somehow held it together and finished his twenty-five missions on July 19. Now he, too, was missing.

As the day wore on, the men couldn't escape reminders of their missing comrades—the empty tents, short mess lines, and absence of familiar faces and voices. Some of the 93rd men sorted and boxed the personal effects of lost comrades. Among those assigned that grim duty was twenty-two-year-old Donald Hudspeth, a 328th Squadron gunner from Yadkinville, North Carolina. He was a member of the crew that had flown *Hell's Wench* down from England only a few days earlier. Addison Baker had pulled rank and appropriated the aircraft for the Ploiesti raid, handpicking a crew of 93rd veterans to accompany him. Baker's action had allowed Hudspeth to live at least one more day, although it also put him in the painful position of boxing up the personal effects of the enlisted men who had died in his place.[5]

The day's only bright spot came in the afternoon with the arrival of two crews that had made emergency landings on Sicily. One of them was a 328th Squadron crew; the other was a 409th Squadron aircraft, *Queenie*, piloted by Lew Brown and South Dakotan Homer Moran, who had shared the Spain adventure with Ben's crew.[6]

Brown and his men had sweated out a harrowing return flight from Ploiesti after being shot up over the target. Struggling to gain altitude as they approached the mountains south of the Danube, Brown ordered his men to throw out everything they didn't need, to lighten their load. Disappearing into a wall of clouds, they flew blindly for about an hour before reaching clear skies along the Ionian coast of Albania and Greece. Quick calculations convinced Brown and his navigator and flight engineer that their best bet was to find a landing spot on Sicily rather than risk running out of fuel over the Mediterranean. They made it to Sicily, and after patching up their battered bomber as best they could, they set off for their desert base with nine five-gallon gasoline cans filled with Sicilian wine. They shared forty gallons with their comrades and kept five gallons for themselves, but no one was in the mood to celebrate.[7]

Brutus Hamilton had spent a good part of the day piecing together what the men had experienced at Ploiesti, and a dark portrait had emerged. He captured the bleak mood among the officers and men at the conclusion of his lengthy diary entry, in a coda that recounted fragments of what he had learned during his conversations of August 2. "All men are agreed that [the raid] was the worst experience they had ever undergone," Hamilton concluded.

Ben moved through the day as if he were in a fog. He had no energy and no appetite. His body ached, as if he had been punched in a boxing match.[8] His wretched mental and physical state mirrored that of most of the men who had flown the Ploiesti raid.

Ninth Air Force headquarters in Cairo was in contact with 93rd officers on the ground and knew well the dark mood that had settled over the camp. The men had lost their beloved group leader, Addison Baker, and one of the group's most popular original members, John Jerstad. They all had lost friends and brothers-in-arms, and there was no place to turn in the camp without being reminded of those who were no longer with them. It was clear to the ranking 93rd officers and Ninth Air Force brass that they needed to get the Ploiesti survivors away from the camp as soon as possible.

ON TUESDAY, AUGUST 3, SEVERAL PLANE loads of Ploiesti survivors boarded flights to Cairo for three days of rest and relaxation. In the 93rd camp that evening, a new replacement crew arrived with four bags of mail addressed to men in the 93rd. On most occasions, mail call was a joyous occasion, especially given the infrequency of deliveries during their temporary deployment to North Africa. But on this occasion, the joy was tinged with sadness as names were called and officers set aside the mail of the missing.[9] The letters would be returned after being stamped with the heartbreaking words: "RETURN TO SENDER. MISSING IN ACTION."

Later that evening, Ben and other men in the 93rd camp once again heard the drone of an approaching aircraft. This time, a B-24 landed in the darkness and out climbed Hap Kendall and his crew. Their escape from Ploiesti had been a stroke of serendipity.

Having been interned in Spain with the Epting crew, Kendall had ruled out landing in neutral Turkey and reliving the same experience. He asked his navigator to plot a course for Sicily. About two hours later they spotted Sicily's Pachino Peninsula, recently liberated by British forces, and picked out a fighter airstrip as their salvation. With engines backfiring, control wires and hydraulic lines severed, and wing flaps shredded, Kendall and his copilot executed a white-knuckle landing. Without flaps, they ran off the end of the short runway and plowed into a pup-tent bivouac, barely missing British airmen who scrambled for their lives. Kendall hit a P-40 fighter before lurching to a stop in a vineyard. Emerging from their battered bomber to howls of protest from their ersatz British hosts, Kendall and his men, including his devout Mormon navigator, spent the rest of the night getting drunk on homemade Sicilian wine. When they finally got *Lucky* patched up enough to continue on their way, they made sure their cargo included a vat of the local vintage.[10]

Ben escaped the camp on an August 4 flight that transported several dozen Ploiesti survivors to Alexandria for three days of rest. For Ben and the others, the respite was a godsend. They lounged in big hotel rooms with servants at their summons, guzzled beer and whiskey, gorged themselves on gourmet cuisine, and danced with vivacious French and Greek girls.[11]

But no amount of creature comforts could heal the psychological wounds suffered by the men who had flown the Ploiesti raid, and their return instantly rekindled memories of lost comrades. In addition to the emotional toll, Ben and others still felt the physical effects—general soreness, insomnia, and nightmares being the most common manifestations.

If rumors swirling through the desert camp on their return from Egypt could be believed, Ben and others struggling with the physical and psychological shocks of the Ploiesti raid wouldn't have long to recover. According to camp scuttlebutt, the 93rd was poised to undertake another momentous raid. Those who survived this next mission could expect a coveted reward: release from their desert purgatory and a return to England.

Chapter 29

LIMBO

Completing twenty-five combat missions had become an increasingly perilous quest for Eighth Air Force bomber crews by August 1943. As the summer weeks wore on and the bombers attempted bigger and bolder raids into Germany, or attacked high-value targets like Ploiesti, the twenty-five-mission requirement became ever more elusive.

As terrible as Ploiesti had been, the raid had brought Ben to the brink of number twenty-five. But now, on the verge of his ticket home, he found himself in a strange limbo. Ben returned from Egypt not knowing when he would fly his next mission, or with whom he would fly it. The only thing he knew with certainty was that he wouldn't be flying with Jake Epting and the men who had become his brothers over the past eight months.

Epting and bombardier Al Naum had completed twenty-five missions before Ploiesti, and so they would be moving on as soon as orders were cut. That was also the case with Ben's closest friends on the crew, radio operator Red Kettering and navigator Edward Weir. They had reached the coveted milestone the moment that *Tupelo Lass* rolled to a stop at the 93rd's Site 7 airfield on their return from the low-level raid. Now, with his friends leaving and the 93rd camp awash in new faces, Ben searched for a worthy pilot whose crew he could join for one more mission.

The new crews had moved into the tents previously occupied by men who hadn't returned from Ploiesti. Red Kettering was awaiting orders for his next move, so he still shared a tent with Ben and the four gunners that Epting had added after their return from Spain. There were a few other familiar faces among the enlisted men wandering around the camp: Bill Dawley, who had recovered from his head injury and was now Hap Kendall's tail gunner; Ples Norwood, the young *Red Ass* mechanic who followed Ben's path to a combat assignment and flew several missions with the Epting crew; and Dick Ryan, the married father from Massachusetts who had been an original member of the Epting crew and whose quest to complete twenty-five missions had been waylaid by his extended stay in Spain. Ryan had finally been released in June but hadn't made it back to the 93rd before the group headed to North Africa. He had recently rejoined the 93rd in Libya as a replacement gunner.

Only hours after Ben and other Ploiesti survivors returned from Alexandria, another rumor swept the camp: Dick Wilkinson and his missing crew were alive and well. The news was confirmed: Wilkie and his men had made it to neutral Turkey, where they were now interned.

The good news about Wilkie had lifted Ben's spirits, but that evening came the ominous news alerting combat crews to expect a mission on Sunday, August 8. There was no word about what the target would be, or who would fly the raid, but speculation swirled. Some of the men noted that the auxiliary fuel tanks installed in their bomb bay for the long flight to Ploiesti hadn't been removed. At the very least that suggested a long mission. The men tried to steel themselves for whatever awaited them.

IN FACT, THE MISSION THAT AWAITED THE 93rd would be the longest bombing raid of the war to date—even longer than Ploiesti.

The target had been in the crosshairs of American and British strategic planners for years: an industrial complex, twenty miles south of Vienna, Austria, that produced one-third of the Luftwaffe's current monthly output of Messerschmitt Me-109 fighters. The Wiener Neustädter Flugzeugwerke had been organized by Herman Göring's Air Ministry in 1938, following Hitler's annexation of Austria, and the factory's first Me-109 was delivered in March 1939.

After the installation of conveyor belts in early 1942, Wiener Neustadt production soared to 130 planes a month. By year's end, plant workers had turned out 1,303 fighters—49 percent of total Me-109 deliveries in 1942. By the following summer, Wiener Neustadt workers had nearly doubled their monthly output from the previous year, yet Göring's Air Ministry pushed for even more. The plant had been assigned a new monthly target of 330 fighters.[1]

For Hap Arnold, the soaring German fighter production posed a threat to his January promises at the Casablanca war conference. Patience had never been one of Arnold's virtues, and he had recently sharpened his criticism of his Eighth Air Force commander, General Ira Eaker.

The pressure on Arnold and Eaker only intensified in May following the TRIDENT war conference in Washington, DC. The most significant decision reached at the conference was an Anglo-American agreement on a date for Operation OVERLORD, the cross-channel invasion of northwest France. The invasion was set for May 1, 1944, but the timetable hinged on the ability of the American and British air forces to achieve air superiority over Western Europe.

Shosuke and Naka Kuroki pose with eight of their ten children circa 1931.
Ben, standing second from left, was fourteen or fifteen when this photo was taken.
Military Division, National Museum of American History, Smithsonian Institution.

Ben was a shy child who gradually
found self-confidence as a teenager
at tiny Hershey High School.
He played baseball and basketball
and was elected vice president of his
graduating class of twelve students.
*Military Division, National Museum
of American History,
Smithsonian Institution.*

In the years before Pearl Harb
Ben played baseball for an a
Japanese American team in
summer when he wasn't driv
a long-haul produce tr
or working on the fa
Ben is seated second from rig
*Military Division, Natio
Museum of American Histc
Smithsonian Instituti*

the weeks following the Pearl Harbor attack, Ben completed his hellish Army Air Forces basic training in Texas in early 1942 and was assigned to clerical school in Fort Logan, Colorado. *Military Division, National Museum of American History, Smithsonian Institution.*

In April 1942, Ben completed clerical training and was ordered to Barksdale Field, Louisiana. hoped for a combat assignment but was a lowly clerk when he was attached to the 93rd Bomb Group, a B-24 outfit. *Military Division, National Museum of American History, Smithsonian Institution.*

Two bigoted sergeants schemed to transfer Ben from the 93rd when the group was ordered to Fort Myers, Florida, to complete training. Ben tearfully pleaded his case and was allowed to remain with the 93rd. In Florida, he slowly earned the trust of his comrades.
Military Division, National Museum of American History, Smithsonian Institution.

Ben was assigned to the 93rd's pool of teletype operators, even while he continued to dream of proving his [lo]yalty to America as an aerial gunner. [H]e proudly posed in his flight gear in Florida heat in the summer of 1942. *Military Division, National Museum of American History, Smithsonian Institution.*

[Afte]r arriving in England in [Dec]ember 1942, Ben begged [a] combat assignment. [Afte]r a trial flight on a crew [with] a temporary need for a gunner, [Ben] insisted on a photograph to [com]memorate the occasion. *[Mili]tary Division, National Museum [of A]merican History, [Smit]hsonian Institution.*

Ben joined a combat crew on the eve of the 93rd's December 1942 departure for North Africa. The 93rd men were ordered to fly missions in support of the Operation TORCH landings out of a base outside Oran, Algeria, but foul weather forced their relocation to a desolate Sahara Desert base in eastern Libya known as Gambut Main.
Military Division, National Museum of American History, Smithsonian Institution.

Ben and his 93rd comrades flew raids on Axis shipping targets in North Africa and Italy for two mon─ In this photo, a crew is being briefed for Ben's sixth mission, a raid on Palermo, Italy, on January 7, 1
Military Division, National Museum of American History, Smithsonian Institution.

Living conditions in the Libyan desert camp were primitive. The 93rd men lived in tents, ate outdoors, and survived on a few cups of water a day. Sandstorms, rain, and cold made conditions even worse.
Military Division, National Museum of American History, Smithsonian Institution.

During the 93rd's return trip to Eng[...]
in late February 1943, Ben and his [...]
were forced to make an emerg[...]
landing in Spanish Moro[...]
Ben, kneeling second from left, s[...]
about two months in Spanish capti[...]
with a colorful international [...]
of interned Allied air[...]
Military Division, National Mus[...]
of American His[...]
Smithsonian Institu[...]

After his release by Spanish authoritie[...]
Ben was debriefed in London. Before [...]
rejoined the 93rd, former Hollywood f[...]
star Ben Lyon interviewed Ben for the
popular *Stars and Stripes in Britain* ra[...]
show. Ben's stirring story of patriotism
and courage was beamed across Ameri[...]
Military Division, National Museum o[...]
American History, Smithsonian Institu[...]

Ben rejoined the 93rd at a pivotal moment in the Eighth Air Force campaign against Nazi Germany. Casualties and combat stress had depleted the ranks of units, and German air defenses were exacting a rising toll on the American raiders. This photo shows the crew of the 93rd B-24 known as *The Exterminator* donning flight gear for an April 1943 mission, just days before Ben rejoined the group. *US Army Air Forces (USAAF)/National Archives and Records Administration (NARA).*

In mid-May 1943, the men of the 93rd welcomed a new group commander: Lieutenant Colonel Addison Baker, right, a renowned stunt pilot in Ohio before the war. Baker was a beloved squadron commander in the 93rd prior to his promotion. A little more than two months later, Ben witnessed Baker's horrifying death during the low-level Ploiesti raid. *US Army Air Forces (USAAF)/National Archives and Records Administration (NARA).*

Ben's first month back with the 93rd was marked by a near-death experience over the Bay of Biscay and mystifying low-level practice flights over the English countryside. On June 25, Ben and his comrades once again set off for North Africa. Their new home was a desert camp outside Benghazi, Libya. The harsh living conditions were a shock to the newcomers, but not for Ben and other veterans of the previous North Africa deployment. *Military Division, National Museum of American History, Smithsonian Institution.*

After three weeks of missions against Italian targets in support of the Sicily invasion,
Ben and his comrades resumed low-level practice flights in the Libyan desert. On August 1, 1943,
Ben and his crewmates were among the first Americans to bomb the Axis oil refineries at Ploiesti,
Romania—a day that would be remembered as Black Sunday because of the devastating American losses.
US Army Air Forces (USAAF)/National Archives and Records Administration (NARA).

In the aftermath of the Ploiesti raid, American air commanders arranged for the survivors
to escape their depressing desert camps for a few days of rest and relaxation in Egypt.
Ben and several 93rd comrades spent their furloughs in Alexandria, Egypt, trying to forget
the horrors they had witnessed. The men savored clean sheets and fine cuisine, drank heavily,
flirted with lovely foreign women, shopped for souvenirs, and posed for photographs.
Ben borrowed a local policeman's fez for one snapshot. But their escape from the pain of Ploiesti
proved fleeting, and the 93rd resumed combat operations in the second week of August 1943.
Military Division, National Museum of American History, Smithsonian Institution.

The Ploiesti mission marked the dissolution of the Epting crew when Ben's pilot and other crewmates completed their twenty-five-mission tours and drew new assignments. Ben finished twenty-five missions later in August and volunteered to fly another five. During the darkest days of the Eighth Air Force campaign, Ben flew sporadic missions for two months before finally taking off from this base at Hardwick, England, for his thirtieth mission, on November 5, 1943. *US Army Air Forces (USAAF)/National Archives and Records Administration (NARA).*

Ben's thirtieth mission—a raid on Münster, Germany—was nearly his last when an enemy shell shattered his top turret. The shrapnel barely missed Ben's head and his oxygen mask was torn from his face. He was turning blue from hypoxia when a crewmate found him on the floor of the B-24 and revived him. Later, Ben posed nonchalantly for a photograph with his shattered turret. He no longer had to be persuaded that it was time to head home for some rest and relaxation. *US Army Air Forces (USAAF)/National Archives and Records Administration (NARA).*

After spending the December holidays with his family in Nebraska, Ben reported to
Army Air Forces Redistribution Center Number Three in Santa Monica, California, in early 1944
await his next assignment. He passed the time playing pinball and Ping-Pong, strolled along the beach,
and gave interviews to reporters interested in documenting the presence of one of the few people
of Japanese descent free to move about California at the time.
Military Division, National Museum of American History, Smithsonian Institution.

In late January 1944, Ben's scheduled interview on a national radio show hosted by singer and movie s
Ginny Simms was canceled at the last minute by NBC Radio executives and the War Department for fe
that Californians might object to such a prominent platform being offered to a person of Japanese
ancestry. After Ben delivered a patriotic speech before San Francisco's Commonwealth Club in which
denounced the anti-Japanese backlash in America, the War Department hastily rescheduled Ben's
appearance on *The Ginny Simms Show*. Ben's celebrity soared following the broadcast. Secretly, the W
Department planned to use America's first Nisei combat hero to help counter a draft-resistance movem
among Japanese American men currently incarcerated in government "relocation" camps.
Military Division, National Museum of American History, Smithsonian Institution.

When Ben arrived in California in early 1944, he had only a vague notion of the terrible fate that had befallen the West Coast residents of Japanese descent. More than 110,000 people had been rounded up in 1942 and sent to interior camps in remote locations. One of the largest camps was at Heart Mountain, Wyoming, in the windswept Bighorn Basin. More than 10,000 people from California were confined behind barbed wire at Heart Mountain. The camp opened in August 1942, and household possessions arrived by train a month later. The crates were delivered to each family's "apartment" in one of scores of cramped and drafty barracks that dotted the camp. *War Relocation Authority/National Archives and Records Administration (NARA).*

Overnight, the Heart Mountain camp became Wyoming's third largest city.
This photo was taken on the evening of September 19, 1942, barely a month after the arrival
of the former California residents of Japanese descent.
War Relocation Authority/National Archives and Records Administration (NARA).

A high school was established for Heart Mountain teenagers uprooted from their lives in California
Thrust into a communal life, with meals taken in large mess halls,
family units began to fray and disintegrate.
War Relocation Authority/National Archives and Records Administration (NARA).

To create a semblance of normalcy
for children and adolescents,
the incarcerated adults established
Boy Scout troops and other
extracurricular activities.
*Military Division, National Museum
of American History,
Smithsonian Institution.*

With the arrival of bitter winter weather,
ponds were created in the camp's interior
so the former California residents could
learn to ice skate. War Relocation Authority
photographer Tom Parker depicted life
as carefree and idyllic for the incarcerees.
Parker was careful not to photograph
the armed guards, the watchtowers, or the
barbed-wire perimeter that ringed the camp.
*War Relocation Authority/National Archives
and Records Administration (NARA).*

By 1943, resistance to the incarceration regime had taken root at Heart Mountain and other camps. One pocket of resistance at Heart Mountain was the Poster Shop, where artists and art students created posters for safety campaigns and information purposes. One of the Poster Shop employees was a former Pasadena Community College art student named Yoshito Kuromiya. Yosh, as he was known to family and friends, developed his skills at Heart Mountain under the tutelage of Japanese American artist Benji Okubo. Yosh also underwent a gradual process of political radicalization that put him on a collision course with Nisei war hero Ben Kuroki.
War Relocation Authority/National Archives and Records Administration (NARA).

Yosh Kuromiya at work in Heart Mountain Poster Shop in 19⋅
War Relocation Authority/National Archi⋅ and Records Administration (NAR

The Roosevelt administration in Washington hailed World War II as a fight against global fascism while depriving Americans of Japanese descent of their rights and incarcerating them in camps like Heart Mountain. This image captured by War Relocation Authority photographer Tom Parker shows older Heart Mountain incarcerees studying English in a classroom decorated with a poster that proclaims "Democracy at Work."
War Relocation Authority/National Archives and Records Administration (NARA).

Ben arrived at the Heart Mountain camp in April 1944 with vague orders from the War Department. A Nisei draft-resistance movement centered in the Heart Mountain camp had prompted an FBI raid and dozens of arrests only days earlier. Among the young men from Heart Mountain being held in Wyoming jails on federal draft evasion charges was the young artist Yosh Kuromiya.
War Relocation Authority/National Archives and Records Administration (NARA).

Ben received a hero's welcome at Heart Mountain. At far left, a poster reads: "Welcome Sgt. Kuroki."
Ben's hosts quickly made it clear that the purpose of his trip was to encourage draft-age Japanese
American men in the camp to enlist in the army for combat with the all-Nisei
442nd Regimental Combat Team in Italy.
War Relocation Authority/National Archives and Records Administration (NARA).

In a series of speeches before groups small and large at Heart Mountain, Ben urged Nisei men
to enlist in the US Army and to prove their patriotism and trustworthiness in combat.
His message fell flat with the growing draft-resistance movement, whose supporters demanded a
restoration of constitutional and civil rights for all camp incarcerees before submitting to military servic
Military Division, National Museum of American History, Smithsonian Institution.

Ben visited three incarceration camps in the spring of 1944, delivering speeches in which
he urged young men to reclaim the honor of Japanese Americans by volunteering for combat duty.
Many camp residents viewed Ben as a model Nisei and sought his autograph.
Others greeted Ben with hostility and angry questions and accused him of collaborating
with a government that had unjustly stripped Japanese Americans of their constitutional rights.
Military Division, National Museum of American History, Smithsonian Institution.

As soon as he was released from recruiting duties, Ben sought a combat assignment in the Pacific.
Ben was jubilant when his quest finally received the personal blessing of Secretary of War
Henry Stimson. After a few days at home for a final furlough, Ben returned to his Nebraska base
for final preparations. When Ben posed for a crew portrait on November 30, 1944,
his long-sought Pacific deployment was only days away. Six days before this photograph
was taken, B-29 Superfortress crews based in the Northern Mariana Islands struck
the first blow against the Japanese home islands, bombing an aircraft engine plant
in the Tokyo suburb of Musashino, ten miles from the Emperor's Palace.
Military Division, National Museum of American History, Smithsonian Institution.

In the last week of December 1944, Ben and his B-29 crew landed at the massive B-29 complex at North Field on Tinian Island. Tinian was one of the Northern Mariana Islands from which the climactic air campaign against Japan would be waged. *US Army Air Forces (USAAF)/ National Archives and Records Administration (NARA).*

As US Army Air Forces B-29 bombers roared over Tini night and day, vestiges of Japanese colonialism a prewar occupation stood alongside vestiges of the islan indigenous civilization. The Japanese had transformed Tini into a center of sugarcane cultivation before the w By the time Ben arrived on the island, the cane fie provided cover for Japanese military holdou *US Army Air Forces (USAAF)/National Archi and Records Administration (NAR*

Pilot Jim Jenkins had embraced Ben as a member of his crew in the late summer of 1944, and they had forged a close relationship by the time they posed beneath the nose of the *Honorable Sad Saki* on Tinian in early 1945. After several weeks of training flights, Ben and his crewmates began to log missions against Japanese targets on outlying islands before flying long raids on Japan's home islands. *Smithsonian National Museum of American History (NMAH).*

he B-29 was a luxury aircraft mpared to the B-24, but Ben's cific missions had their own rticular stresses, including ng and perilous hours over e Pacific Ocean. Ben had nded with two previous crews, d he went through the same ocess again as the old man the *Honorable Sad Saki* crew. *ilitary Division, National Museum American History, nithsonian Institution.*

The firebombing raids on Tokyo and fears of being mistaken for an enemy soldier on Tinian pushed Ben to the brink of a mental breakdown in the spring of 1945. He was hospitalized in Hawaii for a few days, then returned to Tinian to continue flying missions against Japan in the closing months of the war. *Military Division, National Museum of American History, Smithsonian Institution.*

After completing mission number 27 in the Pacific in late July 1945, Ben was interviewed by Technical Sergeant Harold J. Brown for the *Fighting AAF* radio show. The interview aired on radio stations across America on Sunday evening, August 5—around the same time the B-29 Enola Gay dropped its atomic bomb on Hiroshima, Japan. *US Army Air Forces (USAAF)/ National Archives and Records Administration (NARA).*

Ben was in a military hospital on Tinian, recovering from a serious head injury, when the Enola Gay landed on Tinian on the morning of August 6, 1945, after dropping its atomic bomb on Hiroshima.
US Army Air Forces (USAAF)/National Archives and Records Administration (NARA).

Within hours of arriving in America in October 1945, Ben was flown to New York City to deliver a speech at the *New York Herald Tribune* Forum. Afterward, Ben received interview requests from major newspapers and radio stations. Among the prominent journalists who interviewed Ben was Ed Sullivan, an entertainment columnist for the *New York Daily News.* Sullivan later became the legendary host of America's longest-running television variety show.
Military Division, National Museum of American History, Smithsonian Institution.

During his visits to Washington, DC in 1945–1946, Ben sat for a portrait by the artist Joseph Cummings Chase. This portrait is among more than one hundred works by Chase that now hang in the National Portrait Gallery in Washington.
Military Division, National Museum of American History, Smithsonian Institution.

After his discharge from military service in February 1946, Ben launched what he called his 59th Mission Tour, delivering speeches on racial intolerance and prejudice and highlighting the issue in interviews.
Military Division, National Museum of American History, Smithsonian Institution.

's 59th Mission Tour coincided with the release of a biography
tten by war correspondent Ralph G. Martin. Shortly after the
ase of the book in October 1946, Ben stopped in a Brentano's
Wilkes-Barre, Pennsylvania, to sign copies and greet customers.
itary Division, National Museum of American History,
ithsonian Institution.

During his 59th Mission Tour,
Ben addressed scores of civic
and school groups. He enjoyed
posing for photographs and
signing autographs. One of the
Armonk, New York, students
in this photograph renewed
her correspondence with Ben in
2002 after he became the subject
of news stories recalling his
World War II service.
Military Division,
National Museum
of American History,
Smithsonian Institution.

Ben received a warm welcome from University of Nebraska chancellor Reuben G. Gustavson after beginning work on his journalism degree at Nebraska's flagship university in June 1947. Gustavson, who worked on the Manhattan Project at the University of Chicago during World War II, had racially integrated the university's dormitories the year before Ben's arrival.
Military Division, National Museum of American History, Smithsonian Institution.

By the late 1950s, Ben and Shige owned two weekly newspapers in Michigan and were the proud parents of three daughters. From left: Kristyn, Julie, Kerry.
Julie Kuroki.

In a 1995 visit to Heart Mountain, Yosh Kuromiya posed with his watercolor of the haunting peak that called to him from beyond the perimeter of barbed wire and armed guards. "I thought it was a thing of beauty and that maybe it was the only sanity that I was experiencing at the time," he said.
Irene Kuromiya.

006, Ben and Shige and their youngest daughter, Julie, far left, were guests of President George W. Bush First Lady Laura Bush at a White House state dinner for Japanese Prime Minister Junichiro Koizumi.

Military Division, National Museum of American History, Smithsonian Institution.

en and Shige returned to Lincoln, Nebraska, in 2007 to attend the premiere of a documentary film about his life. The documentary aired nationally on PBS later that fall.

Military Division, National Museum of American History, Smithsonian Institution.

President George W. Bush honored Ben at a 2008 White House ceremony attended by
Nisei war veterans as part of the annual celebration of Asian/Pacific Islander Heritage Month.
Ben acknowledged the President's personal tribute with a salute. Afterward,
President Bush warmly greeted the first Nisei war hero of World War II as Ben fought back tears.
Military Division, National Museum of American History, Smithsonian Institution.

The farm where Ben grew up outside Hershey, Nebraska, remained largely unchanged as of 2023. *Mike Theiler.*

The flow of the North Platte River near Ben's childhood home experiences dramatic fluctuations se days because of upstream dams and diversions for crop irrigation. On a hot summer's day in 2023, children splashed in the river where Ben had swum and fished and was saved by his best friend Gordy Jorgenson after falling through the ice during a winter duck hunt. *Mike Theiler.*

The former incarceration camp at Heart Mountain, Wyoming, is now a national historic landmark. Camp survivors, family members, and scholars converge on Heart Mountain each summer in an annual pilgrimage. Exhibits, lectures, and a documentary film recall President Franklin Roosevelt's unjust decision to incarcerate West Coast inhabitants of Japanese descent. *Mike Theiler.*

The plan to achieve that air superiority was officially known as the Eaker Plan, but it just as easily could have been called the Arnold Plan, for it originated with a target list drawn up by the air chief's advisers. In any event, the Combined Chiefs fine tuned the plan in their Washington discussions and set it in motion in June under the codename POINTBLANK. The initial directive set the first priority for American and British bomber forces as "the destruction of the German Air Force, its factories and supporting installations and its ball-bearing plants."[2]

With Arnold's pressure mounting, Eaker complained bitterly about the diversion of his entire force of B-24 bombers to North Africa to carry out the raid on the Ploiesti oil complex—one of seventy-six priority targets enumerated in the POINTBLANK directive. Even before the raid was carried out, Eaker was focused on destroying the Luftwaffe's two prized single-engine fighter factories: the Wiener Neustädter Flugzeugwerke and a factory in Regensburg, Germany. In mid-July, a plan had been drawn up for American bombers to attack these two facilities in one coordinated raid. Eighth Air Force B-17s would attack the Regensburg factory from bases in England. The five North Africa–based B-24 groups, including the 93rd and two other groups wrested from Eaker for the Ploiesti raid, would attack the Wiener Neustadt complex.

As the attack loomed, Eaker's forces were recovering from the loss of ninety-four aircraft on nine strikes during July. In the final week of July alone, Eaker lost seventy-three aircraft—nearly all of them B-17 Flying Fortresses—on four raids into Germany. It had been a bloody stretch, but the POINTBLANK timetable required Eaker to keep pushing his men hard through the final weeks of the European summer. After a year of American raids against German targets, the outcome of what Hap Arnold had sold as a game-changing air campaign remained in doubt. But the coming days could change all that. A successful double-strike raid on the factories that manufactured more than half of Hitler's single-engine fighters could be the long-sought turning point in the air campaign against Nazi Germany.

Once again, Ben and his 93rd comrades were poised to make history.

AS THE NIGHT OF AUGUST 6 WOULD REVEAL, the struggle to process the psychological trauma of the Ploiesti raid wasn't limited to citizen-soldiers like Ben. Twenty-five-year-old Major Joseph Scranton Tate, Jr., had graduated alongside the 93rd's K. O. Dessert and George S. Brown in the West Point Class of 1941, fulfilling a destiny set for him since birth.

Tate had entered the world in February 1918 on a dusty army post in West Texas, where his father was a young lieutenant who had graduated from West Point the previous spring. Much of Joseph Jr.'s early life revolved around the army: living on army posts or visiting them, waiting on his father to return from overseas deployments, or hearing stories about the army from his grandfathers, both retired army colonels with whom Joseph spent much time. One of his great-grandfathers was a retired army general.

He was steeped not only in the ways of America's military aristocracy, but also the upper echelons of politics, business, and high society. His maternal great-grandfather, Joseph Augustine Scranton—born in Connecticut and educated at Phillips Academy and Yale—had received his first political appointment from Abraham Lincoln in 1862, a job as internal revenue collector in the Pennsylvania city that bore the Scranton family name. Joseph Augustine Scranton would go on to become a Republican power broker, five-term member of Congress, and prominent newspaper publisher and editor.

Like his father, grandfather, and great-grandfather, Joe Tate, Jr., was raised in a world of elite prep schools, masquerade parties, formal dinners, and debutante balls. He underwent adolescent polishing at Kent School in Connecticut, and then followed family tradition by entering West Point in the summer of 1937. At the academy, he was a decent student and outstanding athlete, playing football and lettering in ice hockey and lacrosse. After graduation in 1941, he entered the Army Air Forces. A younger brother, Frederic, would graduate a year behind Joe at West Point and also enter the army air service. Joe ended up flying four-engine bombers, while Frederic became a fighter pilot.

On the 93rd's debut mission to Lille, France, in October 1942, Joe Tate and his crew, flying a ship they had christened *Ball of Fire*, survived fighter attacks coming and going. With oxygen, gasoline, and hydraulic lines cut and the aircraft filling with explosive fumes and trailing a plume of gasoline, Tate and his copilot executed an emergency landing on an RAF landing strip just beyond the Cliffs of Dover. Courage in combat, like so many other things, seemed to come easily for Joe Tate. When Addison Baker was promoted to command the 93rd in May 1943, Tate was elevated to Baker's former position as 328th Squadron commander.

Baker's loss over Ploiesti hit Tate especially hard. He had flown off to Egypt on leave with his comrades, but was still struggling to process the terrors of Ploiesti when he returned. On the night of August 6, Tate dreamed that he was attacking Ploiesti again—this time on a solo raid with his crew. In the terrifying mission that unfolded in his dream, Tate's aircraft was riddled by enemy fire. He ran from the cockpit to the back of the plane, tearing his shirt into strips to make tourniquets he used to administer first aid to his grievously injured men. When his tentmates finally shook him awake, Tate discovered that he was being restrained by his comrades. He had ripped his pajama top and mosquito netting to shreds.[3]

With Ploiesti still weighing on Ben and many other 93rd men, Sunday, August 8, loomed as D-Day for another big mission. As the tension built, the crews were informed on Saturday evening that the mission was postponed to Monday because of weather. Tension built again throughout Sunday, but the mission was postponed once more because of weather. Late on Monday evening, the crews were put on notice: Be prepared to take off at first light.

For Ben, the on-again off-again agony of what loomed as his twenty-fifth mission ended that Monday evening when the list of men scheduled to fly the raid was issued. His name wasn't on it. He was a man without a crew once again, with all the uncertainty that entailed. Whenever the big raid finally happened, Ben would still be anxiously awaiting his final mission.

THE 93RD'S AGONIZING PATTERN OF ALERTS, early wake-ups, and predawn briefings dragged on through midweek.

In England, Ira Eaker battled frustration as well. The first eleven days of August had come and gone without his B-17s dropping a single bomb on the enemy. Eaker couldn't afford to let more summer days pass with nothing to show for it, and so the elaborate plan for a coordinated strike on Hitler's two most important Me-109 plants was scrapped. Instead, Eaker seized a window of favorable weather over Western Europe on August 12 to dispatch 330 B-17s to bomb targets in western Germany's Ruhr Valley and the city of Bonn. It was a costly day's work for Eaker's crews, with another twenty-five B-17s lost.

While the 93rd crews scheduled to strike the German Me-109 plant in Austria waited nervously for the green light, twenty-six officers and men celebrated the orders they had awaited since surviving the Ploiesti raid. They had officially been relieved from combat duties and were to depart for England that evening. The lucky souls included four of Ben's longtime crewmates: Jake Epting, Al Naum, Edward Weir, and Red Kettering. The following day, Thursday, August 12, Ben and other 93rd men gave their departing comrades a rousing send-off as they boarded trucks for the short ride to the airfield to begin their journey back to England.

It was a bittersweet occasion for Ben. He was happy for friends who had survived their tours. And yet, he couldn't help but feel sad as the men with whom he had shared eight months of combat disappeared into the distance.

NOT LONG AFTER THE DEPARTURE OF HIS friends, Ben was awakened by the bustle of activity in the camp in the predawn hours of Friday, August

13, 1943. The 93rd's record-breaking raid on the Me-109 fighter factory in Austria was finally happening.

The orders had been issued at 2:00 a.m., and that had unleashed a flurry of preparations by officers charged with overseeing the pre-mission briefing and mechanics and ordnance crews tasked with loading bombs, fueling aircraft, and fine-tuning engines for the early morning takeoff. The combat crew members who managed to sleep through the commotion were awakened at 4:00 a.m. and hustled off to breakfast, followed by a final briefing at 0530.

The weather in the Vienna area remained a concern, and that resulted in the takeoff being pushed back to 0715. But finally, with the veteran 330th Squadron pilot Packy Roche leading the formation and the new 93rd commander, Colonel Leland Fiegel, at his side as copilot, twenty-four crews of the 93rd climbed into the morning sky. A violent sandstorm two days earlier had fouled numerous aircraft engines, and six 93rd bombers turned back on the outbound flight because of engine troubles. A seventh 93rd Liberator landed on Malta with a fuel leak.

For the men who watched the crews depart, an even more nerve-racking day than that of a typical mission day followed. The outbound flight to Wiener Neustadt was eleven hundred miles, and even with auxiliary fuel tanks an attempt by the bombers to return to their desert airstrips outside Benghazi risked calamity. The plan called for the crews to proceed to Tunis after bombing the target, shaving 150 miles off the return and thus reducing the risk of fuel exhaustion. The six aircraft with engine problems returned to the desert airstrip during the course of the day, but after that the men in the camp settled in to a long day of waiting. That evening, Ben and the other men on the ground went to bed without hearing any news of how their comrades had fared.

Ben awakened to another morning of unsettling silence. The empty tents and short mess lines reminded the men of that terrible morning following the Ploiesti raid, but the preliminary reports on the morning of August 14 were good. The raid had gone well, and all but one bomber that attacked the target had landed safely in Tunis.

Gunner Donald Hudspeth, a twenty-two-year-old North Carolinian who had been sweating out the delays, had finally notched the first mission of his combat tour. Hudspeth had gotten a good taste of what lay ahead. He had trouble with his oxygen mask during the flight, and his aircraft, a battle-scarred 93rd original named *Shoot Luke*, had developed a fuel leak during the bomb run. Hudspeth had experienced flak for the first time, but it hadn't been bad—the Germans had been caught by surprise and didn't offer much resistance. Hudspeth and his crewmates had dropped their bombs and made their getaway. During the return flight over Italy,

Hudspeth had seen his first enemy fighter, but the pilot had kept his distance. To the joy and relief of Hudspeth and his crewmates, *Shoot Luke* landed at Tunis at 7:30 in the evening.[4]

Back in the 93rd camp, the joy of the initial report of a successful mission was tempered by the news that one crew from Ben's 409th Squadron was missing. The aircraft was piloted by a Texan named Alva (Jake) Geron, a lanky former Texas Tech basketball player. Ben knew Geron only by sight, but Dick Ryan, his good friend from the Epting crew, had been flying with Geron as a replacement gunner. Geron had lost three gunners on the Ploiesti raid—one killed and two wounded—and two other men had contracted dysentery, so he had flown the raid to Austria with five replacements. Dick Ryan had taken over one of Geron's guns, and now he was missing.

Ben and other friends of the missing men sweated out the next few days until further word arrived. The news could hardly have been better. Jake Geron had made an emergency landing in neutral Switzerland, and he and his entire crew—Dick Ryan included—were now safe and enjoying the carefree lives of internees in the Swiss Alps.[5] By the time the good news about Dick Ryan's new adventure reached the 93rd camp, Ben had some news of his own. He was poised to join forces with an old friend from his sojourn in Spain for the climactic mission of his combat career.

Chapter 30

MORAN CREW

Twenty-seven-year-old Homer Moran was one of several 93rd copilots to earn promotions following the August 12 departure of the officers and enlisted men who had completed their combat tours. A year earlier, Moran had accompanied the 409th Squadron to England as a spare pilot, and through the fall and winter he had worked to earn the trust of peers in sporadic one-off assignments. By February, Moran was still looking for a permanent crew assignment when he boarded *Red Ass* at Gambut Main for the fateful flight that ended in miraculous fashion in Spanish Morocco.

After his release from Spanish custody and return to England in late March, Moran had finally landed a regular gig as Lew Brown's copilot, filling the position vacated by the stress-debilitated Robert Quinlivan. Moran had flown the Rome and Ploiesti raids at Brown's side as the *Queenie* copilot. They had escaped Ploiesti with heavy battle damage and sweated out the return until their emergency landing on Sicily. With Brown headed back to England, Moran took command of *Queenie* and her crew.

Throughout the 93rd, Moran was widely known as one of two Native American pilots flying with the group. The 328th Squadron's Joe Avendano was a member of the Apache tribe and the fifth of twelve children born to migrant workers in Southern California. Moran was a member of the Sicangu or Brulè band of the Lakota people. He was the fourth of nine children born to a farm laborer and homemaker on South Dakota's Rosebud Indian Reservation.

For his first twenty years of life, Moran only occasionally had ventured beyond the boundaries of Rosebud. But as a tall, lithe teenager, he found his ticket off the reservation: basketball. He sharpened his game in high school with boys bearing traditional Sioux names like Felix Knife, Chris Yellow Robe, Dennis Walking Bull, and Vincent Crazy Bear. At the age of twenty, he earned a scholarship to Northern State Teachers College in Aberdeen, South Dakota.[1]

Moran made a name for himself at Northern State with his good looks, engaging personality, and athletic prowess. On the basketball team, he became an all-conference starting guard by his junior year in 1938–39. As a senior, classmates elected him "most popular man" on campus and teammates chose him as their captain. But his peers and the local press always viewed Moran through a racial lens. The Sioux Falls *Argus-Leader* often reverted to stereotypes when writing about Moran, calling him the "Wandering Sioux of Northern Teachers" or Homer "Scout" Moran. Even more cringeworthy was the *Argus-Leader* piece that described Moran as "a full-blooded Sioux Indian [who] brings all his redmen sorcery to the court."[2]

His teammates, many of whom were the children of German immigrants, invariably called him "Chief." As a six-foot-two senior, Moran helped guide his team to the South Dakota College Conference title and a spot in the National Intercollegiate Basketball tournament in Kansas City. Their first-round matchup proved especially memorable for Moran because he played with a broken bone in his hand. Moran and his teammates kept the game close against their much taller opponents from Texas until late in the fourth quarter, ultimately losing by eight points.[3] That was the last game of his college career. Later that spring, Moran lettered on the track team in the throwing events. And then, his years at Northern State ended in mystery.

When commencement exercises were held on May 30, 1940, Moran wasn't among the students who received a diploma. His name didn't appear on any lists of students earning a degree in the school's programs of varying length. He slipped away quietly, as if he had never been there. He returned to the Rosebud reservation and the bleak prospects that awaited a young Brulè man in his mid-twenties, even one with college credits and athletic success to his name.

Education had been beyond the reach of most of the Moran family, making it nearly impossible for Homer's parents and siblings to extricate themselves from the poverty that was a legacy of the Lakota people's forced transition from lives of hunting and gathering to farming and herding. Neither of Homer's parents had advanced beyond the eighth grade, and none of Homer's closest siblings graduated from high school. His fourteen-year-old brother Richard had completed only three years of elementary schooling at the time of the 1940 federal census.

The 1940 census found the Moran family living on the reservation in a rural rental home valued at $5. Only one of the seven family members listed as residents held a job: Homer's twenty-year-old sister Bertha, who described herself as a "servant" in a "private home." Another sister, twenty-two-year-old Mary, identified herself as a seamstress who was "seeking work." When Homer registered for the draft in Rosebud on October 16,

1940, someone drew a line through the spaces on the form for his employer's name and address.

Basketball had given Homer Moran his first extended glimpse of life beyond the reservation. By 1941, it was clear that military service was his best hope to escape Rosebud.

On September 17, 1941, Moran enlisted in the army. He would be one of four Moran brothers who wore the uniform in World War II. One became an army medic and ended the war on Okinawa. Another was an Army Air Forces cook. A third was an army engineer in Europe.

Homer was posted in San Diego when the Japanese bombed Pearl Harbor. In the aftermath, Moran's unit was sent to Los Angeles to secure defense plants from saboteurs and a feared Japanese invasion. Among other tasks, Moran and his comrades installed antiaircraft batteries around the Burbank airport, known at the time as the Lockheed Air Terminal.

Lockheed used the facility to test aircraft that its workers assembled in nearby factories. Moran had never been in an airplane, but after weeks of watching P-38 fighters and various bombers take off and land, he and his buddies decided to apply for flight school. Within a month, Moran began pilot training in Oxnard, California, north of Los Angeles.[4]

In July, he earned his wings in expedited fashion at the army's Victorville advanced flying school in San Bernardino County, east of Los Angeles. He was sent to Florida to learn to fly B-26 medium bombers, but after less than a week he was transferred to a B-24 unit in Fort Myers that was poised to deploy overseas. It was his introduction to the 93rd Bomb Group.

Moran accompanied the 93rd's flight echelon to Grenier Field, New Hampshire, where the crews picked up new B-24s. He still had never flown in a B-24 before being ordered to New York City, where he boarded the *Queen Elizabeth* with the group's ground echelon.[5] Now, less than eighteen months after his first flight in a single-engine trainer, Homer Moran was poised to command a four-engine bomber crew in combat.

Ben knew the outline of Homer Moran's backstory from their weeks together in Spain. They hailed from the same part of the country—the Kuroki farm was about 140 miles due south of the Moran residence on the Rosebud reservation—and they had gotten along well. Ben would never trust another pilot as much as he trusted Jake Epting, but, given the choice between Homer Moran and one of the green pilots that had been with the 93rd only weeks, Ben preferred to take his chances with the big South Dakotan. An association with the Moran crew offered Ben a bonus: He would be reunited with a friend from the Epting crew, former *Red Ass* mechanic Ples Norwood, now serving as Moran's flight engineer and top turret gunner.

The details were worked out. When the Moran crew took off on its next mission, Ben would join them in his quest to complete his combat tour.

AROUND MIDDAY OF SUNDAY, AUGUST 15, shocking news reached the 93rd camp. Two days earlier, one of the new pilots assigned to the group—a well-liked Minnesotan with a flair for flying—had fallen ill with a sore throat and had been taken to a military hospital in Benghazi. Now word arrived that twenty-eight-year-old George Larson was dead. The cause of death was listed as a "throat infection," but the truth was that Larson had contracted polio during a trip into Benghazi or an encounter with a local vendor. He was such a vibrant, handsome fellow that comrades were shaken by his loss. Other 93rd men had contracted mysterious and debilitating illnesses over the previous weeks, and Larson's death put the camp on edge.

Some of the men wouldn't hear the news about George Larson's untimely passing until later in the afternoon, for they had headed off to the nearby seashore for a swim. Some of the men splashed in the surf while others gathered to watch a swim meet between the 93rd and a British Halifax bomber group based nearby. After much spirited cheering, the meet ended in a tie. "It was all good fun," diarist Brutus Hamilton declared.

In the late afternoon, the men were put on alert for a mission the following morning. Homer Moran and his crew occupied a spot in the lineup. Ben wouldn't have to wait long for his shot at number twenty-five. At a briefing that evening, he learned their target was an important Axis airfield at Foggia, twenty miles inland from Italy's eastern Adriatic coast.

It was getting late by the time the men retired to their tents. If all went according to plan, Ben would be off for Italy with Homer Moran at first light.

Chapter 31

A DISAPPOINTING FINALE

At five o'clock on Monday morning, August 16, 1943, Ben and his comrades awakened in the cool darkness, dressed, and shuffled off to breakfast and a final briefing. Around 6:45 a.m. local time—0445 GMT—the lead ship took off.

In the cockpit of *Queenie*, Homer Moran and his copilot, Lieutenant Henry Podgurski, guided their B-24 down the Site 7 runway along with two other bombers and rose above the dun-colored desert. In the twenty-three-year-old Podgurski, Moran had a cockpit partner with seasoning that far exceeded his years. Most pilots and copilots were college boys, many of whom had been introduced to a cockpit in a campus course. The working-class Podgurski had come from a very different background. He had earned his spot in *Queenie*'s cockpit by logging more than three hundred flight hours with the Royal Canadian Air Force.

Tall and thin—his draft record listed him as six-foot-two and 155 pounds—Podgurski was the child of Polish immigrants. He had grown up in an ethnic enclave that centered family, Polish heritage, and Roman Catholicism in his life. Podgurski's parents ran a Polish restaurant in Manor, a town in Westmoreland County, Pennsylvania, just east of Pittsburgh.

At the time he registered for the draft on July 1, 1941, Podgurski was a skilled laborer in the Westinghouse Manufacturing Company's sprawling East Pittsburgh plant. By 1941, production was shifting hard to defense work, and workers at the plant specialized in building huge waterwheel generators and other power equipment required for President Roosevelt's massive defense buildup.

Hitler's 1939 invasion of Poland had caused great anguish in the Polish American communities of America. By the fall of 1941, with America still nominally neutral, Podgurski enlisted in the Royal Canadian Air Force on October 2. After a year of training, he earned his wings in Canada, and in the autumn of 1942, he deployed to England aboard the *Queen Elizabeth*.

By early 1943, with Ira Eaker desperate for pilots to replenish his Eighth Air Force losses, Podgurski transferred into the US Army Air Forces. He took his oath in London and began service with the 93rd on March 24, 1943. He had recently earned a promotion from flight officer to second lieutenant by virtue of his work as a copilot in the July raids on Italian targets and then the Ploiesti low-level raid. Now, the blue-eyed, brown-haired Polish American flier sat beside Homer Moran as *Queenie* joined the formation circling above the Libyan desert.

In the back of the aircraft, Ben enjoyed a reunion of sorts with former comrades from the Epting crew. In addition to Ples Norwood, Moran had added a pair of gunners from the post-Spain incarnation of the Epting crew: Harold Dafoe, the twenty-two-year-old fur trapper from the St. Lawrence River Valley in Upstate New York, and James Wisniewski, a husky twenty-one-year-old from Detroit.

As the twenty-four 93rd aircraft formed in a circling carousel, Moran eased *Queenie* into its assigned spot in the first flight of six aircraft. In all, more than ninety B-24s had been assigned to bomb one of the main airfields outside the southern Italian city of Foggia. Also assigned to the mission were the 93rd's two sister units on loan from the Eighth Air Force—the 44th Bomb Group and the 389th—and the 376th Bomb Group.

In the aftermath of the final Axis surrender in Tunisia in mid-May, the German and Italian air force bases surrounding Foggia had emerged as a key target for the Allies. American and British aircraft had bombed Foggia's civilian airport and rail station in three raids in the final days of May. Another raid followed on June 21. Allied bombers hit the Foggia railway station again on July 15 and July 22, killing or injuring nearly nine thousand civilians in those two raids alone. After several raids, Foggia's weak air defenses had given the city and its nearby complex of airfields a favorable reputation among American and British bomber crews. "We were told that the air raid would be a 'milk run,'" recalled 44th gunner Charles J. Warth.[1]

A milk run—aircrew slang for an easy mission—would be just fine with Ben and his crewmates today. Lounging in the area around the top turret, his assigned position since the July 9 raid on the Ponte Olivo airfield on Sicily, Ben settled in for the four-hour flight to Foggia.

AS THE B-24S FLEW NORTHWARD ACROSS the Mediterranean, their sights set on a target above the heel of the Italian boot, more than fifty US B-25 medium bombers and one-hundred-odd P-40 fighters based in Tunisia had their crosshairs centered on the toe of the Italian mainland. More specifically, these aircraft had been assigned to attack the Straits of Messina, where the final hours of the final act of the battle for Sicily was playing out.

In the thirty-seven days since American and British soldiers had splashed ashore the southern beaches of Sicily, Allied forces had slowly pushed the island's defenders northward, and then northeast. After unrelenting combat through the heat of late July and early August, the remaining German and Italian defenders had withdrawn to a defensive pocket formed by the island's Messina Peninsula. There, the Axis forces prepared for a last stand, with the port of Messina as their lifeline through which men and materiel continued to flow.

Field Marshal Albert Kesselring, the supreme German commander in Italy, had urged the Wehrmacht leadership in Berlin to avoid another mass surrender of troops, like those at Stalingrad in February and Tunis in May. On July 26, the Berlin high command dispatched a hand-carried order to Kesselring, granting his request. The order directed Kesselring to prepare to reverse the flow of Sicily's lifeline so that German soldiers and equipment could be evacuated by water, across the Straits of Messina, to the toe of the Italian mainland.

Kesselring had entrusted the defense of the Straits of Messina to forty-five-year-old Colonel Ernst-Günther Baade, a battle-scarred veteran of the North Africa campaign. A teenage cavalryman in the First World War, Baade had initially fought in North Africa with the 15th Panzer Division. In April 1942, he took command of the Wehrmacht's 115th Rifle Regiment and saw extensive combat in Libya and Egypt. He earned renown for going into battle wearing a Scottish kilt and carrying a claymore, a two-handed Scottish sword, before he was seriously wounded in the first battle of El Alamein in July 1942.[2]

After a lengthy recuperation in Germany, Baade reported to Rome to serve as a Wehrmacht liaison to the Italian army's supreme command. On July 14, four days after the Allied landings on Sicily, Kesselring dispatched Baade to the island to oversee the defense of the vital Straits of Messina. Under Baade's direction, five hundred guns were installed on both the Sicilian and Calabrian shores to secure the straits from Allied air, naval, and ground attacks.

The evacuation orders of July 26 set in motion a flurry of activity around the straits. German engineers prepared camouflaged ferry sites on both shores and assembled a fleet of thirty-three barges, seventy-six motorboats, and a dozen Siebel ferries powered by twin pontoon-mounted airplane engines.[3] In the first week of August, the evacuation quietly got underway with the safe passage of twelve thousand German military officers and civilian officials and four thousand vehicles.[4]

At 6:00 p.m. on Wednesday, August 11, Baade launched the final evacuation, Operation LEHRGANG (Curriculum). As German and Italian forces withdrew to successively shorter defensive lines on the Messina Peninsula, elements of the Hermann Göring Division slipped away from the island aboard Baade's evacuation fleet. By the flickering light of oil lamps, concealed from Allied aircrews by overhead screens, the evacuation continued for six nights.[5]

The Allied response to the eventual evacuation of forty thousand German and seventy thousand Italian soldiers from Sicily remains one of the war's most mystifying episodes. Historian Rick Atkinson notes that "Allied commanders had had no coordinated plan for severing the Messina Strait when HUSKY began, nor did any such plan emerge as the campaign reached its climax."[6] Allied ground and naval commanders were distracted by planning for the looming invasion of the Italian mainland, while Allied air commanders were already consumed by their quest to secure air superiority in Western Europe.

The efforts that were made unfolded in piecemeal fashion. The supreme Allied air commander in North Africa, British air chief marshal Arthur Tedder, initially committed US general Carl Spaatz's two combat air forces in North Africa to block the escape, but an August 2 order prohibited the use of Spaatz's B-17s. Within a week, the orders changed again.

Despite the errors and missed opportunities that unfolded over the next two weeks, daylight of August 16 found American and British troops within a dozen miles of Messina and closing—unaware that only a few hundred enemy troops remained in their path. At 5:30 that morning, the two most senior German commanders still on the island—the one-armed General Hans-Valentin Hube, overall commander of Sicily's defense, and General Walter Fries, commander of the 29th Panzer Grenadier Division—crossed to Calabria. With only a few boatloads of soldiers still to be evacuated, Hube and Fries had left the rearguard defense of the remaining ferry sites in the hands of some two hundred grenadiers.[7]

It had taken the Italians several days to catch wind of the German plan. Hitler had ordered the evacuation to proceed in secrecy for fear that the government that had replaced the dictator Benito Mussolini after his July 25 arrest would withdraw from the Axis Pact of Steel upon learning of the plan to abandon Sicily. Once Italian commanders discovered the German plan, they separately initiated their own escape, aided by the massive train ferry previously targeted by American bombers—a vessel capable of carrying three thousand men per trip.[8]

As Ben and his comrades flew northward across the Mediterranean, they were oblivious to the drama playing out some one hundred miles to their west. In the fateful hours ahead, the Italian commander of Messina's port would depart after setting time bombs to destroy his docks, and the two hundred German grenadiers assigned to slow the approaching invaders would drive off a small US Army patrol—men of Company I, 7th Infantry

Regiment—before falling back in the gathering darkness to board one of the final launches of Operation LEHRGANG. On one of those last boats to leave Sicily, German engineers lowered a bottle of wine into the sea and then drank a toast of the chilled vintage as they approached the Calabrian shore.[9]

Only much later would the magnitude of the Allied error at Messina be revealed, its bloody ramifications punctuated by the deaths of thousands of American and British soldiers in combat with some of the forty thousand Germans who escaped Sicily. But these were not the concerns of Ben and his comrades as they steeled themselves for whatever awaited at Foggia on this mid-August morning.

THE MORAN CREW'S MEDITERRANEAN crossing proceeded without incident, and a few minutes past 8:00 a.m., the American B-24s reached Italy's southeastern coast. To their left lay the forested Apennine peaks and valleys of the Basilicata region. To their right the whitewashed hill towns of the Puglia region and the shimmering Adriatic Sea beyond. They had covered six hundred miles from their desert base, and Foggia lay about a hundred miles ahead—a thirty-minute flight at their current cruising speed. They were now on high alert for enemy fighters. Someone aboard *Queenie* spotted two enemy fighters off in the distance, but they ignored the 93rd bombers and barreled toward the formation of B-24s flying behind them.

About thirteen minutes after crossing the Italian coast, the mission went awry for the Moran crew. *Queenie*'s number three engine—the closest starboard engine to Ben's top turret—began smoking and spewing oil. Homer Moran and Henry Podgurski shut off the malfunctioning engine and feathered the propeller to reduce drag and eliminate the possibility of a windmilling prop. They were only twenty minutes from the point where they would begin their straight-line sprint to the target, but the guidance to pilots in such a case was clear: If you can't keep up with the formation, turn back. At 8:57 a.m., flying at an altitude of eighteen thousand feet, Moran eased *Queenie* from the leading edge of the 93rd formation and banked to the southeast. Now *Queenie* began a long and solitary flight back to Benghazi.

Their return route took them south-southeast over the Ionian Sea. Around forty minutes after turning back, still flying at seventeen thousand feet, *Queenie*'s bombardier jettisoned his load of thirty 100-pound bombs into the sea. Moran now began a steady descent in the hopes of avoiding prowling enemy fighters—a risk that was fairly high off the coast of Greece. The gunners fired five test rounds from each gun and prepared for action.

At 10:20 a.m., eighty minutes after turning back, they had descended to thirty-five hundred feet and were flying about thirty miles off the coast of Greece when they spotted a life raft floating in the sea, about a mile away from an oil slick. They couldn't tell if anyone was in the raft, or what had caused the slick.

They flew on for another three hours without incident. A few minutes past one o'clock the coast of Libya came into sight. At 1:24 p.m., *Queenie* rolled to a stop at the Site 7 airfield. They had been airborne eight hours and thirty minutes. They hadn't hit their target, but they had flown into enemy territory. That fact and their time aloft meant that each member of the Moran crew would be credited with a combat mission for the August 16 raid on Foggia.

For nearly two-and-a-half hours, Ben and his crewmates sweated out the return of the men they had set out with that morning. Finally, a few minutes before 3:00 p.m., the sound of engines could be heard in the distance and dark specks appeared in the sky to the north. Over the next hour, every plane that had been in the 93rd formation when *Queenie* aborted the mission landed. All had made it back, and there had been no casualties.

Fate had favored the 93rd on this day. They had encountered anti-aircraft fire over the target that the crews variously rated as moderate to medium intensity. They had also encountered more than thirty enemy fighters. And at least ten enemy fighters had attacked from the rear, but they had come no closer than six hundred yards. The 93rd's gunners reported shooting down at least ten enemy fighters, the group's best day of gunnery since entering combat.

Their comrades of the 44th Bomb Group weren't as fortunate. The Eight Balls, as they were known, had been flying off to the right of the 93rd when they came under attack by as many as fifty enemy fighters. The 44th lost seven bombers in the fight that followed.

As night fell over the Libyan desert, a range of emotions filled the men of the 93rd. After takeoff that morning, Brutus Hamilton and several other officers had driven into Benghazi to attend the funeral of pilot George Larson, the polio victim. A new batch of mail arrived by plane later in the day. As always, the letters from home elicited joy, sadness, homesickness, and, sometimes, heartbreak. Edward Sand, a young 328th Squadron gunner, was shaken by the news that one of his friends back home in Detroit had been killed in action in the Pacific.[10]

Nightfall brought a USO show headlined by an A-list movie star and comedian, Jack Benny. As a full moon hung overhead, the 93rd men laughed and hooted and groaned as Benny told raunchy jokes, played a spirited violin, and bantered with his troupe and the audience.

Almost exactly a year earlier, Ben had pleaded with 93rd officers to be allowed to accompany the group on its overseas deployment. He had talked his way into a combat role with a B-24 crew, and now he had completed twenty-five missions—the set length of an Eighth Air Force combat tour.[11] But the war was far from over in August 1943, and, in Ben's mind, he still had much to prove. Although he never spoke of it, the disappointing fashion in which his twenty-fifth mission played out undoubtedly weighed on him. Perhaps that fact, as much as anything, explains the audacious decision Ben was poised to make.

Chapter 32

AN ENEMY AT PEAK STRENGTH

For the first time since beginning his combat tour the previous December, Ben awakened on August 17 with the satisfying knowledge that he had proven his detractors wrong. All the men who had mocked him and made snide comments about the color of his skin or shape of his eyes; the men who had questioned his loyalties, his trustworthiness, his courage; the bigoted 93rd sergeants who had twice tried to force him from the group, first in Louisiana and then Florida. He had proven them all wrong. He had pleaded for the opportunity to fight, and, when that opportunity arrived, he proved his mettle. He hadn't ducked tough assignments. He had bombed the Fascist capital, braved the murderous defenses of Ploiesti, and delivered blows against a dozen other enemy targets. Now he could walk away and never fly another combat mission, if that's what he wanted.

But he wasn't sure that was what he wanted.

For a while now, Ben had been thinking about what he would do when he reached twenty-five missions. All his former crewmates and other comrades in the 93rd never doubted what they would do. Ben's best friend, Red Kettering, couldn't wait to return home to see family and friends. They had laughed and joked with each other the previous week as Red prepared to begin that journey. "Don't forget to look up my folks in Nebraska—I've already written them to give you a delicious meal of fish heads and rice," Ben had joked.[1] When his home leave was up, Red would have his choice of cushy assignments, perhaps training new bomber crews or selling War Bonds or recruiting. Ben could expect the same, if that's what he wanted.

But an idea had begun to form in Ben's head. He would volunteer for another five missions. It would be his way of going above and beyond to prove his patriotism, to leave no doubt as to his loyalties. He would do it for his kid brother Fred, who had been booted out of the air service to dig trenches. From those first hours following the news of Pearl Harbor, he and Fred had aspired to prove their love of country by fighting for America, but Fred had been denied the chance. Now Ben could strike a symbolic blow on his brother's behalf. He would fly another five missions in Fred's honor.[2]

The final call wasn't Ben's to make. He made his way through the desert camp to the squadron headquarters tent to present his plan to K. O. Dessert. The 409th Squadron commander listened carefully to Ben and then gently pushed back. "Go home," Dessert urged. Ben's orders for his return to America had already been cut.

Ben respectfully protested. He tried to explain himself—why combat meant so much to him in the first place, and why flying another five missions meant so much to him now. Dessert heard him out and relented. Ben could remain with Homer Moran and his crew for another five missions.[3]

THE 93RD FLEW TWO MORE MISSIONS from their base in the Libyan desert, a pair of tactical raids aimed at the enemy air and rail systems in Italy. Fifteen 93rd Liberators were assigned to an August 19 raid on Foggia's rail marshaling yards and fourteen of the group's B-24s were assigned to an August 20 raid on an air storage depot eighteen miles north of Naples. The 93rd didn't lose any aircraft on either raid. The Moran crew—Ben included—sat out both raids.

Rumors were rife the group would soon be leaving the Libyan desert. Speculation swirled about what was next. Would they return to England? Relocate to Tunis? Italy, maybe? What seemed clear was they finally were poised to leave their godforsaken Sahara camp. Their departure would happen none too soon for the 93rd's weary men and worn aircraft.[4]

By mid-August, a number of 93rd men were battling psychological problems. Among them was Bill Dawley, the *Red Ass* gunner who had been wounded in the head on Ben's first raid the previous December. Dawley had returned to combat in February 1943, and had made the second trek to North Africa as a gunner on Hap Kendall's crew. He had survived the Ploiesti raid, but afterward found himself struggling with what is now recognized as post-traumatic stress. "I was getting pretty shaky," Dawley later recalled.[5]

Dawley was thinking of taking himself off combat duty when he went to talk to the 409th Squadron's operations officer, who happened to be Jake Epting. "I'm quitting," Dawley told his former pilot. Epting patiently tried to talk Dawley down. "You're going to end up with guard duty or buck private or KP [kitchen patrol] the rest of your days," Epting said.

Dawley didn't like the sound of that. He thought it over and when his crew was next assigned a mission, he showed up for the briefing and reported to his aircraft as if nothing had happened. When Hap Kendall taxied out for takeoff, Jake Epting spotted Dawley standing in the waist window and gave him an approving nod. Dawley continued his quest for twenty-five missions.[6]

Within days, the 93rd's long-awaited orders finally arrived.

ON THE MORNING OF AUGUST 26, 1943, Ben and his comrades bade farewell to the desert and began the first leg of their welcome journey back to England.

Over the course of the long flight westward across North Africa, places fraught with memories of close calls and comrades lost flashed beneath Ben: There was Tripoli, the target of Ben's tenth mission with the Epting crew on January 21 and the mission on which Lew Brown had lost four men; Biskra, the Algerian provincial capital which they had overflown on the flight to Benghazi two months earlier, when the mysterious Big One that had brought them back to Africa had yet to claim so many comrades; Oran, the first frenetic city that Ben had experienced in North Africa the previous December; Oudja, the Moroccan border city that the *Red Ass* crew had overflown in the frantic minutes before Jake Epting executed his miraculous landing in a mountain valley about seventy miles away; and Marrakech, Morocco, Winston Churchill's beloved "Paris of the Sahara," their final stop before bidding farewell to Africa. They had covered 1,741 miles during the day and landed around dusk.

The next morning they headed for England's Cornwall peninsula. They were still airborne when darkness fell. The trip took a dire turn when sand-scoured engines faltered on several aircraft.[7]

Ben was among those experiencing a harrowing end to this latest North Africa adventure. For a time, it seemed to Ben, Homer Moran, and Ples Norwood that they were reliving the near-fatal flight that had marked their previous departure from North Africa in February. In the dark, Moran kept a close watch on a failing supercharger that made one of his engines glow like a blazing fire. "I never sweated so much in my life," he later recalled.[8]

Safely on the ground at RAF bases in Cornwall, many of the 93rd men celebrated their return to England by getting drunk at the officers' and enlisted clubs of their British hosts. The cool air, green surroundings, dark beer, English women, paved streets, sturdy barracks—all were welcome sights to men worn out by the rough living of these past weeks.

To a man, the 93rd veterans welcomed their return to England, without much thought for the deadly implications of what that meant. They had left behind a theater defended by a shattered and dispirited enemy, but Western Europe was a different ballgame. Ben would be flying his bonus missions against a German fighter force and air defense system that was approaching peak strength.

Chapter 33

THE KILLING MONTH

Ben's quest to fly another five missions with the 93rd seemed star-crossed almost from the beginning. When the weather actually allowed the 93rd to take off on a raid, some mechanical problem would force Homer Moran to turn back. On other days, either the Moran crew wasn't scheduled to fly or the weather grounded the entire group. Ben faced one frustration after another. The 93rd logged only three raids during the first half of September, and then in mid-September the group was ordered back to North Africa. More bad weather wreaked havoc on operations and the group logged only five missions during this two-week assignment. When Ben returned to England on October 4, more than forty days after joining Homer Moran's crew as top turret gunner, he had logged only one of his five bonus missions.

Ben had barely settled back into his Hardwick Nissen hut when General Ira Eaker set in motion a series of raids in a final attempt to cripple key German industries before bad weather cloaked the continent. The first blow was scheduled for October 8, two weeks to the day since Ben had logged his twenty-sixth mission over Pisa, Italy. The Moran crew was among twenty-one 93rd crews—four of them commanded by pilots making their combat debut—assigned to what Eaker had designated a "maximum effort" against strategic German targets. The specific objectives were submarine pens, shipyards, and a Focke-Wulf Fw-190 fighter factory located around the city of Bremen.

It was yet another brutal day for the Eighth Air Force, with Eaker's forces losing thirty bombers over Bremen and the nearby Vegesack district. But once again, through skill and selfless acts of courage, the 93rd defied the odds. Ben and his comrades made it back to Hardwick without the loss of an airplane or the death or serious injury of one of their men. Ben recorded his twenty-seventh mission in his log.

BEN DIDN'T HAVE LONG TO WONDER when he might fly again or whether his luck would hold. The 93rd was put on alert for a mission shortly after the planes that bombed Bremen and Vegesack landed, and the Moran crew once again was among those on the list to fly.

When the curtain was pulled back in the briefing room the following morning to reveal the day's target, the historic significance wasn't lost on Ben and other 93rd old-timers. They were headed to East Prussia and the ports along Poland's Baltic coast—the deepest penetration into Europe that the Eighth Air Force had yet attempted from England.[1] As with the previous day's mission, it would be another "maximum effort," with the Eighth's B-17s and B-24s coordinating their efforts to hit four targets: the German industrial cities of Anklam and Marienburg and the Polish ports of Gdynia and Danzig (now Gdansk).

The 93rd drew as its target the submarine base at Danzig, on the Baltic Sea. Around three hours after seventeen 93rd Liberators took off from Hardwick, the formation neared Danzig. The target was covered by smoke and heavy flak, but that didn't deter Moran. The gunners watched their bombs disappear into the murk, and then braced to fight their way home through prowling enemy fighters as Moran banked their aircraft to the west.

But the enemy fighters never materialized, or at least not in the numbers or with the ferocity and determination feared. Some of the crews saw seven or eight twin-engine Ju-88 fighter-bombers, but the enemy fliers merely watched the 93rd formation and waited for stragglers to drop from it. Although the 93rd aircraft maintained a tight formation for the most part, coming and going, the final tally at Hardwick revealed two missing bombers.

One of the missing crews was from the 409th Squadron, and they were men well known to Ben. The pilot was a Ploiesti veteran, Miles League, and his ship was *Satan's Sister*. The men were last seen over Bornholm Island, headed for Sweden, raising hopes that they had made an emergency landing. The other bomber was *Piccadilly Filly*, piloted by one of the new 93rd pilots, Thomas W. Atkinson, and less was known about its immediate fate. As it turned out, League and his entire crew had reached neutral Sweden on three engines and made a successful belly landing at a local air base.[2] Atkinson had also reached Sweden, in even more miraculous fashion, but at a dearer cost.

Piccadilly Filly had limped away from the target with two engines out and damage to its tail section and controls. For reasons unknown, Atkinson's navigator, Second Lieutenant Farren F. Shafer, bailed out through the nosewheel hatch and dropped into the frigid sea, never to be seen again. Atkinson instructed the rest of his men to stay put while he figured out their next move. They contemplated ditching at sea, a dangerous proposition under the best of conditions, but decided to remain with *Piccadilly Filly*. Atkinson and his copilot kept the crew aloft with their two portside engines long enough to complete the twenty-mile crossing to the Swedish coast, where the pilots executed a crash landing. "Lieutenant Atkinson, only twenty-one years old, saved our lives," gunner Nicholas Caruso recalled years later.[3]

As tragic as the day had been for the 93rd, it was worse for the other Eighth Air Force groups who flew the raid. Twenty-four of 430 aircraft were shot down, with 124 men killed in action, 131 taken prisoner, and 19 interned.[4]

It was the first anniversary of the 93rd's combat debut, and the group's publicist—Ben's friend Cal Stewart—interviewed several men for a story he wrote for release to news correspondents. Among the 93rd men Stewart interviewed was the Japanese American farm boy whose promotion to a combat crew he had chronicled in a newspaper article ten months earlier.

"The Traveling Circus, in what was probably the longest hop by Libs in the ETO [European Theater of Operations], raided the sub pens at Danzig, one of the oldest cities in Europe," Stewart's latest story began. Stewart followed with a quick succession of quotes from several 93rd men who had flown the raid. First up was Ben, described by Stewart as "a tired-looking gunner" who had logged his twenty-eighth mission on the Danzig raid.

The back-to-back raids had underscored for Ben the perils of his commitment to fly five extra missions. The raids he was now flying weren't nearly as long as the 93rd's raids to Ploiesti or Wiener Neustadt or Rome, but the targets in greater Germany were more heavily defended. In response to Cal Stewart's questions about how the summer missions from Libya compared with those the 93rd now faced, Ben offered a calibrated response. "You have to be on your toes here," Ben said, using a popular sports analogy. "Not like it was in Africa."[5]

After back-to-back raids, Ben and the Moran crew got October 10 off, but the 93rd was in action for a third consecutive day. The 93rd contingent assigned to fly the mission—including another six new pilots—enjoyed an easy day, but their assignment to draw German fighters away from their B-17 comrades failed. The Flying Fortress groups lost another thirty aircraft in an attack on the German city of Münster, bringing the Mighty Eighth's losses over three days of raids to eighty-eight bombers and nearly nine hundred men.

October 11 marked the fourth consecutive day of action for the 93rd, with another planned raid into Germany, but weather forced a cancellation.

Yet another attempt was made the following day to bomb the German city of Emden, and nine 93rd aircraft got aloft before the raid was canceled because their Thunderbolt escorts couldn't get off the ground.[6]

After another day lost to inclement weather, the 93rd crews were alerted to prepare for a mission the following day, October 14. Rumors were soon confirmed. The 93rd was to be part of another double-strike raid on Regensburg and Schweinfurt, the infamous targets that had cost Ira Eaker sixty B-17s in August. The Liberators had been relegated to low-risk diversion duties on a costly Stuttgart raid the previous month and the Münster raid earlier that week, but they would be full partners with the Flying Fortresses in this latest attempt to cripple German production of Me-109 fighters at Regensburg and ball bearings at Schweinfurt.

The plan called for the 93rd commander, Colonel Leland Fiegel, to lead a combined force of sixty Liberators to Schweinfurt, but things unraveled for the B-24s almost from the outset. Only eighteen of twenty-four 93rd Liberators got airborne, and only two of the three B-24 groups assigned to the raid—the diminished 93rd force and the 392nd Bomb Group contingent—arrived at the rendezvous point over the North Sea.

Escorted by a squadron of P-47 Thunderbolts, the Liberators angled south over the Dutch coast and the countryside of occupied Holland. The Liberators had just crossed into German airspace over Aachen when the Thunderbolts reached the limits of their range. The Liberators would be on their own for their remaining ninety minutes of circuitous flight to Schweinfurt and the critical first hour of the return journey to England.

About twenty minutes farther south, flying over Luxembourg before making a hard left to Schweinfurt, Fiegel made a fateful decision. His planned force of sixty Liberators was now down to twenty-two aircraft after the botched rendezvous and assorted mechanical mishaps that had prompted other Liberators to head for home. Rather than press on to a target that struck fear in the hearts of Eighth Air Force men after the August raid, Fiegel changed plans. With Fiegel in the lead, the Liberators banked to the north in a diversionary maneuver aimed at drawing enemy fighters away from Regensburg and Schweinfurt.[7]

As Fiegel was leading his Liberators on a flight down and back up Germany's western fringe without any losses, more than three hundred Eighth Air Force B-17s were locked in three hours and fourteen minutes of costly combat. The American bombers inflicted significant damage on the Me-109 factory at Regensburg and the ball-bearing factories at Schweinfurt, but it came at a high price. The Germans shot down twenty-eight B-17s on the way to their targets and another thirty-two on the return flight.[8]

The loss of 642 American airmen on what was soon being called Black Thursday had a devastating impact on the mental health of the Eighth Air Force bomber crews. "After Black Thursday, morale in the Eighth plummeted to a new low and commanders worried about a crew revolt," historian Donald L. Miller wrote in his classic history of the Eighth Air Force campaign, *Masters of the Air*. "'I will never fly another mission, regardless of the cost,' a gunner told his friends in the privacy of their Nissen hut, where twelve of the twenty cots were empty that night."[9]

At a moment when Ben was trying to survive three more raids, the second double-strike attack on Regensburg and Schweinfurt had plunged the American daylight bombing campaign into crisis.

IRA EAKER'S BOMBER CREWS WERE ALREADY consumed by anxieties that had been percolating since the bloody August strikes on Regensburg and Schweinfurt, followed by the September raid on Stuttgart, and the October raids that had culminated with Black Thursday.

While Hap Arnold publicly expressed nonchalance about the soaring Eighth Air Force casualties, he quietly tried to limit the release of casualty figures to monthly totals rather than a raid-by-raid tally. At the group level, commanders sent dispirited crews to rest homes in the English countryside—"flak farms" as they were known among airmen—to avert breakdowns under the weight of combat stress. The efforts weren't entirely successful. One crew returned from a flak-farm holiday and its members announced that they all wished to be relieved from combat duty.[10]

Bad weather gave the crews a much-needed respite in the second half of October, and many men headed to London on leaves to try to decompress.

Ben's quest for thirty missions stalled amid the latest extended bout of bad weather. The 93rd saw limited action, flying diversions on October 18 and 19 before another diversion was aborted on October 20. Ben flew none of these missions.

After ten days of horrible weather, with pressure from Hap Arnold building once again on Ira Eaker and flowing down to the group level, the 93rd got aircraft airborne on October 30 for a raid on the Ruhr Valley industrial city of Gelsenkirchen. The Moran crew didn't fly the mission, which proved to be an anticlimax when the 93rd bombers were recalled after flying to the target area but not releasing their bombs for fear of inflicting too many civilian casualties by bombing blind through heavy overcast. On the return flight, two 93rd men died when a pilot flying beneath the fifty-foot weather ceiling touched the ground with a wing and the aircraft cartwheeled.

The monotonous diversions, stand-downs, cancellations, and recalls wore on the men. Mercifully, Black October, as the month had become known to some—or "The Killing Month," as one 93rd man christened it—finally ended. In two desultory months with the Moran crew, Ben had completed only three missions. Now November arrived with Ben's personal crusade linked to the larger Eighth Air Force campaign in this autumn of agony.

Chapter 34

DEATH DENIED

Ben began the month of November 1943 knowing that finishing thirty missions wasn't going to be easy. Not only was he flying against the toughest enemy defenses outside of Ploiesti, the autumn weather over Western Europe was making every flight a deadly game of chance. Once reaching their bombing altitude, gunners like Ben faced subzero temperatures that froze any exposed skin in seconds. And there was always a good chance on a mission that jammed guns or some other mishap might require a gunner to remove his gloves to fix the problem. The cautionary tale that stuck in Ben's mind was that of his former 93rd comrade and predecessor on the Epting crew, gunner Ed Bates, who had returned home in February after the partial amputation of several fingers necessitated by severe frostbite.

The first two days of November passed without a mission, extending to nineteen days the 93rd's stretch without a completed mission. Finally, on the afternoon of November 2, Ben learned a mission was scheduled for the following day, and the Moran crew was on the list.

The November 3 raid marked a historic milestone in the Eighth Air Force bombing campaign. Strengthened by a surge of bombers and crews, Eaker massed 566 Flying Fortresses and Liberators to attack the port of Wilhelmshaven. It was the largest force the Eighth Air Force had yet assembled for a single raid, and, in another first, the bombers were escorted to the target and back by P-38 Lightning fighters—"Little Friends," as they would become known. Most noteworthy of all, the raid was carried out despite the target being covered with clouds. The planes were guided by specially trained Pathfinder crews equipped with radar and radio devices that facilitated navigation and bombing in overcast conditions.[1]

Leading the 93rd contingent of thirty crews into Germany today was twenty-five-year-old Russell DeMont, a well-muscled six-footer with a square jaw, a shock of wavy brown hair, and cinema-star looks. DeMont had been unfazed by combat, but that wasn't the case with two of the officers on his crew when he arrived in England a few months earlier. He had picked up a new bombardier just before the second Wiener Neustadt raid on October 1.

His original bombardier had performed superbly in practice missions back in the States, "but when we got overseas and got into flak and fighters he was so scared that he couldn't see anything," DeMont said.[2] The same was true of his original copilot, who was terrified in combat. As they neared their target, the copilot would lay one flak jacket on the floor beneath his seat and sit on another flak jacket, with his feet scrunched on top of the seat, "so that nothing could hit him from below," DeMont said. "He just wasn't worth anything over the target." Both men had been sent off to one of the "flak farms" and hadn't come back.

Now, flying with his new copilot and bombardier, DeMont was attempting to lead his 93rd comrades to Wilhelmshaven to bomb German naval facilities along the granite-walled harbor. Encountering cloud cover over the target, the specially trained Pathfinder crews dropped marker flares to signal the other bombers when to release their ordnance.

Most of the bombs fell on the city proper rather than the port area, but the ability of the 482nd Bomb Group Pathfinders to get the B-17s and B-24s over the target in such sloppy weather stunned the Germans and offered the promise that American bombers would no longer be immobilized by weather. "From this day forward, American strategic bombing was radically transformed," observed historian Donald L. Miller.[3]

Bombing through the clouds didn't do much for accuracy, but it did have one benefit: It kept enemy fighters at a distance, and that reduced American losses on the November 3 mission. The other Eighth Air Force groups lost seven bombers on the raid. Russell DeMont got the 93rd crews to the target and back to Hardwick without a single casualty or lost aircraft.[4]

The raid on Wilhelmshaven was a momentous event not only for the Eighth Air Force, but also for Ben. After two frustrating months, Ben was one mission away from becoming one of an elite cadre of American airmen to complete thirty combat missions against Nazi Germany.

BEN NEVER SPOKE IN ANY OF HIS INTERVIEWS or oral histories about his emotions as he awaited his thirtieth mission, but it's reasonable to assume he was anxious. In any event, he didn't have long to wait. The day following the Wilhelmshaven raid the 93rd received a mission alert, and once again Homer Moran and his men were on the list of assigned crews.

The Eighth Air Force had planned a pair of coordinated strikes on targets in western Germany for mission number 121. This would be another five-hundred-plane raid, with B-17s bombing the railroad marshaling yard and oil plants at Gelsenkirchen, Germany, and B-24s hitting the rail marshaling yard at Münster, about forty miles to the northeast. Münster lay only about 270 miles east of Hardwick, near Germany's frontier with Holland, so it would be the shortest mission Ben had flown during his year in combat, with a planned flight time under five hours. It would also be Ben's closest brush with death.

Leading the 93rd's twenty-seven-plane contingent for the mission was Ben's squadron commander and Ploiesti pilot, K. O. Dessert. Three 93rd men were flying their final mission: Ben, flying with Homer Moran in *Queenie*, and two 330th Squadron gunners, each of whom was flying his twenty-fifth mission.

Dessert and his 93rd bombers got airborne and proceeded to the rendezvous point to meet the other Liberator groups and their escorts. The five-hundred-plane force would have a roundtrip escort provided by Eighth Air Force P-38 Lightnings and P-47 Thunderbolts. A ninety-minute flight brought the B-24s to the Münster area for the final run to the target. Flying through accurate antiaircraft fire of moderate intensity at around twenty thousand feet, *Queenie* and the other 93rd ships released their bombs directly over the heart of the old medieval cathedral city.

About ten feet behind Moran, Ben was blasting away at attacking German fighters with his top turret guns in the moments after the release of the B-24's bombs when an antiaircraft shell exploded just above him. The last thing that Ben remembered was a loud impact: *BAM*. A chunk of jagged metal smashed into the turret and shattered the Plexiglas dome around Ben's head.

The force of the explosion ripped Ben's oxygen mask from his face and knocked him unconscious. The onset of fulminant hypoxia is rapid with a sudden loss of oxygen at twenty thousand feet and Ben's organs began to falter. His heart rate slowed and his skin began to turn blue. Death was imminent.[5]

IN THE COCKPIT OF *QUEENIE*, HOMER MORAN had his hands full. He would later recall the flak he encountered over Münster as the worst he ever experienced. He also had to contend with head-on fighter attacks, a nerve-racking experience. "It seemed like the fighters were coming right at you," he said. "You could see the cannon fire off the wings."[6]

As he tried to outrun the enemy threats, Moran suddenly sensed that something wasn't right. He asked one of the men to check on Ben.[7] Radio operator Robert L. McConnell, a twenty-five-year-old truck driver from Johnstown, Pennsylvania, found Ben unconscious in his turret. Whether he was dead or alive wasn't clear.

McConnell began dragging his unresponsive comrade to the radio workspace. Ben suddenly regained consciousness and began thrashing "like a wild drowning man."[8] Ben was definitely alive, but he was in and out of consciousness. McConnell laid Ben near the radio table, fitted him with an oxygen mask, and covered him with blankets. Moran descended slightly, making sure to remain within the protective field of fire of his comrades.

Revived by the oxygen, Ben stirred. He saw he was lying on his back in the radio room with his friend Bob McConnell anxiously hovering over him. Although buried in blankets, Ben shivered. He felt fuzzy-headed and everything around him seemed out of focus.[9]

"Don't worry, you'll be all right," the relieved radio operator assured him.

For much of the return flight, Ben remained in a fog. His head and his vision cleared gradually. After not finding any wounds on Ben's head and body, McConnell joked that he could work on him with his radio tools and make sure he got a Purple Heart.

Moran and his men had been airborne only four-and-a-half hours when they landed at Hardwick. As Moran eased *Queenie* to a stop, medics were waiting to load Ben into an ambulance and whisk him to the base infirmary for a thorough examination.

Ben's luck had held yet again. Not so for many of his comrades. Eleven bombers were lost in the coordinated raids on Münster and Gelsenkirchen. The tally of casualties listed 11 airmen killed in action, 57 wounded, and 119 missing.

By evening, Ben was feeling fit enough to join a celebration organized by Moran. They pedaled to a nearby pub on their bicycles and proceeded to drink, sing, laugh, and toast Ben's triumph. Ben had participated in similar celebrations before, but never as the guest of honor.

His mind flashed back to all the adventures and ordeals of the past year— his first terrifying experience with flak; the horror of watching comrades plunge to their deaths; the months at Gambut Main and the desert camp outside Benghazi; the history-making raids on Rome and Wilhelmshaven; the heartbreak of Ploiesti; the good men who had made the ultimate sacrifice along the way. He thought of his closest friends from the past year—the men of the Epting crew—and wished they were here to share this night with him. "In the midst of everything," wrote Ben's wartime biographer, "he suddenly felt alone."[10]

IN THE AFTERMATH OF THE MÜNSTER RAID, Ben was once again interviewed and written up by combat correspondents. A number of US newspapers ran a photograph of a smiling Ben holding his shattered turret dome. He seemed nonchalant about his latest brush with death, but his big smile for the camera concealed his physical and mental exhaustion. He had logged 265.5 hours of flight in thirty combat missions over the past eleven months, and he was drained. "I wanted to come home," Ben later recalled. "That was enough."[11]

Ben's separation from the Eighth Air Force took the rest of November, and he was present for some of the grimmest days the 93rd would experience during that bleak autumn. In a raid into Germany only eight days after Ben completed his tour, the 93rd lost five Liberators to enemy fire and had forty-three men killed. Seven were taken prisoner.

As the gray month wore on, Ben was poked and prodded by doctors, analyzed by mental health experts, and debriefed by intelligence officers. He drank and danced and wept with his brothers-in-arms who were still trying to complete their own combat tours. He visited his favorite haunts in Norwich and London, then he bade farewell to his comrades.

In late November, Ben and about a dozen other Eighth Air Force men who had recently completed their combat tours received orders to report to an English port—in all likelihood, Liverpool—for their passage home. Arriving by train, they boarded a New York City–bound troop ship whose passengers included shattered American airmen suffering from combat-related neuroses. Steaming away from the River Mersey docks on December 1, 1943, out into the Irish Sea, Ben set off for America.[12]

Chapter 35

HOMECOMING

Ben's assignment to the Epting crew and departure for combat duty in North Africa had coincided with the first anniversary of the attack on Pearl Harbor. Now he was returning home a celebrated war hero in the shadow of another Pearl Harbor anniversary.

For Ben, Pearl Harbor had unleashed a strong sense of mission. For many other Americans, the attack had triggered dark feelings of fear and loathing directed toward people of Japanese ancestry, at home and abroad. Ben had only a vague understanding of the impact the attack had had on Japanese immigrants and their American-born children back home. They had borne the brunt of the Pearl Harbor backlash. Occasionally, he'd read a newspaper story about some hateful comment from a politician back home that caused his blood to boil. But it was impossible for Ben, and most other Americans, to comprehend the injustice inflicted on more than 110,000 people of Japanese ancestry on the West Coast. In the months ahead, Ben would find himself in the middle of the controversy over what some politicians on the home front euphemistically called "the Japanese question."

But those searing events still lay in Ben's future. For now, he was excited to be coming home. He was confident his new status as a decorated combat veteran—indeed, the first Japanese American war hero—would shield him from the bigotry and prejudice that he had experienced in the army before his overseas deployment.

Throughout his return journey across the Atlantic, Ben was constantly reminded of the war's human toll, even among those fortunate enough to have survived their time in combat. Ben and the small contingent of Eighth Air Force airmen who had completed combat tours with bodies and minds in relatively good shape represented a minority aboard the transport. Most of the passengers had suffered emotional and psychological trauma and had been classified as "psychoneurotics," in the preferred terminology of the time.[1]

On December 7, after a six-day passage, the vague outline of Long

Island and the Jersey Shore took shape on the horizon. Then the Manhattan skyline came into view. Ben's transport steamed past Sandy Hook and threaded its way through the Verrazano Narrows before emerging into the Upper Bay at the mouth of the Hudson River. Ahead loomed a breathtaking sight: the majestic Lady Liberty, torch in hand, bathed in glorious sunlight.

The combat veterans—men forever scarred by war—stood at the rails in silent awe. Tears of joy and relief streaked the cheeks of some. One of the trauma cases sat on the deck sobbing. Ben was among the misty-eyed men at the rail, soaking it all up. Years later, in the twilight of his life, Ben would distill his unforgettable homecoming from Europe to a single understated sentence: "It was a beautiful sight when I saw the Statue of Liberty, I'm telling you."[2]

IN NEW YORK CITY, BEN BOARDED A cross-country train and settled in for a fourteen-hundred-mile journey through the American heartland. After a stop in Chicago, he continued on to Omaha. He could have remained on the train all the way to North Platte, but he had some business to attend to in Lincoln, so he got off the train and made a fifty-mile detour. Ben made his way to the State Capitol and, without an appointment, walked into the governor's office. He explained to aides that he wanted to thank the governor for comments he had made a few months back.

The incident that had moved Ben to delay his homecoming occurred the previous June at the thirty-fifth National Governors' Conference in Columbus, Ohio. US victories in the Pacific in the first months of 1943 had prompted discussions about whether the Roosevelt administration should consider releasing Japanese and Japanese Americans who had been forcibly evicted from their West Coast homes in the months following Pearl Harbor.

California had been ground zero for the wave of angry anti-Japanese sentiment that swept across America, and the backlash had spurred President Franklin Roosevelt to issue Executive Order 9066 on February 19, 1942. The order allowed the military to deem people of Japanese ancestry a national security threat. They were removed from an "exclusion zone" that included all of California and parts of Washington, Oregon and Arizona, and confined to interior camps ringed by barbed wire and armed guards. About two-thirds of them were US citizens born in this country.

One of the most outspoken advocates for the expulsion of people of Japanese ancestry from the West Coast had been California's current Republican governor, Earl Warren. As the state's attorney general, Warren had claimed that the presence of these people in California was "the Achilles' heel of the entire civilian defense effort." In Warren's view, the Japanese Californians were engaged in a "studied effort" at sabotage that had gone undetected because of "their method of living." Warren's support of the expulsion and confinement of California's Japanese and Japanese American residents had been on full display in his 1942 campaign for governor, which he won in a landslide, with 57 percent of the votes cast.

Six months after his inauguration, when proposals to release people of Japanese ancestry from the camps gathered support in the late spring of 1943, Earl Warren had used the power of his office and his influence in national Republican circles to broadly paint people of Japanese ancestry as security threats. At the National Governors Conference that June, Warren fulminated against allowing California's exiled Japanese residents to return to their homes. "If the Japs are released, no one will be able to tell a saboteur from any other Jap," Warren declared. He added, "We don't want to have a second Pearl Harbor in California. We don't propose to have the Japs back in California during this war if there is any lawful means of preventing it."[3]

Nebraska governor Dwight Griswold, also a Republican, pushed back against Warren's diatribe. "Thousands of Japanese have been released with the approval of the FBI without one particle of trouble," Griswold declared.[4]

Griswold's public comments impressed Ben. There weren't many voters of Japanese descent in Nebraska, so Griswold had little to gain politically by picking a fight with the powerful governor of California. It seemed to Ben that Governor Griswold had taken a principled stand because it was the right thing to do, and he wanted to personally thank him.

After introducing himself and explaining why he was there, Ben soon found himself in conversation with the governor and one of his top aides. After a warm and cordial meeting, Ben resumed his journey home.[5]

Later that day, Thursday, December 16, 1943, Ben was reunited with his parents and siblings on the family farm outside of Hershey.

BEN RECEIVED A HERO'S WELCOME IN Hershey and North Platte. On his first full day home, he visited Hershey High School, where "he gave a very interesting talk before the high school students Friday and was enthusiastically received by the students," the North Platte *Tribune* reported.[6]

Hershey was a place of mixed memories for Ben. He hadn't enjoyed farm work and didn't miss it. He missed hunting with his friend Gordy Jorgenson along the North Platte River and hanging out with his friends at Hershey High School, but not the hard life he and his family had known. His father was now seventy-one and his mother was sixty-seven. Their lives had been marked by stress, struggle, and hard physical labor, and they showed their age.

Ben's oldest brother, George, had assumed day-to-day responsibilities on the farm. Only one other sibling remained in Hershey: Ben's youngest sister, seventeen-year-old Rose, was a senior at Hershey High School. The other girls—Fuji, Cecile, Wilma, and Beatrice—had migrated to Chicago and were now married.

Making the rounds of his old haunts in Hershey and North Platte, Ben basked in the adulation of the news coverage that had preceded his homecoming. During his brief stopover in Omaha, he had seen his picture in the window of Brandeis, the city's largest department store, as part of a display honoring "NEBRASKA'S HEROES." The Hershey drugstore owner asked Ben if they could borrow his war medals for a public exhibition.[7]

One morning after his arrival, Ben was awakened by a visitor. He was a prominent local rancher and justice of the peace, Blaine Runner, a tall, rugged man with blue eyes and a towering local legend who'd earned a Carnegie Medal for heroism in his early twenties when he rode his horse into a prairie fire to save two local girls from the wind-whipped flames. Runner presented Ben with a bottle of twenty-year-old bourbon, one Hershey hero to another.[8]

Ben had hoped to see his best friend from high school, but Uncle Sam had Gordy Jorgenson in his grip. Gordy had married one of their Hershey High classmates in 1941 and she had given birth to a baby boy in April 1942. Gordy had tried to enlist in the navy later that year, but failed the physical exam because of a heart defect. The army was happy to have him, and Gordy was now training for a Pacific deployment. Ben visited Gordy's mother instead.

One of headiest experiences for Ben during his time at home was the media interest in interviewing him. From his earliest attempts to enlist in the armed forces after Pearl Harbor, Ben's tale of seeking combat to demonstrate his loyalty had proven to be an irresistible story to journalists. Stories and photographs of Ben had sporadically appeared in Nebraska newspapers after his enlistment. He had been the subject of a few newspaper items after his December 1942 assignment to a combat crew, and he had briefly enjoyed a national spotlight when he was interviewed in London by movie star Ben Lyon for his national radio show in the US.

After spending much of the summer and fall in the military backwaters of North Africa, Ben had reverted to his lowly status as just another faceless Nebraska farm boy. Then, in early October 1943, shortly after Ben's return to England from this third and final North Africa deployment, a twenty-seven-year-old correspondent in the London bureau of the United Press news agency got wind of his story. The correspondent's name was Walter Cronkite.

The B-17 Flying Fortress bases were much more convenient for London-based correspondents looking to make reporting day trips into the English countryside, but Cronkite made the trek out to Hardwick to interview Ben. His angle was the story of a humble Japanese American B-24 gunner finishing twenty-five missions and then asking to keep flying. Cronkite had not only found the only Japanese American aerial gunner in the Eighth Air Force, he had found a gunner who couldn't get enough of aerial combat.

Six days after Ben completed his thirtieth mission on November 5, Cronkite's profile of him appeared in one of Nebraska's state capital newspapers, the *Lincoln Journal Star*. The story hailed Ben as "one of the fightingest men in Uncle Sam's air force." Cronkite described how Ben had ended up flying five extra missions and offered further insight into why he was willing to keep risking his life. "My debt to the United States is greater than that of most of these other fellows," Ben explained to Cronkite. "My debt is greater—and my obligations larger. That's why I wanted another tour of duty."[9]

WALTER CRONKITE'S STORY HAD uncovered an interesting twist in Ben's story. This son of Japanese immigrants wasn't content to fight only Hitler and Mussolini. He wanted to fight his blood kin in Japan. From a journalistic viewpoint, a good story got even better: Japanese American boy wants to bomb Tokyo to prove his patriotism.

Ben had told Cronkite that he had already raised the idea of a Pacific deployment with the army, and had gotten a cool reception. "The army tells me that the danger would be too great if I were captured, but if they won't let me fly I'd like to go to officers' training school and perhaps get into the intelligence section," Ben said.[10]

Cronkite's story had clearly piqued the curiosity of his London-based competitors, and they picked up on the latest twist about Ben's close call on the last of his five extra missions. The photograph of Ben holding his shattered turret circulated among the American correspondents in London, and more items followed. In November, the Associated Press news service distributed a photograph of Ben in his leather flying suit alongside *Tupelo Lass*. "Sgt. Ben Kuroki of Hershey, Neb., is the only Japanese American flying in the European theater—and he's plenty good," the photo cutline declared. Building on Cronkite's story, the AP photo cutline added this nugget of news: "He's returning to the States for further training before going to fight the Japs in the Pacific."[11]

The *North Platte Telegraph* ran a December 3 article about Ben's close call over Münster, based on the shattered turret photo, which the paper said had been shared with it. (The paper didn't say how it got the photo, and it didn't publish the image.) On December 11, AP circulated still another photo of Ben, this one showing him as he bade farewell to four ground crewmen in England "before leaving for the United States." The photo cutline noted Ben would "return for training which will enable him to fight the Japs in the Pacific."[12]

By the time that Ben arrived in Hershey, he was a big story in Nebraska. The state's most powerful radio station, Omaha's WOW, sent a reporter to interview him. A United Press reporter rewrote a *North Platte Daily Bulletin* story about Ben that repeated the narrative about him going to fight in the Pacific. "Ben Kuroki, after a lot of practice, is on his way west to help his native country blast apart the native country of his ancestors," the UP article began. The article quoted Ben: "I didn't join the army with the intention of fighting in Europe. I joined to avenge Pearl Harbor."[13]

While the army had balked at Ben's request to fly combat missions in the Pacific, Ben persisted. No longer the quiet hayseed from Nebraska pleading for a chance to fight, he was mobilizing public opinion to pressure the army to send him to the Pacific.

JUST BEFORE CHRISTMAS, BEN WAS among twenty local boys at home on military furloughs who were feted by North Platte businessmen at the local country club. During the ceremonies, Ben and the other young men made brief remarks about their military experiences. Ben covered the highlights of his combat tour before pivoting to a subject that was increasingly on his mind: the treatment of Japanese and Japanese American people in wartime America. Ben "thanked the people of North Platte for their tolerance and kindness toward American-born Japanese," according to a short item in the Omaha *Morning World-Herald*.[14]

Ben had received orders to report to an Army Air Forces reassignment center in Santa Monica, California, by January 5. In his final days at home, he was a guest of honor at a dance sponsored by Japanese American youth in the North Platte area. The festive affair was a high note as Ben prepared to return to duty.[15]

On January 3, 1944, Ben said goodbye once again to his parents and boarded a train for Los Angeles. When the train stopped in Denver late that evening, reporters were waiting at the station to snag an interview with the Japanese American war hero.

Reporters for the Associated Press, United Press, and International News Service agencies all filed stories with the same theme. "An American-born Japanese who participated in European bombings as a turret gunner on a Liberator said today he hopes his new assignment in San Diego eventually will include duty in the Pacific so he can fight the Japanese 'face-to-face,'" the Associated Press dispatch began. The INS dispatch included a quote from Ben that offered a fuller explanation of his quest for a Pacific deployment. "I want to fight the Japanese face-to-face," Ben said. "I am a good American and I want to help avenge Pearl Harbor."[16]

Notably, none of the reporters who interviewed Ben in Denver mentioned another dramatic and historic twist in his saga: More than twenty months after President Franklin Roosevelt had set in motion the mass expulsion of people of Japanese descent from the West Coast, a Nebraska farm boy was about to become one of the first Japanese Americans—if not the first—to effectively contest the policy.

Chapter 36

MOST HONORABLE SON

Arriving in Los Angeles late on January 4, 1944, Ben made his way to the Edgewater Beach Hotel in Santa Monica. Overlooking the Pacific Ocean, the eight-story hotel was one of six beachfront properties recently acquired by the army to create a complex designated Army Air Forces Redistribution Center Number Three. The Santa Monica facility was one of three such centers in the nation, serving as a combination of "flak farm" and processing center. On his return from a combat tour, an air force veteran would spend several weeks at one of the centers, undergoing physical and psychological assessments that would determine his next assignment.

At the Santa Monica center, an airman could pass time between assessments in any number of ways. He could swim, surf, or stroll along the beach. Women's Army Air Corps personnel staffed the Edgewater and the other hotels housing airmen. They had transformed the Edgewater's fourth floor into a crafts center where men could take classes in leathercraft, watercolors, floral design, charcoal and pencil drawings, or stencil and textile painting. The Santa Monica–Ocean Park Chapter of the American Red Cross organized dances and other social events to occupy the evenings of airmen.[1]

Ben was delighted to discover that his Edgewater roommate was Ed Bates, who had preceded him on the Epting crew. As Ben had learned, Bates had been plagued by bad luck in combat. On the 93rd's first mission—the October 9, 1942, raid on a locomotive factory in Lille, France—he had suffered severe frostbite in his fingers and landed in the hospital for several weeks. His medical leave set in motion the shuffling on the Epting crew that ultimately opened a spot for Ben in early December 1942.

While most 93rd crews were at Gambut Main on the group's first temporary assignment to North Africa, Bates had rejoined the squadron that had remained in England and was flying missions out of Hardwick. On a February 1943 raid into Germany, he suffered an even more severe case of frostbite. To halt the potentially lethal spread of gangrene, doctors amputated parts of several fingers. Bates was shipped back to the US for further treatment and rehabilitation. Only recently had he been declared fit for limited duty and ordered to Santa Monica to await a noncombat assignment.

Ben and Ed had never overlapped on the Epting crew, so they didn't know each other well. But they soon discovered they had much in common. They came from large families. They had Nebraska roots. And they had endured poverty and hardships growing up. Ed's father had been a struggling farmer in Nebraska in the 1920s when he moved his wife and growing family to the Pacific Northwest for a fresh start. The family settled in Walla Walla, Washington, just north of the Oregon border. In Walla Walla, Ed's father struggled to support the family with various odd jobs, including working as a caretaker at a local college.

As the oldest son in a family with eleven children, Ed dropped out of high school after two years to help support his siblings. In the fall of 1941, he enlisted in the army and began his Army Air Forces training. Blond-haired and blue-eyed, Ed carried a solid 160 pounds on his five-foot-ten-inch frame. Among his peers, he cultivated a reputation as a hard-drinking hell-raiser who wouldn't hesitate to settle disputes with his fists. But it would be hard to find a more loyal friend than Ed Bates.

Ed had arrived at Santa Monica not only with the physical and psychological trauma of his own injuries but also the weight of a crushing family tragedy. His closest brother in age, Stanley, younger by two years, had enlisted in the army on October 9, 1942—the same day that Ed saw his first action in Europe and suffered his first case of frostbite.

Stanley had been assigned to the 37th Infantry Division's 148th Infantry Regiment, which originally had been designated for duty in Europe before being rushed to the Pacific to help stem the initial Japanese advance. In July 1943, Stanley entered combat with the 148th in the battle for a Japanese airfield at Munda Point, New Georgia, in the Solomon Islands.

Ed was back in the US undergoing medical treatment on his mangled fingers when word arrived that Stanley had been killed in action on July 31. The family would eventually learn that Stanley died in the climactic fight for the Munda airfield. He had been wounded in the shoulder, but refused to leave the line of battle and continued fighting until he was killed. Only days before departing for Santa Monica, Ed had learned that his brother was being posthumously awarded the Distinguished Service Cross, the army's second-highest valor award.

In long walks along the Santa Monica beach and over meals and drinking sessions, Ben and Ed reminisced about their lives before the war, their time with the 93rd, and what lay ahead for them. It had been nearly two years since Californians of Japanese ancestry had been forced into confinement camps, and so Ben's presence shocked many people they encountered. Sometimes passersby did a double take or whispered something to their companion.[2]

These encounters mortified Ben. He had hated those hostile or questioning looks early in his army service, and now he had to relive these encounters nearly every day. Ed sensed that Ben's heritage and humble origins had left him with an inferiority complex. He made it his mission to remind Ben that he was a worthy American and comrade. When they went out at night, Ed made sure that everyone around them knew that Ben had flown thirty combat missions in Europe and Africa and now wanted to fight in the Pacific."[3]

For Ben's part, the death of Ed's brother became one more reason he had to fight the Japanese. Ed's injuries prevented him from avenging his brother's death, but Ben could do it for him. Ben vowed that the first Japanese Zero he shot down would be for Stanley Bates.[4]

TWO WEEKS INTO HIS STAY AT THE Edgewater, Ben was still awaiting word about his next assignment when he sat down for an interview with a local reporter for the United Press news agency. The resulting story moved across the UP wire with a Los Angeles dateline. The story flatly declared that Ben "would next be in action in the Pacific against the Japs." A slightly rewritten version described Ben as "headed for a crack at the Japs."

For the most part, the latest article rehashed Walter Cronkite's story, but there was one new revelation: Ben's 93rd crewmates had nicknamed him "Most Honorable Son."[5] Also previously unreported were descriptions of the ostracism and distrust that Ben had faced in the army. Recalling his difficult early days in the Army Air Forces, Ben told the reporter, "I'd go into the mess hall and everybody would just stare at me. It just about drove me crazy." Even after he got overseas with the 93rd Bomb Group, Ben said he struggled "to be accepted as a loyal American." In England, he had completed gunnery training and was seeking a combat assignment, but "pilot after pilot refused to accept him as a crew member," the article reported. "Finally Maj. J.B. Epting Jr. took him on."

These revelations didn't reflect well on the army or the 93rd Bomb Group. Given the military's efforts to avoid negative publicity during the war, one can imagine army public relations officers blanching at Ben's willingness to air their dirty laundry.

The latest article was also accompanied by a photograph of Ben in his leather flight suit. A number of newspapers around the country ran the photograph without the article. One of the most popular captions above the published photograph was "Most Honorable Son." Other captions used by newspapers included "Fighter" and "Amerjap Hero."[6]

Ben's candor in this latest interview suggested a growing confidence on his part to share even the more unpleasant aspects of his story. It also seemed to reflect his growing awareness of the leverage he had as a Japanese American war hero, and how he might use that leverage to pry the assignment he wanted from the army.

THE LATEST STORY ABOUT BEN AND THE fact that he was now in Santa Monica awaiting his next assignment attracted the attention of other California journalists as well as leading citizens and civic groups. Ben received more interview requests and even speaking invitations. The prestigious Commonwealth Club of San Francisco—a national platform coveted by politicians, business leaders, and other prominent figures—reached out to Ben about speaking to the group's elite membership, and a date was booked for early February.

Singer and film star Ginny Simms, host of a national radio show originating from the NBC Radio City studios in Hollywood, invited Ben to appear for a live interview on Tuesday, January 25. Simms concluded her interviews with service members by allowing the individual to place a live long-distance call to a person of their choosing. Ben chose his best friend from the Epting crew, radio operator Red Kettering, now based at Scott Field in Belleville, Illinois. A thrilled Ben alerted family and friends of his upcoming appearance, but two hours before the appointed hour an army public relations officer informed him the interview had been canceled. NBC executives feared the "Japanese American question" was too controversial in California. The *Los Angeles Times* reported that the order canceling the interview was issued by the head of the War Department's radio branch, Colonel Ed Kirby.[7]

The clumsy cancellation of Ben's interview generated news coverage that embarrassed the War Department and NBC. Newspapers across the country ran stories about the flap under headlines like "American-Jap Gunner Yanked off Radio" and "War Department Bans US Japanese Hero from Hollywood Radio." But there was more to the War Department's sudden decision to muzzle Ben, and the details would ignite a new wave of anti-Japanese outrage.

IN THE TWENTY MONTHS SINCE US AND Filipino forces had surrendered in the Philippines, several news organizations had pieced together accounts of what would become known as the Bataan Death March and other atrocities committed by Japanese forces. But the War and Navy departments had barred publication of the stories, fearing the accounts would provoke even worse treatment of American and Filipino POWs.

On Thursday night, January 27, as coverage of Ben's canceled interview continued to appear in newspapers around the country, senior officials at the War and Navy departments in Washington, DC, notified news organizations that the ban on atrocity stories had been lifted. The following morning, Friday, January 28, Americans awoke to front-page newspaper stories describing in chilling detail the Japanese atrocities committed against American and Filipino troops after their April 1942 surrender at Bataan in the Philippines.

In California, major newspapers devoted extensive coverage to the topic. There were two full pages of coverage in the *Los Angeles Times* and four pages in the virulently anti-Japanese *San Francisco Examiner*, flagship of the proudly nativist Hearst newspaper chain. The graphic coverage continued on Saturday, January 29, with the *Los Angeles Times* devoting another three pages to atrocity stories and the *San Francisco Examiner* five pages to the atrocities and angry American reactions. Among the reaction pieces were calls for continued "control" of Japanese and Japanese Americans in the US and a firm wartime ban on the return of thousands of incarcerated Californians of Japanese ancestry to their homes.

As AMERICAN NEWSPAPERS AND NATIVIST politicians remained focused on the Japanese atrocity stories, Ben agreed to an interview with a reporter from the *Hollywood Citizen-News*. In the published piece, Ben sounded alternately frustrated and hopeful that a majority of Americans rejected the bigotry that made NBC executives and the War Department fear giving a high-profile platform to a Japanese American.

Ben acknowledged that the incident made him wonder whether American attitudes toward its citizens of Japanese descent had changed in the two years since he had been forced to plead for acceptance by the Army Air Forces and then fight for a combat assignment.

"It's the same old story," Ben said. "My brother and I had to fight to enlist. Then I had to fight to get a chance to fight. And now—again."[8]

Ben's mood brightened as he talked about his positive encounters with fellow airmen in California and, more recently, even civilians.

"The soldiers have been swell," he said. "I'm one of them."

Expressions of goodwill from strangers had lifted his spirits. People recognized him from newspaper photos and offered congratulations or wished him well. Others invited him to their homes. The anti-Japanese bigots were only a small minority, Ben told the reporter.

"How can I feel bitter when nearly every day people here who recognize me from pictures which have been published stop me on the street, congratulate me, and say nice, encouraging things to me?" Ben said. "I get all sorts of letters from residents here, and many of them invite me to their homes. This proves that only a small portion of the people here are lined up against me."[9]

It was a hopeful note, but Ben was shocked by the hateful reaction to the atrocity stories published in the past week. He was reconsidering the wisdom of traveling to San Francisco to deliver his speech before the Commonwealth Club in the coming week.

Would his speech be misconstrued by conservative forces as an intentionally provocative act? After all, San Francisco was the hometown of William Randolph Hearst, publisher of the fiercely anti-Japanese *San Francisco Examiner* and architect of a thirty-year campaign to purge America of people like Sam and Naka Kuroki and their children. How would Hearst and other like-minded Californians react to a Japanese American being given the Commonwealth Club microphone, especially in the midst of the atrocity revelations?

Ben hadn't felt such despair since his first weeks in the Army in early 1942. In some ways, this latest turn of events felt even worse. Now, for the first time in his life, Ben felt fear because of the color of his skin and his ancestral origins. "I felt it wasn't safe to walk the streets of my own country," he said.[10]

Chapter 37

RESIST THE DRAFT

Many people of Japanese descent living in America in World War II felt that fear long before Ben's epiphany. Among them were Yoshito Kuromiya, his parents, and three siblings—all living behind the barbed wire and armed guards of the Heart Mountain Relocation Center in the high desert of Wyoming in late January 1944.

On that first Sunday in December 1941, eighteen-year-old Yosh, as he preferred, was shopping for a used car with his older brother in Pasadena, California. They were on their fourth or fifth lot when a red-faced man burst from his office, screaming and shaking his fist in their direction. "We don't sell to sneaky Japs!" the car salesman bellowed at the brothers. Not until Yosh and his brother retreated to their car and turned on the radio did they learn about the attack on Pearl Harbor.[1]

Yosh was only six months out of Monrovia High School in northern Los Angeles County at the time. Living in the heart of the country's largest concentration of people of Japanese descent, he was studying art at Pasadena Junior College. Carefree and handsome, with a well-oiled pompadour and eyes that sparkled beneath his wire-frame glasses, Yosh felt no guilt or shame about Pearl Harbor.

Even as the anti-Japanese backlash built in America in the weeks following the attack, and family and friends fretted about where it was all headed, Yosh remained unconcerned. He brushed off the backlash as a "hysterical overreaction" that would quickly pass, and dismissed the talk about a roundup of Japanese Americans. "What's the big fuss about my being of Japanese heritage?" he would muse. "We didn't bomb Pearl Harbor. We're Americans."[2]

Years later, Yosh would ruefully acknowledge his misplaced innocence. "I was so naïve," he said.[3]

AT THE TIME OF THE FEDERAL CENSUS taken in the spring of 1930, Los Angeles County was home to about thirty-five thousand people of Japanese ancestry—about one-third of the people of Japanese descent living in America at the time. Hisamitsu and Hana Kuromiya were among the thousands of Japanese immigrants who had settled there to work and raise their families. The couple had married on January 13, 1916, in their native Okayama prefecture on Japan's main Honshu Island, and eight days later boarded a ship for America.[4] Seattle was their port of arrival, but Hisamitsu and Hana soon made their way to Southern California. Hisamitsu found work as a gardener and the couple started a family. Yosh was their third son and fifth child, including one stillborn baby.

The Kuromiya family sunk roots in northern Los Angeles County, living in rented houses in the towns of Sierra Madre and Monrovia, at the base of the San Gabriel Mountains. In an effort to assimilate, Hisamitsu became James Kuromiya. The children attended public schools with white children and the boys played basketball and other sports. Yosh and his older brother Hiroshi spent their 1929 summer vacation with family in Japan, returning home to Monrovia just in time to experience the economic catastrophe of the Great Depression.

Living frugally, the Kuromiya family weathered the Depression's hard times. Many Japanese immigrants and their children worked in farming, and by 1941 people of Japanese ancestry grew nearly 40 percent of California's truck crops. Others found employment in agricultural produce distribution, and ethnic Japanese businessmen came to dominate the Los Angeles fruit and vegetable supply network prior to the war.[5] Among them was James Kuromiya, who opened a produce stand.

Fishing, gardening, and clerical work in Little Tokyo communities in various West Coast cities also offered livelihood opportunities. The path to white-collar jobs proved much harder for Japanese Americans, despite their high education levels. By 1940, only 960 people of Japanese ancestry were employed as professionals in California.[6]

Despite their second-class status, Japanese immigrants and their children became the target of resentment in the American West during the Depression years because of their relative economic success. Political and military events in Asia—reported to the American public through the biased lens of an American press that tilted pro-China and anti-Japan—further fueled anti-Japanese attitudes. Japan had invaded Manchuria in 1931 and established the puppet state of Manchukuo. Six years later, Japan launched a full-scale and notably brutal war of conquest against China.

Tokyo's militarism exacerbated the anti-Japanese backlash in America, especially with a white majority on the West Coast that was already inclined to distrust and dislike Japanese people. Japan's expansionist actions and Hitler's European aggression prompted Congress to approve the first peacetime draft in US history, and on October 16, 1940, five days before his twenty-third birthday, Yosh's older brother Hiroshi was among the Americans who registered for the draft. Hiroshi had yet to be drafted by December 1941, but he was planning to be married. That's why he was shopping for a used car with his younger brother on the morning of December 7.

By February 1942, there were almost daily headlines in the *Los Angeles Times* reporting how some politician or group was demanding the expulsion of people of Japanese ancestry from the state. Yosh was stopped by police one night as he was driving home. Police issued a verbal warning for violating the curfew and travel restrictions on Japanese people, but let Yosh go.[7]

On Saturday morning, February 21, the Kuromiya family awoke to the news that President Franklin Roosevelt had signed Executive Order 9066. The army now held the once-unimaginable power to expel people of Japanese descent from California or any other state.

BEN HAD UNWITTINGLY WITNESSED THE first moments of a nationwide roundup of Japanese set in motion by the Pearl Harbor attack when he had watched two men in dark suits lead Mike Masaoka from the basement of the North Platte church. Masaoka would spend only one night in a North Platte jail cell before his political benefactor, Utah's Democratic US senator Elbert Thomas, got him released. "I was taken to the railroad station and put on a westbound train without so much as an apology," Masaoka later recalled.[8]

After being pulled from his train for questioning during a stop in Cheyenne, Wyoming, Masaoka reached San Francisco on December 11. He found the Japanese American Citizens League headquarters swamped with frantic appeals from the families of men who had been detained, and within days his own efforts to win their release attracted the renewed attention of the FBI. Masaoka and another national JACL leader, Saburo Kido, were hauled into the agency's San Francisco bureau for harsh interrogations periodically. While other activists and community leaders tried to secure the release of detainees, Masaoka turned his focus to reassuring Americans that Japanese immigrants and their US-born children could be trusted.[9]

As events would soon prove, Masaoka's campaign was a fool's errand.

In the aftermath of Roosevelt's executive order, General John L. DeWitt, the dour commander of the Western Defense Command, set in motion the mass removal of every person of Japanese descent in California and most in Oregon, Washington, and Arizona. The orders presented Masaoka with a tough choice. Should he urge Japanese Americans to resist the roundup? Or should he encourage them to cooperate in hope the Roosevelt administration would come to its senses? In a fateful decision, Masaoka and the JACL leadership supported the roundup.

FOR THE KUROMIYA FAMILY, THE unthinkable happened in May 1942. Carrying suitcases crammed with clothes and a few cherished possessions, they left their home at 201 West Huntington Drive in Monrovia and boarded army trucks. They were driven fourteen miles east to a holding camp on the Pomona Fairgrounds.

The Pomona Assembly Center was the innocuous name given to the makeshift facility. It was one of two Los Angeles County camps created to temporarily confine people of Japanese descent. The Pomona camp opened on May 7 and, during its four months of existence, housed as many as fifty-four hundred people—most of them forced from their homes in the urban California counties of Los Angeles, San Francisco, and Santa Clara.

In August 1942, most of the Pomona incarcerees were transported by train to a dusty, windswept camp in the remote Bighorn Basin of northwest Wyoming. It was called the Heart Mountain Relocation Center, another euphemistic name that sought to gloss over the staggering violation of civil and constitutional rights underway.

Located twelve miles north of the town of Cody and about twenty miles south of the Montana state line, the camp was named for a massive slab of limestone and dolomite that rose 8,123 feet above the basin floor, like a landlocked Rock of Gibraltar. In time, the camp would be surrounded by barbed wire and nine guard towers. For now, though, it sprawled across 740 acres of government land, eight miles east of its namesake. There were 468 wooden barracks, 39 mess halls and utility buildings, a 150-bed hospital, schools, recreation halls, and livestock pens.

Yosh would forever remember the misery of his first Heart Mountain winter. "As a native Californian, I was ill-equipped to deal with the biting winds, subzero temperatures, and knee-deep snows," he later wrote. "The snow did not fall gently in Heart Mountain. It came horizontally like icy spears across the barren plains to crash into the tar-papered barrack walls."[10]

Inside the drafty barracks, families lived crammed into small areas grandly called "apartments." Privacy was virtually nonexistent and the furnishings crude. Many residents cobbled together their own furniture from scrap lumber. Everyone slept on an army cot.[11]

There was no running water or cooking facilities in the barracks. Instead, residents were forced to walk, sometimes in subzero temperatures or choking dust storms, to separate utility buildings to perform personal hygiene routines and wash their clothes in communal facilities. Meals were also communal affairs served in mess halls.

Stripped of their homes and livelihoods, adults tried to ease the transition for their children. Heart Mountain High School opened in the fall of 1942 with an enrollment of fifteen hundred students. There was a band and school newspaper, sports competitions, dances, and other social events. Boy Scout and Girl Scout troops were formed, sports leagues organized, and drama, arts, and crafts activities offered. Japanese cultural activities took place, but without the support of camp administrators.

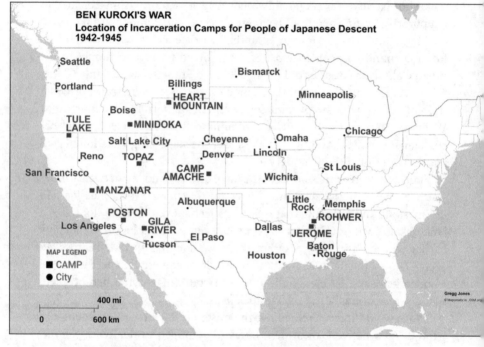

Location of incarceration camps for people of Japanese descent, 1942–1945

The worst part of life at Heart Mountain was the uncertainty. How long would this nightmare last? No one could say.

FROM THE BEGINNING, A NUMBER OF Heart Mountain incarcerees weren't content to meekly accept their fate. Their words and acts of resistance exposed young men like Yosh to the notion of confronting the US government. Communal living accelerated this process. Young people began to take their meals with friends rather than their families, and some began to challenge established views on politics, race, and patriotism.

In one of the first acts of violent resistance, a frustrated inmate working as a cook attacked a white worker with a kitchen knife on September 6. A few weeks later, outraged incarcerees banded together to protest the arrest of thirty-two children for sledding outside camp boundaries. More acts of resistance followed.

Amid the tensions, the army tried to recruit volunteers to build a barbed wire fence around the camp perimeter—ostensibly to keep stray cattle away. Working-age men refused to help. Three thousand people signed a petition declaring that the fence confirmed that Heart Mountain was a "concentration camp," and its inhabitants were "prisoners of war."

As the first anniversary of the Pearl Harbor attack approached, protesting inmates at Manzanar, in the California wilderness near Death Valley, attempted to take their frustrations out on leaders of the Japanese American Citizens League. The protesters besieged the camp police station. Security forces responded with gunfire, killing two inmates and wounding nine.[12]

The incarcerees had willingly accepted the initial orders to abandon their homes and livelihoods to gather in "assembly camps." They had boarded the trains that carried them to remote "relocation camps" like Heart Mountain. But their willingness to accept without protest their loss of constitutional and civil rights had begun to crumble as 1942 drew to a close.

Since the attack on Pearl Harbor, the War Department had engaged in a fierce internal debate over whether to accept Japanese Americans into military service. Ben had barely made it into the army while the deliberations were still underway. On January 5, 1942, the army discharged most Nisei soldiers or assigned them to menial duties. Later that month, the War Department reclassified draft-age Nisei as ineligible for military service. And on March 30 the War Department stopped inducting Japanese Americans into the armed forces altogether.

Privately, the Roosevelt administration continued to weigh the merits of allowing Nisei men to serve. Ever sensitive to political risk, Roosevelt delayed a decision until after the November 1942 midterm elections. With anger mounting, Army chief of staff General George C. Marshall approved an all-Nisei combat unit on the first day of 1943. Twenty-seven days later, Secretary of War Henry Stimson lifted the service ban on Japanese Americans and announced the formation of an all-volunteer Nisei combat unit, the 442nd Regimental Combat Team.[13]

The following week, the War Relocation Authority began requiring every camp resident seventeen years of age or older to complete a loyalty questionnaire. Question No. 27 asked if the person would be willing to serve in combat whenever and wherever ordered. No. 28 asked if the person would forswear any allegiance to the Emperor of Japan.

For many young men in the camps, the questionnaire provoked a crisis of conscience. Many were willing to serve, but only if they and their families were released and their rights restored. Others deeply resented that they were being asked to declare their loyalty to America when the same question wasn't being put to other Americans.

Despite the misgivings, more than 90 percent of camp residents answered yes to questions 27 and 28. In all, more than 65,000 draft-age Nisei men in the camps answered "yes" to both questions; 13,000 answered no to at least one question, and 6,733 answered no to both questions.[14]

In July 1943, under pressure from the army, members of Congress, and even some officials of the Japanese American Citizens League, the War Relocation Authority (WRA) acted to punish the men whose questionnaire answers had been deemed unacceptable. They would become known as the No-No Boys because of their responses to questions 27 and 28. Beginning in October, more than twelve thousand men, women, and children labeled as "disloyals" were transported to a newly created segregation center at the existing Tule Lake incarceration camp in Northern California. The camp had been transformed into a maximum-security prison, with an eight-foot-high double fence and a military police battalion equipped with armored cars and tanks.[15]

Overnight, the Tule Lake camp became a cauldron of resistance and dissent.

In early November, the tensions came to a head during a visit by WRA national director Dillon S. Myer. When five thousand inmates gathered outside the administration offices to show support for their demands, the camp director called in troops. The ensuing crackdown was christened the Tule Lake Riot in newspaper coverage. Martial law was declared in the camp and military police hunted down the leaders of the protests and imprisoned them in the camp stockade without charges or trial.

AS THE LOYALTY QUESTIONNAIRE THREATENED to plunge the Heart Mountain camp into turmoil in early 1943, Yosh Kuromiya immersed himself in his artistic pursuits. After initially working as a trash collector at the Pomona assembly center, Yosh found work in the sign shop. At Heart Mountain, he found a similar outlet for his art producing the camp's information posters.

Yosh's work introduced him to a community of Japanese and Japanese American artists and illustrators incarcerated in the Heart Mountain camp. They included painter and illustrator Benji Okubo, painter and muralist Hideo Date, Disney animator Rokuro (Bob) Kuwahara, painter Shingo Nishiura, and painter, lithographer, and photographer Riyo Sato.[16] Yosh began attending art classes taught by these talented professionals. He fell under the tutelage of Okubo, an accomplished oil and watercolor painter.

As Yosh honed his artistic skills, administrators pressed camp inmates to complete the loyalty questionnaires and volunteer for the army. Yosh had answered question Number 27 with a conditional yes, expressing willingness to serve in the US armed forces if his civil and constitutional rights were restored. His answer to question Number 28 was unambiguous: He disavowed any allegiance to a Japanese emperor he had never venerated in the first place.[17]

Meanwhile, camp militants became increasingly bold. A Nisei inmate named Frank Inouye established a group called the Heart Mountain Congress of American Citizens and forwarded a list of demands that included a restoration of civil rights and rejection of racially segregated army units as a prerequisite for enlistment.

Enthusiasm for the army recruiting efforts was minimal in the camps. The population of Heart Mountain had reached a peak of 10,700 people in January 1943, and WRA national director Dillon Myer had predicted that as many as 2,000 Nisei men in the camp would volunteer for military service. The actual number was 38.[18]

The yearlong army enlistment drive managed to attract only about 1,200 recruits from the ten camps in the continental United States—a number reduced to 805 after factoring in the results from physical exams and the loyalty questionnaire. At the same time the War Department was trying to find Nisei recruits willing to die for the country that had incarcerated them, 800 Nisei men in the Heart Mountain camp renounced their US citizenship.[19]

In August 1943, the all-Nisei 100th Battalion—an army outfit composed of Nisei men from Hawaii—quietly sailed for Europe and then on to North Africa. Within days of the September 3 invasion of the Italian mainland at Salerno, the 100th was taking casualties in combat. A growing sense of urgency infused the War Department's recruiting campaign.

In November, as fighting raged in Italy, resistance in the camps intensified. Around the time a violent confrontation broke out at the Tule Lake segregation center, at Heart Mountain a former high school teacher from Los Angeles Country, Kiyoshi Okamoto, formed what he called the Fair Play Committee of One to challenge the legality of the forced incarceration. Okamoto began building a following with mess hall lectures about the unprecedented violation of rights represented by the camps.

In January 1944, with the army recruitment drive a failure and 100th Battalion casualties rising in Italy, Secretary of War Henry Stimson ordered a resumption of the draft for Nisei men. In Heart Mountain, the response was emphatic. Six days after Stimson's order, Kiyoshi Okamoto partnered with his growing group of disciples to reorganize his Fair Play Committee of One as the Fair Play Committee. Their goal was to resist the draft of Nisei men from the camps.

Twenty-one months behind barbed wire had transformed Yosh Kuromiya. The lectures of the Fair Play Committee activists had resonated with him, and he resolved that if he received a draft notice, he would refuse to serve until his rights had been restored.[20]

Yosh had grown up more than a thousand miles from Ben Kuroki, and their lives could hardly have been more different to that point. If not for the war, their paths likely would never have crossed. But now, in early 1944, these two sons of Japanese immigrants were on a collision course.

Chapter 38

COMMONWEALTH CLUB

Ben was a bundle of nerves as he and his military minder arrived in San Francisco on February 3 for his appearance before the Commonwealth Club of California the following day. He had never delivered a formal speech in his life, and he wasn't looking forward to it. The War Department's cancellation of his interview with Ginny Simms nine days earlier had shaken Ben. The public backlash to the lurid news reports about Japanese maltreatment of American prisoners of war had unsettled him even more. With the country again seething with anti-Japanese rage, Ben felt as if the clock had been turned back to the early days of the war.

In the days since the atrocity stories had appeared, a noisy collection of politicians and civic leaders had called for the continued incarceration of Japanese Americans for the duration of the war. Some had even urged that camp inmates be permanently barred from their West Coast homes. Others demanded that the No-No Boys in the camps be stripped of their American citizenship and deported to Japan. The public mood had darkened so quickly that Ben now doubted the wisdom of challenging the anti-Japanese bigots from the Commonwealth Club stage.

San Francisco had figured prominently in the Kuroki family's American saga. The city had given Sam Kuroki his first taste of America's limitless promise nearly forty years earlier, and it had also exposed him to the scourge of anti-Japanese bigotry. Frazzled nerves aside, Ben swelled with pride at the prospect of being welcomed as an honored guest by such a prominent institution in the city where his father had begun his life in America.

Since its founding in 1903 as a forum for public discourse, the Commonwealth Club had become a coveted platform for figures of prominence—a place where the city's elite gathered to hear top businessmen, bankers, professors, politicians, generals, admirals, foreign dignitaries, and diplomats address important issues. Through the war years, the club had maintained its relevance. Vice President Henry Wallace was scheduled to address the club three days after Ben.

If the Commonwealth Club was emblematic of San Francisco's progressive streak, publisher William Randolph Hearst embodied the city's split personality as the birthplace of anti-Asian hate in America. Hearst's father was a wealthy mining engineer who owned several gold mines and other businesses and later served as a US senator from California. The younger Hearst was twenty-four when his father handed him the keys to the *San Francisco Examiner*, a daily newspaper the family patriarch had acquired as payment for a debt.

Grandly christening his paper "Monarch of the Dailies," young William Randolph hired talented writers, including Mark Twain, Jack London, and Ambrose Bierce. With the *Examiner* as his flagship, Hearst established himself in New York City in 1895 by purchasing the failing *New York Morning Journal*. Plying readers with stories of sensational human drama, Hearst amassed fabulous wealth and power while promoting his political and social views to millions of Americans. As he swung from left to right politically, Hearst never strayed far from his embrace of nativism. California's descent into anti-Chinese and anti-Japanese bigotry didn't originate with Hearst, but the *Examiner* and other Hearst papers fanned the flames.

After suffering a series of financial blows during the Great Depression, Hearst had returned to California. By 1940 he had become something of a recluse, holed up in his remote estate, Wyntoon, in the shadow of Mount Shasta in the state's northern reaches. The attack on Pearl Harbor had revived his longstanding animus for Japanese Americans, and Hearst's *San Francisco Examiner* became a leading advocate of the mass expulsion and incarceration campaign carried out by the Roosevelt administration. Now Hearst's *Examiner* was stoking national outrage over Japanese military atrocities.

On the evening of February 3, still uncertain about delivering his speech, Ben left his room in the Palace Hotel and made his way to the lobby newsstand. Perusing the papers, he was horrified by the bold headlines about Japanese atrocities. He hurried back to his room.

Ben had felt the pressure building since the cancellation of his Ginny Simms interview, and now the emotional weight of these past days overwhelmed him. His Commonwealth Club appearance was a horrible mistake, he feared.

AFTER A RESTLESS NIGHT, BEN SLIPPED on his dress uniform and made his way downstairs to the ballroom where the Commonwealth Club hosted its luncheons. It was known as the Gold Ballroom or simply the Gold Room, and much history had been made in the cavernous hall over the past two decades. Franklin Roosevelt had delivered a speech to the club from the

Gold Room stage in the closing days of his 1932 presidential campaign. And just the previous month, California governor Earl Warren, a frequent Commonwealth Club guest, had spoken from the Gold Room stage in one of his regular appearances.

Ben was battling his nerves as he walked into the packed ballroom. News accounts would report more than seven hundred people on hand to hear the remarks of the celebrated Japanese American war hero. The audience included the Bay Area's most prominent politicians, entrepreneurs, educators, writers, artists, and journalists. Near the front of the room sat the bespectacled steel tycoon Henry Kaiser, Sr., one of America's wealthiest men and the owner of seven West Coast shipyards that had played a pivotal role in the Allied military turnaround in the Pacific. Guests at nearby tables included Stanford University president Ray Lyman Wilbur as well as two top University of California Berkeley officials, president Robert Gordon Sproul and provost Monroe Deutsch.

Like most elite associations of the day, the Commonwealth Club denied membership to women. But there was at least one woman in the audience as Ben entered the room, photographer Dorothea Lange. She was tanned from years of outdoor work, and was given to covering her cropped blond hair with a beret cocked at a jaunty angle. Two years earlier, she had witnessed the roundup and incarceration of California's Japanese population, and she had been intrigued by Ben's story, which had been recounted yet again that week in a *Time* magazine profile. Now she waited to hear what the country's first Japanese American war hero had to say about the injustices being committed against people like him on the home front.

Nervously glancing around the room, Ben saw only a blur of faces. What did these people think about him after reading the stories about Japanese soldiers torturing and summarily executing surrendered American and Filipino forces in the Philippines? Introductions were made and he stepped uncertainly to the microphone. As he began speaking, Ben felt fear rising in his throat.

In a shaky voice, he apologized for his lack of polish as a public speaker. He began to tell his story in simple, earnest language. He described his life in Nebraska before the war, his horror after learning of the Pearl Harbor attack, his efforts to enlist. Softly, he described the misery of his first months in the army—the epithets, the ostracism, the loneliness.

As he spoke, Ben began to relax. He sensed warmth from the audience, not hostility. Questioning eyes now appeared to be empathetic.

He recalled his efforts to remain with the 93rd Bomb Group, his fight for a combat assignment, his heartbreak at being told he would not accompany his comrades to England. He recounted his tearful pleas and the compassion shown by those officers who accepted him as a loyal American. He described how he finally landed a crew assignment as a gunner and the terror and transcendent sense of belonging that combat had given him. He described the horrors of the Ploiesti raid and the pain of losing friends and comrades. "When you live with men under combat conditions for fifteen months you begin to understand what brotherhood is all about, what equality and tolerance really mean," he said.

Ben spoke candidly about the anti-Japanese bigotry he had encountered. The recent atrocity stories had rekindled dark forces in the country, and neither his uniform nor his medals shielded him from this renewed wave of hate and prejudice. And then, words that shocked and shamed the audience: "I don't know for sure that it is safe for me to walk the streets of my own country," he declared.

He ended by speaking about his goal to avenge the Japanese attack on Pearl Harbor and the atrocities in the Philippines by serving a combat tour in the Pacific Theater. "When I visit Tokyo, it will be in a Liberator bomber," Ben vowed, "and I won't be flying alone."

Audience members leapt to their feet and unleashed a thunderous ovation. For ten minutes, the room pulsed with applause. Tears streamed down the cheeks of Henry Kaiser and others. Twice, Ben was summoned back to the podium to acknowledge the crowd's appreciation. Afterward, Kaiser, Dorothea Lange, and other famous and powerful people crowded around Ben to shake his hand, acknowledge his service, and wish him well.[1]

Ben's speech had been a spectacular success. The national wire services and Bay Area newspapers carried his words across the country. His star soared. He was not only a war hero, but a fearless opponent of injustice and bigotry at home. Overnight, he became a focal point of the national discussion over America's treatment of Japanese Americans. It was one of the most thrilling moments of his life, but it didn't last long. Even as Ben left San Francisco, the government was taking aim at Nisei militants in the Heart Mountain camp who had vowed to resist the military draft. Ben was about to be thrust into the cross fire.

Chapter 39

"NO TURNING BACK"

On February 8, as Ben basked in the triumph of his Commonwealth Club speech, sixty Nisei men convened an urgent public meeting in a mess hall at the Heart Mountain Relocation Center in Wyoming. The men were members of the camp's Fair Play Committee, and many of them had received draft notices by mail in the previous days.

The committee leaders resolved to contest the army's conscription of Japanese American men on two grounds: It was illegal for the government to compel military service by men who had been stripped of their constitutional rights, and it was illegal to force the men to serve in racially segregated army units. Members of the Fair Play Committee were eager to force a legal test of their arguments. Their challenge wasn't based in disloyalty or pacifism. They simply believed they shouldn't be required to serve the same government that was denying their basic rights.

Among the men who attended the meeting was twenty-year-old Yosh Kuromiya. A little less than two years earlier, on June 30, 1942, Yosh had registered for the draft during the first weeks of his family's initial incarceration at the Pomona Assembly Camp. The back of Yosh's draft card listed the same basic information as that of any of the millions of men serving America around the globe: race ("Oriental"); height (five-feet-five-inches); weight (110 pounds); eye color (brown); hair color (black); and complexion (light brown).

What Yosh's draft card didn't reflect was the fact that he and other Nisei men had been physically fit yet declared ineligible for service for no other reason than their Japanese ancestry. But circumstances had changed. Now the army needed Nisei men to fight and die on the Allied front lines in Italy.

The government had undergone a change of heart about the desirability of the military service of these men, but the men themselves now held radically different views about their willingness to serve. Held under armed guard like prisoners of war by their own government, Yosh and many of the other Nisei men at Heart Mountain now regretted their acquiescence to the evacuation orders of 1942. "I was quite determined that I could not, in good conscience, bear arms under the existing conditions," Yosh later recalled. "But I also had trepidations about protesting alone."

Yosh decided that he needed to attend a Fair Play Committee meeting to hear the thoughts of other Nisei men facing the draft.[1]

As Yosh approached the mess hall for the meeting in early February 1944, he was struck by "the absence of the usual clatter of dishes, pots, and pans. There were no familiar shrieks of children nor incessant chatter of gossip. Also missing was the pungent aroma of steaming rice, homemade *takuan* [pickled radish] and not-so-fresh fish, which would escape every time someone would open a door to enter or leave. There was only a deep rumbling of subdued voices, interrupted occasionally by the squeal of a table or bench dragging on the concrete floor."[2]

Cigarette smoke hung heavily in the air as Yosh entered the room. Failing to spot any familiar faces, he slipped between two strangers on a wooden bench near the back of the mess hall. At the front of the room, Fair Play Committee leaders sat at two tables, conversing and exchanging papers.[3]

A slight, middle-aged man called the meeting to order. Kiyoshi Okamoto was the pugnacious founder of the original Fair Play Committee of One and an early advocate of resistance to the incarceration regime. "He was so atypical of the quiet, contained Japanese image, I was immediately enthralled by his demeanor, his forthrightness, animation, and (hopefully) his sincerity," Yosh recalled. "His language was brutally crude, sprinkled generously with four-letter expletives, but the content was essentially an articulation of my own deeper thoughts, values, and feelings."[4]

Yosh left his first meeting of the Fair Play Committee preoccupied with the momentous choice that confronted him. He began regularly attending committee meetings in camp mess halls whose managers were sympathetic to the resistance cause. He paid $2 to formally join the group, and at each subsequent gathering moved closer to the front so he wouldn't miss a word spoken by the leaders.[5]

Yosh and many other young men inside the camp were deeply impressed by what they viewed as the courage and selflessness of the Fair Play Committee leaders. But the editors of the camp newspaper, the *Heart Mountain Sentinel*—fundamentally conservative men who were ideologically aligned with the views of the Japanese American Citizens League and committed to cooperation with camp administrators—denounced the draft resistance movement as dangerously misguided. Opposition to the draft resistance became a fault line within the camp community.

As word of the Heart Mountain Fair Play Committee's draft resistance spread eastward through "free zones" where Japanese Americans had not been incarcerated, a few courageous souls voiced support. In Denver, James Omura, the thirty-one-year-old English-language editor of the influential *Rocky Shimpo* newspaper, published a February 23 editorial that offered moral support to the Heart Mountain dissidents.

On Sunday morning, February 27, the first group of Heart Mountain draftees boarded an army bus to be driven to their pre-induction physicals. The compliance of the men was a stinging rejection of the Fair Play Committee's call for resistance. Committee leaders convened a meeting to discuss their next move.

In the first week of March, some four hundred people crowded into one of the Heart Mountain mess halls for the watershed meeting of the Fair Play Committee. By now, the resistance had spread beyond the ranks of draft-age Nisei men to include embittered parents who feared the combat loss of a son in service to the government that had imprisoned them. "After being evacuated to this relocation center from the outside I have lost everything in worldly goods," said one such parent, the father of two draft-age Nisei sons. "All I have left is my family. I'd rather have [my boys] go to prison and I know that they will come back alive someday."[6]

Now Fair Play Committee leaders called for its members to move from words of protest to direct acts of resistance. One of the leaders, a twenty-seven-year-old Los Angeles grocer named Frank Emi, declared that there had been enough rhetoric. It was time to take a stand against the draft. Group members overwhelmingly agreed. In a statement drawn up and printed on fliers and posters, the committee put its advocacy of draft resistance in writing: "We feel the present program of drafting us from this concentration camp is unjust, unconstitutional, and against all principles of civilized usage. Therefore, we members of the Fair Play Committee hereby refuse to go to the physical examination, or to the induction, if or when we are called in order to contest the issue."[7]

On March 6, the Fair Play Committee scored its first victory when two Heart Mountain inmates refused to board the army bus that would ferry them to their physical. Before the week was out, twelve Heart Mountain inmates had refused to report for their physicals. With concern soaring in Washington, the FBI opened an investigation of the Fair Play Committee.

YOSH KUROMIYA'S MOMENT OF DECISION arrived a few days later, in mid-March, when he received a notice ordering him to report for his army physical exam. At the next Fair Play Committee meeting, he took a seat in the front of the room. As the meeting progressed, one of the leaders called for a show of hands from those who had received their pre-induction physical notices since the last meeting. Yosh raised his hand. One of the men at the head table asked Yosh to share with the audience what he intended to do.

Rising to his feet, Yosh nervously began to speak. He didn't share the fact that his father supported his opposition to the draft and his mother was pleading with him to avoid a conflict with the federal government. With all eyes focused on him, Yosh said that he had received a notice from the army ordering him to board a bus for his physical on the morning of March 23. Summoning his courage, Yosh announced his decision: He would not be on that bus when it exited the Heart Mountain camp.

The room erupted in cheers so loud that the windows rattled. "I felt a million eyes on me and as exhilarating as it was, my knees began to buckle," Yosh recalled.[8] Startled by the ovation, he sank to his seat.

As the draft resistance movement gathered force, the federal government finally decided to act. On Wednesday, March 22, federal warrants were issued charging twelve Japanese Americans at the Heart Mountain Relocation Center with failure to report for their army physicals.

The following morning, as the bus rolled out of Heart Mountain without Yosh and the latest group of draft resisters aboard, US Marshals swept through the camp to arrest the first group of a dozen men on federal charges of draft evasion. In the days that followed, Yosh Kuromiya and several dozen other men were arrested on federal warrants.

"I had passed the point of no return," Yosh recalled years later. "It was cast in stone. There would be no turning back."[9]

THE ARRESTS DIDN'T STOP THE DRAFT resistance movement. In fact, with each passing week, the number of Heart Mountain resisters grew, until more than sixty had been charged. The threat of federal prosecution seemed to have a diminishing impact on the spread of the draft rebellion in Heart Mountain. With the need for Nisei recruits growing more urgent by the day, the War Department decided to ramp up its effort to counter the draft resistance movement. By late March, War Department officials had a plan to counter the Heart Mountain draft resistance movement. They would use Ben Kuroki as the poster boy for Japanese American patriotism and send him to Heart Mountain to break the back of the draft resistance.

Chapter 40

HEART MOUNTAIN

Ben's Commonwealth Club speech won him powerful friends and celebrity status. But he still hadn't landed the Pacific combat assignment he so publicly sought. Instead, while higher authorities in Washington and the Army Air Forces tried to figure out what to do with their Japanese American hero, Ben found himself shunted from the spotlight in Los Angeles to a temporary assignment at Fresno's Hammer Field.

But the publicity surrounding Ben's speech had moved the War Department to reconsider its clumsy handling of the canceled NBC Radio interview in late January. Officials abruptly arranged for Ben to travel to Hollywood for a live February 24 appearance on *The Ginny Simms Show*. The day before the speech, Ben boarded a train in Fresno for the two-hundred-mile trip to Los Angeles. In the Mojave Desert, heavy rains washed out the tracks, so Ben set off for the nearest highway and hitchhiked the final seventy miles to Hollywood.[1]

His interview with Ginny Simms was beamed across America, and Ben touched on all the familiar themes of his inspiring story. He described the crews he had fought with as the embodiment of the American melting pot. "We all looked different, but we felt the same, and we were all heading for the same target," Ben told Simms. "We were Americans." Ben concluded with another public appeal to be allowed to fly raids against Japan. He couldn't wait "to head for the Pacific and knock the rice out of my ancestors," in his pithy description.

But the War Department wouldn't budge. Shortly after his appearance on *The Ginny Simms Show*, Ben was transferred to an Army Air base in Pueblo, Colorado, to train B-24 gunners. Ben would later say he found the duty more nerve-racking than flying thirty combat missions in Europe and North Africa. Nearly every day, wailing sirens signaled the crash of another inexperienced pilot and crew. "It was hair-raising," Ben later recalled. "And I'd go up with them over these turbulent mountains in Colorado to teach the gunners to fire their guns and they would all get airsick and wouldn't fire a shot."[2]

About a month into his Colorado assignment, Ben was summoned to the camp adjutant's office and given oral instructions. He was to visit three War Relocation Authority camps on behalf of the War Department and the army. He wasn't shown any written orders or given detailed instructions, and there was only a vague mention of recruiting young men to fight. How he was supposed to do that wasn't clear. All Ben knew was the names of the three camps he was supposed to visit. First on the list was Heart Mountain, Wyoming, five hundred miles north of Pueblo.

Ben wasn't aware that the camp was in turmoil or that battle lines had been drawn among camp residents. He certainly didn't know that militant elements within the camp were contemplating acts of violence against inmates perceived as collaborating with the government responsible for their imprisonment. Thousands of miles from the closest battlefront, Ben was walking into a different kind of war zone.

SHORTLY AFTER MIDDAY ON MONDAY, April 24, some three thousand incarcerees at the Heart Mountain Relocation Center gathered near the front gate of the sprawling Wyoming camp to greet the honored guest. The *Heart Mountain Sentinel* had written lavish articles and editorials about the visitor. A big handwritten sign was positioned near the gate to make a favorable first impression: "Welcome Sergeant Ben Kuroki." A dark-colored army sedan approached. Peering out through a back window, Ben was shocked. "The armed guards were wearing the same uniform I was wearing," he later recalled. "And inside, behind barbed wire, were my own people."[3]

Ben arrived at Heart Mountain with only the vaguest idea of the ordeal the inhabitants of the camp had experienced, and no concept of the conditions under which they had been confined. Now he was shaken by the sight of men, women, and children who looked like him, packed into flimsy wooden barracks in this windswept place, guarded by rifle-toting US Army soldiers as if they were enemy combatants.

As Ben tried to process his surroundings, the Heart Mountain camp director and a community council representative fawned over him in a brief formal ceremony. The crowd of camp residents applauded politely, as if they were attending a ribbon-cutting ceremony back in their California hometowns. Later that evening, Ben was feted at a banquet attended by two hundred Japanese American community leaders.

The warm welcome Ben received at Heart Mountain belied the fault lines that had fractured the camp community. Moderate elements committed to cooperation with the federal government on the military draft and other matters were at ever sharper odds with the growing faction of militants who had now dedicated themselves to opposing the incarceration regime on all fronts.

Passions within the camp had been further inflamed by a rolling government crackdown on the resistance movement in the weeks since the arrests of Yosh Kuromiya and several dozen other men on federal draft evasion charges. In early April, federal agents abruptly transferred Kiyoshi Okamoto, the Fair Play Committee founder, to the segregation center for "disloyal" Japanese at Tule Lake, California. By late April, federal authorities had arrested fifty-three men at the Heart Mountain camp. These young men, Yosh Kuromiya among them, were now being held in scattered Wyoming county jails awaiting trial on federal draft evasion charges.

Despite all this, hundreds of Heart Mountain residents continued to support the draft resisters. Fair Play Committee leaders urged other men to defy the draft as they received their physical exam summons. But the militants had gone beyond words. In recent days, they had denounced the editors of the *Heart Mountain Sentinel* as collaborators who had cast their lot with their government oppressors, and a number of violent clashes had put the camp on edge.

Ben knew none of this when he arrived at the Heart Mountain camp.

AWAKENING AT HEART MOUNTAIN ON Tuesday, April 25, Ben was hustled by his handlers to speaking events and meet-and-greets arranged by administrators and community leaders. He toured the camp's wooden barracks, mess halls, schools, churches, baseball fields, basketball courts, and other recreation areas.

Within a day or so, Ben understood why he was there. He was to encourage Nisei men to enlist, or at least not resist the draft. In conversations with small groups of draft-age men and in public speeches, Ben shared his story of patriotism, perseverance, and courage. Many young men hung on every word, and mesmerized children sat at his feet. "A lot of boys and girls—especially the girls—were asking for [Ben's] autograph," recalled camp resident Eiichi Sakauye.[4]

Although he was treated like a movie star by many inmates, Ben quickly became aware of the deep divisions within the camp. He was shocked when members of the Fair Play Committee began to interrupt and heckle him during his speeches. They accused Ben of collaborating with the very people who had deprived camp residents of their rights. "While most Nisei treated me as their first war hero, the dissidents seemingly despised me and some even resorted to derogatory name-calling," Ben recalled. "Their leader called me a bull-shitter."[5]

Camp administrators and community leaders asked Ben to talk to a group of Fair Play Committee members in hopes of persuading them to drop their resistance to the draft. "There might be trouble," Ben was told, and so extra guards were assigned. He gave his talk without disruption, but he wasn't changing many minds.

At one of his meetings with Heart Mountain dissidents, Ben bluntly told his hostile audience that if they thought Japan was going to win the war, as some did, they were "crazy." Bluntly, Ben warned them of a looming catastrophe for the land of their ancestry. "Japan is gonna get bombed off the map," Ben flatly declared.[6]

Some of the audience members booed and hissed his words.

The hostile reactions pained Ben. He fervently believed that the Nisei inmates should follow his example and prove their loyalty to America through military service. In the case of the Heart Mountain Nisei, joining the army and serving with the 442nd Regimental Combat Team "was going to help" the people of Japanese ancestry in America, Ben insisted.[7]

His words infuriated the Heart Mountain militants. Most of them were Californians and better educated than Ben. They viewed him as unsophisticated and uninformed. Their families had lost nearly everything but their lives. Ben and his family hadn't experienced anything like the harm they had suffered.

Even worse, in their eyes, Ben seemed oblivious to the anguish felt by some of the incarcerees, and that infuriated them. "He'd never been in camp," said Jack Tono, a Heart Mountain dissident who was eventually convicted of draft evasion and spent two years in a federal prison. "He's a Nebraska boy, and here we'd lost everything and then [were] thrown into camp. He's coming out, preaching to us what the hell we should be doing."[8]

The fury toward Ben built during the week. In the eyes of the resisters, Ben was a race-traitor who had broken faith with his own people for a few medals and the approval of their oppressors. "There was guys in camp wanna kill [Kuroki]," said Tono. "He's lucky he went out of there alive."[9]

ON THURSDAY, APRIL 27, BEN ADDRESSED a large mass meeting at the camp high school. There were more events on Friday and Saturday. After a full weekend of activities, he delivered his final speech on Sunday, April 30, at a farewell ceremony in his honor. Standing on an outdoor platform before an American flag poster, he thanked the residents for their hospitality and called for young men in the audience to honor Japanese Americans by joining the army.

Ben had done everything asked of him at Heart Mountain. He had done his best to convince draft-age inmates that they should enlist, or at least not resist the draft. Some men heeded his exhortations and enlisted.

Others complied with their draft summons under duress, fearing the costs of challenging the federal government. At one point, Ben had boarded a bus loaded with departing Heart Mountain recruits to wish them luck. "I was met with stony silence," Ben said, laughing nervously at the memory of the tense encounter.[10]

While Ben's visit was judged a success by camp administrators and the army, he had not broken the spirit of resistance that coursed through Heart Mountain and was spreading. On the day Ben climbed into the back of an army sedan and rolled back through the barbed wire that confined the camp inmates, another six Heart Mountain incarcerees refused to report for their pre-induction physicals.[11]

Chapter 41

A TURNING POINT

Ben spent the remainder of the spring of 1944 on the road, doing recruiting and public relations work for the War Department and the War Relocation Authority. His itinerary took him to other incarceration camps and to Chicago, where a growing number of Japanese Americans had settled after their early release from confinement over the past year. At each stop, Ben delivered speeches recounting his personal story of patriotism, perseverance, and combat valor.

More controversially, Ben urged Nisei men in his audiences to enlist in the army as the ultimate answer to those critics who questioned their love for America or their loyalty to its cause. Although he didn't face physical threats in the camps he visited after Heart Mountain, Ben encountered resistance to his argument that unconditional military service was the antidote to the prevailing bigotry and prejudice. Increasingly, these unpleasant encounters weighed on him.

The next stop for Ben after Heart Mountain was the Minidoka Relocation Center near Hunt, Idaho. As Ben quickly discovered, there was a dreary monotony to the camps: bleak locations; flimsy wooden barracks, mess halls, and other crude facilities; carefully tended vegetable gardens and flower beds; and arts and cultural displays that reflected the brave efforts of incarcerees to celebrate their heritage and resurrect pieces of the lives they had lost.

Among the Minidoka incarcerees on hand to witness Ben's arrival was a twenty-eight-year-old Southern Californian named Minoru (James) Sakoda. At the time of the Pearl Harbor attack, Sakoda had been studying psychology at the University of California at Berkeley.

His parents had returned to Japan in the previous decade, and so Sakoda went to Los Angeles to reunite with his siblings. When the West Coast roundup began in March, he and his siblings were first sent to the Tulare Assembly Center in California's San Joaquin Valley and then to the permanent incarceration camp at Tule Lake in the state's northern extremes.

Not long after arriving at Tule Lake, James Sakoda was hired by a

Cal Berkeley acquaintance, sociologist Dorothy Swaine Thomas, who had launched a multidisciplinary project known as the Japanese American Evacuation and Resettlement Study (JERS). Sakoda was one of more than two dozen field-workers assigned to gather data from four assembly centers, six incarceration camps, and several resettlement communities outside the exclusion zone. The project would eventually produce three books published by the University of California Press.[1]

When Tule Lake became the segregation facility for perceived "disloyals" from other WRA facilities, Sakoda asked to be transferred to the Minidoka camp in Idaho to be with his fiancée. He arrived there in September 1943 and was married shortly afterward. In the months since, Sakoda had focused his research for the Cal Berkeley study on incarcerees who chose to remain in the camp rather than accept offers to work or study in the outside world.[2]

As Ben made his recruiting rounds at Minidoka, Sakoda was struck by the airman's unwillingness to consider the views of his audience members—especially the immigrant Issei who still harbored a deep reverence for their homeland. Many of these people believed that Japan was winning the war and would ultimately prevail and free them from the camps.[3]

Ben repeated his comments about Japan not only facing defeat, but destruction from American bombs. His words shocked the Issei inmates and hardened attitudes against him, especially since many viewed Ben as the face of the Washington war machine that would send their sons to their deaths. Nisei men didn't share their parents' reverence for Japan, but they considered rejecting the draft a principled stand against a profound injustice.[4]

Although Ben received a warm welcome from some inmates and signed scores of autographs, he "wasn't a hero" to many others, Sakoda said. "He was something—somebody—they despised. The ones who really welcomed Ben Kuroki as a hero were the young kids and the young girls who saw him as he was supposed to be seen."[5]

Despite the backlash, Ben continued to insist that combat service by Nisei men was the surest way to change American attitudes toward people of Japanese descent.

"I'd much rather be fighting than doing this civilian work, but I'd like to do what I can to help," Ben told Sakoda. "I won't be discouraged."[6]

AFTER SPENDING THE FIRST WEEK OF MAY at Minidoka, Ben traveled to Chicago to address employees of the War Relocation Authority and former incarcerees who had been allowed to resettle in Illinois. The visit was especially joyous for Ben because he got to see four of his five sisters—Fuji, Cecile, Wilma, and Beatrice—who had married and were living in Chicago.

While Ben was in Chicago, the legal case involving Yosh Kuromiya and other Heart Mountain draft resisters took a dramatic turn. On May 10, a grand jury in Cheyenne, Wyoming, indicted sixty-three resisters on federal draft evasion charges. The grand jury also indicted seven leaders of the Fair Play Committee and *Rocky Shimpo* journalist James Omura on federal charges of conspiracy to counsel draft evasion. A trial date for the resisters was set for June.

After several pleasant days in Chicago, Ben headed home to Nebraska to visit his parents. He arrived in Hershey on Monday, May 15, for what was supposed to be a fifteen-day furlough, but he had been home only a day when an army telegram ordered him back to his base in Colorado. The abrupt change of plans had been triggered by developments in Italy. The five-month battle for Monte Cassino, western anchor of the German army's Gustav Line south of Rome, had reached a climax.

During the initial January-February assaults on Monte Cassino, the all-Nisei 100th Battalion had become known as the Purple Heart Battalion because of its heavy losses. Throughout the spring, the army had replenished the 100th with men from another all-Nisei unit training in Mississippi, the 442nd Regimental Combat Team. On May 1, all but the 442nd's depleted 1st Battalion had sailed for Italy. Once Monte Cassino was captured, the 442nd would join forces with the 100th for the push up the Italian peninsula.

With Nisei casualties expected to spike during the summer fighting season, the War Department was hard-pressed to enlist—or draft—more Nisei recruits. The army needed Ben to deliver their recruits.

Arriving at his Colorado base on Wednesday, May 17, Ben was handed his orders: He was to travel to the Topaz War Relocation Center in Delta, Utah. There, he would urge another pool of draft-age Nisei men to join the climactic fight against Nazi Germany.

AT TOPAZ, BEN RECEIVED HIS MOST exuberant welcome yet. The camp newspaper, the *Topaz Times*, published a special edition that celebrated every aspect of Ben's life. "He's Human Too; He Keeps a Charm, Likes Steak, Played Center Field," announced the headline of a gushing story that described Ben as "our finest example of Nisei manhood" and "an excellent sport with a contagious grin."[7]

The paper reprinted an excerpt from Ben's Commonwealth Club speech as well as the February *Time* magazine profile. "Foremost an American," declared the headline over a *Topaz Times* editorial that pronounced Ben "the living example of what a Nisei should be—an American first, a Nisei second." Continuing in this vein, the editors rhapsodized: "He belongs to all America. After many struggles he attained his deserved and rightful role. This is the stuff which heroes are made from."[8]

The paper urged camp residents to "learn a lot from Ben Kuroki. We Nisei of the relocation centers are too prone to tag ourselves as Nisei first and only secondly as Americans. Undoubtedly our trials and circumstances have magnified our Nisei status. But it is up to us to emerge from our shells of self-pity into full-fledged Americans. Sergeant Kuroki is the kind of citizen we in the relocation centers can prepare to become in the world outside."[9]

For five days, Ben was feted and celebrated. He delivered speeches, attended banquets, picnics, and cookouts, met with students of all ages, comforted patients in the camp hospital, attended a USO luncheon with the parents of Nisei soldiers, and dined with the local Lion's Club. "Everywhere he visited admiring crowds congregated around him, and autograph hounds trailed him," the *Topaz Times* reported.[10]

When it was time for Ben to leave, some eight hundred residents gathered at the main gate for what the *Topaz Times* described as a "rousing sendoff." His car was swarmed by last-minute autograph seekers as the camp's Boy Scout drum and bugle corps set pulses racing.[11]

For Ben, the Topaz sendoff was a high note on which to end his unsettling assignment.

BEN RETURNED TO CHICAGO AGAIN IN early June to speak to War Relocation Authority employees and representatives of the various camps and resettled Nisei. The growing sense across America that 1944 might be the year of victory was intensified by the events of June 6, when Allied forces stormed ashore the beaches of Normandy, France, to begin the liberation of Europe. Some of the young men inspired by Ben to enlist would be in combat before the summer was out, and some would die. As for Ben, he was weary of his work as an army recruiter and pitch man. Rather than live on past glory and suffer the brickbats of his fellow Nisei, he was ready to get back to fighting the war.

As Ben headed home to Nebraska to resume his aborted furlough, the war in the Pacific entered a decisive phase. US forces were poised to launch a series of attacks on Japanese-held islands, from Biak off the coast of New Guinea to the Northern Mariana Islands of Saipan, Tinian, and Guam. General Hap Arnold was keeping a close eye on the Northern Marianas as the launching pad for his climactic air campaign against Japan, utilizing his state-of-the-art long-range bomber, the B-29 Superfortress, which had made its combat debut on June 5 by taking off from bases in British India to bomb Japanese railroad facilities in Bangkok, Thailand. The B-29s were poised to bomb the Japanese homeland from China, but Arnold viewed the Northern Marianas as the preferred launching pad for operations against Japan.

On June 15, 1944, US soldiers splashed ashore on Saipan to begin a twenty-four-day battle. Arnold's chessboard was set: As soon as the Marianas were secured, Seabees would set to work on Saipan, Tinian, and Guam, building airfields capable of handling America's biggest bomber. Once that was accomplished, Arnold would begin his decisive campaign on the Japanese homeland from the Northern Marianas.

BEN'S DETRACTORS IN THE INCARCERATION camps had scorned him as a collaborator and race traitor, but his Commonwealth Club speech had galvanized a national conversation about restoring the rights of incarcerated Japanese Americans. A crusade to close the camps and release the incarcerees was being led by a group of prominent California progressives calling themselves the Pacific Coast Committee on American Principles and Fair Play. The group's leaders included University of California Berkeley president Robert Gordon Sproul, UC provost Monroe Deutsch, and Stanford University president Ray Lyman Wilbur. All three had attended Ben's Commonwealth Club speech and had been moved by his words. Their efforts were being supported by an influential friend of First Lady Eleanor Roosevelt, photographer Dorothea Lange, who had written Ben's family a lovely letter praising his speech.[12]

But dark forces continued to oppose the lifting of wartime restrictions on those people of Japanese descent who had been forcibly removed from the West Coast exclusion zone. A few days after Ben concluded his visit to Topaz, a speaker stood at the same Commonwealth Club podium where Ben had spoken three months earlier and vehemently argued against closing the incarceration camps. "We're not against the Japs for what they are, but for what they do," thundered former California state legislator Seth Millington, who was now a leader of the fiercely pro-incarceration Native Sons and Daughters of the Golden West.

Drawing a distinction between loyal and disloyal Japanese, Millington singled out the club's February speaker as a role model. "As to Sergeant Ben Kuroki, he flew for his regular twenty-five missions against the Germans and volunteered for five more," Millington said. "And so far as the Native Sons and American Legion are concerned, he has demonstrated his loyalty, and he and any other man like him can live next door to us for the rest of his life." But, Millington added, America's "disloyal" Japanese should be exiled to Japan "on the first boat."

Pressure on Franklin Roosevelt to close the camps mounted through the summer of 1944, but the political cost was always foremost in the mind of the American president. Facing reelection in November, Roosevelt knew that opinion polls showed a majority of Americans favored confining people of Japanese descent for the remainder of the war. Ninety percent of Los Angelenos polled earlier in the year favored continued army control of people of Japanese descent. Sixty-one percent favored the permanent exclusion of all Japanese from the Pacific Coast. Sixty-five percent favored a postwar constitutional amendment that would result in the deportation of all Japanese immigrants.[13] With those sentiments in mind, Roosevelt ducked the issue as Election Day approached.

Forty days after winning election to a fourth term, Roosevelt finally acted. On December 17, 1944, US Army major general Henry C. Platt issued Public Proclamation No. 21, ordering an end to the "internment" of Japanese Americans, effective the second day of 1945. Unwilling to accept responsibility for the shameful incarceration order he had personally approved in 1942, Roosevelt had delegated the announcement to a subordinate.

Civic leaders and activists who had spent more than two years trying to convince Roosevelt to undo his incarceration of Japanese Americans would later describe Ben Kuroki's Commonwealth Club speech as a turning point. As activist Ruth Kingman described it, Ben's speech "was the beginning of [the] change of the whole attitude in California."[14]

Chapter 42

HONORABLE SAD SAKI

July 1944 found Ben back in Colorado training B-24 crews how to survive in combat, while stewing over his own unrequited goal to serve a tour in the Pacific. His view of military service had always been infused with the spiritual themes of atonement and redemption. But now he also harbored a taste for Old Testament retribution. In his mind, he would avenge the lives lost at Pearl Harbor and Bataan and he would avenge the death of Stanley Bates. In recent weeks, his thirst for vengeance had become almost insatiable after receiving devastating news from home: His friend Gordy Jorgenson had been killed fighting the Japanese in the South Pacific.[1]

At the same time, a recent incident had convinced Ben he still hadn't done enough to earn the respect and trust of his fellow Americans. He was passing through Colorado during his recent travels and flagged down a taxi at the Denver train station. A passenger already in the taxi took one look at Ben in his bemedaled dress uniform and snarled, "I won't ride with no lousy Jap!" The man slammed the taxi door in Ben's face, unleashing a wave of shame and self-doubt.[2]

Ben concluded he still hadn't done enough to prove himself to his fellow Americans, or at least to some of them. He resolved to bomb Tokyo to prove beyond any doubt where his loyalties lay. He wouldn't rest until he landed a Pacific combat assignment.

IN AUGUST 1944, BEN RECEIVED ORDERS to report to the 505th Bomb Group in Harvard, Nebraska. On his arrival, Ben was assigned as the tail gunner on a B-29 Superfortress crew.

The crew was commanded by Lieutenant James Jenkins, a five-foot-ten, twenty-six-year-old Michigan native. Jenkins was born in the state's rural interior but spent most of his life in and around Detroit. He graduated from Detroit's northside Cooley High School in 1936, and, when his parents divorced, he moved to Flint, Michigan, with his mother and her new husband. In Flint, he found work as a parts manager at a local auto garage. When he registered for the Selective Service draft in October

1940, twenty-one-year-old Jim was back in Detroit, working in the General Motors Company's Chevrolet Division retail store in the city's bustling New Center area.

Jenkins entered the Army Air Forces after Pearl Harbor, earned his pilot's wings, and got married. He learned to fly B-17s and became an instructor at the army's advanced flying school at Pampa, Texas, as the American bombing campaign in Europe entered its darkest months. Now he was commander of B-29 Crew 84-10, as it was known in 384th Squadron records.

Jenkins was asked by his superiors whether he would be willing to take on a tail gunner of Asian descent. "I didn't know he was a Japanese American when I first saw him," Jenkins recalled of his introduction to Ben Kuroki. Once he became aware of Ben's ancestry, Jenkins thought about the complications of taking on a Japanese American gunner. He finally decided it was the right thing to do. When he wrote his mother to tell her about his new tail gunner, Mabel Jenkins expressed her disapproval of "that man."[3]

As Ben began to bond with members of his new crew, he found his comrades baffled by his decision to request another combat tour when it wasn't required of him. "What's the matter with you?" some of them asked. Why keep going?[4]

Ben tried to explain the obsession that burned inside—his compulsion to prove himself loyal, his desire to avenge compatriots and friends who had been cut down by Japanese bullets and bombs. He tried to explain why he was willing to put his life on the line by undertaking a combat tour in another theater when no one was asking him to do so. If he struck a blow against Japan and showed his willingness to shed the blood of his own ancestral kin, no one could ever again call him a "lousy Jap" or question his loyalty to his country.

WHEN BEN ARRIVED AT HARVARD Army Air Field, the 505th Bomb Group was still taking shape. The group was comprised of three squadrons: the 482nd, 483rd, and 484th. Ben's squadron, the 484th, had been created in Florida with only a few men and officers before moving to Harvard the previous spring.

After nearly freezing to death in some of his B-24 missions over Europe, Ben could hardly believe the creature comforts and cutting-edge technology of the B-29. America's new super-bomber was a truly revolutionary aircraft—bigger, heavier, and more spacious than the B-17 or the B-24, capable of flying farther, faster, and higher. The Superfortress was the first American aircraft with pressurized compartments and a centralized fire-control system that allowed gunners to remotely operate turrets from the comfort of the fuselage.

The B-29 had been conceived before America's entry into World War II as a high-altitude strategic bomber. Hitler's aggression in Europe led Hap Arnold to seek and receive permission to put the bomber into production, but the program was plagued by technical problems and never saw action in the campaign against Nazi Germany. Eventually, with the program's cost dwarfing that of the Manhattan Project by more than $1 billion, the B-29 would be directed at Japan.

Despite the thirty combat missions Ben had under his belt, the B-29 presented a learning curve. On a B-24, each gunner was on his own. On the B-29, computers allowed gunners to synchronize their fire to best defend against an enemy threat. The isolation of the tail gunner's position on a B-17 or a B-24 presented its own unique psychological challenges in combat. As Ben discovered, the B-29 promised similar isolation. The tail gunner occupied a pressurized compartment separate from the main fuselage. That required Ben to remain in his self-contained cocoon until the aircraft descended to an altitude that allowed unpressurized flight.

By the end of August, the crews were working through their training checklists. In October, they began to undertake three-thousand-mile cross-country flights. Maintenance problems disrupted the training schedule at times, and the loss of eleven men in a fatal accident at Ben's old B-24 base at Barksdale Field, Louisiana, reminded the men of the perils of their work. By the beginning of November, the 505th Bomb Group crews had completed their training.

Finally, on November 6, 1944, the group's ground echelon—maintenance crews, mechanics, armorers, and other support staff—departed Harvard Army Air Base for Seattle, where they were to board a transport ship bound for the Pacific.

The combat crews were to follow on a staggered basis after Thanksgiving—everyone except Ben Kuroki, that is. Ben had been informed that he wouldn't be allowed to accompany his crew to the Pacific. Ominously, Ben was told the order came "from the top."

BEN HAD BEEN WARNED EARLY IN HIS B-29 training that the War Department had an ironclad ban on Japanese Americans flying combat missions in the Pacific Theater. Undeterred, he requested an exemption based on his combat record and was confident it would be granted, but on September 27, he had received a letter from Colonel Warren Williams, deputy chief of staff of the Second Air Force, responsible for bomber crew training west of the Mississippi River. "I hate to give you the bad news, but I have done everything humanly possible to get you overseas in the Pacific Theater, but the War Department absolutely refuses to grant permission," Williams wrote. At the bottom of the page, Williams scribbled a postscript. "We went right to the top and they would do nothing," he wrote. "Sorry."[5]

Two years earlier, when faced with the prospect of being left behind by the 93rd Bomb Group, Ben's only option had been to beg for reconsideration. Now, with a national profile and friends in high places, Ben unleashed his allies on the White House and the War Department. On October 17, one of Ben's Commonwealth Club friends, Monroe Deutsch, vice president and provost at the University of California, Berkeley, sent a telegram to Secretary of War Henry Stimson, urging a dispensation for the decorated Japanese American airman. Stimson refused to budge. Ben dashed off another flurry of letters to powerful friends he had made over the past year, but the War Department still refused to rescind its policy.

In early November, with deployment only a few weeks away, Ben played his last card. Accompanied by pilot Jim Jenkins and other officers on his crew, Ben tracked down Congressman Carl Curtis, a New Deal Democrat, at a meeting in a town fifty miles from their base. Ben explained his predicament: His crew was scheduled to depart for the Pacific in a matter of days, but the War Department refused to let him go. Could the congressman help?

Ben and the congressman talked for a while. Curtis asked Ben about his life before the war, and Ben shared his family story. Curtis was impressed with Ben and the obvious bond he had forged with his crew. The congressman brought the conversation back to Ben's wish to fight the Japanese in the Pacific. "Is this really what you want to do?" Curtis asked. "Yes, I do," Ben replied. "I am an American."[6]

Curtis had heard enough. He drafted a telegram to the army chief of staff, General George C. Marshall, and urged that Ben be allowed to fly and fight in the Pacific. He also fired off telegrams to Secretary of War Stimson and General Arnold.

On Thursday, November 16, Secretary of War Stimson sent letters to Monroe Deutsch, Congressman Curtis, and other influential advocates who had written appeals on Ben's behalf. "I am now happy to inform you that, by reason of his splendid record, it has been decided to exempt Sgt. Kuroki from the provision of the policy to which I earlier referred," Stimson wrote.[7]

Ben would be allowed to serve in the Pacific after all.

AROUND DECEMBER 15, BEN AND THE other members of the Jenkins crew loaded their gear aboard their B-29. They were poised to depart Harvard

Army Airfield for the final time when men who identified themselves as army intelligence officers accosted Ben and asked him to prove he had permission to deploy to the Pacific. Ben frantically dug into the pile of gear stowed inside their B-29 in search of his B4 military garment bag. He pulled a copy of Secretary of War Stimson's letter from the bag and showed it to the men. While the purported intelligence officers contemplated their next move, Jim Jenkins gunned the engines and took off with Ben aboard.

A similar scene played out during a stop at Mather Field, outside Sacramento, California. Once again, Jenkins settled the issue by getting his crew aboard and taking off before the shadowy inquisitors could take Ben away for questioning.[8]

During a layover in Hawaii, the 505th crews performed the ritual of naming their aircraft and having a base artist paint their preferred mascot on the nose. Most of the crews opted for a sexually suggestive name and a nude woman as their talisman. The Jenkins crew decided to pay tribute to their courageous tail gunner. They had previously nicknamed Ben "The Honorable Sad Saki," a mashup of the popular *Sad Sack* comic book character popular with army readers and the beverage saki, the fermented rice wine that many Americans associated with Japanese culture. Henceforth, their glistening silver B-29 would be known as *Honorable Sad Saki*.

In the final week of December 1944, with Ben's steadfast advocate Jim Jenkins in the command pilot's seat, *Honorable Sad Saki* climbed into the skies over Hawaii. The shimmering waters of Pearl Harbor and the sunken hulk of the battleship USS *Arizona* flashed beneath them as *Honorable Sad Saki* banked to the west and an unknown destination in the Northern Mariana Islands. Since December 7, 1941, the ghosts of Pearl Harbor had haunted Ben, as if he somehow shared personal responsibility for the deeds of the Japanese armed forces. In his anguish and his shame, Ben had convinced himself that only by confronting Japan in combat could he prove his patriotism and atone for the deaths of more than ninety thousand Americans in three years of Pacific combat.

Chapter 43

TINIAN

In the final week of 1944, after a journey of 3,700 miles west across the Pacific Ocean from Honolulu, Ben Kuroki and the crew of *Honorable Sad Saki* reached their destination: Tinian, a thirty-nine-square-mile chunk of coral-encrusted limestone in the Northern Marianas chain. The island's most important feature was its proximity to Tokyo—a distance of fifteen hundred miles, or a fourteen-hour roundtrip flight for a bomb-laden B-29 Superfortress. Deployed to England for the early days of the Eighth Air Force bombing of Nazi Germany, Ben now found himself in the vanguard of the climactic air campaign against Japan.

Ben and his comrades emerged from *Honorable Sad Saki* for an introduction to their new home. In their first hours on the ground, they formed several impressions, none of them good. The island was hot, humid, and dangerous. The crew had no place to sleep, and no shelter from the tropical sun. Had anyone been expecting them? There was no evidence of it.

American soldiers had captured Tinian on August 1, 1944, after eight days of fighting that claimed the lives of 328 US soldiers and nearly 9,000 Japanese. Many of the Japanese soldiers had committed suicide rather than surrender. As soon as the island was secure, Navy Seabees came ashore and began clearing the island's sugarcane fields to transform Tinian into a massive B-29 base. The entire northern end of the island was now covered by nearly eleven miles of runways, taxiways, and hardstands—enough to accommodate the four groups of the 313th Bombardment Wing, which included Ben's 505th Bomb Group.

With the Seabees still focused on accommodations for the B-29s rather than their crews, Ben and his comrades set to work building a bivouac. For the enlisted personnel like Ben, canvas shelter halves would have to suffice until pyramid tents could be secured. Exercising the privilege of rank as always, the officers appropriated the sole Quonset hut near the airfield.

As the men worked, air-raid sirens periodically sent them scurrying for cover. The attackers were Japanese fighters and Bettys, twin-engine bombers that roared overhead to hit targets on the larger island of Saipan, whose southern tip lay only three miles off Tinian's northern shore.

Tinian, Saipan, and the smaller island of Rota had been important sugar-producing islands under Japanese administration before the war, and lush fields of seven-foot-tall cane surrounded the 505th bivouac. Rumors swept the group that some of Tinian's Japanese defenders had survived the fighting and were hiding in caves and cane fields, waiting to strike the American airmen and their B-29s. Nervous sentries reacted to random sounds and imagined threats by firing wildly into the fields, especially after nightfall.

Jim Jenkins and the *Honorable Sad Saki* crew feared their Japanese American gunner would be mistaken for an enemy soldier and shot on sight by a trigger-happy sentry. They pleaded with Ben to wear his US Army helmet at all times and they accompanied him to the mess tent and latrine. Ben stopped going to the latrine after dark. "I deserve a Purple Heart for bladder damage," he joked with Jenkins and their squadron commander after a few days.[1]

Ben managed to make light of his predicament, but the danger was real. He had prepared himself for all imaginable challenges in the Pacific, but being mistaken for an enemy soldier and shot by his own comrades wasn't one of them. With that grim possibility hanging over him every waking minute, Ben began to steel himself for actual combat against Japanese forces.

TEN WEEKS BEFORE BEN AND HIS crewmates landed on Tinian, Brigadier General Haywood "Possum" Hansell arrived on neighboring Saipan to head the bombing campaign designed to seal Japan's defeat. Hansell went to work getting his inexperienced Superfortress pilots and gunners prepared for action. He first directed bombing raids on Truk atoll, providing an opportunity to practice formation flying and overwater flight while going up against light enemy defenses. After two raids on Truk he sent his crews to bomb airfields on the fortified Japanese island of Iwo Jima, a more formidable target that tested the daylight visual bombing skills of his men and their first night return. Hansell's crews exhibited wildly inaccurate bombing in six training missions against Truk and Iwo Jima, but those problems would have to be worked out on the job.[2]

Hansell's primary objective was the destruction of Japanese aircraft engine and assembly plants. His force had just over one hundred bombers on hand when Hansell issued his Twentieth Air Force crews their first strategic assignment: a strike on the Nakajima Aircraft Company's engine plant in the crowded Tokyo suburb of Musashino, ten miles northwest of the Emperor's Palace.

The raid took place November 24. Leading the way was a B-29 named *Dauntless Dotty*, piloted by a pair of celebrated B-17 pilots. Brigadier General Emmett "Rosie" O'Donnell, who had been a B-17 squadron commander in the Philippines at the time of the Pearl Harbor attack, was the lead command pilot. Seated next to him in the copilot's seat was Major Robert K. Morgan, who had piloted the *Memphis Belle* during the first year of the Eighth Air Force campaign against Nazi Germany.

On the flight to Tokyo, seventeen of 111 B-29s that got airborne aborted for various reasons. Another six failed to bomb because of mechanical issues. The aircraft that reached Tokyo rocketed into their bomb run with a 120-knot tailwind that increased their ground speed to about 445 miles per hour. The wind coupled with clouds that obscured the Nakajima plant led most of the aircraft to head for alternate targets. Only twenty-four B-29s bombed the Nakajima plant, while sixty-four dropped their ordnance on docks and urban areas.[3]

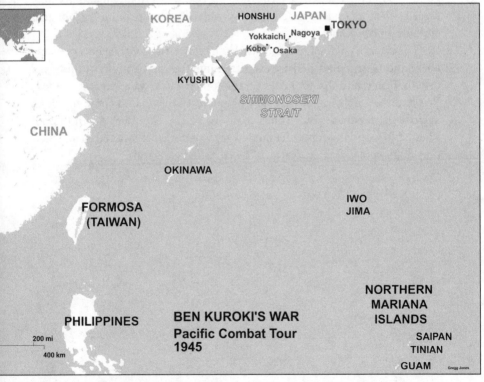

Pacific combat tour, 1945

The first Tokyo raid by Hansell's forces—and the desultory results—were harbingers for what was to come. The B-29s executed occasional strikes on Iwo Jima's airfields and some experimental incendiary raids on urban areas, but the high-altitude, daylight precision raids on aircraft factories in Japan fell far short of expectations. Clouds and high winds repeatedly undermined bombing accuracy.

By early January 1945, Hansell's boss, the chronically impatient four-star general Hap Arnold, had seen enough. He relieved Hansell and replaced him with General Curtis LeMay. Arnold dispatched his hand-picked hatchet man, General Lauris Norstad, to deliver a blunt warning. "If you don't succeed," Norstad told LeMay, "you will be fired."[4]

Ben and the vanguard of the 505th Bomb Group had arrived in the waning days of Hansell's command. The 313th Wing commanders on the ground had quickly sized up the new arrivals as deficient in key areas. They devised a month-long training program to whip the raw crews into shape flying simulated practice missions. On January 21, 1945, Curtis LeMay's first full day as chief of the XXI Bomber Command, Ben logged his first mission as a B-29 gunner, bombing a Japanese airfield on the island of Truk. Ben and his crew logged two more raids in the closing days of January, twice bombing Japanese airfields on Iwo Jima.

For veterans of the European air war like Ben, the contrast between Japanese and German air defenses was striking. German antiaircraft fire was usually heavy and disciplined, and the fighter pilots were equally skilled. Ben had seen nothing of that skill or intensity in his first three missions against the Japanese. But would that still be the case over Japan's home islands? Ben and his comrades could only wonder what awaited them when they finally got a chance to attack the Honshu heartland.

Chapter 44

DÉJÀ VU

On February 4, 1945, Ben and the men of *Honorable Sad Saki* were among 129 crews that took off from the Marianas to attack Kobe, Japan's sixth largest city and most important port. The city was a shipbuilding center, but its workers also manufactured steel, railway machinery, rubber, and munitions. Its rapid growth had occurred in more recent times, and thus much of the construction was less vulnerable to fire. But Kobe's population density and proximity of industrial and residential areas made the city an intriguing test of Lauris Norstad's conviction that saturating Japanese cities with incendiaries would be the best use of the B-29s.

As *Honorable Sad Saki* approached Kobe with Ben in his pressurized tail compartment, Japanese air defenses filled the skies with heavy and accurate flak and about two hundred fighters. The raid could have ended badly for Ben and his comrades, but the Japanese air defenses were surprisingly inept. Despite their favorable numbers, the Japanese managed to shoot down only one B-29, while damaging thirty-five. Sixty-nine B-29s reached the target, dropping 159.2 tons of incendiaries and 13.6 tons of fragmentation bombs.

The incendiary raid proved far more destructive than precision attacks by B-29s had been thus far. Fires ignited by the American incendiaries destroyed or seriously damaged 1,039 buildings in Kobe's southwest industrial district. Civilian casualties were described by the air command as "only moderate," but 4,350 people were rendered homeless. Five of Kobe's major military factories sustained damage and one of its two major shipyards saw operations reduced by half. Among other industrial losses, Kobe's production of fabric and synthetic rubber was wiped out.

For Ben and his comrades, the raid was a milestone: They had flown fifteen hundred miles across the open Pacific to rain fire and destruction on Japan's Honshu heartland, and they had returned to their base on Tinian without a scratch.

Despite the effectiveness of the incendiary-heavy raid on Kobe, LeMay and his commanders promptly reverted to the high-altitude, precision attacks they knew best from Europe. The bombing accuracy was as poor as the previous attempts to cripple Japan from higher altitudes, and the Americans paid dearly with the lives of their crews.

February 10 was an especially costly day for Ben's comrades in the 505th Bomb Group. Their target was another Nakajima Aircraft assembly plant, this one in the southern Tokyo suburb of Ota. Twenty-one 505th aircraft took off for the raid. Eighteen reached the target, but only ten returned. Two B-29s collided over the target and crashed. Another was last seen being pursued by ten or so Japanese fighters. One disappeared without a trace on the return flight. And three others ditched in the Pacific, with all members of two crews rescued and four members of the third crew, including the pilot, lost. One 505th B-29 had crashed on takeoff.

Back on the ground, Ben and a handful of other veterans of the air war against Nazi Germany felt a dark flash of déjà vu as the 505th airmen and ground crews processed the pain of their losses.

THE FEBRUARY 4 KOBE RAID HAD only intensified Hap Arnold's interest in the use of incendiaries against Japanese cities. Eight days later, Norstad suggested to LeMay a major incendiary attack on Nagoya "to secure more planning data."[1] LeMay didn't need an interpreter to divine the meaning of the message: Arnold was getting impatient.

February 19 proved to be an auspicious day for the B-29s. As the Marianas-based Superfortresses winged their way to Tokyo, Marines stormed the beaches of the Japanese stronghold at Iwo Jima. In Washington that same day, Hap Arnold issued a B-29 target directive that elevated incendiary attacks on the Japanese cities of Nagoya, Osaka, Kawasaki, and Tokyo to a priority level only second to precision attacks on aircraft engine factories. Underscoring the command-level interest in incendiary attacks, another "test raid" on Nagoya was ordered for February 25. Once again, bad weather forced a diversion to alternate targets around Tokyo.

As February drew to a close, Ben had logged eight missions in his Pacific tour. The long flights over open ocean were nerve-racking, but weak Japanese air defenses compensated for it. In any event, fortune had smiled on the crew of *Honorable Sad Saki*. From his perch in the tail compartment, Ben had seen only one Japanese fighter in his five-plus weeks of combat.

In a letter he wrote home in late February, Ben shared only the bare outlines of his latest adventure. "There are still a few of my dishonorable ancestors running loose on this island, but they don't give us much trouble," he reported. But his lighthearted tone grew darker as he wrote, and his words revealed a growing weariness with the strain of war. "I'm sure if more people could see the actual tragedies of battlefronts, they would be resolved to make this the last war," he wrote.[2]

As Ben revealed a glimpse of his combat stress, the B-29 campaign against Japan was poised to take an especially grim turn. In his eagerness to prove his patriotism to anyone inclined to doubt him, Ben had often spoken nonchalantly about bombing Tokyo as payback for Pearl Harbor. At that very moment, far up the chain of command, planning was underway for an attack like none ever inflicted in the history of warfare. Ben would be among the eyewitnesses to Tokyo's night of unimaginable horror.

Chapter 45

FIREBOMBING TOKYO

In the early twilight of Friday, March 9, 1945, Ben sat in his tiny tail compartment as *Honorable Sad Saki* rumbled along a runway at Tinian's North Field. He was about to be part of Curtis LeMay's radical reset of the B-29 bombing campaign against Japan.

The mission began with the planes of the 314th Wing's two bomb groups taking off from Guam at 5:35 p.m., followed by the 313th Wing bombers on Tinian forty minutes later. The last to follow were the 73rd Wing aircraft on Saipan. In all, it would take two hours and forty-five minutes to get 334 B-29s airborne and headed north in the gathering darkness.[1]

As the armada thrummed through the night, the bombers encountered a wicked storm front. The B-29s disappeared into heavy clouds, heaving and pitching in pockets of turbulent air. Emerging into clear skies, the navigators finally identified the looming landfall of Japan's main Honshu island. From there, they marked the point where they would begin their final dash to the target. The three wings of the attack force were staggered at altitudes ranging from 4,900 to 9,200 feet, which made the crews especially nervous. They now approached Tokyo at the lowest altitude, and in some of the clearest weather they had encountered in their attempts to bomb the Japanese capital.

Inside *Honorable Sad Saki*, tensions ran high. Many of the B-29 men were convinced that LeMay was sending them to their deaths by ordering them to attack the Japanese capital at an altitude that put them within easy reach of enemy fighters and flak. Would they be blasted from the sky by antiaircraft fire or enemy fighters? Was LeMay's gamble a masterstroke or a death sentence? Ben and the *Honorable Sad Saki* crew were minutes from finding out.

LEADING THE B-29 ATTACK FORCE closing on Tokyo were trained pathfinder crews. A few minutes past midnight, they unleashed their M47 incendiary bombs over assigned aiming points within a densely populated target rectangle that roughly measured four miles by three miles. The first red blotches of fire became visible to the trailing aircraft closing on Tokyo and quickly spread in the stiffening winds. The B-29s attacked in single file, one after the other, some of them fanning out to unleash their firebombs on areas untouched by flames. Smaller fires merged into pulsing forests.[2]

Japanese air defenses had been surprised by the American tactics, and they opened fire in halting fashion. Searchlights scanned the skies, trying to illuminate American bombers for the benefit of ground gunners. As the bombs fell and flames spread, antiaircraft batteries were consumed by fire and the flak guns fell silent. Several dozen Japanese fighters mounted only forty attacks as the bombers rumbled overhead. Forty-two B-29s were damaged by flak and fourteen American bombers were shot down or forced to ditch at sea—far less than feared. LeMay's gamble had already paid off.

It was 3:45 a.m. as the last B-29s passed over Tokyo. By then, a firestorm raged throughout the target zone. Boiling smoke and turbulent heat waves forced the final Superfortresses to bomb blindly through the maelstrom.

On the ground, firefighters were overwhelmed within a half hour. Before the night was out, flames had consumed 95 fire engines and killed 125 firemen. By daybreak, sixteen square miles of Tokyo had been consumed by fire. The carnage was staggering: 83,793 killed (with some estimates twice that number) and tens of thousands of people injured; 267,171 buildings destroyed and more than 1 million people rendered homeless. Radio Tokyo bitterly denounced the raid as "slaughter bombing."[3]

In the light of day, American photo reconnaissance flights revealed the extent of the destruction. Curtis LeMay was triumphant. Hap Arnold, for once, was pleased.

"Congratulations," the air chief cabled LeMay. "This mission shows your crews have got the guts for anything."[4]

From his perch in the tail of *Honorable Sad Saki*, Ben had watched the deadliest air raid in human history unfold—with awe at first, and then shock and horror as a red glow wreathed the Japanese capital. "I was in the tail turret, so as we leave the target I swear for an hour it was just a huge red glare," Ben later recalled. "You know, you could just see the whole city burning."[5]

BUOYED BY THE TOKYO RESULTS AND the vindication of his terrifying new tactics, LeMay pressed his advantage. Barely twenty hours after his weary B-29 crews had completed their post-mission debriefings, swigged a shot of whiskey, and collapsed onto their cots, they were dispatched again to inflict the same fiery punishment on another Japanese city.

On the night of March 11–12, Nagoya was in the crosshairs of the B-29 crews. On March 14, Osaka was the target. On March 16–17, Kobe. On

March 18–19, Nagoya was hit again. Over a ten-day flurry, LeMay's B-29s flew 15,950 sorties, dropped 9,373 tons of incendiary bombs and razed thirty square miles of Japan's four largest cities. LeMay lost only twenty-two planes on the raids.

The fighter opposition and antiaircraft fire continued to be much less than what Ben had experienced in his raids on German targets, but the danger was real. Ben and his comrades resorted to black-humor bantering when they discussed the threat of getting shot down. When Ben's crewmates teasingly suggested that he stick close to them on the ground so they could protect him from getting shot "by some of these trigger-happy guys," Ben had a ready retort: "Yeah, but when we get on the mission and we get shot down, you better stay close to me because I'll bring you rice and fish heads."[6]

AS THE FIGHTING IN THE EUROPEAN Theater in March 1945 culminated with the collapse of Nazi Germany, the air campaign against Japan entered a new phase. The B-29s now alternated between incendiary attacks on major cities and precision attacks on specific industrial and military targets. On March 27, the American air onslaught against Japan introduced another line of attack when Ben's 313th Wing launched the first in a series of missions aimed at mining the Shimonoseki Straits, the vital shipping passageway that separated the Japanese islands of Honshu and Kyushu. The aim was to disrupt the flow of food to the Japanese people, and the mining raids achieved the intended effect. In April, the mining was expanded to shipping channels and harbors under the codename of Operation STARVATION.

Along with the mining raids, the 313th Wing's operations were expanded to include raids on the southern island of Kyushu. Ben and his comrades bombed airfields that were being used by kamikaze pilots for attacks on American ships in the Okinawa campaign.

On the night of April 13–14, Ben and the crew of *Honorable Sad Saki* flew their third firebombing mission against Tokyo. During the raid, 327 B-29s dropped 2,120 tons of incendiary and high-explosive bombs. The raid burned another 11.4 square miles of the capital and destroyed 170,546 buildings. Civilian evacuations and improved response times by Japanese authorities limited casualties to only a fraction of those inflicted in the first firebombing raid against Tokyo, but that was little consolation to the families of the 2,459 Japanese people who died in the April 13–14 raid.

BY APRIL, BEN WAS BREAKING UNDER the stress. When he was on the ground, he feared being mistaken for an enemy soldier and shot by his comrades. When he was in the air, he feared being blown from the sky, lost at sea, or, worst of all, captured and tortured by the Japanese. The moral and ethical dimensions of his work had also begun to trouble him. In the safety of his Tinian bunk after each raid, Ben would drink a shot of whiskey to help him sleep, but sleep became increasingly elusive, and he was tormented by nightmares.[7]

In one of his recurring dreams, Ben was pulled from a jeep by American soldiers and accused of being a Japanese soldier in disguise. They prodded him with their bayonets as he tried to convince them he was a B-29 gunner. A sergeant demanded his identification, but Ben couldn't find his papers. "Honest to God, I'm an American," he insisted. "I'm from Nebraska." "Shoot him," one of the corporals coldly suggested as Ben pleaded for his life. A jeep driven by a friend of Ben's rolled up, but the driver disavowed Ben. Ben was still screaming the jeep driver's name when he awoke.[8] In another dream, Ben confronted a big soldier who called him a "dirty Jap" and began punching the fellow. When Ben woke up, he was pounding his cot with his fists.[9] In other dreams, Japanese soldiers armed with knives were sneaking up on his tent, and sometimes they were actually stabbing him.[10]

The April 13–14 Tokyo raid brought Ben to the breaking point. He became more erratic, his mind going blank at times. He remembered the broken airmen who had been aboard his ship from England and knew he needed help. He went to the squadron flight surgeon and unburdened himself. The surgeon offered to put Ben on the priority list for a rest camp, but he was concerned enough that he reported the encounter up the chain of command.

The following day, the group surgeon informed Ben that he was being removed from combat and shipped home to train crews in aerial gunnery. "You've done more than your share in this war," the group surgeon said. Ben thought of all the people who had lobbied the War Department on his behalf to get him a Pacific assignment, the people he had recruited in the incarceration camps now fighting and dying in Europe, the friends whose deaths he had vowed to avenge. Ben told the medical officer, "I know what my body can take and all I need is a rest, sir."[11]

The surgeon relented. Instead of a transfer back to stateside duty, he arranged a furlough for Ben and his crewmates. Escorted by his closest friends on the *Honorable Sad Saki* crew, Ben boarded an army transport bound for Hawaii.

Chapter 46

WOUNDED ENEMY

In Honolulu, Ben spent his first few days in a military hospital under observation and undergoing tests. Army Air Forces public relations officers now rarely missed a chance to use Ben to generate favorable publicity, and so they arranged for him to visit the offices of the *Honolulu Star-Bulletin* for an interview and photograph. "We bombed Tokyo a week ago," Ben told a reporter, alluding to the April 13–14 firebombing raid, "but we're not supposed to say anything more about that." The *Star-Bulletin* ran a photo of Ben with his *Honorable Sad Saki* crewmate LeRoy Kirkpatrick on April 23.

Ben hinted at the lack of resistance the B-29s now faced. "Japan airpower is becoming weaker every day," he told the reporter. "Iwo Jima has made possible all our recent air actions. Those Marines did a wonderful job. They're responsible for saving hundreds of lives of B-29 men who made emergency landings there." As he always did, Ben shared the spotlight with his crewmates and asked the reporter to include their names in his story. The reporter obliged.[1]

Since leaving the US in December on his latest overseas deployment, Ben had remained in the public eye. Millard Lampell, a young writer and radio producer of national renown now serving as an Army Air Forces sergeant, had fictionalized Ben's story in a radio play that recently aired across the country. Weaving Ben's story into a recurring radio series called *First in the Air*, Lampell had titled his drama "The Boy from Nebraska." The play noted that Ben hadn't been wounded by enemy combatants, but he had suffered injuries from domestic bigots. The story culminated with Ben encountering a racist barbershop owner in Arizona who had a sign in his shop window: "JAP KEEP OUT YOU RATS." The narrator gravely intoned, "He means the boy from Nebraska."

The publicists at the War Relocation Authority helped keep the spotlight on Ben by issuing a press release that noted his exploits in the Pacific and described him as "recuperating from these raids in a Honolulu hospital." The United Press news agency in Washington had written a dispatch based on the release that highlighted the fact that Ben was "the first

Japanese American to help bomb Tokyo." In fact, the UP dispatch noted, he was the only Japanese American flying combat missions in the Pacific.

Although he hadn't actually interviewed Ben, the United Press correspondent assured the American public that the heroic Japanese American airman was "eager to get back to combat." The piece ended with a grandiloquent kicker, proclaiming that as soon as Ben Kuroki wrapped up his Honolulu holiday he would be "dropping more Tokyo roses on Tokyo Rose."[2]

Aside from his newspaper interview, Ben spent his days in Honolulu relaxing. He met up with a few friends and played tourist with LeRoy Kirkpatrick. They took photographs of palm trees and manicured gardens, and Ben posed for a tourist snapshot on the grounds of the Hawaiian royal family's Iolani Palace.

Ben was still in Honolulu in late April when the stunning news from Europe broke: Adolf Hitler had committed suicide in Berlin rather than witness the fall of his capital to the Russian hordes. Shortly afterward, Ben boarded his return flight for the Marianas with his crewmates. They were back on Tinian when another thunderclap broke on May 8: Nazi Germany had surrendered, concluding the war in Europe.

All eyes were on the Pacific and the final showdown with Japan.

As Ben returned to combat in early May 1945, the end of the war was coming into focus. The guns had fallen silent in Europe, and the ground forces of Japan were in retreat in the Pacific.

B-29 crews were now pouring into the Marianas. There had been four hundred B-29s based on the islands in March. By August there would be one thousand.[3] As new crews arrived from US training bases, the 313th Wing headquarters arranged for the transfer of battle-tested crews into inexperienced outfits. Among the veterans tapped to provide guidance to the new arrivals were Jim Jenkins and his *Honorable Sad Saki* crew. Bidding farewell to their comrades in the 484th Squadron, Jenkins and his men now became one of the lead crews of the 680th Squadron of the 504th Bomb Group.

A new unit wasn't the only change that greeted Ben on his return to Tinian. The military population on the island was soaring from a few thousand men when Ben arrived to 26,500 by the summer.[4] With each passing day, battle-scarred Tinian seemed to lose some of the aura of danger that had caused such stress for Ben and his comrades when they had arrived.

Along with the waning risk of an encounter with a Japanese army holdout (or a jittery American sentry), creature comforts increased for the B-29 crews. Gone were the crude lean-tos and tents that had been the only shelter available to Ben and his comrades when they first arrived. Now they slept and lounged between missions in all-weather Quonset huts that shielded them from the sun and the monsoon rains. Touring USO troupes and military ensembles performed in theaters and on open-air stages. Ben could check out a book from the group lending library, or join an athletic league to compete on baseball, basketball, or volleyball teams.

The extracurricular activities helped the men fill their idle hours, but the nature of their work was changing, too. The original vision of conquering Japan with high-altitude "precision-bombing" raids was a distant memory, as was the high-minded talk about waging an air campaign that spared unnecessary civilian casualties. Now incinerating Japan's most important industrial cities, killing factory workers, and breaking the morale of the Japanese people had become American objectives. The air campaign had been conceived as preparation for a ground invasion of the home islands, starting with Kyushu in November. But, as Pacific War air historian James Boyle wrote, with some hyperbole, by May "many American commanders, mostly air officers," had come to believe that the B-29 bombing campaign "would make an invasion unnecessary."[5]

The stakes were enormous. The epic battle for Okinawa was underway fourteen hundred miles northwest of Tinian just as Ben returned to combat. For the American high command as well as the soldiers and Marines on the ground, the fight for Okinawa was a nightmarish glimpse of what was likely to come—unless the air campaign could bring Japan to its knees without an invasion.

WITH THIRTEEN MISSIONS UNDER HIS belt by early May, Ben's Pacific combat tour so far hadn't been nearly as harrowing as the worst raids he flew in Europe and North Africa. Casualty rates for the B-29 crews were a fraction of those incurred by the B-17 and B-24 groups of the Eighth Air Force in Ben's final weeks in Europe in the fall of 1943.[6]

Still, Ben had been around long enough to know that survival in aerial combat came down to luck. It would only take a dime-size piece of flak to kill him or disable *Honorable Sad Saki*. But luck had been a constant companion for Ben throughout the war, and he returned to action in May 1945 with the conviction that his luck was going to hold.

On May 11, 1945—three days after Germany's unconditional surrender in Europe—the B-29s flew their last strike against Japanese kamikaze airfields on Kyushu. That same day, Fleet Admiral Chester Nimitz, commander in chief, Pacific Ocean Areas, released the Marianas-based B-29s from support of the Okinawa campaign. With an eye toward destroying

Japan's industries, LeMay ordered his B-29 group commanders to prepare for more firebombing raids on Japan's principle urban areas.[7]

On May 14, LeMay's B-29 incendiary raids resumed in spectacular fashion with a joint daytime strike by all four Marianas-based air wings. The target was the north urban area of the Japanese city of Nagoya. It was the largest B-29 force mustered against Japan to date, with 529 aircraft taking off for the target. The area included LeMay's top precision target, the Mitsubishi Aircraft Engine Works, and other high-value industrial targets, including the Mitsubishi Electric Company and a branch of the Nagoya Arsenal.[8] The raid was the lead story in the *New York Times* later that day: "500 'Superforts' Blast Nagoya." Within forty-eight hours, the B-29s hit Nagoya again, this time focusing on the city's southern area. The two raids effectively destroyed the city's most important manufacturing concerns and prompted another 170,000 people to flee Nagoya.[9] LeMay crossed Nagoya off his list, but he had other targets in his sights.

On May 23 and 25, the B-29s completed the destruction of Tokyo. Yokohama was gutted on May 29 and Osaka on June 1. In each case, the Superfortresses faced almost no enemy fighter resistance. Only twenty of the 1,433 B-29s dispatched to bomb Japan between March 24 and May 19 were lost to any cause—numbers that underscored the extent of Japan's military decline.[10]

For Ben, the growing sense that Japan was on the verge of defeat was a personal triumph. He had proven his loyalty to America by taking the war to the land of his ancestors, and he had refused an early ticket out of harm's way. He had weathered that crisis and, as victory loomed, was fulfilling his responsibilities as *Honorable Sad Saki*'s tail gunner. But if Ben had learned anything from his months of aerial combat, he knew that disaster was never far away for a bomber crew, even against a wounded enemy.

Chapter 47

A WAR WITHOUT MERCY

The early hours of June 5, 1945, found Ben in the tail compartment of *Honorable Sad Saki*, cruising northward across the Pacific Ocean through overcast skies and sporadic showers. Jim Jenkins and his men had been among 531 B-29 crews that climbed into their aircraft after a late evening briefing and began taking off from Marianas runways before midnight.

General Curtis LeMay had committed all four of his XXI Bombardment Command wings in a "maximum effort attack" on Kobe, Japan's sixth largest city. Before the war, Kobe was Japan's most Westernized and cosmopolitan city—an international enclave with a taste for Hollywood films and American baseball and a curiosity about foreign cultures that was rare in much of Japan. Kobe also began the war as one of Japan's most important industrial cities. Factories produced fighter planes, tanks, diesel and marine engines, ship turbines, and locomotives. The city's shipyards turned out battleships, cruisers, aircraft carriers, and submarines. Its international port was Japan's busiest.[1] Now Curtis LeMay aimed to wipe Kobe off the map, or at least burn it to the ground so that its factories and workers would no longer be able to contribute to Japan's war machine.

Since returning from Hawaii, Ben had settled back into his routine with the Jenkins crew. No pilot would ever measure up to Jake Epting in Ben's estimation, but Jim Jenkins had proven himself a steady hand in combat. His command qualities had not gone unnoticed. Jenkins would be pinning a captain's bars on his khaki blouse in a few days. But combat was all about surviving the moment, and Jenkins had his hands full in this morning's soupy Pacific skies.

The force would eschew the single-file attack mode used during night raids in favor of a conventional four-plane defensive formation. As one of the most experienced pilots in the 680th Squadron, Jenkins faced the tricky task of herding his flight into formation amid these unexpectedly precarious weather conditions. He accomplished this, and dawn found the 680th Squadron Superfortresses approaching Japan's southern islands in clearing skies.

Without warning, shore batteries opened a heavy barrage of fire. No sooner had Jenkins and his trailing crews survived this threat than scores of enemy fighters attacked with startling aggressiveness. For the first time in five months of Pacific combat, Ben and his comrades found themselves fighting for their lives against resolute enemy fighters. Of the more than 500 Superfortresses that had taken off from the Marianas seven or so hours earlier, 473 now approached the city at a ground speed averaging 325 miles per hour.[2]

Driving ahead through the onrushing enemy fighters, Jenkins was poised to pass control of *Honorable Sad Saki* to bombardier Ken Neill when they discovered their aiming point was obscured by a wall of smoke. Rather than bomb blindly, Jenkins pushed through the blacked-out area. On the other side of the veil, Neill unleashed his load of incendiaries.[3]

Jim Jenkins had delivered his deadly ordnance as briefed, but more flak and fighters awaited the crew. In their desperate southward dash out of the target area, *Honorable Sad Saki* faced another "withering barrage" of anti-aircraft fire. They were hit repeatedly, but *Honorable Sad Saki*'s engines and other vital systems remained in working order. Jenkins emerged from the ring of flak to encounter more enemy fighters. In a running battle, Ben and his comrades made their escape.[4]

The mission had been a near-tragedy for the Jenkins crew, but once again, Ben's luck had prevailed. Such luck eluded eleven of the 473 B-29s that reached Kobe: Nine were lost to flak or fighters, or a combination of both, and two disappeared due to mechanical failures.

From the results-oriented perspective of Curtis LeMay, the raid on Kobe was another mission accomplished. The B-29s had blanketed Kobe with 3,006 tons of incendiaries and 71 tons of high explosives, killing more than 3,600 people and injuring another 10,000. The resulting fires incinerated 4.35 square miles of the city.[5] Nearly 180,000 people were rendered homeless by the raid.

Kobe was eliminated from LeMay's priority list of urban targets.

LIKE MOST BOMBER CREWMEN DURING World War II, Ben didn't agonize over the morality of his work. He had asked for this assignment, and he was determined to do his duty. That meant dropping bombs on targets determined by higher-ups, and most of those targets were in congested urban areas where civilians lived. During the war, and even decades later, Ben never publicly questioned America's policy of incinerating Japanese civilians in the final months of the Pacific War. But evidence suggests the topic was on his mind.

In his 1946 book about Ben's wartime exploits, journalist Ralph Martin shared Ben's inner reflections about the Japanese people dying beneath the American bombs and incendiaries—people who looked like him and maybe even thought like him. People who perhaps shared "his hate of Fascism, his love of democracy. All of them, the good and the bad and the innocent—under the bombs."[6]

Interviewed by documentary filmmaker Bill Kubota in the late 1990s, Ben seemed shocked to learn how many Japanese civilians had died in the firebombing raids. "The thing that surprised me the most was I didn't realize the tremendous toll that we'd taken [on Japanese civilians]," he told Kubota. And then, Ben flashed back to his thoughts as he peered down at the columns of smoke billowing from Japan's burning cities. "Sometimes I felt sorry for all the women and children in those situations," Ben said. "There was no way they could escape. We just dropped tons and tons of incendiaries on them."[7]

That's as close as Ben ever came to expressing regret about the firebombing in his public comments.

AMERICAN MILITARY PERSONNEL—prisoners of war captured at places like Wake Island, Guam, Bataan, and Corregidor—were also on the ground in Kobe on June 5, 1945, and they, too, were trapped in the inferno. They were the largest group of American prisoners remaining in Kobe: the doctors, staff, and patients at a facility officially designated Hospital Number 30, but commonly known as the Kobe POW Hospital.[8]

Ten 500-pound cluster bombs splattered the hospital grounds, a mile north of Kobe's harbor, on high ground at the base of the lush Rokko Mountains. A navy dental officer, Lieutenant (junior grade) Stanley W. Smith, was in the operating room when he saw "a blinding flash." He came to beneath a pile of timbers and debris, as fire consumed the building.[9] The doctors and corpsmen freed trapped patients and carried them up the hill and placed them alongside Japanese civilians, many of them badly injured, sitting and lying along the road. The American doctors and corpsmen tended to the injured, administering shots of morphine to badly burned victims. When the flames subsided in the late afternoon, the American medical personnel returned to the blackened ruins of their hospital. Miraculously, only three Americans had been killed. Seventeen POWs suffered burns of varying degrees. And four sustained cuts and other injuries.[10]

In the weeks that followed, a brutal coda to the Kobe raid of June 5, 1945, played out.

One of the eleven B-29s lost on the raid was a 444th Bomb Group aircraft named *Black Jack Too*. The B-29 collided with a Japanese fighter, but all eleven crew members managed to parachute from their stricken bomber.

One of the airmen suffered fatal head injuries during his landing and died on the night of June 5. The others were captured over the next few days and ended up at the Tokai District Army headquarters in Nagoya, about 120 miles northeast of Kobe.

On June 28, the ten surviving crew members and two survivors of a B-29 crew shot down during a May 29 raid were loaded into a military truck and driven into the nearby countryside. One by one, the eleven American airmen were led away to a secluded spot and beheaded by Japanese soldiers.[11]

Other Americans shot down during the Kobe raid met the same fate. The B-29 *Indian Maid* of the 482nd Bomb Squadron, 505th Bomb Group, was hit by flak over Kobe. Five men went down with the plane, but six bailed out and were captured. On July 20, 1945, two of the *Indian Maid* survivors—Sergeant James N. Fitzgerald and Sergeant Harvey B. Kennedy, Jr.—were executed by Japanese soldiers at Shinodayama Military Parade Ground near Osaka. Japanese authorities reported after the war that the other four members of the *Indian Maid* crew who had been captured on the ground died in captivity.[12]

The Japanese military had routinely treated American prisoners of war with brutal contempt since the beginning of the conflict, but the firebombing campaign had encouraged even harsher treatment of captured American airmen. Ben's crewmates had joked with him about the welcome he could expect from the Japanese if he were ever captured. But now execution awaited captured American airman in much of Japan. No one could expect mercy.

Chapter 48

OUT OF LUCK

The fierce attacks mounted by Japanese fighters over Kobe on June 5 were a last stand of sorts. Curtis LeMay's B-29s would never again face such resistance. The city was still burying its dead and tending to its horribly injured people when LeMay dispatched his B-29s back to Osaka Bay on June 7. In the crosshairs of Ben and his comrades of the XXI Bomber Command was the city of Osaka. The bombers of Ben's 313th Wing and two others were loaded with M69 incendiaries while the 58th Combat Wing Superfortresses carried thousand-pound high-explosive bombs. The 58th crews had a target of particular importance: the Osaka Army Arsenal, an important ordnance source for Japanese ground forces in the home islands.

Heavy clouds kept enemy fighters out of the fight, and 409 Superfortresses attacked without a single loss to enemy fire. The cloud cover forced the B-29s to bomb by radar, but it made no difference to the unfortunate souls on the ground: 2.21 square miles of Osaka were burned to the ground. The fires destroyed 55,333 buildings, only 1,022 of which were industrial in nature.[1]

Eight days later, on June 15, the B-29s returned to Osaka Bay for a final attack. Once again, the Marianas wings managed to get more than five hundred Superfortresses airborne for a mission. There wasn't enough of Osaka left to make the city the sole target, so part of the force took aim at the industrial suburb of Amagasaki, home of a major aircraft factory, large synthetic oil refineries, important power plants, and other industrial targets.[2]

The B-29s spent two hours and eleven minutes over Osaka and Amagasaki and didn't see a single enemy fighter. Only one bomber was damaged by enemy fire. The Superfortresses dropped 3,157 tons of incendiaries on the mission, burning an additional 1.9 square miles of Osaka and 0.59 square miles of Amagasaki.

The June 15 raid allowed LeMay to mark off the last of Japan's six most important industrial cities from his list of targets. Tokyo, Kawasaki, Kobe, Nagoya, Yokohama, and Osaka had been reduced to blackened ruins. Phase

I of LeMay's campaign to destroy Japanese industry and force Tokyo's surrender without an invasion was complete.[3]

ON JUNE 17, LEMAY LAUNCHED PHASE II of his plan to destroy Japan's ability to continue the war. This phase centered on the destruction of dozens of secondary cities that now assumed responsibility for much of Japan's remaining war production efforts. The list of these cities was not only much longer, but also presented much smaller targets. As a result, LeMay intended to commit one B-29 wing to one city for each mission. For the opening act, LeMay launched attacks against four cities: Omuta, Hamamatsu, Yokkaichi, and Kagoshima.

Ben's wing, the 313th, was assigned to bomb Yokkaichi, a small port city on Ise Bay, about eighteen miles southwest of the major industrial city of Nagoya and sixty-five miles northeast of Osaka. By the spring of 1945, Yokkaichi's proximity to the major industrial cities of Nagoya, Osaka, and Kobe had put the local population on notice of the peril posed by *B-san*—Mr. B—as America's terrifying Superfortress was known. In the early hours of June 18, 1945, Mr. B appeared in the skies over Yokkaichi. Instead of their war-weary compatriots in Nagoya, the residents of Yokkaichi were the target.

Ben and the men of *Honorable Sad Saki* were among eighty-nine 313th Wing crews that dumped some 584 tons of incendiaries on Yokkaichi from 1:13 a.m. to 3:05 a.m. In the resulting inferno, 736 civilians died and 1,500 were injured. Some 47,000 people were made homeless. The B-29s destroyed 1.23 square miles, or about 60 percent, of Yokkaichi in those early hours of June 18, 1945.[4]

On June 22, after eighty-three days of combat, organized Japanese resistance ended on Okinawa. The casualties were staggering. US forces lost 12,520 men killed or missing and 36,631 wounded in action. More than 77,000 Japanese soldiers died, and an estimated 30,000 or more Okinawan conscripts were killed after being pressed into action by the Japanese. Estimates of civilian deaths ranged from 40,000 to 150,000 Okinawans.

Planning was already underway for Operation DOWNFALL, the Allied invasion of the Japanese home islands. The first phase—Operation OLYMPIC—would begin in November 1945 with the invasion of Kyushu, in the south. The second phase was scheduled for the following spring: Operation CORONET, the planned invasion of Honshu, culminating with the capture of Tokyo. The Okinawa casualty figures underscored the importance of the air campaign if America hoped to avoid the astronomical casualties an invasion promised.

LeMay didn't have to be reminded of this. He pushed his B-29 crews harder. The initial June 17–18 raids on secondary cities became a template for the weeks that followed. On average, the Marianas-based B-29 crews flew two incendiary raids a week, torching four cities a night, taking off in the late afternoon, arriving over their targets in the early morning, and saturating the smaller cities with tons of napalm and magnesium-based incendiaries. Within a matter of weeks, LeMay's intelligence officers were struggling to come up with targets of sufficient size and importance.[5]

Arnold supplemented LeMay's B-29 raids with attacks by other air assets in the Pacific, including the Fifth and Seventh Air Forces and the VII Fighter Command. These units attacked naval and military installations, economic targets, and smaller cities and towns. The aim was to destroy Japan's main cities, "with the prime purpose of not leaving one stone lying on another," as one Twentieth Air Force staff officer later said. The Allied Combined Chiefs of Staff envisioned a higher strategic goal: the destruction of Japanese society.[6]

With the Japanese hanging by a thread, LeMay introduced one final twist to his campaign. On the night of July 27, six B-29s took off from the Marianas with 660,000 leaflets packed into M26 bomb cases. The Super-forts dumped the leaflets over eleven Japanese cities, warning inhabitants that they were going to be bombed in the coming days and that they should flee. On the following night, B-29s hit the first six cities listed in the leaflets. It was an audacious move by LeMay: announcing his target to the Japanese in advance, challenging them to stop the mighty Mr. B. On July 31, twelve cities were warned. Four were firebombed the following day by 627 B-29s. On August 4–5, the same drama played out, and another four Japanese cities were firebombed. Systematically, LeMay and his B-29s had destroyed "the Japanese mind," as one American air commander put it. In the Phase II attacks that began on June 17, LeMay's B-29s burned fifty-eight cities with 54,184 tons of incendiaries.[7]

Ben had achieved his goal of bombing Japan, but his quest to prove his patriotism had also made him a participant in what remains the deadliest air campaign in human history. The US Strategic Bombing Survey conservatively estimated following the war that the firebombing raids carried out by American B-29s in the spring and summer of 1945 had killed 330,000 people and injured 476,000. Some estimates put the death toll from the fire-bombing raids and two atomic bomb attacks at 1 million Japanese civilians.

As AUGUST APPROACHED, BEN HAD nearly seven months of Pacific combat to his credit. He was closing in on the impressive thirty missions he had flown in Europe. He had just completed mission number 27 when he was asked to do an interview for a popular Army Air Forces radio show *The Fighting AAF*. The show was broadcast nationally across America and had made a star of the field reporter covering the B-29 campaign against Japan.

The thirty-three-year-old reporter, Technical Sergeant Harold J. Brown, was tall and lanky, and spoke in a melodious baritone that was pitch-perfect for radio. A native of Lincoln, Nebraska, Brown had moved with his family to California as a child and gotten his start in radio in California's Central Valley before the war. He had broadcast high school baseball games in Fresno and risen to become manager and on-air announcer for station WERN in Bakersfield before enlisting in the Army Air Forces. He had taken on the B-29 assignment with gusto, and only days earlier had flown a firebombing mission to Japan while standing behind the pilot as a wall of flak rose ahead in their path. By the time he asked to interview Ben, Brown had earned an Air Medal for completing five combat missions with Superfortress crews.[8]

Standing near the tail of *Honorable Sad Saki* on the tarmac at Tinian's North Field, Brown covered some of the familiar ground with Ben before drawing out some of his latest experiences in the Pacific. Even though Ben had flown his last Tokyo raid in April, that was the angle that the show's producers back in New York City decided to play up for the show they were putting together with Ben's interview as the centerpiece.

As Ben and Hal Brown chatted, a still photographer prowled around them. The image that the AAF public relations office in Guam wired back to Washington for release showed Ben in his khaki fatigues, sleeves of his blouse rolled up to his elbows, sunglasses case on his belt, and a regulation ball cap protecting his head from the tropical sun. He was speaking into a bulky black microphone that Brown held in his left hand. The backdrop of the shot was Ben's home in the air those past months: the tail section of *Honorable Sad Saki*.

By the time the *Fighting AAF* interview aired on radio stations in America on Sunday night, August 5, Ben's remarkable luck had run out, and his Pacific combat tour had taken a shocking turn.

Chapter 49

UNSCRIPTED ENDING

This wasn't how Ben's war was supposed to end.

He had flown fifty-eight combat missions on three continents, triumphed over death again and again, survived more close calls than he could count. Whether his good fortune was attributable to providence or some other cosmic force, Ben was a survivor. And then, he was on the ground, blood gushing from his head, his life hanging by a thread.[1]

That late July afternoon had been like any other when he wasn't flying a mission. The men lounged around, wrote letters, played cards, shot the bull, drank beer. Ben was sitting in a Quonset hut, drinking with some of the boys, when things got a little raw. They playfully insulted each other all the time, but on this occasion one of Ben's buddies crossed a line. The friend was a Native American airman that everyone called Chief, and the banter that he and Ben sometimes exchanged had a racial tinge to it. But Ben was no longer willing to ignore the slur that had been directed at him so often since Pearl Harbor, and Chief had not only used the slur, but questioned Ben's courage. "You damn Nebraska Japs can't fight anyone," Chief said, or something like that, as Ben and other witnesses later recalled.[2]

Ben looked at Chief to see if he was joking, but when his friend didn't smile, Ben blew up. "You can call Tojo a 'damn Jap,' but don't call me one," Ben retorted. Angry words followed. They went outside and talked a bit. Passions cooled, and soon they were back inside, drinking and bantering as if nothing had happened.

They were sitting around a table and Chief was slicing bread for sandwiches with a carbon-steel bayonet when Ben exclaimed, "I'm not afraid of that knife." He didn't mean anything by it, but Chief took umbrage. Without a word of warning, he slashed the top of Ben's head with the bayonet. Ben fell to the floor, blood gushing from a deep gash. An airman stopped Chief from finishing Ben off while someone ran to summon the Jenkins crew officers. Bombardier Ken Neill ran into the hut and saw Ben sprawled on the floor, the top of his head laid open with a horseshoe-shaped wound.

Comrades tried to stanch the bleeding with a towel while Ben slipped in and out of consciousness. There was a short jeep ride, then an ambulance. Ben later remembered lying on a hospital operating table, plasma coursing into his body through intravenous tubes. The doctors saved his life. "I can't believe I survived that one," Ben later said. "If it had been a half an inch deeper or lower I would have been finished."[3]

BEN WAS STILL IN THE HOSPITAL AS friends and family in Nebraska tuned in to Omaha's KOWH radio station at 7:30 p.m. on Sunday evening, August 5, 1945 to catch his interview on *The Fighting AAF*. Because of the time difference, it was already late Monday morning, August 6, on Tinian. At that very moment, the *Enola Gay*—an enigmatic B-29 that had occupied a North Field hardstand near *Honorable Sad Saki* since July 6—was on its way back to the island following its epochal mission.

On forays to the North Field officers' club in recent weeks, Jim Jenkins had bumped into some of the pilots of the 509th Composite Group, the outfit to which *Enola Gay* was assigned. But the 509th men kept to themselves. It was easy enough for Jenkins and his men to see that the 509th crews had some sort of special status, for their aircraft weren't equipped with gun turrets and they didn't fly combat missions with the other B-29s. "You guys are damn quiet about what you're carrying," Jenkins had remarked to the *Enola Gay* commander only a week or so earlier. "Why don't you tell us?" Thirty-year-old Colonel Paul Tibbetts had evenly replied, "Oh, I couldn't do it, couldn't do it. Call it an island buster."[4]

Tibbetts had been in the command pilot's seat when the *Enola Gay* had taken off from North Field at 2:45 a.m. the morning of the 6th with a single 9,700-pound bomb in its bay. They had flown a northwest course, passing over Iwo Jima, then proceeded to Japan's Honshu island. At 9:15 a.m. Tinian time—8:15 a.m. in Japan—the *Enola Gay*'s bombardier, a North Carolina boy named Thomas Ferebee, unleashed his solitary bomb over Hiroshima, a city the Americans had purposely spared from the firebombing raids. Tibbetts put *Enola Gay* into a banking dive, and about fifty seconds later the bomb christened Little Boy exploded in a blinding flash some nineteen hundred feet above Hiroshima's two-story Shima Hospital.

In a cataclysmic instant, at least sixty thousand lives were extinguished by an atomic bomb.

At 2:58 p.m. Tinian time, after an uneventful return flight, Tibbetts eased *Enola Gay* onto a North Field runway and taxied to a stop. He and his crew emerged from their aircraft to a rousing welcome by a hundred or so Army Air Forces officers, news reporters, and photographers. At an impromptu tarmac ceremony, General Carl A. "Tooey" Spaatz, Hap Arnold's new commander of US Strategic Air Forces in the Pacific, awarded

Tibbetts the Distinguished Service Cross. General Curtis LeMay offered his praise and congratulations.

On the other side of the world, President Harry S. Truman revealed the first atomic bomb strike in a low-key radio announcement to the nation that began in remarkably understated fashion: "A short time ago, an American airplane dropped one bomb on Hiroshima and destroyed its usefulness to the enemy."[5]

A second atomic bomb mission—this one flown by the 509th B-29 *Bockscar* against the city of Nagasaki—took off from Tinian's North Field three days later. On August 14, as rumors of Japan's imminent surrender swirled, LeMay unleashed a final punishing flurry of B-29 raids on Japan. An Associated Press dispatch from Guam, where LeMay was now assigned as a deputy to Spaatz, raised further hopes that the end was at hand: "Superfortresses have struck Japan with a five-thousand-ton demolition attack. Headquarters indicated that the B-29s will continue their crushing blows until a final official surrender notice is received."

That notice of surrender was delivered in extraordinary fashion hours later in a radio broadcast to the Japanese people by Emperor Hirohito himself. World War II was over.

BEN WAS STILL RECOVERING FROM HIS injuries when Japan's surrender was announced. The news set off a mad scramble among the B-29 crews on Tinian, and orders were cut for Jim Jenkins to fly his crew back to the States. Ben was heartsick when the *Honorable Sad Saki* took off from Tinian's North Field for the final time without him.

In September, Ben was finally cleared to return to the States, but all available B-29s were long gone. It took him weeks to get out of the Marianas, but in early October, Ben finally boarded a humble Liberty ship for the Pacific crossing to San Francisco. After twenty-one days at sea, Ben was exuberant to see the Golden Gate Bridge. The "boy from Nebraska," as the AAF play had christened him in the spring, was now twenty-eight years old, a veteran of fifty-eight combat missions, and recipient of three Distinguished Flying Crosses. With no thoughts of future plans beyond getting off the Liberty ship and getting out of the Army Air Forces, Ben stepped ashore along the same waterfront where his father had entered America as a young immigrant forty-two years earlier.

Chapter 50

A GREATER CAUSE

The scene as Ben came ashore in San Francisco was far different than what he had experienced on his return from Europe in December 1943. A Women's Army Corps band was dockside playing "Hail, Hail, the Gang's All Here," and on the ferry transporting troops across the bay to a transit camp, a USO troupe provided live entertainment. At the camp, a colonel welcomed the returning GIs with a rousing speech. As soon as that was out of the way, the men dashed off to indulge in all the deferred pleasures suddenly at their fingertips, including hot showers, sheets, and all the steak and ice cream they could eat.

Ben had just reached his bunk when he was summoned to the orderly room. "Sergeant Kuroki, you're flying to New York immediately to meet General Marshall," a solicitous captain informed him. The captain didn't have further details. Still clad in the sweat-stained khakis he had been wearing since leaving the Marianas, Ben hustled to the nearest air base and boarded a waiting B-24. Shortly after they were airborne, he fell asleep.[1]

Arriving in Newark, New Jersey, that evening, Ben was accosted by an eager lieutenant as he stepped onto the tarmac. The lieutenant directed Ben to a waiting army sedan, and the car threaded its way through traffic and crossed the Hudson River into Manhattan.

The lieutenant's orders were to deliver Ben to the posh Waldorf Astoria Hotel. Unshaven, his shoes scuffed and moldy, his uniform a rumpled mess, Ben asked the driver to drop him at a back entrance. When the registration clerk finally figured out that the scruffy airman was legitimately connected to a big event about to get underway at the hotel, he directed a bellhop to lead Ben to his room.

Ben was sprawled on the bed when his phone rang. It was the secretary of a *New York Herald Tribune* executive, Helen Rogers Reid, who also happened to be the wife of the newspaper's owner and a prominent patron of liberal causes. Could he please come to Mrs. Reid's room right away? Reid, it turned out, was the founding chair of the annual *Herald Tribune* Forum, a prestigious gathering in its fourteenth year. She had read about

245

Ben's Commonwealth Club speech the previous year and thought he would be a perfect speaker for the current events forum. She had reserved a spot for him on the opening night two days from now. Could she count on him?

Everything was settled the following morning. Ben had twenty-four hours to clean up and pull together the speech of his life. With $100 wired from his brother George and a money order from Reid, Ben got a haircut, shave, polished shoes, and a crisp new uniform to showcase his medals and ribbons. Tapping her liberal circle, Reid had arranged for Millard Lampell, the journalist and playwright who had penned the AAF drama about Ben's life earlier in the year, to help write Ben's remarks.

During a frenetic day's work, Lampell and Ben crafted a powerful speech. On Monday evening, October 29, Ben slipped a copy into his pocket and made his way into the crowded Waldorf Astoria ballroom for the night of his life.

As BEN MOUNTED THE STAGE, AN USHER introduced him to an instantly recognizable figure: a tall, emaciated man with four stars on his shoulders and the Medal of Honor around his neck. It was Jonathan Wainwright, commander of the American and Filipino defenders of Corregidor Island in the Philippines until their surrender on May 6, 1942. Wainwright had endured three years of brutal Japanese captivity and had recently returned to a hero's welcome. President Harry Truman hosted Wainwright at the White House on September 10 and surprised him by awarding him the Medal of Honor. Three days later, Wainwright was showered by cheers and ticker tape as he rode through the streets of Manhattan in an open limousine. Now this living, breathing symbol of Japan's wartime brutality offered Ben a nod of greeting. In his nervous state, Ben reached out to shake the general's hand rather than salute him.

Glancing around the stage, Ben felt intimidated. Along with Wainwright and army chief of staff General George C. Marshall was the celebrated air general, Claire Chennault, who had commanded the US Fourteenth Air Force in China during the war. Representing America's allies were President Sergio Osmeña of the Philippines and Australia's foreign minister, Dr. Herbert Evatt. The other speaker was Navy Captain Harold Stassen, former Minnesota governor and recent Pacific naval combat veteran, now poised to resume his political career.

Just as he had been unnerved by the news coverage of Japanese atrocities in the Philippines on the eve of his Commonwealth Club speech, Ben now felt the eyes of the audience bore into him as he sat next to the brutalized hero of Bataan and Corregidor. After sitting anxiously through Marshall's keynote address, Wainwright's remarks, and other speeches, Ben finally stepped to the podium. He was so nervous that he initially forgot to make eye contact with the audience and rushed through his written pages.

Gaining control of his churning emotions, Ben slowed his pace and began to connect with the people in the room. Ben's epic journey had never lacked for poignancy, but Millard Lampell's pen had elevated his oft-told tale to an American allegory. It was still the inspiring story of a humble Japanese American farm boy who had risked everything to prove his love of country. But now it also became a summons to the nation to redirect the commitment mounted against foreign fascism into a fight at home to forge a more perfect union for *all* Americans.

"Not only did I go to war to fight the Fascist ideas of Germany and Japan, but also to fight against a very few Americans who fail to understand the principles of freedom and equality upon which this country was founded," Ben declared.

I've had fifty-eight bombing missions now, and I'm still tired enough so my hands shake, and plenty of nights I don't sleep so good. I'd like to go home to Nebraska and forget the war, and just lie under a tree somewhere and take it easy. It's hard to realize that the war is not over for me. Not for a lot of us Jewish Americans, Italian Americans, Negro Americans, Japanese Americans. While there is still hatred and prejudice, our fight goes on. Back in Nebraska on our farm, when I planted a seed, I knew that after a while I'd get a crop. That's the way it was with a lot of us in this war; we went to plant the seeds to bring in a crop of decency and peace for our families and our children.

Back in high school in Nebraska, one of the things they taught me was that America is a land where it isn't race or religion that makes free men. That's why I went to Tokyo. I went to fight for my country, where freedom isn't color, but a way of life, and all men are created equal until they prove otherwise. That's an old idea we have in Hershey, Nebraska, just down the highway from Cozad, which is near North Platte.

The room exploded with thunderous applause reminiscent of Ben's Commonwealth Club speech nearly two years earlier. Embarrassed, Ben finally returned to his seat. The gaunt General Wainwright extended his hand with an approving smile. As the audience continued to convey its appreciation, Ben bowed awkwardly. With the reaction reverberating throughout the room, a smiling Helen Rogers Reid motioned for Ben to stand once again to acknowledge the crowd's approbation.

OVERNIGHT, BEN'S SPEECH ELEVATED his profile in a way that none of his wartime interviews ever had. He had established himself in the vanguard of a postwar movement to create a more just and equitable America.

Ben was inundated with interview and speaking requests. He decided the time was right for a book about his exploits and so he asked Millard Lampell if he would write it. Lampell begged off, but he found a reporter friend who was interested.[2] During the war, Ralph Martin Goldberg had written for the army's *Stars and Stripes* newspaper and *Yank* weekly magazine under the pen name Ralph G. Martin. A Jewish kid from Brooklyn, Martin viewed Ben's story as a saga that could speak to important American themes beyond the battlefield. He soon struck a deal with Harper & Brothers Publishers in New York and set to work interviewing Ben.

Everybody, it seemed, wanted a piece of Ben.

At the *Herald Tribune* Forum, Ben had seemed to be handling the spotlight in stride. Privately, he was struggling. He felt terribly alone and wanted nothing more than to go home. That line in his speech about lying under a tree somewhere and taking it easy wasn't just a rhetorical flourish. He felt like he was breaking down again. He was so tense and nervous that he found it a challenge to pick up the phone and order room service at the Waldorf Astoria.[3]

He received orders summoning him to Washington, DC, and it was all he could do to drag himself aboard his train at Penn Station.

At the Pentagon, Ben met with Colonel Howard Rusk, director of the Army Air Forces convalescent and rehabilitation services. Ben pleaded for a furlough that would allow him to go home for a few days. Rusk agreed to do what he could. Before leaving Washington, Ben was invited to dinner with Dillon Myer, director of the War Relocation Authority, which was in the process of closing its network of incarceration camps and releasing the inmates. Ben arrived at Myer's home, expecting a private dinner, only to encounter a host of other guests. Ben kept losing his focus. At one point he heard a bugler blowing taps somewhere in the distance and broke down, "crying and shivering, his cheeks twitching uncontrollably."[4]

After his disastrous dinner, Ben caught a train to New York City with one final obligation before his furlough. Army Public Affairs had agreed to make Ben available for an interview on *Report to the Nation*, a national CBS radio show originating in New York City. At Penn Station, Ben asked the Travelers Aid USO desk for help in booking a hotel room. "Are you a Chinese or Japanese American?" the attendant asked. Ben was taken aback. "I'm just asking because I wanted to save you embarrassment," the attendant explained. "There are some hotels here that won't accept Japanese Americans."[5]

Ben found a hotel that would have him and made his way to the Manhattan studio for his Saturday night appearance on *Report to the Nation*. He shared top billing with big-name British actor Boris Karloff, and held himself together.

As he prepared to leave New York on Sunday, November 4, Ben made news with the publication of an interview he had given to a United Press correspondent in Washington. In the interview, Ben had waded into a spiraling controversy involving the American Legion, the country's biggest veterans' group. Local Legion chapters were denying membership to Black veterans in the South and Japanese Americans on the West Coast. Ben told the UP reporter that Nisei soldiers might have to form their own group to make sure their story was told.[6]

By taking on the powerful American Legion, Ben enhanced his standing even more with prominent liberals, civil rights activists, and advocacy groups. But Ben's head was elsewhere. Boarding his train in New York City, he began the first leg of his journey home.

BACK HOME IN HERSHEY, BEN TOOK long walks around the farm and surrounding fields and then ventured into town. He stopped by his high school and gave a talk to students. He made a tearful visit to console Gordy Jorgenson's mother.[7]

Each day's mail brought reminders of the important work that awaited him on the East Coast. Among the requests he fielded was one from the University of Pittsburgh, asking to use his *Herald Tribune* Forum speech for teaching tolerance to high school students. Another request came from the mass circulation *Reader's Digest* magazine, which wanted to reprint his speech in its January 1946 issue. There were countless letters from ordinary people he had inspired.

On his return to New York City, Ben and other Japanese American veterans were feted by the Japanese American Citizens League with a banquet at the celebrated Delmonico's restaurant. The following evening—November 22, Thanksgiving—Ben appeared on the national *America's Town Meeting* radio show. During the broadcast, he continued to passionately make the case for an America that lived up to its highest ideals. "The enemy is Fascism, whether it's in Germany or a congressman from Mississippi," Ben declared.[8]

Ben's plainspoken convictions once again impressed listeners. "Magnificent in its exposition of true Americanism and eloquent in its denunciation of racial and religious discrimination was the speech of Sergeant Ben Kuroki, the American war hero of Japanese strain, during the Town Hall meeting, last night," commented the *New York Daily News*.[9]

In early December, Ben was invited to offer comments at a daylong conference on managing the civilian transition of more than a million Army Air Forces personnel. The event was held at Mitchel Field, Long Island. Among the senior military leaders who shook Ben's hand were Army General Omar Bradley, now serving as President Truman's veterans administrator, and four-star general Carl Spaatz and three-star Jimmy Doolittle. Millard Lampell's *Boy from Nebraska* radio drama was played for the audience and Ben was called to the stage. He was given a standing ovation, with the legendary generals leading the applause.

For the rest of the year and into January, the Army Air Forces kept Ben busy speaking to civic groups and clubs across the country. Ben had taken up residence in a YMCA in Lower Manhattan, and he returned from his travels to stacks of laudatory mail.

In mid-February 1946, Ben reported to Fort Dix, New Jersey, to receive his discharge. He had given four years and one month to the Army Air Forces, and Uncle Sam had gotten his money's worth. As Ben signed his name on the discharge form and collected his final paycheck, he felt an overwhelming sense that the work he had started on the stage of the *Herald Tribune* Forum wasn't finished. He had a stack of invitations to speak to civic clubs, schools, and other religious and community groups around the country. He couldn't turn away from this opportunity to help shape a better America. He would have to do it on his own dime, but he felt just as passionate about this new mission as he had felt about serving as a combat gunner.

Ben loved America, but these past four years had illuminated the imperfections of the American experiment. His parents had come to this country as immigrants more than forty years earlier. They had worked and paid taxes, and yet federal law prevented them from becoming US citizens. State law in Nebraska prevented them from owning land. Why? Why were Black Americans and Japanese Americans forced to fight in segregated units during the war? Why couldn't they eat in certain restaurants or stay in certain hotels? These questions haunted Ben, and he believed they should haunt other Americans.

He had fought to prove his loyalty to America. Now he would fight for a cause that was bigger than he was, and far more important than his personal quest for respect and acceptance—a cause that went to the heart of what America was, and what America would be.

Chapter 51

FIFTY-NINTH MISSION

Two weeks after Ben was honorably discharged from the Army Air Forces, the Sunday magazine of the Omaha *Morning World-Herald* newspaper ran a full-page article on Nebraska's celebrated war hero. "Ben Kuroki's 59th Mission," the main headline read. And then, in smaller type: "Nebraska Nisei Hero Turns on Race Hatred." The piece marked the rejuvenation of one of Ben's most important wartime friendships, as the author was none other than Cal Stewart, the 93rd Bomb Group public relations officer who had done so much to highlight Ben's combat exploits throughout his time with Ted's Travelling Circus. Stewart had returned to Nebraska in the fall to resume his newspaper career, and he had pitched a piece on the high-flying Nisei war hero to the state's largest newspaper.

Stewart had caught up with Ben in New York City to flesh out his story about the war hero's transition to crusading activist. Ben was living in a small room in the massive YMCA on West 23rd Street in Lower Manhattan. It was known as the McBurney YMCA, and it was one of New York City's largest residence clubs, with 279 rooms on ten floors, a gymnasium, swimming pool, handball courts, and meeting rooms for various social, civic, and artistic activities.[1] Stewart cast Ben's place of residence as further evidence of his humble grounding. "He has many admirers who would willingly install him in a more elaborate set-up in a fashionable downtown hotel," Stewart wrote. "But he prefers the congenial cosmopolitan and friendly atmosphere of the YMCA. Because, he's the boy from Nebraska."[2]

No longer a soldier, Ben had taken to wearing business suits at his appearances. But he counted his Army Air Forces uniform as one of his most cherished possessions. It hung in the closet of his room, still adorned with his medals and ribbons.

Ben had arrived in San Francisco the previous October with only a vague notion of returning home to Hershey and resuming his life on the farm. But the reaction to his speeches and public appearances had caused him to rethink his plan for the future—or at least his immediate future. He even had a catchy title for what he planned to do.

"My hands still shake a little, but I've got one more mission to go," Ben had said during his Thanksgiving evening broadcast interview. "There is still the fight against prejudice and race hatred. I call it my fifty-ninth mission, and I have a hunch that's one mission I won't be fighting alone."[3] It was a clever reference that likely originated with Millard Lampell, but Ben liked it, and now Cal Stewart—creator of the 93rd's catchy "Ted's Travelling Circus" moniker back in England—fixed a name for Ben's crusade in the public mind.

Ben shared his rough plan for the rest of the year: He would knock out as many speaking engagements and interviews as he could through the spring and summer, and then head home to resume his life. He had shown little interest in college before the war, in part because of his tight finances, but now, with the GI Bill of Rights signed into law by Franklin Roosevelt in 1944, Ben didn't have to worry about paying for his higher education. He had begun to imagine himself as a college boy. Come fall, Ben told Stewart, he hoped to enter the University of Nebraska's College of Agriculture. "I figure it this way: Farming is what I know best," Ben said. "There have been lots of changes in farming methods since I went away, and if I'm going to be a good farmer, I've got a lot to learn."

Stewart had his own thoughts on what Ben should do with his life, and, if he didn't share them with Ben during this visit, he did at some point in the months ahead. For now, Ben had a plan for the rest of 1946. But his life since Pearl Harbor had rarely gone according to script, and neither would his journey back to civilian life.

AMONG THE PERQUISITES THAT HAD suddenly fallen his way over the past four months, Ben had become the most prominent Japanese American in the public eye by early 1946. He had been just an unremarkable Nisei farm boy when he attended the speech of Japanese American Citizens League leader Mike Masaoka in the North Platte church basement on December 7, 1941. Now Ben was being given access to bigger platforms than Masaoka.

Masaoka had emerged from the war with painful political baggage stemming from the JACL's decision to encourage cooperation with the West Coast roundup of people of Japanese descent. Masaoka would later contend that he and other JACL leaders had been assured by Roosevelt administration officials that the removal of people from their West Coast homes would only be temporary and there had been no talk of mass incarceration.[4] Whatever the reality, Masaoka would be forever tainted by the incarceration.

During the war, Masaoka served in the army as publicity officer for the 442nd Regimental Combat Team. One of his brothers lay buried in a

European grave and two others carried the scars of combat wounds. In early 1946, Masaoka resumed his role as JACL's national leader, and he set to work organizing the group's ninth biennial convention in Denver. When the gathering got underway on February 28, one of the speakers was Ben Kuroki, billed as "a Nisei war hero of World War II."

The convention highlighted the postwar issues of importance to people of Japanese descent, including a timely and just peace treaty with Japan and repeal of the federal law that barred Ben's parents and tens of thousands of other Japanese immigrants from obtaining American citizenship. Another priority was government compensation of individuals who had suffered financial losses in the roundup.

Ben's crusade against bigotry was of particular interest, because so many Asian Americans and other Americans of color faced discrimination and race hatred in their daily lives. The return of Nisei and Black troops from overseas had highlighted examples of these festering issues, including acts of violence committed against Black veterans as they returned to their homes in the South.

The lead story in the JACL newspaper, *Pacific Citizen*, on March 23 highlighted the appalling treatment of wounded Nisei veterans returning from combat in Europe. Forty-four wounded Nisei veterans of the 442nd RCT, including nine amputees, had endured shoddy treatment during their weeks-long stay in a California military hospital. As if that weren't bad enough, the Nisei veterans had been forced to travel in the hold of the navy transport *President Hayes* on their passage from San Francisco to Honolulu.[5]

That same March 23 issue of the *Pacific Citizen* reflected Ben's soaring profile in the Japanese American community. An article about a Nisei veterans appreciation gala in Salt Lake City scheduled for the following week noted two main speakers: Mike Masaoka and Ben Kuroki.[6] Another article reported that Ben had been invited to join the provisional committee for a new veterans group devoted to minority veterans. Overnight, Ben's war record had given him a seat at the table.

THE LEGACY OF THE DRAFT RESISTANCE movement that Ben encountered at Heart Mountain in April 1944 was another issue that hung over the Japanese American community in the war's aftermath. The movement had quickly spread to eight of the ten camps in the continental US. Eventually, some three hundred incarcerated men refused to undergo their preinduction physical or otherwise defied their summons to serve.

The Heart Mountain dissidents seized the national spotlight in two high-profile trials. The young artist Yosh Kuromiya was one of sixty-three men from Heart Mountain who went on trial on federal draft evasion charges at the US District Court in Cheyenne, Wyoming, on June 12, 1944. The men waived their right to a jury trial, placing their fate in the hands of Judge T. Blake Kennedy. On June 26, Judge Kennedy found all sixty-three defendants guilty and sentenced them to three years in federal prison.

The second trial involving the Heart Mountain dissidents got underway in Cheyenne on October 23, 1944, with seven leaders of the camp's Fair Play Committee and the sympathetic Nisei journalist James Omura accused of conspiring to encourage draft evasion. On November 1, a jury found the seven Fair Play Committee leaders guilty and acquitted Omura. The following day, the seven committee leaders were sentenced to federal prison terms ranging from two to four years.

Both groups of Heart Mountain defendants appealed. When the Tenth Circuit Court of Appeals in Denver affirmed the convictions of Kuromiya and his codefendants, they were serving their sentences at the federal prison at McNeil Island, Washington. On December 26, 1945, that same court of appeals reversed the conviction of the seven Heart Mountain Fair Play Committee leaders, concluding the court erred in not allowing the jury to consider the civil disobedience argument offered by the defendants. Federal prosecutors declined to retry the seven men and they were released from Leavenworth Prison in Kansas.

Yosh Kuromiya and most of his codefendants from the Heart Mountain resisters case remained behind bars at McNeil Island until July 14, 1946, when they were released with time off for good behavior.

Nisei draft resisters from other camps had faced trials in federal courts in Arkansas, Colorado, Idaho, and Utah, and all were convicted and given prison terms that ranged from six months to thirty-nine months. The resisters at a camp in Poston, Arizona, were convicted on the eve of the war's end and were sentenced to one-penny fines by a lenient judge.

The only Nisei draft resisters to prevail in federal court were twenty-seven defendants from the Tule Lake Segregation Center. US District Judge Louis E. Goodman of the Northern District of California concluded after a brief trial that it was "shocking to the conscience" for the federal government to have jailed American citizens on suspicions of disloyalty and then prosecuted them for refusing to be forced into military service.[7]

On December 24, 1947, President Harry Truman pardoned all wartime draft resisters, expunging the conviction of Yosh Kuromiya and the other sixty-two men from Heart Mountain convicted of evading the draft. But not even a presidential pardon could erase the stigma the draft resisters and No-No Boys faced in their highly conformist and close-knit communities. In a March 1946 letter to the editor published in the *Pacific Citizen*,

Ben called on his Nisei peers to "stop bickering over the past." But Ben had underestimated—or even completely dismissed—the depths of anguish and anger that many Nisei and Issei in America felt over the injustices committed against them by the US government during the war. Ben had faced bigotry during the war, but he and his family had not been forced from their land or incarcerated, and he seemed unable to make that distinction.

Back in the fall of 1944, as he was trying to win War Department approval for his deployment to the Pacific, Ben had been ordered to Cheyenne to testify as a prosecution witness in the conspiracy trial of the seven leaders of the Heart Mountain Fair Play Committee and journalist James Omura. In the end, Ben wasn't called to the stand, but he had condemned the draft resisters to a newspaper reporter outside the courthouse after the trial. The activities of the Japanese American draft resisters were "a stab in the back," Ben declared. "These men are Fascists in my estimation and no good to any country. They have torn down all the rest of us have tried to do."[8]

Since Pearl Harbor, Ben had been tormented by his fears of what other people, especially white Americans, thought of him. Did they see him as a loyal American or a "lousy Jap"? That fear had driven his actions for the past four years, and he continued to struggle with these insecurities in the war's aftermath. He never wavered in his wartime belief that Nisei men should swallow the government injustices they had suffered and seek a combat assignment like he had to prove their loyalty to America.

Most of the young men, including Yosh Kuromiya, had defied the draft out of principle, not ideology, but Ben could never accept that. The draft resisters and the No-No Boys and their supporters would never forget nor forgive Ben. The day would come, far in the future, when their voices would be heard.

FROM HIS ROOM IN THE MCBURNEY YMCA, Ben arranged interviews and speaking appearances, read and responded to stacks of mail, and attended meetings in his new role as an activist for veterans' affairs and racial justice. His war experiences continued to appeal to radio interviewers and producers. The radio station WMCA in New York City broadcast a dramatization of Ben's battle experiences on the popular *New World A-Coming* program, which had a Black host and frequently featured stories on discrimination experienced by African American veterans. Ben's story was also featured on the *Treasury Salute* radio program, which was sponsored by the US government as part of its drive to pay off war debts.

Through Millard Lampell, Helen Rogers Reid, and other liberal contacts, Ben became one of the leaders in an effort to enlist returning veterans in a campaign to advance a progressive agenda. At the forefront of the movement was the upstart American Veterans Committee (AVC), which presented itself as a progressive alternative to the conservative American Legion and Veterans of Foreign Wars. AVC had adopted the motto of "Citizens First, Veterans Second," and it made opposition to racial discrimination a core issue. The AVC's organizing campaign was aided by some marquee political names, including Franklin Roosevelt, Jr., and Philip Willkie, son of the late Republican presidential candidate Wendell Willkie.

Ben was involved in the formation of yet another veterans' group, this one calling itself the National Veterans Organization. This group was founded by minority veterans with the specific goal of addressing issues experienced by minority veterans. As accounts from around the country made clear, these problems were systemic: Local Veterans Administration officials had provided little or no assistance to minority veterans in some parts of the country. While a white veteran could enlist his local American Legion or VFW chapter to help him with the VA, the American Legion and VFW had effectively turned their backs on minority veterans by allowing local chapters to bar non-whites from membership.[9]

The National Veterans Organization leadership committee that included Ben lobbied the Veterans Administration and its national head, General Omar Bradley, to aid minority veterans. They specifically asked Bradley to press regional VA administrators to hire minority staff at local facilities. But the Truman administration was treading carefully on civil rights matters because of a backlash from Southern Democrats, and Bradley took his cue from the White House. Although discrimination and segregation were rife in the country's VA facilities, Bradley would only *encourage*— not command—regional administrators to make more minority hires.

As Bradley and his chief medical director rationalized, they couldn't force local VA facilities to "depart from community patterns too rapidly," as one newspaper put it.[10] It was clear to Ben and other minority veterans involved in these groundbreaking efforts that the problems they had exposed weren't going to be fixed overnight. Still, they had succeeded in turning a national spotlight on the racist and discriminatory practices faced by minority veterans.

BEN HAD AMPLIFIED THE VOICE OF minority veterans, but many Americans in early 1946 didn't believe that bigotry was the country's most pressing issue. At every turn there was talk of Communist subversion aimed at conquering America. The January 25, 1946, issue of the *Nashville Banner*, one of the newspapers in Tennessee's state capital, offered a snapshot of these fears. Among the stories was one about the War Department stepping up its drive "to purge subversive civilian employees from Army posts." Another warned of "communistic activities" in the Tennessee Valley Authority, the New Deal–era electrification program. Still another story reported that the Grand Exalted Ruler of the national Elks social fraternity had vowed before a gathering of seven hundred Nashville Elks that the organization "will fight communism and all other un-American blocs until hell freezes over."

Some prominent East Coast elites were soon running scared. Agnes Meyer, a liberal journalist married to the publisher of the *Washington Post*, wrote a five-part series for the paper in the summer of 1946, praising the work of a leftist Chicago community organizer named Saul Alinsky. By the following January, Meyer was warning a gathering of "women's patriotic groups" in Washington, DC, that "communism and socialism are on the march throughout the world" and "their fanaticism must be met with a positive and realistic program if we are to win the battle."[11]

Ben and others publicly challenging America's status quo on racial, social, and economic matters found themselves in the line of fire by early 1946. There were suggestions from some quarters that those publicly highlighting America's shortcomings were "pinks" or "reds" who were softening the country up for a Soviet-directed Communist revolution. Smears were hurled at some of Ben's new friends and associates. A prominent conservative columnist and writer, Westbrook Pegler, accused the American Veterans Committee of being leftist or even Communist.[12] Although Ben was a homespun conservative at heart, he was sailing into a gathering storm.

For now, Ben earnestly threw himself into his activism. Named to the planning board of the American Veterans Committee, Ben began speaking at organizing rallies around New York City. Addressing several hundred veterans and their supporters at a March 20 rally at a Brooklyn high school, Ben declared that "an attack against any minority is an attack on the United States of America."[13] He would repeat variations of that line in speeches over the next year. He also addressed the International Convention of the YMCA in Atlantic City, New Jersey, and shared an Upper West Side stage with Mike Masaoka at a Manhattan event where he was introduced as a JACL "special representative and national speaker of minority problems."[14]

At some point early in 1946, Ben was introduced to the novelist Pearl S. Buck, the daughter of American Christian missionaries to China who had already been honored with a Pulitzer Prize for her 1931 novel about China, *The Good Earth*, and the Nobel Prize for Literature in 1938. During the war, Buck had created the East and West Association to assist the Allies by promoting a better understanding of the people and cultures of China and India. In the war's aftermath, Buck and her foundation had taken a strong stand against continued European colonial rule in Asia while supporting the fight against bigotry and racism at home.[15]

Ben's Fifty-Ninth Mission Tour was exactly the sort of thing that Buck and her association sought to support, and so an arrangement was reached: Ben would continue his speaking tour with the association's endorsement and some financial support.

Chapter 52

A PATH IN PEACE

During a swing through the West in early 1946, Ben was invited to a dinner at Mike Masaoka's house in Salt Lake City. Although Ben had a date, one of the other guests caught his eye. She was a beautiful University of Utah student whose brother-in-law had roomed with Masaoka at the university several years earlier.

After dinner that night, Masaoka took the group to a local dance hall. Ben and the student were both awkward dancers, so they paired off and spent much of the evening together. Ben learned the short version of her life story. She was about to turn twenty-two. She was born and raised around Pocatello, Idaho, about fifty miles from Minidoka, one of the camps he had visited in 1944. And, like Ben, her father had been a farm boy who had immigrated from Japan in 1904.

Her name was Shige Tanabe, and Ben was smitten.

On his first visit to meet Shige's parents in Idaho, Ben made a memorable impression. Euphoric at regaining the liberties of his pre-army life, Ben had taken to smoking cigars and drinking beer. He arrived at Shige's house with a six-pack and stashed it in the refrigerator—not realizing that Shige and her family were devout Mormons who didn't drink and didn't smoke. "I think the family was always in a state of shock," Shige later recalled of her dating life with Ben. "He wasn't the normal boyfriend."[1]

In a matter of weeks, the cigar-smoking, beer-drinking, non-Mormon boyfriend proposed to Shige. She accepted, and on August 9, 1946, they married in the town of Tyhee, Idaho.

After a brief honeymoon, Ben returned to the East Coast with Shige to continue his speaking tour. The East and West Association had given him the title of executive secretary of the Washington Council, but it sounded more impressive than it was. While the association helped arrange events, Ben paid most of his own expenses. He was burning through his savings.

In October, two months into their marriage, Ben and Shige celebrated the release of Ralph G. Martin's book, *Boy from Nebraska: The Story of*

Ben Kuroki. It was an exhilarating time, and the book received favorable reviews in major publications.

"Ben Kuroki is now on what he calls his fifty-ninth mission—the fight against prejudice here at home," wrote the *New York Times* reviewer. "All who believe democracy has a future must wish him well. Ralph Martin has told his story simply and clearly. It is a good book. It should be widely read."[2]

Throughout the fall of 1946, Ben traveled the middle Atlantic states, speaking to high school students and civic clubs about the importance of racial tolerance in a healthy democracy and promoting his book in radio interviews and bookstore signings. At a series of appearances in Binghamton, New York, in November, Ben and a popular Greek actress shared speaking honors as part of World Friendship Day, an event sponsored by the East and West Association to promote "international understanding and goodwill."[3]

After Thanksgiving, Ben and Shige headed west for the holidays. They spent several days in Nebraska, where Ben delivered more speeches, including one at the University of Nebraska's main campus in Lincoln. He detoured to the northern Nebraska town of O'Neill to introduce Shige to his friend Cal Stewart, now publishing a local weekly newspaper. The couple spent time with Ben's family in Hershey, then continued on to Idaho.[4]

After ringing in the New Year with Shige's family, Ben prepared to return to the East Coast. His savings were nearly depleted and speaking invitations were drying up. His Fifty-Ninth Mission Tour had been an extraordinary capstone to his combat exploits, but Ben was looking ahead to his next challenge.

THE FINAL ACT OF BEN'S CRUSADE unfolded over twenty-nine days in early 1947. Traveling to five states and the District of Columbia, Ben delivered his well-honed speech—"The Unfinished Fight for Democracy"—and gave interviews. On some days, he spoke to four different groups, with audiences ranging in size from the dozens to the hundreds.

He kicked things off with an appearance on *Americans All*, a radio program hosted by Tomlinson D. Todd, a prominent Black civil rights activist in Washington, DC. Ben appeared on the show with US senator Glen H. Taylor, a progressive Democrat from Idaho. For his segment, Ben was interviewed by Grace Yaukey, sister of the novelist Pearl Buck. "It seems to me so terribly important that if America is to be the leader of world democracy we should set a true example at home," Ben solemnly declared.[5]

After a stop in New York City, Ben proceeded to Wallingford, Connecticut, for events on February 9. A few days later, he traveled to the Berkshires of western Massachusetts for two events in Pittsfield. He spoke to congregants in the Sunday morning services at the First Methodist Church and then addressed an evening crowd at the First Congregational Church. Before an audience of five hundred that evening, Ben built to a soaring finish. "To make the United States the proving ground that people can all live together in peace and without prejudice is our great obligation," he said. "To quote Franklin Roosevelt, Americanism is not and never has been a matter of race and religion. Americanism is a matter of the heart and mind."[6]

The following day, February 17, Ben returned to Binghamton, New York, for the biggest event of his finale. Ben had made his public speaking debut almost exactly three years earlier at the Commonwealth Club in San Francisco, nervously taking the podium before a well-heeled audience of one thousand in San Francisco's finest luxury hotel. His appearance at the *Herald Tribune* Forum had been before another high-powered crowd in New York City's most elegant hotel. Now, although the crowd size in Binghamton equaled or exceeded those in San Francisco and New York City, Ben found himself living a classic Americana moment: a farm boy from Nebraska who had made something of himself, addressing a salt-of-the-earth audience in a high school gymnasium near the confluence of the Susquehanna and Chenango Rivers in Upstate New York.[7]

Ben rose to the occasion with another inspiring event. "Though many Fascists were killed during the war, we have not killed fascism nor the tenets of racial superiority," he declared as he built to a climax. He called out organizations like the Ku Klux Klan as the obvious face of fascism in America, but warned that the American ideal was being undermined in more subtle ways, including by unjust laws.[8]

He called out the discriminatory immigration laws that barred his parents from American citizenship, "even though they have lived here forty-five years, raised ten children, and given two of those children to Army service." He called out the lack of legal protections that allowed people of color to be barred from "certain New York City hotels" or restaurants or other public facilities. When he declared with rising vehemence that "an attack on one minority is an attack on all minorities," the overwhelmingly white audience burst into applause. He concluded with a summons to those before him and the country at large: "I do not believe that war has brought peace, and I urge you to join the Fifty-Ninth Mission, the fight against intolerance here in America."[9]

The pace of Ben's appearances picked up for the remainder of the month. In Fredericksburg, Virginia, scene of a great Civil War battlefield that saw 1,300 Union soldiers killed and 9,600 wounded, Ben spoke four times during the course of a day.

He made his final stop on March 3 in Gettysburg, Pennsylvania, another town whose name would be forever linked to the four-year struggle to preserve the Union and extinguish slavery. Members of the International Club of Gettysburg College had invited Ben to their campus, and he met some of the students in a gathering at the home of the college president.

As a photographer snapped away, Ben sat on a couch beside the president of Gettysburg College, Dr. Henry Hanson. To Ben's right was an Arab student from Palestine. Over his right shoulder stood a Pennsylvanian of German ancestry who had served with the navy in the Pacific during the war. Over Ben's left shoulder, bending forward slightly to follow the conversations, was a dark-skinned student from the Philippines, which the US had finally granted independence the previous year after forty-six years of colonial rule. Next to the Filipino stood a young man from China, then a student from France and a student of Indian ancestry from British Guiana.[10] It was an all-male group, but otherwise symbolic of the diverse America that Ben had sought to celebrate in his Fifty-Ninth Mission Tour.

Later, three hundred people crowded into the Brua Chapel on campus to hear Ben deliver the speech that was etched into his heart and mind. His story was the story of so many Americans, he explained. "I am fighting against discrimination not only against the Americans of Japanese descent, but also discrimination against any other minority. For an attack on one minority is an attack on all minorities. And an attack on minorities is an attack against all America."[11]

The big idea that Ben had tried to convey to his audiences was that America's success in the fight against fascism and other totalitarian ideologies hinged on the morality of its actions at home and abroad. As the weeks had passed, he had inserted into his speech examples of postwar injustices committed against returning veterans of color. These included the confiscation of land from Japanese American veterans in California, who had acted as legal proxies for parents targeted by alien land laws, and the beating and lynching of Black veterans in the South.

"The United States should be a leader of democracy—but stealing land from ex-GIs because their parents are Japanese, or killing Negroes, does not speak well for America to the world," Ben said. "We can't afford to lose our position morally as an exponent of democracy, for the news of our discrimination spreads everywhere in the world immediately. Those who continue race prejudices are few—but so were the groups that put Hitler and Tojo into power."[12]

It had been another good day for Ben, but he was physically and emotionally spent. The country was hurtling toward a second Red Scare in the aftermath of President Harry Truman's losses in the midterm elections four months earlier and the rapid deterioration of US-Soviet relations. Eighteen days ahead, in the most infamous act of his presidency, Truman would sign Executive Order 9835—the so-called Loyalty Order—setting in motion a witch hunt for Communists in the federal government. The Cold War abroad had unleashed icy winds at home, and progressive crusades like Ben's Fifty-Ninth Mission Tour faced growing peril.

Tired, nearly broke, and discouraged that his tour hadn't produced policy changes or other tangible results, Ben was ready to go home.

IN JUNE 1947, ONLY WEEKS AFTER returning home, Ben entered the University of Nebraska as a student on the GI Bill. His brothers, older and younger, had attended the university before him, but none of them got the attention that Ben received. The university chancellor personally welcomed Ben to campus, invited him to his office for a chat, and posed for photographs.

A reporter at the *Lincoln Evening Journal* got wind of the presence of the renowned war hero who had enrolled in the summer session and arranged an interview. "You might say that Ben, one of America's most heavily decorated war heroes, is back home and broke," the reporter began his article.[13] Ben was honest about his tight finances. He expected to "sweat out" four years of college. "I doubt that the GI subsistence payments will be enough to see us through," he said. "One of these days, we'll be needing a washing machine and a lot of stuff like that. Anyway, I'm going to get a part-time job somewhere."

The reference to a washing machine was a scoop for the reporter: Shige was expecting their first child.

Ben freely admitted that he had hoped to have a greater impact on American attitudes with his crusade. "It was a pretty thankless undertaking," he said. "It was discouraging." But he hadn't abandoned his hope of fostering change in America. With encouragement from Cal Stewart, Ben had decided that a career in journalism, rather than farming, would give him a voice in the struggle for America's soul.

Whatever his disappointments, Ben didn't regret devoting the past two years of his life to challenging Americans to broaden their minds on matters of race and justice. "I'd do the same thing over again," he declared. He had given everything he could to his Fifty-Ninth Mission Tour. Posing for a photographer with textbooks tucked under his right arm, Ben was off and running in his new quest to serve his country through the pursuit of journalism.

The shy Nebraska farm boy had become a celebrated war hero, inspirational speaker, progressive crusader, aspiring journalist, husband, and father-to-be. The war was over, and Ben Kuroki had found his path in peace.

Chapter 53

PUBLISHER, REPORTER, EDITOR

In the spring of 1950, with Shige now caring for a pair of baby girls, Ben prepared to graduate from the University of Nebraska with a degree in journalism. He had gotten some hands-on experience at Cal Stewart's weekly paper in O'Neill, and he was inspired. He could have applied for a reporting position with one of the big papers in Lincoln or Omaha, or sought a job with a smaller paper around the state. But Ben had bigger plans. He wanted to follow in his friend's footsteps and publish his own local newspaper.

With Shige's blessing, Ben scouted the area and discovered that the longtime owner of a weekly paper in the town of York, fifty miles west of Lincoln, was ready to retire. Within a week, and without discussing his plan with Cal Stewart, Ben took out a loan and signed the papers to buy the *York Republican* and its antiquated printing presses.

Ben was a newspaper publisher. And then it hit him: Now what?

In his college journalism classes, Ben had learned how to report and write and edit a newspaper story. But he had only a vague idea of what being a small-town weekly publisher entailed. As the publisher of the *York Republican*, he would be in competition with an established daily newspaper owned by a statewide chain. The can-do self-confidence he had honed in the military had served him well in combat, but now, with his family's future on the line, those defining traits had led him out on a limb.

Ben drove the 150 miles to O'Neill to lay out his predicament to his friend.

Stewart put the word out to Nebraska newspaper friends, many of them World War II veterans themselves. Within a week, more than forty ink-stained community newspaper publishers and editors converged on York to undertake what Stewart dubbed Operation Democracy. They sold ads, reported and wrote stories, and designed pages. They had initially planned a special edition of eighteen pages, but Stewart's squadron sold so many ads that the number of pages spiraled. By the time the special Operation Democracy Edition of the *York Republican* hit the streets on June 8, 1950, the community could peruse forty pages of news, sports, editorials, features, and photographs.[1]

Word spread beyond Nebraska of the extraordinary launch of the Nisei war hero's newspaper career. Ben had kept a low profile since ending his Fifty-Ninth Mission Tour and returning to Nebraska in the spring of 1947. Now he was once again the hot interview sought by journalists from national publications such as *Time* and *Life*, the *New York Times*, and state and regional newspapers.

Some of the reporters asked Ben why he had chosen small-town life over a city. "I wanted to go someplace where I could find security, a home where my kids would be respected," he told a reporter for the *St. Louis Post-Dispatch*. "I just wanted to be accepted by the community and live in peace."[2]

Ben seemed to feel the need to reassure his local readers that he didn't buy the paper as a platform for his Fifty-Ninth Mission crusade. "The story has gone out that I wanted a paper as an organ to keep up my fight against intolerance, but that's not the point at all," Ben said. "Of course, the paper will be against such things, as any good newspaper should be, but all I want is to put out a good community newspaper."[3]

Heartened by the support of his fellow journalists, Ben was also relieved by the local reception he received. York residents had warmly welcomed Ben, Shige, and their two daughters. "It almost scares me," Ben said, "because it seems almost too good to be true."[4]

A full-page story about Operation Democracy in the *St. Louis Post-Dispatch* on June 18 called the launch "the last chapter in the story of Ben Kuroki."

But Operation Democracy would prove to be only the first in a series of extraordinary chapters in Ben's postwar life.[5]

As Ben feared, the magical start of his newspaper career was too good to be true.

Only a month after the Operation Democracy launch, on Saturday evening, July 8, Ben and Shige were entertaining one of Ben's war friends at the local country club when an unusually heavy summer rain fell. It kept falling, and within hours York was inundated with a record thirteen inches of rain. The Blue River burst its banks. When Ben ventured out into the night with his staff photographer to report on the freak floodwaters, his car got washed away. By Sunday, a good portion of York had experienced heavy damage.[6]

Cal Stewart once again rallied community newspaper editors to give Ben a hand with the publication of a special flood edition.[7] Ben survived the flood, but it was a harbinger of the hard times ahead. The financial challenge of making the *York Republican* a viable enterprise proved too great, even with a $10,000 loan from his younger brother Fred.[8] After eighteen months, Ben surrendered to a challenge for one of the few times in his life. On January 11, 1952, he announced the sale of the *York Republican*.[9]

He was closemouthed about his next move, but he turned up in Shige's home state of Idaho within a few months as editor and part-owner of another weekly newspaper, the *Blackfoot Bulletin*. After more than two years in Idaho, Ben left that venture and returned to Nebraska to take a job as a reporter with the *North Platte Telegraph-Bulletin*.

If Ben felt deflated, his work for the *Telegraph-Bulletin* didn't show it. The paper published his first bylined story on December 22, 1954: "Fair Skies, Rising Mercury Greet First Day of Winter," read the headline. "White Christmas Unlikely." Ben had learned his craft well, and the article was solidly reported and concisely written. Over the months that followed, he wrote stories about such varied topics as the subzero camping trip of local Boy Scouts, the retirement of a beloved parks commissioner, and the poignant naturalization ceremony for three local residents.

Nearly exactly a year after hiring Ben, the North Platte paper broke the news of their restless reporter's next move. "Ben Kuroki, courthouse and police reporter for the *Telegraph-Bulletin* since Nov. 27, 1954, left Saturday to take over as editor and publisher of the Williamston, Michigan, *Enterprise*, which he has purchased," the story reported.

Ben's Michigan sojourn spanned a decade. In October 1957, he added to his journalistic empire in the suburbs of Michigan's state capital by starting a tabloid weekly in a nearby township. Once again, Fred chipped in $10,000 to help his big brother realize his dreams.

In 1960, the *Detroit Free Press* published a profile on the Lansing-area newspaper publisher with a fascinating back story. Ben was now forty-three years of age and his wiry frame had filled out. He wore his hair in a military-style crew cut, smoked cigars, and read with the aid of horn-rimmed glasses. He had become an avid golfer and served on the board of directors of his local country club. He dabbled in local politics, winning a seat on the Williamston City Council. He was a member of a local Methodist church, and he and Shige now had three daughters: Kerry, Kristyn, and Julie.

The *Free-Press* story revealed another interesting twist in Ben's life. His certified public accountant happened to be his former B-29 pilot in the Pacific, Jim Jenkins, who lived in the Detroit suburb of Pontiac. "Jim tells me that I'm a good editor, but I'm not so hot as a businessman," Ben quipped.[10] It sounded like a joke, but Ben knew it was also true.

As a spunky small-town newspaper editor, Ben had found his footing. He wasn't afraid to ruffle feathers with tough editorials. At one point, the Williamston City Council voted 4–3 to demand an apology from their local newspaper publisher for a critical editorial deemed unfair by the offended council members. Ben refused and responded directly to his readers in another editorial. "There will be no apologies in the battle for your right to know," Ben wrote.[11]

In 1964, twenty years after Ben's tour of the incarceration camps, the Japanese American Citizens League honored him for his postwar crusade against intolerance at the group's nineteenth biennial convention in Detroit. "People were gripped by wartime hysteria," Ben told a reporter from the *Detroit Free Press*, trying to explain how the liberal Franklin Roosevelt and his Democratic administration came to round up 110,000 people of Japanese descent and confine them to camps. "Propaganda whipped them up."[12]

That same year, Ben revealed his deepening conservatism by endorsing Republican Barry Goldwater for the presidency in a signed column. Goldwater lost in a landslide.

By 1965, labor troubles and tight finances had brought Ben and Shige to the brink once again. In April, they abruptly announced the sale of their two weekly newspapers in the Lansing suburbs and revealed plans to relocate to the West Coast. The family's move to California may have held deeper considerations for Ben and Shige. Their children were growing up in a place almost completely disconnected from their Asian ancestry, and Ben and Shige saw the move to California as a way to change that dynamic.[13]

Ben wasn't unemployed for long. Southern California's *Ventura County Star-Free Press* hired him as an editor, and he began a long and successful tenure with the paper. He was a copy editor, edited the Sunday magazine, and eventually became news editor. While editing and writing stories for the paper, he explored the state that once had been the bastion of anti-Japanese sentiment in America. He camped in the High Sierra near Yosemite, fished for albacore off the Ventura coast, and watched his daughters excel in their various endeavors before they headed off to California universities in pursuit of their dreams.

In 1982, at the age of sixty-five, Ben retired from journalism.

At no point since Pearl Harbor had he experienced such a sudden and disorienting transition. He had a national speaking tour lined up when he left the army in 1946, and then he had college and his journalism career ahead of him. Now he went to work part-time at a golf shop in Ventura, played golf with his buddies and bridge with Shige, and kept in touch with his girls and their lives. But ghosts from the past were stirring.

As with many of his peers, the passage of decades and advancing age increasingly rekindled memories of the war, the terrors of combat and the beauties of comradeship long past. Most veterans hadn't overcome the challenges that Ben had faced, or achieved his fame, and those realities would bring both joy and pain to Ben's life. With the fiftieth anniversary of the Pearl Harbor attack looming in 1991, the shadow of World War II once again fell over Ben.

Chapter 54

HIDDEN HEROES

Ben wasn't like many combat veterans who centered the war as the defining element of their lives and traded on their record at every turn. His innate modesty wouldn't allow that. But Ben was justifiably proud of his war record and the fame he had achieved. In his quiet way, he occasionally let people know he had done his part and had been more than just another faceless grunt.

One of those moments came in 1966 when he walked into the office of the top editor at the *Ventura Star*. Owners of the venerable *New York Herald Tribune* had announced that paper was shutting down, and the news had brought back a flood of memories for Ben. He quietly knocked out a piece about his return from the Pacific in October 1945—about being whisked from San Francisco to New York City aboard an army transport plane and then finding himself on a stage at the Waldorf Astoria Hotel alongside some of America's most celebrated generals. Ben walked into his editor's office at the *Ventura Star* on his day off, with the finished piece in hand. "He dropped a sheaf of copy on my desk and said softly, 'Maybe there's something here that you can use,'" recalled the editor, a World War II navy veteran named Julius Gius.[1]

Gius was stunned by what he read. He recapped Ben's remarkable story for readers, noting Ben had been at the paper a year and neither Gius nor any other of Ben's coworkers had a clue about his spectacular war record or his fame.

A year later, in 1967, Ben was assigned to cover the dedication of a plaque marking one of the incidents that contributed to the roundup and incarceration of Californians of Japanese descent: the shelling of the state's central coast on the night of February 23, 1942, by a Japanese submarine. The plaque commemorating the incident was the project of the Native Sons and Daughters of the Golden West, a vociferous roundup proponent.

Ben wrote a just-the-facts news story about the plaque dedication, but he also turned in a first-person piece about his wartime memories of the Native Sons and Daughters of the Golden West. He was stationed in

England in the fall of 1942 when he picked up a magazine in which the California group was calling for the isolation of all Japanese Americans in a swamp somewhere in a remote corner of America. "I was so mad I volunteered immediately for combat duty as an aerial gunner," Ben wrote, hedging the truth a bit. He had been angling for a combat assignment months before he read about the racist Native Sons proposal.[2]

Only a few weeks after his 1967 brush with the Native Sons and Daughters of the Golden West and the hysteria-inducing submarine attack, four eighth-grade students from a Ventura junior high school came to the *Ventura Star* to interview Ben and Gius for a term paper they were writing on the incarceration of Japanese Americans. It was another moment that transported Ben back in time, something that happened with increasing frequency in the ensuing years.

Ben never spoke about his war service to his girls when they were growing up, but there were hints of the traumas he had endured and the scars he carried. "We had to be super careful about walking around him when he was sleeping," his youngest daughter, Julie, recalled. "If you actually touched him when he was sleeping, he would lash out, reflex-type stuff, thinking that somebody was going to hurt him. But he really didn't talk about it much at all."[3]

As a college student in the late 1970s, Julie became more curious about this hidden chapter of her father's life. She asked him about his war, and it was as if a door had been unlocked. Ben produced a trunk stuffed with photo albums, letters, official documents, and other war memorabilia. It was a treasure trove that revealed an extraordinary part of her father's life that she knew virtually nothing about. Ben allowed Julie to use part of his uniform to fashion the cover of a book she created as an art student. "After that was when he started talking to me about things," Julie said. "As he pulled stuff out of the trunk, he personalized events."[4]

Six years into his retirement, Ben had settled into a life that revolved around family and golf when something prompted him to take his copy of an old wartime book off the shelf. The book was *Air Gunner*, and it told the story of the precarious lives of Eighth Air Force B-17 and B-24 gunners. Ben's combat exploits were among those included by the journalist authors, a pair of army sergeants named Bud Hutton and Andy Rooney. In recent decades, Rooney had achieved fame and celebrity as a curmudgeonly commentator on the popular CBS News show *60 Minutes*. Something prompted Ben to mail his copy of *Air Gunner* to Rooney at CBS News in New York City and to ask the author if he would mind signing the book. When Ben got the book back, Rooney had inscribed it: "To BK, who I'm sure is as great an American in 1988 as he was when I first knew him in 1942—AR 3/25/88."

Around the same time, a national news event moved Ben to write a letter to the editor of the *Los Angeles Times*. The trigger was the US government finally agreeing to make amends to Japanese Americans who had been incarcerated during World War II. After years of lobbying by prominent Japanese Americans, Congress had finally passed legislation for an apology and reparations and President Ronald Reagan had signed it. The *Los Angeles Times* published a letter from Ben in which he recalled being sent on a War Department recruiting mission to the Heart Mountain incarceration camp in 1944. "I vividly remember what a shock it was," Ben wrote. "At the entrance were armed guards wearing the same uniform I was wearing. Inside, behind barbed wire, were 'my own people.'"[5]

What Ben's letter didn't mention was the fact that his visit had stirred controversy within the Heart Mountain community and, in more recent decades, within certain Japanese American circles. The War Department had ordered Ben to visit the camps, and he had complied. Did that make him complicit in the incarceration regime? A collaborator? Ben certainly didn't think so, and neither did many of the inmates who welcomed his visit. But a vocal group of Nisei thought otherwise at the time, and their voices had begun to shape revisionist books and films on the incarceration. Increasingly, the revisionists turned a critical spotlight on Ben.

In early 1990, another ghost from Ben's past came calling. The phone rang one day and on the other end was Charles Brannan, the 409th Squadron adjutant who had helped block an attempt by a couple of bigoted 93rd sergeants who were trying to get Ben out of the group before their deployment to England in the late summer of 1942. Ben's tearful pleas to remain with the group and his subsequent combat heroics had never left Brannan's memory. Now retired in Fayetteville, Arkansas, Brannan tracked Ben down to discuss those events. Afterward, Brannan wrote a letter to the president of the Air Force Association to make sure they were aware of Ben as the fiftieth anniversary commemoration of World War II kicked off. Ben was "one of the Air Force's brave," Brannan wrote. Indeed, in Brannan's estimation Ben "did more for America than people would ever believe unless they were aware of his deeds."[6]

By 1991, museums and historical societies across America were preparing for four years of commemorations marking the fiftieth anniversary of World War II. The Nebraska Historical Society had timed the opening of its World War II exhibition to the fiftieth anniversary of the Japanese attack on Pearl Harbor. During discussions about which Nebraska World War II veteran should deliver the opening night remarks, at the ceremony formally opening the exhibit, the group's leaders decided to invite the Nebraska native son who had been the nation's first Nisei war hero. Ben Kuroki accepted the invitation and flew to Lincoln in early December 1991 to help commemorate the event that changed the course of his life.

ON THE EVENING OF DECEMBER 6, 1991, the largest crowd to ever attend a single event at the Museum of Nebraska History filed into the Nebraska Historical Society's showcase venue in downtown Lincoln to witness the formal opening of one of the society's most ambitious projects ever: "What Did You Do in the War? Nebraskans in World War II," a four-year exhibition marking the epochal events of World War II as seen and experienced by Nebraskans.

Before the festivities got underway, Ben and more than 600 invited guests dined on a buffet of war-era food, including Spam. At the appointed hour, more than 125 VIPs and other select guests were ushered into the museum's auditorium while other invitees gathered around closed-circuit monitors positioned inside the building. More than twenty members of Ben's extended family from five states were among the guests. Also, there were two friends who had vouched for Ben at pivotal moments in his life: 93rd Bomb Group veteran Cal Stewart and retired congressman—and, later, US senator—Carl Curtis, who had secured War Department approval for Ben's Pacific deployment in November 1944.

The director of the Nebraska Historical Society, James Hanson, introduced Ben as one of 110,000 Nebraska men and women who served in the various US military branches in World War II, and Ben—now seventy-four years of age—moved to the podium to deliver his first speech before such a large crowd since 1947.

Ben drew on the themes from his Fifty-Ninth Mission Tour speech as he recounted his wartime service. But he also went out of his way to express pride in his Nebraska heritage. "Nebraska was the American dream for my parents," he said. "During the war, nobody waved the flag as hard as Dad Kuroki."

He was touched by the invitation and went on at length about how much it meant to him. He spoke about how the society might have taken a safer path choosing a Nebraska veteran from the state's white majority to open the exhibition. His leading role in the ceremony was "an honor I considered the very best of my military experience," Ben said. "I somehow feel vindicated. My dogged determination to prove my loyalty to America has been accomplished."

Ben concluded his remarks by remembering his boyhood friend from Hershey, Gordy Jorgenson, one of 3,626 Nebraska natives who had paid the ultimate price during World War II. Ben declared the exhibition open "on behalf of all veterans of Nebraska and especially for my friend, Gordy."[7]

The following morning, December 7, 1991, Ben was still savoring the thrill of his triumphal homecoming when someone alerted him to pick up a copy of the morning's *New York Times*. In an editorial headlined "The Hidden Heroes," Ben's wartime service was celebrated by America's most influential newspaper.

"When the orations are over today, most Americans who fought and died because of Pearl Harbor will have been well and fully remembered," the editorial began. "What happened fifty years ago will have been generously commemorated on television and in print, in speeches and sermons. What remains very much in order is a special tribute to largely unremembered Americans like Ben, an Army Air Force[s] sergeant from Hershey, Neb."[8]

The editorial summarized Ben's record: thirty B-24 missions in Europe, his internment by Spanish forces, and his twenty-eight missions in the Pacific. "Ben was an authentic hero. General George Marshall asked to meet him; so did Generals Bradley, Spaatz, Wainwright and Jimmy Doolittle. He was feted on his return and pressed to make speeches. Yet this, his fifty-ninth mission, needed valor of a different kind. For Ben, as one historian notes, 'couldn't walk into a barber shop in California; he couldn't be sure of getting a hotel room in New York.' His ancestry was Japanese.

"His full name was Ben Kuroki. Like other Japanese Americans after Pearl Harbor, he was at first deemed unfit to serve because of his origin."

The editorial went on to recount the heroics of the 442nd Regimental Combat Team in Europe and the stalwart service of six thousand Nisei soldiers who aided military intelligence efforts in the Pacific. "Prejudice, secrecy, and negligence have denied these brave Americans their full measure of respect and recognition," the *Times* wrote. "All Japanese Americans—those who fought, and the 120,000 who were interned in camps—have earned the apology that President [George Herbert Walker] Bush intends to offer at Pearl Harbor today."

The editorial ended with a Franklin Roosevelt quote that Ben had incorporated into his Fifty-Ninth Mission Tour speech: "The principle on which the country was founded and by which it has always been governed is that Americanism is a matter of mind and heart; Americanism is not, and never was, a matter of race or ancestry."

A few days after returning from Lincoln, Ben received a letter from the Nebraska Historical Society director that he would cherish. "You have won the hearts of Nebraskans," James A. Hanson wrote. "Never so many complimentary remarks. It was a special thrill to read the editorials in Nebraska papers, and the *New York Times* editorial made me fairly burst with pride and admiration."[9]

Ben could hardly have imagined a more thrilling finale to his life's story. Yet even now, at the age of seventy-four, greater honors lay ahead.

Chapter 55

RECKONING, REMEMBRANCE, AND REWARD

Throughout the 1990s, historians and journalists churned out thousands of books on nearly every imaginable aspect of World War II. There were wide-lens looks at the war, close-focus examinations of specific battles or incidents, and biographies by the score. And yet, Ben's story was somehow overlooked in the publishing frenzy.

But he wasn't entirely forgotten.

In 1994, Ben was living in Ojai, a charming spa town in the Ventura County mountains. He spent much of his time on the golf course. As World War II fiftieth anniversary celebrations took place across America, Ben was content to bask in the glow of what he called his "last hurrah"—his 1991 appearance opening the Nebraska Historical Society's World War II exhibition in Lincoln.

When he received an interview request in 1994 from a history professor at California State University, Fullerton, Ben politely declined. The professor's name was Arthur Hansen, and he was an accomplished scholar of the Japanese American experience in America. He had immersed himself in the World War II incarceration tragedy and the resistance to the incarceration. In his research, Hansen had become familiar with Ben Kuroki's story. Hansen was determined to talk to Ben, and so he enlisted his wife to approach Shige through a mutual friend. In that roundabout way, Hansen arranged to sit down with Ben at his Ojai home on October 17, 1994.

Hansen was a masterful researcher and storyteller, and he had developed a philosophy of oral history interviewing. His approach was the antithesis of what he disdainfully referred to as "strip-mining"—the superficial interviews conducted by many journalists and less accomplished historians. Hansen viewed an oral history interview as a mutually enlightening encounter for the interviewer and the interviewee. He structured his interviews to draw out his subject and allow them to relive their life during the course of the conversation. It was a highly effective method.[1]

Rigorous preparation was a hallmark of Hansen's method. He had pored over Ralph Martin's book, flagging the holes, inconsistencies, and questionable facts and carefully preparing his long list of questions. Hansen had requested two days for the interview, but Ben would agree to only one. As it turned out, one day was enough. Over the course of several hours, Hansen covered Ben's story in rich detail. Hansen elicited from Ben a number of revelations, like the fact that Ben's mother, Naka, came to America as a "picture bride," and that professional writers on the army payroll had written Ben's signature speeches before the Commonwealth Club and *Herald Tribune* Forum.

Hansen felt uneasy as he zeroed in on Ben's controversial visits to the three incarceration camps in the spring of 1944. He felt guilty about confronting Ben with questions that he no doubt would find uncomfortable, but his sense of integrity and his commitment to an accurate rendering of history didn't allow him to avoid these uncomfortable moments in Ben's life. Gently, skillfully, Hansen forged ahead.[2]

In Ben's memory, his most intense encounters during his recruiting mission had come at Heart Mountain, the first of his stops. But Hansen had studied the notes of James Sakoda, the Minidoka inmate who was also conducting field research on the camps for the University of California, Berkeley. Sakoda's journals depicted Ben's tour of Minidoka as contentious. When Hansen gently laid out some of Sakoda's notes that suggested Ben's reception at Minidoka was more hostile than commonly portrayed, Ben became defensive.

"That's BS!" Ben exclaimed at one point.[3]

Hansen concluded that the camp visits came in such quick succession for Ben that some of his memories were jumbled. In any event, Hansen had covered the necessary ground to illuminate Ben's collision with the resisters and their conflicting definitions of patriotism. The interview ended in cordial fashion, and they said their goodbyes. Hansen went away thinking that Ben was a good person and a gentleman.

But Hansen couldn't get Ben out of his thoughts. He decided he wanted to write a book about Ben. But first, Hansen had another commitment to fulfill. He was crafting a book from the papers of James Omura, the Japanese American journalist who had supported the Heart Mountain draft resisters and had been acquitted of federal charges during his 1944 trial with the leaders of the Fair Play Committee. Hansen figured he would complete his Omura book in a year or two and then write the story of Ben's life.

In the year after his interview with Ben, Hansen wrote a groundbreaking article about Ben's 1944 visit to Heart Mountain. In 1995, he was invited to an event at Heart Mountain where he discussed Ben's visit and the article he had written about Ben's visits to the camps and his encounters with draft resisters and their supporters. Hansen had essentially concluded that Nisei soldiers like Ben and the Nisei camp inmates who resisted the draft to protest their unjust incarceration represented two strains of patriotism, each worthy of recognition and respect. After his 1995 Heart Mountain presentation, several people approached Hansen to introduce themselves. One of them was convicted draft resister Yosh Kuromiya. They connected immediately, the beginning of a long and cherished friendship.

Hansen continued to think about his Ben Kuroki biography. He and his wife traveled to Nebraska to understand Ben's world in preparation for writing the book. But Hansen was struggling to complete his book on James Omura. He had a heavy course load as a Cal State Fullerton history professor, and there were other competing demands in his life. The two years he had allotted for the Omura project became five, and then five became ten, and ten became fifteen. And still the book defied completion. Finally, in 2018, Hansen held in his hands a copy of *Nisei Naysayer: The Memoir of Militant Japanese American Journalist Jimmie Omura*.

By then, events had overtaken the biography of Ben Kuroki that Art Hansen had been writing in his head for years.

AT THE SAME TIME ARTHUR HANSEN had taken an interest in Ben's story, Ben's friend Cal Stewart had been hard at work for years on the definitive history of the 93rd Bomb Group, the first US Army Air Forces B-24 unit to join the Eighth Air Force in England and the outfit that Stewart had christened Ted's Travelling Circus. Stewart had already made one successful foray into book publishing. In 1959, he sold his weekly newspaper in O'Neill to work full-time on a project he had undertaken with James Dugan, an old army buddy who had published four nonfiction books and forged a profitable writing and film collaboration with the undersea explorer Jacques Cousteau.[4] The topic of the Dugan-Stewart collaboration was a book on the low-level Ploiesti mission of August 1, 1943. For two years, Stewart drove around the country with his family, interviewing Ploiesti veterans. Dugan focused on the writing, and the result was a 1962 Random House release, hailed as the definitive account of the raid.

After completing his work on the Ploiesti book, Stewart moved to Lincoln, where he started a weekly paper and a successful printing business. He was active in the 93rd veterans' association, and in the 1980s began work on his book on the group. The 93rd had flown more missions than any other Eighth Air Force outfit during the war, and the sheer scope of Stewart's effort was staggering. As word of Stewart's project circulated, a mountain of first-person accounts, unpublished memoirs, diaries, letters, and other primary source material found its way to him. Stewart kept chipping away. Finally, in 1996, Cal Stewart's opus—*Ted's Travelling Circus*—rolled off the presses at his Lincoln printing business. Once again, Stewart had done his part to honor Ben's war record, this time by devoting an entire chapter to his story in the book.

Not long after the publication of Stewart's book, two Japanese American journalists became interested in Ben's story. They both had personal connections to it: Frank Abe's father, George, had been incarcerated at Heart Mountain and never forgot Ben's visit in April 1944. Bill Kubota's father, James, had been incarcerated with his family at the Minidoka camp in Idaho and vividly remembered Ben's visit to that camp.

George Abe had immigrated to the US as an unaccompanied thirteen-year-old in 1937, contracted to work on a walnut farm near San Jose, California. When the roundup got underway in 1942, he was sent to the Pomona Assembly Camp in Southern California, then to Heart Mountain. George had been a nineteen-year-old mess hall worker at the time of Ben's visit to Heart Mountain. When the camp closed, a War Relocation Authority officer sent George to Cleveland, Ohio, for resettlement. He married Emma Kiyono Abe, a Japanese woman from his home village in Japan, and they had a son, Frank, in 1951. When Frank was ten, the family moved to Santa Clara, California, where George worked as a landscaper and Emma worked as a dental technician.[5]

After graduating from Cupertino High School, Frank Abe entered the University of California at Santa Cruz and earned his bachelor's degree in theater directing in 1973. He joined playwright Frank Chin's new Asian American Theater Workshop in San Francisco, part of a broader effort by young writers, scholars, and artists to forge an identity rooted in their Asian ancestry. Their effort was known as the Combined Asian American Resources Project (CARP).

In 1976, Abe moved to Seattle to join another theater group, the Asian Exclusion Act, and it was there that his interest in the Japanese American incarceration deepened. Under Chin's guidance, he was one of the organizers of the first Day of Remembrance, in 1978, to draw attention to the injustice of the wartime roundups and kickstart a popular campaign for redress and reparations. Abe helped produce a series of public symposiums on the incarceration camps and was introduced by Chin to the resistance movements inside those camps. The prevailing narrative he had learned in school was that there really hadn't been any resistance.

Abe continued his activism and scholarship after joining KIRO Newsradio in Seattle as a reporter in 1979. In the early 1990s, he and Chin began work on a film project to document the story of the Fair Play Committee and the sixty-three Heart Mountain draft resisters. A pivotal moment in the Fair Play Committee story was Ben Kuroki's April 1944 visit.

Over the years, Abe had become good friends with Arthur Hansen and he knew about Hansen's oral history interview with Ben. Abe needed to get Ben's story on camera for his film and reached out to him. Although Ben knew that Frank Abe viewed the draft resisters in heroic terms, he agreed to the interview after Abe assured him he was committed to giving voice to both sides of the story. On January 31, 1998, Ben and Shige welcome Frank Abe and Frank Chin into their Southern California home.

BEN AND SHIGE'S INTERVIEW WITH the two filmmakers delved into uncomfortable areas Ben had not spoken about for the public record since his interview with Arthur Hansen. The interview wasn't contentious, but it was tense at times. One area that intrigued both Abe and Chin was Ben's feeling that he needed to "prove" his loyalty to America because of Pearl Harbor—a view that Abe and Chin clearly didn't share. That topic first arose when Chin asked Ben about his decision to fly five bonus missions after completing twenty-five missions with the Eighth Air Force. Ben replied, "Well, I just was—wanted to prove myself a little, little more." Chin interjected, "Prove yourself as what?" Ben tried to explain. "Well, wanted to prove my loyalty as a Japanese American."[6]

Abe later revisited the subject and Ben again tried to explain himself. "Well, first of all, I was the same as the Japanese, as the enemy was also Japanese. And I knew I was different. I think the other thing, that I was so upset. I mean, I just felt that Pearl Harbor was terrible, and I think I felt like a lot of the Caucasian kids that wanted to avenge what happened at Pearl Harbor."

Abe asked Ben to explain his 1991 comments at the Nebraska Historical Society event when he described feeling "shame" and his "strange guilt complex" over Pearl Harbor.

Ben said his parents had always taught him "not to bring shame to my own family," and that he viewed the Pearl Harbor attack in that light.

"And yet, you had nothing to do with Pearl Harbor," Abe interjected.

"No, but my ancestors did and that's what come[s] back to reflect on me, is what they did," Ben said.

Abe gently disagreed. "It could be argued that you as a Nebraska-born citizen, American citizen, had your rights, and you had no need to prove anything."

"Well, I suppose you could say that, but I think, you know, you—all of my friends and my high school buddy Gordy Jorgenson, they were all enlisting and . . . anyone with patriotism in his blood would certainly be willing to join the services, I think, at that time in Nebraska, anyway," Ben said.

The exchanges between Ben and his interviewers over his 1944 tour of the camps were the most fascinating of the hours-long encounter. At one point, Abe said he had interviewed some Heart Mountain inmates who recalled Ben encouraging them to volunteer, in spite of their loss of homes and constitutional rights. Abe quoted one of the young men as asking Ben, "So you think it's okay for us to be evacuated and locked up here?"

Ben said he never condoned the roundup and incarceration. "Oh, I didn't think for a minute that it was fair, the way they got locked up or the tremendous losses that they suffered," he said. Ben pivoted, praising the government apology and $20,000 reparations payments to incarcerated individuals. "It's just absolutely great that a country could admit a mistake after so many years," he said. "And then to apologize, it couldn't have happened anywhere else except in the United States. It's a great country."

Turning to the prosecution of the Heart Mountain draft resisters, Abe wanted to know what Ben would have said if he had been called to testify at the autumn 1944 federal trial of the Fair Play Committee leaders. Ben initially demurred, but when pressed harder he said, "I certainly wouldn't have agreed with their stance, for sure."

Abe also questioned Ben about his condemnation of the resisters as "fascists" who were "doing no good." Did Ben still feel that way?

"At that time, I think that was the normal reaction for me because, my gosh, the publicity was terrible that was coming out about the trial and everything," Ben said. "And it was bad enough that the Bataan Death March in the Philippines was being headlined in the newspapers, the Japanese enemy doing those horrible things in the Death March and you know, everything was—there was so much going on at the time that it really made things worse as far as I was concerned."

As Abe persisted, Ben offered a concession. "Well, I think it was pretty strong stuff. I wouldn't say that today." He laughed nervously. "But at the time, being young and gung-ho, you know, waving the flag, being patriotic as I was, I can understand why I said those things."

Abe and Chin had covered some of this same ground with Shige earlier, and she had explained the culture of conformity that existed in the Japanese American community at the time and how that shaped views of the resisters.

Her view of the resisters had evolved with time, Shige offered. "I think I, I have a feeling more of compassion than I [did], that they had their reasons, and they certainly were—had to be very, very brave to have stood by their principles. That isn't easy to do, particularly in war."

Shige added, wistfully it seemed, "In hindsight, don't we all see the errors that we made then?"[7]

BEN'S INTERVIEW WITH BILL KUBOTA later in 1998 focused more on his military service. The interview stretched over two days and Ben covered the span of his life to that point. Bill Kubota's father, James, had been a thirteen-year-old boy in 1944 when Ben visited the Minidoka camp, and he had encouraged his journalist son to tell Ben's story. Kubota was a producer at the public television station in Detroit, WTVS, and his vision was to get Ben's story on film and air it nationally on PBS.

While the Frank Abe film on the Heart Mountain resisters and Bill Kubota's film, tentatively named *The Ben Kuroki Story*, slowly moved forward, Ben and Shige encountered serious health issues. In a ten-day span in 1999, both of them had heart surgery. "We almost lost Shige," a shaken Ben recalled a few years later. "Her heart stopped."

In March 2000, feeling better after their surgeries, Ben and Shige traveled to Honolulu, Hawaii, where Ben addressed the 442nd Regimental Combat Team annual tribute. The heroic story of the 442nd, with its tales of extraordinary valor and "Go For Broke" motto, had eclipsed Ben's story as the definitive Japanese American World War II saga over the decades. The outfit was the subject of a 1951 Hollywood blockbuster, *Go for Broke!*, and a number of books. While the 442nd remained in the public eye, Ben's story had largely receded from public memory. And yet, as Arthur Hansen described it, Ben Kuroki *was* the 442nd before there was a 442nd.

Ben's appearance at the 442nd tribute—and the warm reception he received—was especially gratifying for Ben after experiencing some tensions with the group several years earlier. Ben had declined an invitation to address 442nd veterans in the 1990s because of his desire to keep a low profile, and there were hurt feelings among them over that. It was a healing experience for Ben and Shige to spend a few happy days with surviving members of the 442nd and their families.

Two months later, Frank Abe's film, *Conscience and the Constitution*, had its world premiere in Los Angeles. It was a powerful piece of work and audiences were moved by the accounts of the Heart Mountain draft resisters and the price they paid for their principled stand, both during the war and in the decades that followed. As Ben had expected, he took some criticism from the resisters who appeared in the film. But, true to his word, Abe had given Ben and his story a fair hearing. Afterward, Ben sent Abe a note "to say he appreciated the way we had conducted the interview and that we were welcome to come back to visit him," Abe recalled. "That really meant a lot to me."[8]

Ben's comrades, especially 93rd Bomb Group veterans, viewed him in a far more positive light than the resisters and their supporters. His comrades knew what he had endured on the ground and in the skies, and they viewed him as a great American who had never been appropriately honored by his country.

By 2002, Cal Stewart was at the forefront of an effort to change that.

VETERANS OF THE 93RD BOMB GROUP had begun gathering for annual reunions in the 1950s. In 2002, with the survivors now in their eighties or even nineties, the men of the 93rd and their families converged on Colorado Springs, Colorado, for a reunion. The US Air Force Academy had prepared a plaque commemorating the World War II feats of the 93rd, and the unveiling of the memorial on the academy plaza was to be a highlight of the gathering.

Although Ben had been a dues-paying member of the association for years, he had never attended a reunion. Now, at the age of eighty-five, with Shige at his side, Ben made his first appearance. At the poignant plaque unveiling ceremonies, Ben and his old 409th Squadron commander, K. O. Dessert, represented the group. Ben also delivered formal remarks at the annual banquet. The group's president, retired colonel Alfred Asch, saluted Ben for his "tremendous contribution to freedom and democracy."[9]

At the Colorado Springs reunion, Cal Stewart continued to talk up the idea of securing higher official recognition of Ben's wartime service. A year later, meeting in New Orleans, the 93rd Bomb Group Association veterans formally set in motion an effort to have Ben's highest military decoration—the Distinguished Flying Cross with two Oak Leaf Clusters—upgraded. Ben didn't attend that reunion, but he discouraged talk of nominating him for the Medal of Honor, insisting he didn't meet the very specific qualifications of the US military's highest honor. The 93rd veterans resolved to nominate Ben for the army award just below the Medal of Honor, the Distinguished Service Medal.

After two years of diligent work that included writing letters and gathering testimonials, lobbying politicians and senior military officers in Washington, DC, and enlisting the influence of such luminaries as former president George H. W. Bush, the army finally approved the presentation of the Distinguished Service Medal to Ben.

The ceremony was set for Lincoln, Nebraska, on August 12, 2005. On the eve of the presentation, the *Los Angeles Times* ran a lengthy profile of Ben under the headline "Righting a Wrong, US to Honor WWII Vet's Bravery." Ben and Shige flew to Nebraska for the ceremonies, which rivaled the welcome that Ben had received when he had opened up the Nebraska Historical Society's World War II exhibition fourteen years earlier—an event that Ben had once described as his "last hurrah." The Distinguished

Service Medal was draped around Ben's neck before a crowd of hundreds of well-wishers, including a former high school student inspired by Ben during his Fifty-Ninth Mission Tour in 1946–47. "I had to fight like hell for the right to fight for my own country," Ben said in his remarks. "And I now feel vindicated."[10] The ovation was loud and long.

The following day, the Nebraska Press Association bestowed its President's Award on Ben and the University of Nebraska awarded him an honorary Doctorate of Humane Letters. Feted at a luncheon hosted by the University' of Nebraska Journalism and Mass Communications Department, Ben said, "My humble life has been on cloud nine and words cannot adequately express my gratitude for priceless friends who do not judge a man by his ancestry. At the ripe old age of eighty-eight, I consider myself the luckiest person on this planet. And these two days in Lincoln, Nebraska will be forever cherished. God bless the University of Nebraska. And God bless America."[11]

The honors continued to flow.

In 2006, Ben, Shige, and Julie, their youngest daughter, were guests at the White House State Dinner that President George W. Bush and First Lady Barbara Bush hosted for Japanese Prime Minister Junichiro Koizumi. In 2007, Ben returned to Lincoln, Nebraska, to attend the August 1 premiere of *Most Honorable Son*, Bill Kubota's documentary film about his life. The film aired nationwide on PBS later that fall. Sadly for Ben, he flew back to Lincoln two weeks later to deliver the eulogy for Cal Stewart, who had finally succumbed to his battle with cancer.

Ben returned to Washington the following year for more honors. During the White House Asia Pacific American Heritage Month ceremony in 2008, President George W. Bush delivered a heartfelt tribute to Ben. Ben stood and saluted, and President Bush returned the honor.

During that trip, Ben was also the guest of honor at the Smithsonian National Air and Space Museum for the dedication of an exhibit honoring his service. At a private banquet presided over by the museum's director, General J. R. Dailey, Bill Kubota's *Most Honorable Son* was screened in the Lockheed Martin IMAX Theater. Describing himself as "the luckiest dude on the planet," Ben concluded, "Your public event is the ultimate tribute and your heartwarming gesture epitomizes the goodness of Americans. Thank you and God Bless America."[12]

Julie had become more than her father's caretaker as he traveled the country to accept various honors. She was Ben's sounding board and trusted advisor. Her devotion was total. Among her many cherished memories of their time together was her father's command of the minutia of current events, history, and popular culture that allowed him to cheerfully dominate family games of Trivial Pursuit. He possessed "one of the most wonderful minds I ever met," Julie recalled. "His thinking ability was so off-the-charts brilliant."[13]

By then in his nineties, Ben was among the dwindling number of World War II veterans alive to acknowledge the gratitude of their countrymen. In 2010, Ben received the Audie Murphy Award at the American Veterans Center 13th Annual Conference and Awards Gala in Washington, DC. Two years later, he was inducted into the Nebraska Aviation Hall of Fame.

In the fall of 2014, Ben was ninety-seven when he received an invitation to open a new "Road to Berlin" exhibition at the National WWII Museum in New Orleans. Ben's children thought the trip was too risky for his health, but Ben was determined to go. He phoned the nephew of a 93rd Bomb Group pilot, Joe Avendano, who had flown with him in 1943 and died in a training accident in England in early 1944. Ben explained his predicament to the nephew, Joe Avendano Duran. "Joe, would you be my escort?"[14]

Joe Duran thought it over and discussed it with his wife, Phyllis. They both had gotten to know Ben over the previous fifteen years through their research on Joe Avendano. They weren't sure whether he would survive the rigors of the trip, but they both believed that if Ben Kuroki wanted to go to New Orleans for one more "last hurrah," he had earned that right.

In early December 2014, Joe Avendano Duran escorted a wheelchair-bound Ben through the Burbank airport to their New Orleans flight. Once aboard, a flight attendant asked Joe for more details about Ben's story. Later in the flight, the pilot made his way back to see them. "You're a survivor of fifty-eight combat missions?" the awestruck pilot asked Ben. After a brief conversation, the pilot returned to the front of the plane and then his voice came over the intercom. "We have a special guest with us today," the pilot announced. He gave a brief synopsis of Ben's remarkable story. When he finished, the pilot said, "I'd like everybody to give Mr. Ben Kuroki a hand." The plane erupted in cheers and applause. "Ben couldn't stand up, but he raised his hand and kind of waved," Duran said.[15]

The event at the National WWII Museum came off without a hitch. Once again, Ben was the star of the show. Much to Joe Duran's relief, Ben survived the journey without incident. "It was a great sendoff," Duran said.

This was indeed Ben's last hurrah, or at least his final in-person last hurrah. Within months, his health took a turn for the worse. On September 1, 2015, Ben died at the age of ninety-eight. His passing was noted by several national publications. In a lengthy obituary, the *New York Times* paid tribute to his epic quest to prove his patriotism in World War II. "Ben Kuroki Dies at 98," the headline read. "Japanese American Overcame Bias to Fight for U.S."

EPILOGUE

The doors of the Smithsonian National Museum of American History in Washington, DC, swing open at 10:00 a.m. every day of the year except December 25, and before closing time, five thousand people on average make their way inside. On the northern fringe of the National Mall, along Constitution Avenue between Twelfth and Fourteenth Streets, the 750,000-square-foot facility has been a magical place for me since my second visit as a nine-year-old in the summer of 1968. Like most visitors, I had always spent my visits wandering through the three main exhibition levels, marveling at such artifacts as Abraham Lincoln's stovepipe hat or Dixie Gillespie's trumpet, oblivious to the inner sanctum that occupies two upper levels.

In June 2023, as students on the school year's final tours vied with tourists in the public rooms, Smithsonian curator and project director Jennifer L. Jones escorted me into her hidden world in the Military History division to examine one of the museum's lesser-known acquisitions of recent vintage. In 2008, Ben had bequeathed his papers, scrapbooks, and war memorabilia to the museum. I would be the first outside scholar to examine the collection, she said.

Ben's story had first appeared in my life thirty-three years earlier, in 1990, when I began a quest rooted in my childhood. My mother had endured several scarring traumas early in life, but perhaps the most profound was the disappearance of her oldest brother during a World War II bombing mission. His name was L. H. White, and he was part of the first wave of replacement crews to replenish the depleted ranks of the 93rd Bomb Group in the spring of 1943. Only two weeks before my uncle arrived at Hardwick, Ben had resumed his combat tour with the 93rd after his return from Spain. My Uncle L.H. and Ben were in different 93rd squadrons—L.H. in the 328th, Ben in the 409th—so they weren't close friends. But they would have known each other by sight from the mess hall and mission briefings.

After the 93rd was deployed to the Libyan desert for the Ploiesti raid in late June 1943, L.H. and his crew flew many of the same raids as Ben. They both flew the 500-plane raid on Rome on July 19, and they both survived the low-level Ploiesti raid on August 1. On October 1, 1943, when the 93rd was flying out of Tunis on yet another temporary assignment to

North Africa, they both took off on a long raid to Austria. Their target was the German Me-109 fighter factory at Wiener Neustadt, just south of Vienna. Ben's pilot, Homer Moran, aborted the raid for mechanical reasons and safely returned to base. My uncle was on the only 93rd aircraft that didn't make it back that day, a storied B-24 named *Jerk's Natural*.

My mother was only eleven at the time, and she and her family endured seven years of agony after receiving the MIA telegram from the War Department the same week that Ben nearly died over Münster on his final mission with the 93rd. In early 1950, three months before Ben graduated from the University of Nebraska and began his career as publisher of the *York Republican*, two of my mother's older siblings and her father gathered at a freshly dug grave at Jefferson Barracks National Cemetery, on a bluff overlooking the Mississippi River south of St. Louis, Missouri. On March 13, 1950, L.H. was buried with eight comrades in a single casket. All the families who were there that raw day left doubting whether their boys had really been found. I grew up with the legacy of those doubts and the enduring pain of L.H.'s loss. Like Ben, I became a journalist, and after a decade of reporting experience, I set out to find answers for my mother and her surviving siblings.

Among the 93rd Bomb Group veterans I interviewed were Cal Stewart and Elmer (Bill) Dawley, the gunner who suffered a head wound on Ben's first mission in December 1942. Ben was keeping a low profile during those years, and so I never spoke with him. But I did interview more than one hundred 93rd veterans, and several of them mentioned Ben.

When I set out to tell Ben's story in 2022, I meshed his print interviews over the years with his late-life oral histories and other sources like the Ralph Martin book and the documentary films of Bill Kubota and Frank Abe. I broadened my search for other sources of information and that eventually led me to the National Museum of American History. Jennifer L. Jones made no promises of what I might find as she escorted me into a small office with the first two boxes that Ben had donated. I pulled out an old scrapbook, and Ben's remarkable story came to life.

It meant a great deal to Ben late in his life that a young Japanese American curator at the Smithsonian, Noriko Sanefuji, had taken an interest in securing his collection for the National Museum of American History. After signing his deed of gift in April 2008, Ben began corresponding with Noriko, and she became a valued friend.

In one of his final letters to her, written in October 2013, Ben asked Noriko if she could find him a copy of the old newspaper photograph that showed Ben and Fred standing before the Army Air Forces recruiter at

Grand Island the week after the Pearl Harbor attack, the right hand of each brother raised as they recited the Pledge of Allegiance

Ben had typed the letter himself and he apologized for his mistakes. "This electric typewriter [is] difficult with my shaky hands," he wrote. He also shared with Noriko a letter he had received from the governor of Nebraska. "A final incredible honor and closure," Ben wrote. "Gratifying homecoming for a WWII veteran of Japanese ancestry."[1]

In July 2023, I drove to Lincoln County, Nebraska, to see and feel this remote corner of America that had shaped Ben. I stayed in North Platte, and on consecutive days I drove out to the Hershey farm that Sam Kuroki had leased through the 1930s and 1940s. The land was now irrigated and planted in corn, not the potatoes, tomatoes, and sugar beets that Sam and George had cultivated for years. I knocked on the front door of the farmhouse, and a man with a disheveled appearance and nervous manner answered. I explained why I was there and asked whether I might wander around the place a bit. I didn't expect the man would know Ben's story. I just described the person I was writing about as the first Japanese American hero of World War II. "You mean Kuroki?" the man interjected. Cutting the conversation short, he curtly told me I needed permission from the property owner back on the main road, and shut the door.

On both days that I drove out to the Hershey farm, I also continued a mile farther up the road to the North Platte River, where Ben used to hunt with his friend Gordy Jorgenson. Even with its reduced summer flow, the river is life-giving as it courses through the arid Lincoln County prairie on its way to merging with the South Platte River on the outskirts of the town of North Platte. From the north bank, I gazed at the deeper eddies along the river's southern fringe. I imagined Ben and Gordy blasting away at ducks, Ben breaking through the ice as he stepped onto the river's frozen surface, and then Gordy coming to his rescue.

In the late afternoon, the road across the river came alive with tractors and other machinery as farmers headed back home after their day's work. When the noise died away, all that remained was the sound of rushing water cutting through the bars of sand and gravel, and the symphony of birds, seen and unseen: common yellowthroats, killdeer, cliff swallows, song sparrows, field sparrows, robins, blue jays, mourning doves, and a lone bald eagle, swooping from a tall cottonwood and skimming just above the water on its way downstream.

After the war, Sam and Naka Kuroki had left country life behind and moved into North Platte, and George had continued to farm the Hershey land. I met a former teacher in North Platte who told me that she used to bring her students out to see George's potato farm. The only brother who had stuck around to help George with the farm was Fred, a lifelong bachelor. He became a surrogate father to George's son, Reed. George was a workaholic, and so it was his Uncle Fred who taught him things and told him family stories, Reed told me.

Among the stories that Fred had told Reed was about the Kuroki boys swimming in the ditch that ran along the road in front of the farmhouse. They sometimes caught small carp and minnows in the ditch, and Naka would fry them in a pan and serve them with soy sauce. Fred and Ben both became skilled trappers as teenagers. Fred would never forget one successful year when he amassed a good number of skunk and raccoon pelts. But the family was experiencing hard times and Fred used his profits to buy food for his parents and siblings.

Reed had grown up in the shadow of his Uncle Ben's legacy, but he had ended up with a more complicated view of his famous uncle. For one thing, Ben and George didn't get along, Reed said. He didn't know much more, but it's easy to imagine the source of the tension. Ben tried to get out of the farm chores whenever he could, and George would spend the rest of his life on the farm, abandoning his college dreams of becoming an engineer because of his filial responsibilities as the oldest son. Julie Kuroki told me that her father "felt his older brother hadn't welcomed him back" when he returned from the war. Whatever the source of the breach, it lasted for the rest of their lives.[2]

When Reed went off to the University of Nebraska, Ben's legacy followed him. Two Japanese American brothers from North Platte lived on the same floor of Reed's dorm, and they knew all about Ben. Their fathers were Fred and Norman Ugai, and both fought with the 442nd Regimental Combat Team in Europe. Ben's recruiting work in the camps in 1944 hadn't set well with the Ugai brothers and some other men who ended up in the 442nd, and the brothers had passed on their animus toward the celebrated Ben Kuroki to their sons.

Reed only saw his Uncle Ben four or five times over the decades. At their last reunion, Ben shared two stories. The first was about Gordy saving him when he fell through the ice during their duck hunt along the North Platte River. And the second was about Ben's visit with Gordy's heartbroken mother after the war. "He was pretty broke up," Reed said.

Ben's friend Gordy was long gone, but never forgotten. Gordy's brother, Kenneth, had named his son after his fallen brother, and the nephew Gordy Jorgenson was Reed's best friend. Reed's son was in a lawn business with Dustin Jorgenson, the son of the nephew Gordy. The Gordy

Jorgenson who had fought and died in the Pacific never earned Ben's acclaim, but, like Ben, the shadow of his legacy endured.

Not long before I visited North Platte, James Griffin, director and curator of the Lincoln County Historical Museum, had unveiled a new exhibition called "Japanese of Lincoln County." The exhibition spanned the period from around 1920 to the 1950s. Although Ben would later say he never experienced bigotry growing up in Hershey, anti-Japanese sentiment had deep roots in the area, the exhibits revealed. Nebraska's Alien Land Law, which mirrored similar laws passed throughout the West in the 1920s, had been proposed by a state representative from North Platte. The law, which prevented land ownership by noncitizens, has never been repealed.

The suspicion that immediately fell on local Japanese and Japanese American residents after Pearl Harbor was also on display. The exhibit included a list "of all Japanese families" compiled by the North Platte police chief on Monday, December 8, 1941, and submitted to the FBI office in Omaha later that day. There were twenty-five typed names on the list. Among eight names handwritten at the bottom of the chief's list were the names of Ben and George Kuroki.

One of the panels told the story of the detention of the popular local Episcopal priest, Reverend Hiram Kano, who was confined in multiple internment camps before being paroled and sent to a seminary in Wisconsin. Another detailed how the national anti-Japanese backlash played out in Nebraska. Local residents weren't rounded up and sent to incarceration camps, but their bank accounts were frozen, travel restricted, and cameras, radios, and guns confiscated. Registration with government authorities was also required.

A major focus of the exhibition was the service of the 442nd Regimental Combat Team. Ultimately, twenty-two local men of Japanese descent, including three Kuroki brothers, served in the armed forces. Ben's story was featured in a separate panel that included a photograph of him in his bemedaled uniform and a copy of Ralph G. Martin's *Boy from Nebraska*.

The closing panels highlighted the naturalization of Issei residents in Lincoln County. The Issei citizenship legislation that Ben had advocated during his Fifty-Ninth Mission Tour had been approved by Congress and signed into law by President Truman in 1952, and the following year Sam and Naka Kuroki were among twenty-five Lincoln County residents of Japanese ancestry who passed the naturalization test and became American citizens. A photograph of the newly naturalized citizens, Sam and Naka among them, was on display.

As fate would have it, Sam enjoyed the benefits of his American citizenship for only five years. He died in 1958 and was buried in the North Platte cemetery. Naka lived until 1974, and she is buried beside Sam.

Fred Kuroki died in 2002 in North Platte at the age of eighty-two. George died the following year in Hershey.

The rest of Sam and Naka's children scattered to the winds. When Ben died in 2015, only one of his siblings was still alive: his youngest sister Rose, born in 1926. Like the other Kuroki girls, Rose had lived for a time in Chicago and had married there in 1951. Like Ben, she ended up in California. Thirteen months after Ben's death, on December 4, 2016, Rose Kuroki Ura—the last of Shosuke and Naka's ten children—died in Palo Alto, California.

IT's 467 MILES AS THE CROW FLIES from Hershey, Nebraska, to what remains of the Heart Mountain Relocation Center in northern Wyoming. The small portion of the camp that remains in public hands today has been designated a national historic landmark. Drive north into the Bighorn Basin from the town of Cody on US Highway 14, and about a dozen miles out it suddenly appears on your left.

The site lies only a few hundred yards from the rail line that transported Yosh Kuromiya and other incarcerees to their forced exile in the late summer of 1942. A replica guard tower like those that greeted Ben on his visit rises like a sentry above a cluster of reconstructed barracks. An interpretive center houses interactive exhibits, a gallery, and a small theater.

As I steered my car into an unpaved parking area, dust curling from the powdery soil, I noticed a small building under construction. It's the future home of the Mineta-Simpson Institute at Heart Mountain, named for two boys who met here in the 1940s and went on to notable careers as public servants. Norman Mineta, a future Democratic congressman and cabinet member under presidents Bill Clinton and George W. Bush, was incarcerated with his family at Heart Mountain. Alan Simpson, a future Republican senator, met Mineta through Boy Scout gatherings and sporting events that introduced Cody boys to camp boys. The center named for the friends who became known for bridging their political differences for the common good is envisioned as a retreat space where workshops and programs can be held to "foster empathy, courage, and cooperation in the next generation of leaders," the Heart Mountain website says.

I arrived during the Heart Mountain Pilgrimage, an annual homecoming in which former inmates and their families bond with old friends and remember the injustices that led to their wartime incarceration. Most of the survivors are now in their eighties, and they made the trip with three, or even four, generations of family members.

Inside the interpretive center, after watching the poignant introductory film, *All We Could Carry*, and viewing the exhibits, I struck up a conversation with a young woman wearing a staff badge. Her name was Eva Petersen, and when I mentioned that I was writing a biography of Ben Kuroki, she reacted viscerally. She knew he was a Nebraska farm boy who had become a Nisei war hero, and she knew his visit to Heart Mountain had stirred controversy.

Among those attending the Pilgrimage was a bearded historian named Douglas W. Nelson. As a young graduate student at the University of Wyoming in 1968, Nelson had begun research that would eventually become the definitive history of the Heart Mountain camp on its publication in book form in 1976. Eva tracked down Professor Nelson, and, as Pilgrimage participants and other visitors swirled around us in the Interpretive Center, I listened with fascination as the eminent Heart Mountain scholar discussed the significance of Ben's visit to the camp.

The debate over the resumption of the Nisei draft in January 1944 and the possibility of service in the segregated 442nd Regimental Combat Team was just gaining critical mass when Ben arrived, Nelson said. Ben's visit galvanized the opposing sides. "It was an important turning point here," Nelson told me. "Before that, the extent of the division wasn't as clear as it was during and after Ben's visit."

As Professor Nelson rushed off to an event, Eva and I resumed our conversation. I mentioned that one of the individuals whose story I was drawn to as I did my research on Heart Mountain was the young artist who became a convicted draft resister, Yoshito Kuromiya. "Yosh's daughter is here!" Eva excitedly said. "I'll text her so you can meet her." Before long, the third of Yosh Kuromiya's four daughters appeared.

Gail Kuromiya had a warm and thoughtful way about her. She briefly told me the story of her father's journey after Heart Mountain. Yosh never could have reclaimed his old life, even if he had wanted to, as Gail explained it. Many in the Japanese American community shunned the resisters because they had brought controversy and, in the eyes of many, shame, upon the community. It was the sort of thinking that had prompted Ben to denounce the resisters and the Fair Play Committee leaders as fascists. Yet Yosh remained true to his principles. "Writing and speaking out for the resisters—this was his life," Gail told me.

Yosh worried about how his path might affect his daughters as they grew older, but the girls were strong and they found their way. They inherited Yosh's artistic talent—some of his drawings and watercolor paintings are now held by the Smithsonian National Museum of American History—and they all became graphic designers. As the years passed, they encouraged their father to weave his essays and other pieces on his painful Heart Mountain experience into a book. He finished the manuscript in early 2018 and died within six months. "He handed it off to us and said, 'You girls do what you think is best,'" Gail said.

The daughters found the perfect advocate in Arthur A. Hansen, emeritus professor of history at California State University, Fullerton, and founding director of the Japanese American Project of the Oral History Program and the Center for Oral and Public History. He edited Yosh's memoir, pro bono, and in 2021 the book was published by the University Press of Colorado. *Beyond the Betrayal: The Memoir of a World War II Japanese American Draft Resister of Conscience* was the first book-length account of the Nisei draft resistance movement by an insider.

For the daughters of Yosh Kuromiya, the book was a monument to the role model at the center of their lives. I bought a copy in the Interpretive Center bookstore and asked Gail to sign it. I had told Gail that I intended to tell a small part of her father's story in my book on Ben Kuroki, and she seemed pleased. She penned a gracious inscription in her father's honor. "Best wishes on your new writing endeavor," she wrote. "I think dad would be proud and flattered!"

Before leaving Heart Mountain, I made my way up the hill from the Interpretive Center to a memorial where there are a series of plaques dedicated to those incarcerated in the camp and the 750 men and women who served in the armed forces during the war. Some had been inspired to serve by Ben's exhortations in April 1944, and some had died in combat.

The area around the memorial offers a dramatic view of Heart Mountain, the limestone pillar that rises 8,123 feet above sea level and looms over the area. But something was off as I gazed to the west at the mountain that had given this camp its evocative name.

While doing research at NARA II—the cavernous National Archives and Records Administration facility in College Park, Maryland—I had come across a War Relocation Authority file in the Still Pictures Research Room that contained about two hundred images of daily life at the Heart Mountain camp. I spent hours examining and scanning every image, in part to burn into my memory what it looked like, and in part to fix in my mind the faces of some of the fourteen thousand people who were unjustly confined in this place during America's crusade against global fascism. In the photos I had examined that were taken outside the buildings, the landscape was dusty and barren as it stretched toward Heart Mountain.

Except now, I was gazing out at lush, green fields of alfalfa. How had this happened?

As I puzzled over this mystery, a woman in a floppy hat that shielded her head from the blazing sun power-walked past me along the road. I greeted her and we struck up a conversation. Her name was Cally Steussy, and she was the director of the Heart Mountain Interpretive Center.

The camp had been carved from the federal Bureau of Reclamation's Heart Mountain Irrigation Project, an ambitious endeavor to transform the parched landscape using water from the nearby Shoshone River. In 1937, the Bureau began work on the Heart Mountain Canal, but construction was halted when the war began. After the camp opened, Heart Mountain inmates resumed work on the canal, extending it by a mile and eventually cultivating seventeen hundred acres of land reclaimed from the barren high desert.

Heart Mountain inmates began to leave the camp in January 1945, and the final incarcerees departed on November 10 of that year. By 1946, farmers began to establish homesteads on the former Heart Mountain camp lands. The irrigation project was completed and the barren ground that once lay inside the barbed wire became cultivated fields.[3]

Now the windswept desolation that once greeted camp inmates every day of their incarceration was an undulating blanket of green sprinkled with yellow blossoms and white butterflies, as vivid as a Van Gogh painting. The passage of time couldn't change the tragic history of this place, but the transformation of this desert spoke to the possibility of healing.

As I stood beside the road, looking out at the fields and the dramatic peak eight miles distant, I thought about Ben and his remarkable life. Sam Kuroki had ended up in Nebraska so he could cultivate fields like this, and he had raised his family in an enclave largely insulated from the bigotry and hate that was inflicted on immigrants from China, Japan, the Philippines, and other Asian countries throughout the fifty years leading up to World War II. But the attack on Pearl Harbor had unleashed a tidal wave of pent-up prejudice and bigotry, and this had set Ben on his epic quest to prove himself as a loyal and worthy American. Eventually, his journey led him to this place where the American covenant had been so cruelly betrayed.

The Constitution that he had sworn to uphold when he entered the military after Pearl Harbor had been trampled in the dust at Heart Mountain, and yet Ben struggled to fully acknowledge the injustice that occurred here and in the other camps. It was a regrettable blind spot in a brave and remarkable life, and yet the sort of blind spot that afflicts nearly all of us. "Who am I to judge those who joined the 442nd or those who resisted?" Gail Kuromiya said to me at Heart Mountain—wise words that remain in my thoughts. With his gallant and selfless service, Ben Kuroki earned the honors and accolades that came his way in time. And in the end, this earnest young man from Nebraska and the principled draft resisters from California, each in their own way, embody the highest ideals of a good and great nation.

AFTERWORD

by Jonathan Eig

Muhammad Ali called himself "The Greatest." He joked, in fact, that he began calling himself "The Greatest" before he knew it was true. The scholar Michael Eric Dyson has called Martin Luther King, Jr. "the greatest American who ever lived." I have written biographies of these two superlative figures, as well as baseball's greatest first baseman, Lou Gehrig, and the greatest gangster of the Prohibition Era, Al Capone.

While I have spent much of my writing exploring the great lives, I'm aware, of course, that we live in an age of distrust, if not contempt, for the great-man (or great-person) approach to history, politics, and biography. Too many of history's so-called great figures have turned out to be great purveyors of death. Too many have turned out to be great liars and hypocrites. But I don't see this is as reason to abandon the exploration of great lives. Greatness does not require perfection. Biography serves as exploration of greatness, a careful, nuanced exploration, an exploration of the scope and significance of a life, an exploration of human courage, ambition, and creativity as well as weakness, doubt, and failure.

Ben Kuroki's story is certainly one of greatness. As Gregg Jones tells us in these fascinating pages, Ben was one of ten children born to Japanese immigrants, a high school graduate who appeared headed for a lifetime on the farm in Nebraska, growing potatoes and sugar beets with his father and brothers, until the events of December 7, 1941 changed everything, until he recognized, as all great men and women do, that he had to make a choice about whether to risk his personal security for something bigger.

After the bombing of Pearl Harbor, Ben proved his patriotism by joining the Army Air Forces. But he faced brutally racist attacks and ostracism. Rather than earning assignment to a bomber crew, he got kitchen duty. He persisted. He suffered the abuse of peers and superiors until he earned the chance to fight and made good as an aerial gunner. It was almost absurdly dangerous work, a series of nearly impossible missions flown in preposterously unsafe aircraft. On his first combat mission, Ben saw his crewmate suffer a near-fatal head wound. Yet he wanted more action, and he got it. He risked his life and excelled again and again, as a B-24 waist gunner and top turret gunner in Europe and North Africa, and as a B-29 tail gunner in the Pacific.

Our great heroes are not perfect, nor should we expect them to be. Ben failed to recognize the heroism of those Japanese American men who had been forced from their West Coast homes and confined with their families in remote incarceration camps during World War II and who led a draft-resistance movement. The United States sent Ben to three camps in early 1944, using him as a symbol of patriotism, to persuade Japanese American men to serve in the military. Some called him a race traitor and collaborator, criticism that stuck to him the rest of his life and led him to reflect on whether his own enthusiasm to serve had narrowed his vision of what it meant to be a patriot.

The great-person approach to history draws fire in large part because it risks placing too much emphasis on a few leading figures, and because those figures all too often turn out to be white men. The great-person theory also assumes, in some interpretations, that great people are born, not made, but I don't accept that assumption. In fact, the Ben Kuroki story helps broaden our view of great figures in history. Ben's story will be unknown to most readers. His greatness stems in large part from his position as an outsider and his courageous effort to use his outsider status to break down prejudice. It's the ordinary nature of his life that makes it so special. It's the nuance Jones brings to the saga that makes Kuroki's tale so moving and so worthy of exploration. It's the detail that makes the reader feel he's along for the ride with Kuroki—for a ride that terrifies, troubles, and inspires.

When I was conducting interviews for my Muhammad Ali biography, the comedian and activist Dick Gregory gave me a challenge: Don't bother writing your book, he said, if you can't explain what made Ali—a Black child of the Jim Crow South—think he could get away with calling himself The Greatest. It was solid advice. The biographer's job is to show, first, what makes a person think he can be different. What makes a young man think he can go against the grain, challenge authority, perhaps even change the world? What made Ali think he could fight racism? What made Ben Kuroki think he could prove to all Americans that their Japanese American neighbors could be patriots and even war heroes? What made him think he could be special?

Late in life, Ben explained that many Americans saw him as an enemy, because the Japanese became enemies after the bombing of Pearl Harbor. "And I knew I was different," he said. He made up his mind to prove it in the most dramatic and dangerous possible way.

Ben was widely celebrated late in life for his willingness to be different, to risk everything for his country, for his convictions. He came to terms, however uncomfortably, with the fact that the same country he defended rounded up and imprisoned Japanese Americans. "Oh, I didn't think for a minute that it was fair, the way they got locked up or the tremendous losses that they suffered," he said. He applauded those who stood by their principles and resisted the draft, calling them "very, very brave."

Ben was more than qualified in making that assessment. When we speak of great lives, we ought to speak of moral character, something our leaders today often fail to supply. Ben Kuroki believed in living honorably. He believed that the fate of the free world rested on good character. He wasn't perfect, but he lived life with purpose, courage, and a steady moral compass. Anyone who does that can claim to have lived a great life.

ACKNOWLEDGMENTS

When I wrote my first book thirty-five years ago, I fell in love with the challenge of weaving interviews and historical research into a compelling narrative. I also fell in love with the journey—the knowledge acquired and interesting people encountered along the way.

Such was the case with this book.

Bill Kubota is a longtime journalist and documentary filmmaker in Detroit, Michigan, and he spent the better part of a decade shaping hundreds of hours of interviews into a compelling hour-long documentary on Ben Kuroki's life. When I first reached out to Bill to seek his guidance for a biography of Ben, he took a couple of hours out of his Sunday morning to brief me. Bill also generously shared hundreds of hours of interviews and transcripts. I deeply admire Bill's work, and I am forever in his debt.

Interviewing Arthur Hansen, the acclaimed California State University, Fullerton, history professor emeritus, was a highlight of this project. Before we talked, Art emailed me the one-hundred-page transcript of his 1994 interview with Ben—a document that is a testament to Art Hansen's skill as an interviewer and historian. During our interview, Art shared with me his vivid memories of the day he spent with Ben. His insights and his interview greatly informed this book.

I was introduced to Art by the prodigiously talented journalist, writer, historian, playwright, and actor Frank Abe. Working with project partner Frank Chin in 1998, Frank Abe conducted an extraordinary interview with Ben that became an important component of his powerful 2000 documentary film *Conscience and the Constitution*. The film greatly informed my understanding of the situation Ben encountered on the ground at the Heart Mountain incarceration camp when he arrived there on a War Department recruiting mission in April 1944. Although besieged by deadlines, Frank took time to offer valuable guidance and introductions.

Carroll (Cal) Stewart was a 93rd Bomb Group publicist and journalist during World War II who became one of Ben's early advocates. In the 1990s, I corresponded with Cal and spoke with him by phone as I investigated the saga of my uncle who had been killed in action with the 93rd in 1943. I've consulted Cal's work on the 93rd and Ben throughout this project. His son,

Scott Stewart, shared several documents, including a booklet-length biography that his father wrote about Ben.

Thanks as well to Joe Avendano Duran, nephew of a 93rd Bomb Group pilot killed in England in January 1944, for his many kindnesses. Joe possesses an encyclopedic knowledge of 93rd history from his years of attending 93rd Bomb Group Association reunions. Joe has also done extraordinary research on the wartime service and death of his uncle, and that led him to a long friendship with Ben. I'm grateful to Joe for sharing his recollections of Ben and for reading the manuscript to make sure my account remained true to the history of the 93rd.

In Nebraska, Job Vigil, a reporter for the *North Platte Telegraph* newspaper, kindly introduced me to his golfing buddy Reed Kuroki, son of Ben's oldest brother, George. Reed still lives in Hershey, Nebraska, and he shared memories of his Uncle Ben and other insights and recollections. I'm grateful to him for his assistance. Thanks as well to James Griffin, director and curator of the outstanding Lincoln County Historical Museum in North Platte, Nebraska, and curator of an excellent exhibition on the local Japanese American community.

I'm indebted to a legion of archivists, curators, and staff at various libraries and archives. Special thanks to Jennifer L. Jones at the Smithsonian's National Museum of American History for warmly facilitating my visit to examine the untapped collection of Ben Kuroki's papers, photographs, correspondence, and World War II–related memorabilia. My thanks as well to the staffs of the Manuscript Division and the Main Reading Room at the Library of Congress and the staffs of the Still Photography and Textual Records Collections of the National Archives and Records Administration facility at College Park, Maryland. I'm also grateful to the staff of the Air Force Historical Research Agency at Maxwell Air Force Base, Alabama, where I began doing research on the 93rd Bomb Group in the early 1990s. More recently, I'm grateful to AFHRA Research Team supervisor Patrick J. Charles for providing me with digitized microfilm rolls that allowed me to peruse thousands of pages of records from the convenience of my home. These records allowed me to nail down some loose ends regarding Ben's European service and to discover some new information about Ben's Pacific service.

Early in the project, I tried without success to track down Ben Kuroki's youngest daughter, Julie, in California. We were finally connected through Jennifer L. Jones, and it was my good fortune to be able to listen to some of Julie's memories of her remarkable father. Julie also shared with me the wonderful photograph of Ben and his daughters and procured the signatures needed to publish this image.

It was a thrill to meet and speak with Gail Kuromiya at Heart Mountain National Historic Landmark, and Gail and her sister, Suzi, shared photographs of their father, the artist, activist, and principled draft resister Yosh Kuromiya. Gail also took the time to read through the portions of the manuscript where I tell a piece of her father's story.

In Wyoming, I'm grateful to the staff of the Heart Mountain Wyoming Foundation and the Heart Mountain National Historic Landmark for their noble work to preserve this tragic place that figured so prominently in Ben's story. Although foundation executive director Aura Sunada Newlin was swamped with Pilgrimage Weekend duties when I visited, I had the chance to view the extraordinary exhibits and speak with other staff members. My thanks to director of interpretation and preservation Cally Steussy for our impromptu interview and to executive assistant to the chair Eva Petersen for introducing me to some of the scholars and family members in attendance at the 2023 Pilgrimage. Thanks as well to director of communications and strategy Ray Locker for his generous offer of assistance.

Several people read early drafts of the manuscript. My thanks to my brother Steve Jones for his feedback and encouragement. Thanks as well to Air Force University historian Brian Laslie. Seth Mydans has been my friend and mentor since I was a freelance journalist in the Philippines in the 1980s, and he has read all of my manuscripts and offered invaluable feedback over the decades. Once again, Seth was generous with his time and encouragement. Joey Reaves, a longtime friend, accomplished journalist, author, and former Los Angeles Dodgers executive, devoted many hours to a careful edit of my second draft that proved tremendously helpful. My friend John Reinan offered valuable feedback. Trevor McIntyre has my gratitude for his sharp eye on technical matters and Pacific War history. The Nebraska-born, globe-trotting photographer Mike Theiler accompanied me on an epic road trip through Nebraska and Wyoming, during which he provided good company and captured superb images.

Deepest thanks to authors Jonathan Eig and James M. Scott for their encouragement and counsel during a long dry spell in my writing life. My thanks as well to Doug Swanson for his friendship over the years. I'm also grateful to Patrick O'Donnell for his counsel at a crucial moment. Tracy Frish has been a treasured source of friendship during good times and bad.

This book grew out of the decades I spent investigating the disappearance of my uncle's B-24 crew during a 1943 raid on the German Messerschmitt Me-109 fighter factory at Wiener Neustadt, Austria. In the process, I learned how to do archival research and how to write a historical narrative, and I deepened my knowledge of the first year of the American bombing campaign against Nazi Germany. All of this proved invaluable when I set out to tell Ben's story.

In 2015–16, Beverly Rogers and Carol C. Harter provided generous financial support through the Black Mountain Institute at the University of Nevada, Las Vegas. A BMI-Kluge Fellowship allowed me to spend four months at the Kluge Center at the Library of Congress in Washington, DC. During this time, I explored every thread of my uncle's story and that informed my understanding of what Ben and his 93rd Bomb Group comrades endured in those first sixteen months of almost suicidal unescorted raids into Nazi-occupied Europe. Throughout my time at the Kluge Center, I was inspired by brilliant colleagues. My thanks to you all: Kluge Center intern Katie Rose Turlik; research fellows Adrian Browne, Ivan Chaar-Lopez, Elia Corazza, Andrew Devereux, Mary Dudziak, Eliana Hadjisavvas, Bruce Jentleson, Rhian Keyse, Charlotte Lerg, Katherine Luongo, Dara Orenstein, Mathilde Pavis, Anna Browne Ribeiro, Dan Rood, Lucy Taylor, Joe Thorogood, and Julia Young; Kluge Center staff Mary Lou Reker, Dan Turello, and Jason Steinhauer; and Megan Harris of the Library of Congress Veterans History Project.

At the back end of the fellowship, I spent five months at the Black Mountain Institute, writing and discussing storytelling. Among the highlights of my time at BMI was my introduction to Sally Denton and her amazing family. The author of several outstanding books, Sally facilitated my fellowship and then arranged for me to live rent-free in the basement of her family home in Boulder City. My upstairs host was the extraordinary Sara Denton, Sally's mother, a vibrant ninety-eight years of age as I write this. Thanks also to esteemed Nevada journalist John Smith, former BMI director Joshua Wolf Shenk, BMI staffers Joseph Langdon and Cynthia Reed, and BMI fellows Hossein Mortezaeian Abkenar, John Garth, Walter Kirn, and Okey Ndibe.

The Botstiber Institute for Austrian-American Studies awarded me a grant that allowed me to spend three weeks in Austria in 2017, nailing down facts about the loss of my uncle's crew and deepening my understanding of the impact of the American bombing campaign on Austrian civilians. I'm especially grateful to Dr. Siegfried Beer, renowned Austrian historian and Botstiber board member, and the Botstiber Institute's Valerie Grupp Arapis. In Austria, I'm grateful for the friendship and hospitality of Franz Haüsler, his wife Elizabeth Unterberger Haüsler, and the extended Haüsler-Unterberger families—Opa, Oma, Hansi, Anna Lisie, Angelika, Veronika, and Hubert. Thanks as well to Austrian historians Markus Reisner and Georg Hoffmann for sharing their knowledge on the American bombing of Austria.

Special thanks to the writer and Khe Sanh veteran Michael Archer for his friendship, counsel, and encouragement. Thanks as well to friends Pat Benic, Alan Berlow, Chris Billing, Jay Branegan, Bill Branigin, John Garth, Candy Gourlay, Dale Maharidge, Tod Robberson, David Timberman, Matthew Westfall, and Cris Yabes.

Teaching journalism and storytelling to students at Greenhill School in Addison, Texas, has sharpened my skills over the past six years. I'm especially grateful to 2022 graduates Saara Bidiwala, Jothi Gupta, and Cam Kettles and 2023 graduates Khushi Chhaya, Ivy Stitt, Ava Iwasko, and Emma Nguyen for their exceptional brilliance and passion. Special thanks to bosses Lee Hark, Tom Perryman, and Trevor Worcester and a long list of valued colleagues.

I will be forever grateful to my literary agent Andrew Stuart and editorial consultant Paul Starobin for their support and hard work. James Abbate, my editor at Kensington Publishing, has been a wonderfully kind and energetic partner. My thanks to Seth Lerner and the Kensington art team for designing a powerful cover and to Ann Pryor and the publicity team for all their efforts to share *Most Honorable Son* with a larger audience.

Don and Bonny Edmonds have been cherished friends and mentors since we met shortly after I began my newspaper career in Virginia in 1981. Steve LeVine has been an amazing friend for nearly forty years, and our relationship has been enriched by the ladies in his life: Nurilda (Nuri) Nurlybayeva, Alisha and Ilana, and Dolores. Steve set in motion the events that are now culminating with the publication of this book.

Ali, my wife of nearly forty years, and our son, Chris, are the sun and moon and stars of my world. Ali is an award-winning elementary special education teacher in the third act of her professional life. Chris is a world-class metal guitarist whose national and international tours of the past two years are a testament to his talent and hard work. It's a joy to share the highs and lows of our respective artistic journeys. Ali would tell you I work too much on my book projects. All I can say in my defense is that some force compels me to keep trying to create written works of lasting value. Aided by the generosity and kindness of the aforementioned people, I think this book meets that standard.

NOTE ON SOURCES

Ben Kuroki was interviewed dozens of times by newspaper, magazine, and radio reporters during World War II, and these interviews illuminated Ben's wartime thoughts and experiences. Ben also delivered dozens of speeches during and after the war—some crafted by professional writers with Ben's input, and others, after the war, written by Ben. These speeches—most of which are preserved in Ben Kuroki's papers at the Smithsonian's National Museum of American History in Washington, DC—also provided valuable insights into Ben's journey.

In the 1990s, Ben gave three lengthy interviews. In 1994, he was interviewed by California State University, Fullerton, historian Arthur Hansen. In 1998, he was interviewed separately by documentary filmmakers Frank Abe and Bill Kubota. These interviews proved invaluable in my work on this project.

Ben was also the subject of a 1946 biography. *Boy from Nebraska*, by the war correspondent Ralph G. Martin, is a quick read but flawed. There are no source notes, so the reader is left to assume that Martin's quotes and other facts were obtained directly from Ben. But Ben later indicated that he hadn't read the book, or at least not carefully. Martin's account is contradicted in several instances by available facts. In other instances, I found myself wondering whether Martin took literary license to fill gaps in his narrative. For these reasons, I've limited my use of his work to material I confirmed elsewhere or concluded was highly plausible under the circumstances.

Other primary source material I drew on included my 1990s interviews with more than one hundred veterans of the 93rd Bomb Group. My knowledge of Ben's European tour was deepened by 93rd Bomb Group sortie reports and unit histories at the National Archives and Records Administration and the Air Force Historical Research Agency at Maxwell Air Force Base, Alabama. Through Freedom of Information Act requests I filed with the National Personnel Records Center in St. Louis, Missouri, I obtained personnel files for Ben and a number of his crewmates and comrades.

The Ben Kuroki collection at the Smithsonian's National Museum of American History was an untapped trove that contained correspondence, photographs, and other memorabilia accumulated by Ben. Also useful were diaries kept by 93rd Bomb Group flight surgeon Wilmer Paine and 93rd intelligence officer Brutus Hamilton, and an unpublished narrative written by 93rd pilot Edwin Baker.

My knowledge of the Japanese American incarceration and Ben's 1944 recruiting visits to three incarceration camps was informed by textual records and photographs at the NARA II facility in College Park, Maryland. Another invaluable source on these subjects was the Densho Encyclopedia, the extraordinary online website maintained by Densho: The Japanese American Legacy Project, a nonprofit organization based in Seattle, Washington. Densho's repository of oral histories, photos, documents, and other primary sources and artifacts also deepened my understanding of the roundup and incarceration of people of Japanese descent in 1942.

My grasp of these topics was also greatly assisted by the groundbreaking scholarship of Arthur Hansen, Susan Kamei, Eric L. Muller, Doug Nelson, and Stephanie Hinnershitz, and by firsthand accounts written by Yoshito (Yosh) Kuromiya and Michiko (Michi) Nishiura Weglyn. Finally, the powerful documentary films of Frank Abe and Bill Kubota greatly informed my work.

ARCHIVES AND LIBRARIES

Air Force Historical Research Agency, Maxwell Air Force Base, Alabama

Center for Oral and Public History, California State University, Fullerton, California

Dallas Public Library, Dallas, Texas

Eugene McDermott Library, University of Texas at Dallas, Dallas, Texas

Heart Mountain National Historic Landmark, Powell, Wyoming

Houghton Library, Harvard University, Cambridge, Massachusetts

KDN Films Archives, Detroit, Michigan

Library of Congress, Washington, DC

Lincoln County Historical Museum, North Platte, Nebraska

National Archives and Records Administration, College Park, Maryland

National Personnel Records Center, St. Louis, Missouri

Plano Public Library, Plano, Texas

Smithsonian National Museum of American History, Washington, DC

ENDNOTES

PROLOGUE

1   "The Hershey Senior Class, 1936," *Hershey* (Nebraska) *Times*, May 7, 1936, p. 1.

CHAPTER 1: FIT FOR SERVICE

1   Ben recounted the immigration of his parents, their early lives in America, and how they came to move to Nebraska in an extraordinary oral history interview with the imminent Cal State, Fullerton, history professor (and now professor emeritus) Art Hansen. See Arthur A. Hansen, Center for Oral and Public History, California State University, Fullerton, Japanese American Oral History Project, October 17, 1944. Shosuke Kuroki's fondness for gambling during his Wyoming days is drawn from the author's interview with Reed Kuroki, the son of Ben's oldest brother, George. Reed Kuroki, author interview, November 5, 2022.

2   "Taking a Sight with John Bentley," *Nebraska State Journal*, April 22, 1928, p. 6.

3   The neighbor who looked after Ben was Margaret (Maggie) Harkness Geiken, an Irish immigrant from Belfast who had married a Nebraska farmer named Albert Geiken. "Obituary: Margaret Harkness Geiken," *Cozad* (Nebraska) *Local*, August 29, 1950; also Ralph G. Martin, *Boy from Nebraska* (New York: Harper & Brothers Publishing, 1946), pp. 34–36.

4   Martin, *Boy from Nebraska*, pp. 16–17.

5   At the time of the Pearl Harbor attack on December 7, 1941, Hawaii was fixed as Coordinated Universal Time (UTC) minus ten hours and thirty minutes. As a result, 7:55 a.m. in Honolulu—the moment of the Japanese attack by most accounts—was 1:25 p.m. in Washington, DC, and 12:25 p.m. in Nebraska. On June 8, 1947, Hawaii time was adjusted forward by thirty minutes to conform with the rest of the United States.

CHAPTER 2: "THIS IS URGENT"

1   Mike Masaoka with Bill Hosokawa, *They Call Me Moses Masaoka: An American Saga* (New York: William Morrow and Company, 1987), pp. 69–70.

2   Ben Kuroki interview with Bill Kubota, August 26–27, 1998, unedited footage used in *Most Honorable Son* documentary film, Ben Kuroki Collection, KDN Films Archives.

CHAPTER 3: "THIS IS YOUR COUNTRY"

1   Ben Kuroki interview with Bill Kubota, August 26–27, 1998, *Most Honorable Son* documentary, unedited footage.

2   "FBI Makes Raid on 'Little Tokyo,'" *Kearney* (Nebraska) *Daily Hub*, December 8, 1941, p. 5; "U.S. in Fast Moving Protective Measures Arrest 736 Japanese Aliens—Troops Called on Guard Duty at Defense Plants, Strategic Bridges," *North Platte Telegraph*, December 8, 1941, p. 1.

3   "Alien Japs in Nebraska," *Hershey* (Nebraska) *Citizen*, December 25, 1941, p. 8.

4   "Bonus offered first airman to hit Tokyo," *Lincoln* (Nebraska) *Journal Star*, December 30, 1941, p. 1.

5   "Japanese of Lincoln County," Lincoln County (Nebraska) Historical Museum exhibition, North Platte, Nebraska; for a vivid description of the backlash on the West Coast, see Susan Kamei, *When Can We Go Back to America?: Voices of Japanese American Incarceration During WWII* (New York: Simon & Schuster, 2021), pp. 50–57.

6   Ben Kuroki oral history interview with Tom Gibbs, March 26, 2013, National World War II Museum.

7   Ibid.

8   The saga of Ben and Fred Kuroki's efforts to enlist was documented in newspaper articles in the *North Platte Telegraph*, the *Grand Island Daily Independent*, and other Nebraska newspapers. See "List Men Who Have Volunteered," *North Platte Telegraph*, December 10, 1941, p. 4; "American-Born Sons of Nippon Join Army Here," *Grand Island Daily Independent*, December 16, 1941, p. 4; "American Sons of Japanese Parents Join U.S. Army Air Corps," *Grand Island Daily Independent*, December 16, 1941, p. 5. Later in life, Ben's memory of the timeline became fuzzy, and he described waiting up to two weeks to hear back from the North Platte recruiter before driving to Grand Island to enlist. In fact, as contemporary newspaper accounts make clear, he waited only a day before driving to Grand Island. Ben repeated this incorrect timeline in oral history interviews he gave in the 1990s and early 2000s, and this was repeated in a fifty-five-page biography crafted by Ben's 93rd Bomb Group friend Carroll (Cal) Stewart. Author Ralph G. Martin fashioned an even more garbled account of Ben's enlistment in his 1946 biography. See Martin, *Boy from Nebraska*, pp. 45–48.

9   "Scottsbluff Jap Arrest," Associated Press dispatch, *North Platte Telegraph*, December 23, 1941, p. 6.

10   "Big Arrows Cut in Cane as Jap Planes Attacked Hawaii," United Press dispatch printed in the *Lincoln* (Nebraska) *Journal*, December 30, 1941, p. 1.

11   Ibid.

12   Ibid.

13   "Japanese Turn in Radios, Cameras . . . ," *Lincoln* (Nebraska) *Journal Star*, December 30, 1941, p. 2.

Chapter 4: Alone

1   Wesley Frank Craven and James Lea Cate, eds., *The Army Air Forces in World War II. Vol. 6, Men and Planes* (Washington, DC: Office of Air Force History, 1949), pp. 528–32.

2   Ibid., pp. 530–32.

3   Ben discussed his basic training experiences at Sheppard Field in his interview with Bill Kubota, August 26–27, 1998, for the *Most Honorable Son* documentary, unedited footage, and with Tom Gibbs, March 26, 2013, for the National World War II Museum oral history collection. Martin's *Boy from Nebraska* also describes these experiences and the correspondence of Ben and his brother Fred with family members. See Martin, *Boy from Nebraska*, p. 52.

4   Ben Kuroki oral history interview with Tom Gibbs, March 26, 2013, National World War II Museum.

5   Ibid.

6   Martin, *Boy from Nebraska*, pp. 55–56.

7   Ibid., pp. 59–60.

CHAPTER 5: "ARE YOU AN AMERICAN CITIZEN?"

1   Craven and Cate, *Men and Planes*, pp. 205–206.

2   Details of Ben Kuroki's initial activities at Barksdale Field are drawn from his August 26–27, 1998, interview with filmmaker Bill Kubota for the *Most Honorable Son* documentary, unedited footage, and from Martin, *Boy from Nebraska*, pp. 59–60. The quote from Ben is from the Kubota interview.

3   Ralph Martin places Ben's kitchen duty at Barksdale Field in a two-week period after his arrival, when he was awaiting assignment to an operational unit. See Martin, *Boy from Nebraska*, p. 60.

4   Craven and Cate, *Men and Planes*, pp. 57–58.

5   Martin, *Boy from Nebraska*, p. 61.

6   Ibid.

7   Ibid., p. 62. Martin incorrectly identifies the squadron commander as a "Major Zadalis." His name was Stanley A. Zidiales, and he was a second lieutenant at the time. Zidiales commanded the 409th Squadron from March 26, 1942, to July 12, 1942, when K. K. Compton assumed leadership of the squadron.

8   Exactly how Ben was informed of the reprieve is the subject of conflicting accounts. Ralph G. Martin describes the first sergeant rousing Ben as he slept in his bunk and asking Ben if he would like to remain with the 93rd, to which Ben replied in the affirmative. At this point, in Martin's telling, the first sergeant informed Ben that he would be remaining with the group. See Martin, p. 63. The definitive history of the 93rd Bomb Group offers a slightly different account. "The day before the group left Barksdale, the CO called Ben in again, and told him to pack his barracks bag. He was going with them to Florida," the account reads. See Carroll (Cal) Stewart, *Ted's Travelling Circus* (Lincoln, Nebraska: Sun/World Communications, 1996), p. 43.

CHAPTER 6: "IN NO SENSE READY FOR CONFLICT"

1   "Special Task Force Given Last Touches," Fort Myers (Florida) *News-Press*, May 15, 1942, pp. 1 and 3. Halverson's secret orders called for his detachment to join the Tenth Air Force in China to conduct raids on the Japanese home islands. But a Japanese offensive in China disrupted the plan, and Halverson and his men had

gotten no farther than Egypt when they received a change of orders. On June 11, 1942, thirteen B-24s of the Halverson Project (HALPRO) carried out the first US air raid on Europe when they bombed oil refineries in Ploiesti, Romania.

2   Martin, *Boy from Nebraska*, p. 64.

3   Ibid., pp. 65–66.

4   Biographical material on Chaplain James A. Burris is drawn from federal census and military records, including his 1940 draft registration card, and various newspaper articles. These include "Chaplain Asks Divorce: Wife Ruined His Career, Says Capt. James A. Burris," *Kansas City Times*, August 12, 1944, p. 12, an account of Burris's wartime marital problems that includes useful biographical information; "Major Burris Honored," *Cassville* (Missouri) *Republican*, August 29, 1946, p. 1; and "New Chaplain Is Assigned to MacDill Field," *Tampa Tribune*, May 11, 1947, p. 17.

5   Martin, *Boy from Nebraska*, p. 65.

6   The first German submarine was credited to the 93rd crew commanded by First Lieutenant John L. (Jack) Jerstad, affectionately known to his comrades as Jerk Jerstad. Rollin Reineck, author interview, September 23, 1991. Reineck was the navigator of the Jerstad crew, although he wasn't aboard the aircraft when his comrades sank the submarine in the Gulf of Mexico in June 1942. Crew members later described the submarine sinking in an article for *Air Force* magazine. See Captain Arthur Gordon, "Dream Crew," *Air Force*, October 1943, pp. 8–9. The second submarine was sunk on June 21, 1942, by the 93rd crew commanded by First Lieutenant B. F. Williams. See "B-24 Crew Cited for Sinking U-Boat on June 21 in the Gulf of Mexico," *Palm Beach* (Florida) *Post*, July 26, 1942, p. 2; "Plane Crew Cited for Sinking U-Boat," *New York Times*, July 26, 1942.

7   James Parton, *Air Force Spoken Here* (Bethesda, Maryland: Adler & Adler, 1986), pp. 168–70. Parton was General Ira Eaker's aide-de-camp in England.

8   H. H. Arnold, *Global Mission* (New York: Harper & Brothers, 1949), p. 329.

9   Stewart, *Ted's Travelling Circus*, p. 43.

Chapter 7: Queen of the Seas

1   I consulted several accounts about the RMS *Queen Elizabeth*'s wartime service. These include: Andrew Britton, *RMS Queen Elizabeth*, Classic Liners series (Stroud, Gloucestershire, UK: The History Press, 2013); D. A. Butler, *Warrior Queens: The Queen Mary and Queen Elizabeth in World War II* (Mechanicsburg, Pennsylvania: Stackpole Books, 2002); Chris Koning, *"Queen Elizabeth" at War: His Majesty's Transport, 1939–1946* (Wellingborough, UK: Patrick Stephens, 1985); and *The Two "Queens"—War Service of the Queen Mary and Queen Elizabeth*, Hutchinson's Pictorial History of the War, Vol. 26, pp. 389–92. Also informative was the entry for the RMS *Queen Elizabeth* on the Great Ocean Liners website, accessed at https://www.greatoceanliners.com/rms-queen-elizabeth, and an article on the site about the *Queen Elizabeth* written by Henrik Reimertz. A fascinating wartime account of the *Queen Elizabeth*'s conversion from luxury liner to troop transport is "Thousands of Canadian Workers Make Queen Elizabeth Troop Ship," *The Gazette* (Montreal, Canada), December 6, 1944, p. 16. The Manhattan "Super Piers" from which many U.S. servicemen

departed in World War II are described in "Sailing Away," *New York Times*, March 12, 2006, Section 14, p. 4. An indispensable source on trans-Atlantic convoys during the war is the Arthur Hague Convoy Database, accessed at http://www.convoyweb.org.uk/misc/index.html.

2   Cal Stewart's first encounter with Ben Kuroki aboard the *Queen Elizabeth* was related to the author by Stewart's son. Scott Stewart, author interview, July 24, 2023.

CHAPTER 8: "CHINAMAN BOY"

1   *The Story of the 93rd Bomb Group* (San Angelo Texas: Newsfoto Pub., n.d.), Chapter 2.

2   Ibid.

3   Rollin Reineck, author interview, September 23, 1991.

4   Martin, *Boy from Nebraska*, p. 76.

5   Stewart, *Ted's Travelling Circus*, p. 21.

6   Ibid., p. 22.

7   Martin, *Boy from Nebraska*, p. 78.

8   Ibid.

9   Lieutenant George R. Kaiser, Jr., October 4, 1942, "Historical Narrative of the Four Hundred Ninth Bomb Squadron, 1942, Month of October." Author's collection.

CHAPTER 9: "HEY, THEY'RE SHOOTING AT US!"

1   Stewart, *Ted's Travelling Circus*, p. 3.

2   Ibid., p. 7.

3   Ibid.

4   Theodore Finnarn, author interview, August 10, 1991. An Ohio native, Finnarn was the flight engineer and top turret gunner of *Thunder Bird*. The tail gunner who was so shaken by his first encounter with enemy flak was Jack R. Stover, a carpenter born in Illinois and living in Northern California at the time of his enlistment. The pilot was Charles (Pat) Murphy, the son of a prominent Mississippi attorney, and the copilot was Joe Avendano, a full-blooded Apache from Southern California.

5   Stewart, *Ted's Travelling Circus*, p. 8. The five men who died in the crash of the *Big Eagle* were Lieutenant William Marsh and sergeants James Detoris, Stephen Eppolito, Clayton Kammerer, and Arthur N. Torrey. The pilot of *Big Eagle* was Captain Alexander Simpson and his copilot was Lieutenant Nicholas H. Cox.

6   Stewart, *Ted's Travelling Circus*, p. 14.

7   Ibid.

CHAPTER 10: "LOOK AT ME NOW"

1   Stewart, *Ted's Travelling Circus*, pp. 23–24.

2   Ibid., p. 35.

3   Ibid., p. 35.

4   Bill Kubota, *Most Honorable Son* documentary transcript.

5   Stewart, *Ted's Travelling Circus*, p. 25.

6   Ibid., p. 27.

7   Ibid.

8   Ibid., pp. 27–28.

9   The command pilot of the dramatic flight was First Lieutenant Howard N. Young of Berkeley, California; the copilot was Second Lieutenant Cleveland D. Hickman from nearby Albany, California; and the bombardier was Second Lieutenant Anthony C. Yenalavage of Kingston, Pennsylvania. All three were awarded the Distinguished Flying Cross in February 1943. Young lost an arm because of his wounds, but he would be the only one of the three to survive the war. Their heroics were recounted in "Berkeley Fliers, Strangers Once, 'Blood Brothers' Now," *Oakland* (California) *Tribune*, January 7, 1943, p. 10; "Local Bombardier Gets DFC; Saved Crew by Taking Over Controls of Crippled Ship," *Wilkes-Barre* (Pennsylvania) *Times Leader*, February 17, 1943, p. 3; and "Local Fliers Decorated for Heroism Over Lorient," *Oakland* (California) *Tribune*, February 17, 1943, p. 1.

CHAPTER 11: "ARE YOU SURE YOU KNOW WHAT YOU'RE DOING?"

1   Martin, *Boy from Nebraska*, p. 77.

2   Ibid., p. 80.

3   Theodore Finnarn, author interview, August 10, 1991

4   Art Ferwerda interview with Bill Kubota, September 18, 1998, *Most Honorable Son* documentary, unedited footage.

5   I've tapped several sources for the biographical information on 93rd pilot Richard (Dick) Wilkinson and his father, J. L. Wilkinson. Joe Avendano Duran, nephew of the 93rd pilot Joe Avendano, shared with me recollections of his conversations with Dick Wilkinson in the early 2000s that included discussions about J. L. Wilkinson's ownership of the Kansas City Monarchs. Bill Young and Charles F. Faber have written an excellent biographical piece on J.L. that can be found on the Society for American Baseball Research (SABR) website here: https://sabr.org/bioproj/person/j-l-wilkinson/. Among the sources that Young and Faber tapped for their piece is an excellent profile of J. L. Wilkinson written by Sam Mellinger, "J.L. Wilkinson: He Was a Man Apart," *Kansas City Star*, July 30, 2006, pp. C1, C12. J.L. was inducted into the National Baseball Hall of Fame in 2006, and his biographical sketch on the Hall of Fame's website can be found here: https://baseballhall.org/hall-of-famers/wilkinson-jl. Joseph A. Reaves interviewed Dick Wilkinson for his excellent story in the *Arizona Republic* on the eve of J. L. Wilkinson's induction into the Baseball Hall of Fame: "Negro League Legends Fitting for Call to Hall," *Arizona Republic*, February 25, 2006, pp. C1, C6. I gleaned additional information from several other wartime newspaper articles, including: "Sporting Comment," *Kansas City Star*, August 15, 1943, p. 15, and "K.C. Owner's Son Downed in Raid," *Pittsburgh* (Pennsylvania) *Courier*, January 1, 1944, p. 12.

6   Ibid.

7   Ibid.

8   Richard L. Wilkinson census records, 1940 Selective Service registration card, 1941 enlist records, 93rd BG records.

9   Joe Avendano Duran, nephew of 93rd pilot Joe Avendano, talked with both Dick Wilkinson and Ben Kuroki about Dick's acceptance of Ben as a fill-in gunner on his crew in the late autumn of 1942. In a series of conversations, text messages, and emails on January 6, 8, 11, and 14, 2022, Joe Duran shared with me the recollections of Dick Wilkinson and Ben Kuroki about how Ben had become a replacement on Wilkinson's crew. Joseph A. Reaves also touched on this topic in his interview with Dick Wilkinson for "Negro League Legends Fitting for Call to Hall," *Arizona Republic*, February 25, 2006, pp. C1, C6.

10   Ibid.

CHAPTER 12: A BIG CHANCE

1   Edward Weir interview with Bill Kubota, August 29, 1998, *Most Honorable Son* documentary, unedited footage.

2   Stewart, *Ted's Travelling Circus*, p. 47.

3   Al Asch written account, quoted in Stewart, *Ted's Travelling Circus*, pp. 47–48.

4   Information on the physical attributes of Robert A. Johnson was drawn from his World War II Army Air Corps enlistment record. Details on his crash were drawn from newspaper articles found on the Crawford County, Iowa, IAGenWeb, under the headings "Military-World War II-News About Military Personnel-1943," http://iagenweb.org/crawford/military/ccmilitaryww2.html, accessed on November 12, 2022. Also see Stewart, *Ted's Travelling Circus*, pp. 47–48.

CHAPTER 13: "NOW, I BELONG"

1   Stewart, *Ted's Travelling Circus*, p. 49.

2   Ibid.

3   The presence of the Jewish workers on the ground in Tunis is recounted in Rick Atkinson, *Army at Dawn: The War in North Africa, 1942–1943* (New York: Henry Holt and Company, 2002), pp. 239–40.

4   Atkinson, *Army at Dawn*, p. 218

5   Recollections of Ben's first mission are drawn from Bill Kubota's interviews with Ben Kuroki and Bill Dawley and Ralph Martin's account. See Ben Kuroki interview with Bill Kubota, August 26–27, 1998, *Most Honorable Son* documentary, unedited footage; Elmer (Bill) Dawley interview with Bill Kubota, November 12, 1998, unedited footage; and Martin, *Boy from Nebraska*, pp. 91–94. Dawley said in his interview with Kubota, "The next thing I know, bang, I'm gone. A chunk of flak hit me and that was the end of me."

6   As Ben recalled: "He got hit in the head and we couldn't even help him until we got out of the flak zone and out of the enemy aircraft. [Hap] Kendall came back and was going to give him a morphine injection and I waved him off and told him not to because I remembered what they had taught me in gunner's school in England: A morphine injection to a serious head injury could be fatal." Ben Kuroki interview with Bill Kubota, August 26–27, 1998, *Most Honorable Son* documentary, unedited footage.

7   Stewart, *Ted's Travelling Circus*, pp. 50–51. The three members of the *Ambrose* crew who died in the crash landing were Lieutenants Walter R. Erness and Estell A. Martin and Sergeant Henry M. Elder.

8   Ibid., p. 51.

9   Various accounts about the 93rd's movement from Tafaraoui, Algeria, to Gambut, Libya, all place the movement as occurring in the third week of December 1942, but they differ as to the date. The official 328th Squadron History for December 1942 lists December 20 as the date of the 93rd's movement from Tafaraoui to Gambut. Years later, in his unofficial history of the 93rd, Cal Stewart cites December 15 as the date of the movement. See Stewart, *Ted's Travelling Circus*, p. 51. In their official history, Wesley Frank Craven and James Lea Cate cite December 16 as the day of the arrival of the 93rd bombers at Gambut. See Craven and Cate, eds., *The Army Air Forces in World War II, Vol. 2. Europe: Torch to Pointblank, August 1942 to December 1943* (Washington, DC: Superintendent of Documents, 1948), pp. 97–98. Other 93rd Bomb Group accounts fix December 18 as the date of the group's arrival at Gambut after a flight that began late in the evening of December 17, and that's what I have used.

CHAPTER 14: GAMBUT

1   Craven and Cate, *Europe: Torch to Pointblank, August 1942 to December 1943*, pp. 97–98.

2   Lewis H. Brereton diary entry for December 13, 1942, published as Lewis H. Brereton, Lieutenant General, USA, *The Brereton Diaries: The War in the Air in the Pacific, Middle East and Europe: 3 October 1941–8 May 1945* (New York, William Morrow and Company, 1946), p. 174.

3   Stewart, *Ted's Travelling Circus*, p. 57.

4   Wilmer H. Paine journal entry for December 23, 1942, published by Paine's son as *Flight Surgeon: The Journal of Maj. Wilmer H. Paine 93rd Bombardment Group Eighth Air Force* (W. Paine Jr., 2006).

5   Stewart, *Ted's Travelling Circus*, p. 58.

6   Brereton diary entry for December 13, 1942, *Brereton Diaries*, p. 174.

7   Stewart, *Ted's Travelling Circus*, p. 58.

8   Paine journal entry for December 24, 1942.

9   Brereton diary entry for December 25, 1942.

10   Paine journal entry for December 26, 1942.

11   Paine journal entry for December 27, 1942.

12   Paine journal entry for December 29, 1942; Brereton diary entry for December 31, 1942.

13   Paine journal entry for December 30, 1942.

14   Paine journal entries for December 27–28, 1942.

CHAPTER 15: BROTHERS IN ARMS

1   Paine journal entry for January 1, 1943.

Chapter 16: On to Italy

1   Atkinson, *Army at Dawn*, p. 242.

2   Ibid., p. 245.

3   Ibid., pp. 253–55.

4   Ibid., pp. 258–59.

5   Ibid., p. 260.

6   Ibid., p. 260.

7   Ibid., p. 248.

8   Brereton diary entry for January 4, 1943.

9   Martin, *Boy from Nebraska*, p. 97.

Chapter 17: *Big Dealer*

1   Paine journal entry for January 10, 1943.

2   Stewart, *Ted's Travelling Circus*, p. 50.

3   Associated Press dispatch, "Gunner Helps Bring Crippled Bomber Home by Holding Fuel Line Leak Till Hands Freeze," *Evening Star* (Washington, DC), October 11, 1942, p. 23.

4   United Press dispatch, "Anglo-U.S. Patrols Protect Convoys," New York *Daily News*, November 11, 1942, p. 22.

5   "Former Mines Student Killed," *Rapid City* (South Dakota) *Journal*, January 27, 1943, pp. 1 and 6.

6   Paine journal entry for January 12, 1943.

7   Paine journal entry for January 14, 1943.

Chapter 18: *Double Trouble*

1   Paine journal entry for January 15, 1943. Also see Stewart, *Ted's Travelling Circus*, p. 55.

2   Stewart, *Ted's Travelling Circus*, p. 54.

3   Paine journal entry for January 19, 1943. Also see Stewart, *Ted's Travelling Circus*, pp. 54–55

4   Craven and Cate, *Europe: Torch to Pointblank: August 1942 to December 1943*, p. 102.

Chapter 19: No End in Sight

1   Ibid., pp. 102–3.

2   Details of the 93rd's January 26, 1943, raid on the Messina port area are drawn from Stewart, *Ted's Travelling Circus*, p. 56.

3   Craven and Cate, *Europe: Torch to Pointblank: August 1942 to December 1943*, pp. 102–03; Stewart, *Ted's Travelling Circus*, p. 59.

4   Ibid.

5   Atkinson, *Army at Dawn*, pp. 291–95.

6   Ibid.

7   Major General John W. Huston, USAF Retired, ed., *American Airpower Comes of Age: General Henry H. "Hap" Arnold's World War II Diaries* (Maxwell Air Force Base, Alabama: Air University Press, 2002), pp. 475–76.

8   Ibid.

CHAPTER 20: RETURN TO ENGLAND

1   Stewart, *Ted's Travelling Circus*, p. 65.

2   Paine journal entry for January 26, 1943.

3   Paine journal entry for February 3, 1943.

4   Paine journal entry for January 31, 1943.

5   Paine journal entry for February 9, 1943.

6   Stewart, *Ted's Travelling Circus*, pp. 59–60.

7   Ibid., p. 66.

8   Paine journal entry for February 13, 1943.

9   Paine journal entry for February 15, 1943.

10 Paine journal entry for February 16, 1943.

11 Paine journal entry for February 18, 1943.

12 George Piburn would put his combat experience to good use training crews in the United Kingdom, and he would meet and marry a British woman, Christina Marie Swales. Piburn survived the war and returned to Southern California with Christina, but he would die young. In 1976, Piburn was living in Rancho Palos Verdes in Orange County when a teenage driver rolled their car in an accident a quarter of a mile from Piburn's house. A nineteen-year-old girl was killed in the accident. Police were still at the scene of the accident a short time later when Piburn suffered a fatal heart attack. He was fifty-four years old. See "Crash Victim Dies of Injuries," *Press-Telegram* (Long Beach, California), January 13, 1976, p. 12.

13 My description of the fighting at Kasserine Pass is drawn from Rick Atkinson's detailed account in *Army at Dawn* and other sources. See Atkinson, *Army at Dawn*, pp. 339–92, and "The Battle of Kasserine Pass," an article published by the National WWII Museum on February 5, 2018, and accessed at https://www .nationalww2museum.org/war/articles/battle-kasserine-pass.

CHAPTER 21: MISSING IN ACTION

1   Stewart, *Ted's Travelling Circus*, pp. 67–68.

2   Edward Weir shared the same sentiment in a letter to his father later that week. "We expected to crash into the mountains at any minute," Weir wrote. Edward Weir letter to his father, February 27, 1943, quoted in "Kilgore Flier Interned in Spanish Morocco; Has Narrow Escape as Big Plane Forced Down," *Kilgore* (Texas) *News Herald*, March 28, 1943, pp. 1 and 8.

3   The Epting crew's encounter with the hundred or so horsemen was described in Bill Kubota's interviews with Ben Kuroki, Homer Moran, and Edward Weir for his *Most Honorable Son* documentary, unedited footage. Another source of information was Edward Weir's letter to his father, cited above.

4   Ibid.

5 Edward Weir letter to father, February 27, 1943.
6 Ben Kuroki interview with Bill Kubota, August 26–27, 1998.
7 Edward Weir interview with Bill Kubota, August 29, 1998.

CHAPTER 22: PRISONERS IN A GILDED CAGE

1 My understanding of Francisco Franco's complicated alliance with Adolf Hitler during World War II was informed by four sources: Willard L. Beaulac, *Franco: Silent Ally in World War II* (Carbondale, Illinois: Southern Illinois University Press, 1986); Wayne H. Bowen, *Spain during World War II* (Columbia, Missouri: University of Missouri Press, 2006); Charles B. Burdick, *Germany's Military Strategy and Spain in World War II*, (Syracuse, New York: Syracuse University Press, 1968); and Herbert Feis, *The Spanish Story: Franco and the Nations at War* (New York: Alfred A. Knopf, 1948).

2 Beaulac, *Franco: Silent Ally in World War II*, p. 205.

3 Ambassador Carlton Hayes cable to Secretary of State Cordell Hull, January 15, 1943, published as Document 544, "The Ambassador in Spain (Hayes) to the Secretary of State," in E. Ralph Perkins and N. O. Sappington, eds., *Foreign Relations of the United States: Diplomatic Papers, 1943, Europe, Vol. II* (Washington, DC: US Government Printing Office, 1964).

4 Details of Ben Kuroki's internment in Spain with thirteen 93rd Bomb Group airmen are drawn from Bill Kubota's previously cited interviews with Ben Kuroki, Homer Moran, and Edward Weir. Also see Stewart, *Ted's Travelling Circus*, pp. 103–10.

5 Stewart, *Ted's Travelling Circus*, pp. 106–7.

6 Ambassador Carlton Hayes cable to Secretary of State Cordell Hull, January 15, 1943, as Document 544, "The Ambassador in Spain (Hayes) to the Secretary of State," and Document 546, "The Chargé in Spain (Beaulac) to the Secretary of State," in Perkins and Sappington, eds., *FRUS: Diplomatic Papers, 1943, Europe, Vol. II.*

7 Homer Moran interview with Bill Kubota, September 5, 1990.

CHAPTER 23: TUPELO LASS

1 James Parton diary entry for March 27, 1943, James Parton Papers, Houghton Library, Harvard University, Cambridge, Massachusetts.

2 Ralph G. Martin, *Boy from Nebraska*, p. 134. I've drawn additional details about the near-crash from the Epting crew's after-mission debriefing comments in the crew's sortie report for the May 29, 1943, mission to La Pallice, France, found in the 93rd Bomb Group records, RG 18, National Archives and Records Administration (NARA II), College Park, Maryland.

3 I found this notation on the Epting crew's sortie report for the May 29, 1943, mission to La Pallice, France, in the National Archives. 93rd Bomb Group Records, RG 18, NARA II.

CHAPTER 24: SPECIAL ORDERS NUMBER 174

1   James Dugan and Carroll Stewart, *Ploesti: The Great Ground-Air Battle of 1 August 1943* (New York: Random House, 1962), pp. 44–45; Stewart, *Ted's Travelling Circus*, pp. 127–28. At the time the Dugan-Stewart book was published in 1962, the name of the Romanian city was spelled "Ploesti." It is now Ploiesti.

2   Edward Sand diary entries for June 6, 7, 10, and 14, 1943. Author's collection.

3   William Gros, author interview, October 13, 1991.

4   Robert Lovett to General Henry H. Arnold, memoranda dated June 18 and 19, 1943, Ira Eaker Papers, Manuscript Division, Library of Congress, Washington, DC.

5   General Henry H. Arnold to General Barney M. Giles, directive dated June 22, 1943, Henry (Hap) Arnold Papers, Manuscript Division, Library of Congress, Washington, DC.

6   "Squadron History—June 1943," 328th Squadron records, July 13, 1944. Author's collection.

CHAPTER 25: THE BIG ONE

1   Brutus Hamilton diary entry for June 27, 1943, 330th Squadron, 93rd Bomb Group Records. Author's collection.

2   Edward Sand diary entry for June 27, 1943. Author's collection.

3   Brutus Hamilton diary entry for June 28, 1943. The officer had been a two-time Olympian and silver medalist in the decathlon at the 1920 Olympic Games in Antwerp, Belgium. The Missouri-born Hamilton was track and field coach at the University of California, Berkeley, and was in his early forties when he entered the army after Pearl Harbor and was assigned to the 93rd's 330th Squadron as an intelligence major. Hamilton was a gifted poet and writer and kept a diary that documented the 93rd's exploits as the air war against Nazi Germany ramped up in 1943.

4   Post-mission intelligence report, July 19, 1943, 93rd Bomb Group Records. Author's collection.

5   Rome radio reported the deaths of 166 persons on the ground the day following the raid. Over the next several days, the official death toll rose to 700 people. A 2003 investigation launched by Rome's municipal government concluded that the actual number of deaths in the city's San Lorenzo district alone was more than 1,500.

6   Gelorme Musco's first name is spelled inconsistently in government records and news accounts. He was born "Gelorme Musco," according to birth and census records. In US military records, his name appears as "Jerome" and "Gelrome." On November 13, 1943, the New York *Daily News* ran a feature article about the death of Musco, written by a London-based correspondent for the United Press news service, Walter Cronkite, later of CBS News fame. Cronkite's story began, "All his life Gelrome Musco wanted to see Sicily. His parents were born there. His grandparents still live there. Gelrome today is buried in Sicily, in the little town of Cassible—but he never saw the Mediterranean isle." See Walter Cronkite, "Bury Slain Flier on Isle He Pined to See," New York *Daily News*, November 13, 1943, p. 65.

7   Brutus Hamilton diary entry for July 24, 1943.

8   Edward Sand diary entry for July 31, 1943.

CHAPTER 26: TIDAL WAVE

1   Background information on Charles Stenius Young is drawn from several
     sources, including U.S. federal census records for 1920, 1930, and 1940, and
     Young's Selective Service and army enlistment records. A fascinating source
     was a letter about Young from his great-niece, Kate Jensen, published as "Reader
     Voices: Discovering Uncle Bubba," *Deseret* (Utah) *News*, February 10, 2010.

2   Background information on Ivan Canfield is drawn from U.S. federal census
     records for 1920, 1930, and 1940, and Canfield's army enlistment records.
     Additional information about Canfield is drawn from various news clippings,
     including: "Gulf Coast Training Center Pins Wings on Biggest Flying Classes,"
     Fort Worth (Texas) *Star-Telegram*, January 15, 1943, p. 15; "99 Texans Decorated
     for Participation in Ploesti Oil Refineries Raid," *San Angelo* (Texas) *Standard-
     Times*, November 17, 1943, p. 8; and "Airman's Mother Receives His Medal for
     Raid," *Fort Worth* (Texas) *Star-Telegram*, December 30, 1943, p. 4.

3   I separately interviewed the two *Kickapoo* survivors, Russell Polivka and
     Eugene Garner, and they agreed on most key facts. Both, for example, said that
     Kickapoo lost three engines shortly after takeoff, precipitating the emergency
     that culminated in the deadly crash. Garner described how the pilots guided
     the aircraft over the sea, where they dumped their bombs, before circling back
     to attempt an emergency landing. It was Garner's recollection that they were
     airborne for more than thirty minutes before the attempted landing. Polivka said
     he left the nose compartment and made his way back to the bulkhead area "when
     I knew we were going to crash." As the pilots attempted to land, "there was a
     telephone pole out in the desert and we hit that," Polivka told me. "Cut off a wing
     and the next I knew everything was on fire." Polivka said he escaped through the
     hole where the top turret had caved in. It was Garner's recollection that Polivka
     got stuck in a window while trying to exit the burning aircraft and that he had
     pulled Polivka free and dragged him to a nearby railroad embankment. Garner
     said his burns weren't as severe as Polivka's because he was doused by a five-
     gallon can of hydraulic fluid that burst when the plane broke up. The hydraulic
     fluid didn't burn easily and "insulated" him, Garner said. Ploiesti was Polivka's
     first and last mission of the war. Garner returned to duty about five weeks later
     and flew twenty-five missions with the 93rd. One of Garner's first missions after
     his return to duty was the October 1, 1943, raid on which my uncle, Technical
     Sergeant L. H. White, and eight crewmates were killed. Author interviews with
     Eugene Garner, July 17, 1991, and Russell Polivka, November 19, 1991.

4   Ben Kuroki interview with Bill Kubota, August 26–27, 1998.

5   Edwin Baker, *One of Many*, unpublished memoir dated 1982, p. 16. Baker shared
     his manuscript with me in the early 1990s.

6   The descriptions of the banter among members of the *Tupelo Lass* crew on the
     flight to Ploiesti and the singing of the "Blue Danube" waltz are drawn from
     Bill Kubota's interviews for his *Most Honorable Son* documentary: Ben Kuroki

interview with Bill Kubota, August 26–27, 1998, unedited footage; K. O. Dessert interview with Bill Kubota, October 16, 1998, unedited footage; and Edward Weir interview with Bill Kubota, August 29, 1998, unedited footage.

7   Dugan and Stewart, *Ploesti*, pp. 106–7; Stewart, *Ted's Travelling Circus*, pp. 168–69.

CHAPTER 27: A HELLHOLE OF FIRE, FLAME, AND SMOKE

1   Ben Kuroki interview with Bill Kubota, August 26–27, 1998.

2   Dugan and Stewart. *Ploesti*, p. 112.

3   The gunner who broke down at his waist gun was a member of my uncle's crew, which was flying in *Jerk's Natural*, tail number 41-23711, piloted by Cleveland Hickman. The crew's regular command pilot, William F. Stein, flew as copilot. The breakdown of gunner Kermit Morris was described to me by the crew's tail gunner on the Ploiesti raid, William G. Anderson. "Morris just wilted. [Technical Sergeant L. H. White] had to come back and take over his waist gun. Morris sat down and cried," Anderson told me in the first of several interviews and conversations we had through the 1990s. William G. Anderson, author interview, December 17, 1991. By all accounts, Kermit Morris was never the same after the Ploiesti raid. He flew one more mission then took himself off flying status, although he remained with the 93rd in various ground duties for several months afterward. Morris continued to struggle after the war. He drank heavily and, according to public records, was arrested for public intoxication in New Mexico and California. He died in 1968 at the age of fifty. "He never was the same after the war," his former wife told me. Tootie Summersgill, author interview, December 30, 1990.

4   Ben Kuroki's descriptions of what he saw and experienced over Ploiesti are primarily drawn from his August 26–27, 1998, interview with documentary filmmaker Bill Kubota, unedited footage. Jake Epting described what he saw from the cockpit of *Tupelo Lass* in Dugan and Stewart, *Ploesti*, p. 112.

5   The pilot was 328th Squadron commander Joseph Tate, quoted in Dugan and Stewart, *Ploesti*, p. 117.

6   Ben Kuroki interview with Bill Kubota, August 26–27, 1998. Ben believed the aircraft was *Jose Carioca*, piloted by Nicholas Stampolis with copilot Ivan Canfield. Other accounts described *Jose Carioca* as the aircraft that plowed into the third floor of Ploiesti's women's prison. Regardless of how *Jose Carioca* met its end, there were no survivors.

7   Edwin Baker, *One of Many*, p. 17.

8   Hubert Womble, author interview, November 19, 1991. Womble also provided a written account of his Ploiesti experience to author Michael Hill. See Hill, *Black Sunday: Ploesti* (Atglen, Pennsylvania: Schiffer Military/Aviation History, 1993), p. 66.

9   Ben Kuroki interview with Bill Kubota, August 26–27, 1998.

10   Ibid.

11   K. O. Dessert interview with Bill Kubota, October 16, 1998.

12   Ibid.

CHAPTER 28: THE LONGEST NIGHT

1   Edward Weir interview with Bill Kubota, August 29, 1998.

2   Ben Kuroki interview with Bill Kubota, August 26–27, 1998.

3   Brutus Hamilton diary entry for August 1, 1943.

4   K. O. Dessert interview with Bill Kubota, October 16, 1998.

5   Donald Hudspeth diary entry for August 2, 1943. Author's collection. I spoke with Hudspeth several times during the 1990s and I formally interviewed him on July 9, 1991, and August 12, 1991. He mentioned that he kept a diary, which he then generously shared with me. Hudspeth died in Yadkinville, North Carolina, in 2012 at the age of ninety-one.

6   The 328th Squadron aircraft that returned from Sicily on Aug. 2, 1943 was *Jerk's Natural*, the aircraft named and flown to England by John L. (Jerk) Jerstad, who died over Ploesti. The aircraft had been bequeathed to the William Stein crew, which had joined the 93rd in England in June. My uncle—my mother's oldest brother—Technical Sergeant L. H. White was the radio operator on *Jerk's Natural*. On Oct. 1, 1943, my uncle and eight other men, including William Stein, died during an attempted crash landing in southern Austria after bombing the German Messerschmitt Me-109 factory at Wiener Neustadt, Austria.

7   Homer Moran interview with Bill Kubota, Sept. 5, 1998, *Most Honorable Son* documentary, unedited footage, Ben Kuroki Collection, KDN Films Archives.

8   Ben Kuroki interview with Bill Kubota, August 26–27, 1998.

9   Brutus Hamilton diary entry for August 3, 1943.

10 Elmer (Bill) Dawley interview with Bill Kubota, November 12, 1998.

11 A 328th Squadron pilot who was among the 93rd men sent to Egypt for rest and relaxation following the Ploiesti raid detailed how the men spent their time in a letter to his family. Second Lieutenant George B. Wilkinson to Dear Mother, letter dated Aug. 7, 1943. Author's collection.

CHAPTER 29: LIMBO

1   United States Strategic Bombing Survey, *Wiener Neustädter Flugzeugwerke, Wiener Neustadt, Austria*, 2nd ed. (Washington, DC: Survey, 1947).

2   Parton, *Air Force Spoken Here*, p. 263.

3   Brutus Hamilton diary entry for August 7, 1943.

4   Donald Hudspeth diary entry for August 13, 1943.

5   Alva (Jake) Geron related his experiences on the Ploiesti raid and the August 13, 1943, raid on Wiener Neustadt, Austria, in two interviews with me. Alva Geron, author interviews, December 8, 1990, and August 2, 1993.

CHAPTER 30: MORAN CREW

1   See "Rosebud Indian School Boys Visit the Journal," *Rapid City Journal*, February 7, 1933, p. 5.

2   Homer Moran's basketball exploits were documented by the Sioux Falls *Argus-Leader* and other South Dakota newspapers. The "Wandering Sioux" photo and cutline were published in the Sioux Falls *Argus-Leader*, January 21, 1938, p. 10. Also see "Powerful Northern Squad Coming for Two Contests," Sioux Falls *Argus-Leader*, February 4, 1940, p. 10.

3   See "World's Tallest Team Sets Back Wolves, 60–52," *Rapid City Journal*, March 12, 1940, p. 7; "Northern Beaten 60–52; Hamline Wins; Wayne Out," Sioux Falls *Argus-Leader*, March 12, 1940, p. 6.

4   Homer Moran, interview with Bill Kubota, September 5, 1998.

5   Moran recounted his path to flying B-24s with the 93rd Bomb Group in his September 5, 1998, interview with Bill Kubota. Moran's graduation from the Victorville, California, flying school was noted in a small item in the *Rapid City Journal*. See "Is Pilot," *Rapid City Journal*, July 31, 1942, p. 3.

Chapter 31: A Disappointing Finale

1   Martin Bowman, *Home by Christmas? The Story of US 8th/15th Air Force Airmen at War* (Wellingborough, Northamptonshire, UK: Patrick Stephens, 1987), p. 41.

2   Biographical material on Ernst-Günther Baade is drawn primarily from Samuel W. Mitcham, *Rommel's Desert Commanders: The Men Who Served the Desert Fox, North Africa, 1941–42* (Mechanicsburg, PA: Stackpole Books, 2007), pp. 76–77, and Rick Atkinson, *The Day of Battle: The War in Sicily and Italy, 1943–1944* (New York: Holt Paperbacks, 2007), p. 165.

3   Atkinson, *The Day of Battle: The War in Sicily and Italy, 1943–1944*, p. 165.

4   Atkinson, *Day of Battle*, p. 165. Also see Lieutenant Colonel Albert N. Garland and Howard McGaw Smyth, *US Army in World War II: Mediterranean Theater of Operations: Sicily and the Surrender of Italy* (Washington, DC: Center of Military History, US Army, 1993), pp. 374–76.

5   Atkinson, *Day of Battle*, p. 167.

6   Ibid., p. 168.

7   Garland and Smyth, *Sicily and the Surrender of Italy*, pp. 413–15.

8   Ibid., pp. 413–78.

9   Ibid., pp. 413–16; Atkinson, *Day of Battle*, p. 168.

10   Edward Sand diary entry for August 16, 1943.

11   The length of a combat tour for an Eighth Air Force heavy bomber crew member was set at twenty-five missions in the spring of 1943. The number would be increased in increments of five missions in 1944 as Luftwaffe resistance diminished, until it reached fifty missions by the final months of the war. The length of a combat tour for heavy bomber crews based in North Africa was already at fifty missions in the summer of 1943, but the 93rd, 44th, and 389th B-24 crews—the three Eighth Air Force B-24 groups temporarily based in North Africa from June to August 1943—were still governed by Eighth Air Force rules, and thus their tour of duty was twenty-five missions.

Chapter 32: An Enemy at Peak Strength

1   Martin, *Boy from Nebraska*, p. 149.

2   Ben contemporaneously discussed his reasons for flying five "bonus" combat missions with the 93rd on at least two occasions: in an interview with a *Los Angeles Daily News* reporter in January 1944 and in a speech before the Commonwealth Club in San Francisco on February 4, 1944. The article in which Ben discussed this with the *Los Angeles Daily News* was reprinted as "Ben Kuroki Is in the Limelight: Dramatic Story of War Record Brings Fame on Pacific Coast," *Lincoln County* (Nebraska) *Tribune*, January 27, 1944, pp. 1 and 8.

3   Ben Kuroki interview with Bill Kubota, August 26–27, 1998, *Most Honorable Son* documentary, unedited footage.

4   Several 93rd men mentioned the rumors in diary entries and letters to family members in August 1943. Brutus Hamilton discussed the rumors in his diary entry for August 18, 1943. "Gen. [James P.] Hodges and Gen. [Ira] Eaker are in the Theatre and are no doubt discussing with the IX Air Force just what should be done with us. No announcements yet but plenty of rumors," Hamilton wrote.

5   Elmer (Bill) Dawley interview with Bill Kubota, November 12, 1998, *Most Honorable Son* documentary, unedited footage.

6   Ibid.

7   Descriptions of the 93rd's August 26–27, 1943, return trip from North Africa are drawn from the diary entries of navigator James Reid and gunners Donald Hudspeth and Edward Sand. Author's collection.

8   Homer Moran interview with Bill Kubota, September 5, 1998, *Most Honorable Son* documentary, unedited footage.

CHAPTER 33: THE KILLING MONTH

1   In *Masters of the Air*, historian Donald L. Miller describes the October 9, 1943, raid on Marienburg as "the longest mission of the war up to this point." See Miller, pp. 207–8. To be more precise, Marienburg was the "longest mission of the war up to this point" only for Eighth Air Force bombers flying from England. The one-way distance covered by the American B-17s and B-24s from their bases in England to Marienburg on October 9 was about 525 miles. By comparison, this is less than half the 1,200 miles flown one-way by the 93rd and other B-24 groups from their Libyan bases to Wiener Neustadt, Austria, on August 13, 1943. The first Wiener Neustadt raid would remain the "longest mission of the war" for US bombers based in both the European and Mediterranean theaters. By comparison, Berlin was about 500 miles one-way from the American B-17 and B-24 bases in East Anglia—less than half the distance of the first Wiener Neustadt raid.

2   Details about the emergency landing of Miles League in *Satan's Sister* are drawn from the American Air Museum in Britain database. The entry reads as follows: "9-Oct-43 on mission to bomb Danzig U-Boat production in B-24 42-40610 'Satan's Sister' A/C took flak hits, lost engine on return, diverting to Sweden. A/C Belly landed in Rinkaby airfield, Sweden. Interned."

3   The Nicholas Caruso quote is drawn from Stewart, *Ted's Travelling Circus*, p. 250. In the early 1990s, I interviewed Caruso about his experiences with the 93rd, including the Danzig raid and his landing in Sweden. Nicholas Caruso, author interview, November 18, 1991.

4 The numbers of aircraft and losses on the October 9, 1943, raid by the Eighth
   Air Force are drawn from Kit C. Carter and Robert Mueller, eds., *U.S. Army
   Air Forces in World War II. Combat Chronology: 1941–1945* (Washington, DC:
   Center for Air Force History, 1991), p. 229.

5 The Ben Kuroki quote is from Cal Stewart's contemporaneous story about the
   93rd's October 9, 1943, raid on Danzig, written by Stewart in his role as the 93rd
   Bomb Group publicist. Cal Stewart, "Danzig Story," Public Relations Office,
   Ninety-third Bombardment Group (H) AAF 104, October 9, 1943. Author's
   collection.

6 Stewart, *Ted's Travelling Circus*, p. 251.

7 Ibid., pp. 251–52.

8 Miller, *Masters of the Air*, pp. 208–9. Also see Gerald Astor, *The Mighty Eighth:
   The Air War in Europe as Told by the Men Who Fought It* (New York: Dell
   Publishing, 1998), p. 198.

9 Miller, *Masters of the Air*, p. 210.

10 Ibid., p. 214.

CHAPTER 34: DEATH DENIED

1 Ibid., pp. 234–35.

2 Russell DeMont, author interview, October 6, 1991.

3 Miller, *Masters of the Air*, p. 234.

4 Stewart, *Ted's Travelling Circus*, p. 252.

5 Ben Kuroki and Homer Moran recalled Ben's near-death experience on the
   November 5, 1943, Münster raid in their interviews with Bill Kubota. Ben Kuroki
   interview with Bill Kubota, August 26–27, 1998, and Homer Moran interview
   with Bill Kubota, September 5, 1998, *Most Honorable Son* documentary,
   unedited footage.

6 Homer Moran interview with Bill Kubota, September 5, 1998, unedited footage.

7 Moran's account of the incident was more expansive than Ben's. Moran said he
   heard the top turret guns firing "when it shouldn't have been firing," and so he
   ordered a crewman to "take a look up there to see what was happening." Moran's
   memory on this particular detail may have been faulty, as there is some question
   as to whether Ben's guns would have continued firing after he lost consciousness.
   In any event, Moran said his order resulted in Ben being discovered unconscious,
   his oxygen mask torn from his face. Homer Moran interview with Bill Kubota,
   September 5, 1998, unedited footage.

8 Martin, *Boy from Nebraska*, p. 152.

9 Martin, *Boy from Nebraska*, pp. 152–53.

10 Ibid., p. 153.

11 Ben Kuroki interview with Bill Kubota, August 26–27, 1998.

12 Ben's later recollections about his passage from England to America are sparse.
   In a February 4, 1944, speech before the Commonwealth Club in San Francisco,
   Ben said he left England on December 1, 1943, and reached New York City
   on December 7. Ralph G. Martin offers no details of Ben's return in his 1946
   biography, *Boy from Nebraska*. Ben said this about his return from England in

his lengthy interview with Bill Kubota: "Unfortunately I didn't get to fly home. I had to come home by boat. It took me six, seven days to get back." Preservation of World War II convoy records has been spotty, and I couldn't find any documents that definitively established the date of Ben's departure from England or his arrival in New York City. But a telegram I came across in Ben's papers at the Smithsonian's National Museum of American History supports the timetable that Ben recalled in his Commonwealth Club speech. The timestamp on the telegram that Ben sent to his brother George in Hershey, Nebraska, was "Dec 8, 1227 PM." Ben's telegram read as follows: "Near New York will visit Chicago probably week before arrive home—Ben Kuroki."

CHAPTER 35: HOMECOMING

1 Martin, *Boy from Nebraska*, p. 154.

2 Ibid. Ben's quote is drawn from his August 26–27, 1998, interview with Bill Kubota.

3 "Warren Sees Sabotage Peril in Freeing Evacuees," United Press dispatch in the *Fresno* (California) *Bee*, June 21, 1943, p. 2.

4 Ibid.

5 Ben Kuroki interview with Bill Kubota, August 26–27, 1998.

6 See "Kuroki Here," North Platte (Nebraska) *Tribune*, December 23, 1943, p. 1; "Ben Kuroki Is Home After War Services," *North Platte Telegraph*, December 17, 1943, p. 2.

7 Martin, *Boy from Nebraska*, p. 155.

8 Blaine Runner's heroics were recounted in numerous local newspaper articles at the time. See "Fire Sweeps South Part of County," *North Platte Telegraph*, March 31, 1910, p. 5, and "Blaine Runner Receives Medal," *North Platte Semi-Weekly Tribune*, January 30, 1912, p. 4. His height (six-foot-two) and other physical characteristics are drawn from his World War II draft registration card. Runner's visit to Ben and gift is recounted in Martin, *Boy from Nebraska*, p. 155.

9 Walter Cronkite, United Press dispatch, published as "Nebraska Jap on Liberator is 'fightingest,'" *Lincoln* (Nebraska) *Evening State Journal*, November 11, 1943, p. 1.

10 Walter Cronkite, United Press dispatch, published as "Nebraska Jap on Liberator is 'fightingest,'" *Lincoln* (Nebraska) *Evening State Journal*, November 11, 1943, p. 3.

11 "D.F.C. Attests to His Deeds," *Commercial Appeal*, Memphis, Tennessee, November 28, 1943, p. 23.

12 "Kuroki Has Close Call on His Last Trip to Germany," *North Platte* (Nebraska) *Telegraph*, December 3, 1943, p. 1; "Hershey Boy Jap-American Flier For U.S.A.," *Morning World-Herald*, Omaha, Nebraska, December 11, 1943, p. 2.

13 "Sgt. Kuroki Wants to Avenge Pearl Harbor," *North Platte* (Nebraska) *Daily Bulletin*, December 21, 1943, pp. 1 and 7; United Press dispatch, "No Pleasure Jaunt is Raid Over Ploesti," *Columbus* (Nebraska) *Telegram*, December 21, 1943, p. 4.

14 "Nebraska Notes—North Platte," Omaha *Morning World-Herald*, December 23, 1943, p. 11.

15 "Japanese Y.P. to Honor Sgt. Kuroki," *North Platte Telegraph*, December 30, 1943, p. 6.

16 The dispatches appeared in dozens of newspapers across the United States, including the following: Associated Press dispatch, "American-Born Jap Is Fighter," *Arizona Republic*, January 4, 1944, p. 4; United Press dispatch, "Kuroki Hasn't Yet Realized Ambition," *Columbus* (Nebraska) *Telegram*, January 4, 1944; International News Service dispatch, "Nebraska-Born Japanese Hailed," Omaha *Morning-World Herald*, January 4, 1944, p. 4; and "Sergeant Kuroki Is Hero but Still Very Dissatisfied," *Macon* (Georgia) *News*, January 4, 1944, p. 2.

CHAPTER 36: MOST HONORABLE SON

1 See "Army Takes Over Six Bay Hotels," *Evening Vanguard* (Venice, California), November 25, 1943, p. 1; "Army to Occupy Six Hostelries in Santa Monica," *San Bernardino County* (California) *Sun*, November 26, 1943, p. 2; "Air Force Center Gives Bay Aides New Duties," *Los Angeles Times*, January 2, 1944, p. C2; "Flyers' Center Gets New Chief," *Los Angeles Times*, January 15, 1944; "Army Takes Three More Santa Monica Hotels," *Los Angeles Times*, January 19, 1944, p. A2; "Bay Leaguers Assist Redistribution Center," *Los Angeles Times*, March 26, 1944, p. C4; "Air Wac Recruits Offered Redistribution Center Jobs," *Los Angeles Times*, May 28, 1944, p. B2.

2 Edward Bates interview with Bill Kubota, undated, 1998 or 1999, *Most Honorable Son* documentary, unedited footage, Ben Kuroki Collection, KDN Films Archives.

3 Ibid.

4 Ibid.

5 "Ben Kuroki Heads for Crack at Japs," *Omaha Daily Journal-Stockman*, January 19, 1944, p. 2.

6 Ibid.; also "Jap Gunner Returns with Air Medals," *Eugene* (Oregon) *Guard*, January 20, 1944, p. 9.

7 "Network Tells Why Jap Gunner Barred from Air," *Los Angeles Times*, January 27, 1944, p. 4.

8 "Broadcast Cancellation Bewilders U.S.-Jap Here," *Hollywood* (California) *Citizen-News*, February 1, 1944, p. 9.

9 Ben Kuroki quoted in "Broadcast Cancellation Bewilders U.S.-Jap Here," *Hollywood Citizen-News*, February 1, 1944, p. 9.

10 Ben Kuroki interview with Bill Kubota, August 26–27, 1998.

CHAPTER 37: RESIST THE DRAFT

1 Yoshito Kuromiya and Arthur A. Hansen, ed., *Beyond the Betrayal: The Memoir of a World War II Japanese American Draft Resister of Conscience* (Louisville, Colorado: University Press of Colorado, 2021), p. 40.

2 Yoshito "Yosh" Kuromiya quoted in Susan H. Kamei, *When Can We Go Back to America? Voices of Japanese American Incarceration During WWII* (New York: Simon & Schuster, 2021), pp. 8–11.

3   Yoshito "Yosh" Kuromiya quoted in Kamei, *When Can We Go Back to America?*, pp. 8–11.

4   Biographical information on Hisamitsu (James) Kuromiya and Hana Tada Kuromiya and their children is drawn from US federal census records for 1920, 1930, and 1940 and other documents. These include the federal immigration and naturalization records of Hisamitsu and Hana Kuroyima, the World War I draft registration records of Hisamitsu (by then known as James), the World War II draft registration documents of Yoshito and his older brother Hiroshi, and federal records generated in the Kuromiya family's incarceration during World War II. Yosh Kuromiya's memoir *Beyond the Betrayal*, edited by the imminent historian Arthur Hansen, was indispensable in my understanding of the ordeal experienced by the Kuromiya family.

5   United States. (n.d.), *Personal Justice Denied: Public Hearings of the Commission on Wartime Relocation and Internment 1981*, pp. 42–44. Retrieved April 7, 2023, from http://gdc.gale.com/archivesunbound/.

6   Ibid.

7   Martha Nakagawa, "Yosh Kuromiya, Who Resisted Wartime Draft from Heart Mountain Camp, Dies," *Nichi Bei Weekly*, August 2, 2018.

8   Masaoka with Hosokawa, *They Call Me Moses Masaoka*, p. 71.

9   Ibid., pp. 74–76.

10 Yosh Kuromiya essay, "The Winters of Heart Mountain," dated June 27, 2000, and published in Kuromiya's memoir, *Beyond the Betrayal*, pp. 52–53.

11 Description of life at the Heart Mountain camp is drawn primarily from these sources: Yosh Kuromiya's memoir *Beyond the Betrayal*; Douglas W. Nelson's definitive work *Heart Mountain: The History of An American Concentration Camp* (Madison, Wisconsin: State Historical Society of Wisconsin, 1976); Mieko Matsumoto's article on Heart Mountain for the Densho Encyclopedia ("Heart Mountain," Densho Encyclopedia, https://encyclopedia.densho.org/Heart_Mountain/); and the Heart Mountain National Historic Landmark and Heart Mountain Wyoming Foundation website (https://www.heartmountain.org/history/life-in-the-camp/).

12 Arthur A. Hansen, *Barbed Voices: Oral History, Resistance, and the World War II Japanese American Social Disaster* (Louisville, Colorado: University Press of Colorado, 2018), pp. 33–36.

13 "American Japanese Can Join Army Now," *Philadelphia Inquirer*, January 29, 1943, p. 4.

14 Richard Reeve, *Infamy: The Shocking Story of the Japanese American Internment in World War II* (New York: Henry Holt and Company, 2015), p. 159.

15 Barbara Takei, "Tule Lake," Densho Encyclopedia, https://encyclopedia.densho.org/Tule_Lake/.

16 Details of Yosh Kuromiya's story are drawn from the following sources: Kuromiya's memoir, *Beyond the Betrayal*; Frank Abe's documentary film *Conscience and the Constitution*; the film's Resisters.com website, accessed at https://resisters.com/conscience/the_story/characters/kuromiya_yosh.html; and Martha Nakagawa's obituary, "Yosh Kuromiya, Who Resisted Wartime

Draft from Heart Mountain Camp, Dies," published in the *Nichi Bei Weekly*, August 2, 2018, and accessed online at https://www.nichibei.org/2018/08/yosh-kuromiya-who-resisted-wartime-draft-from-heart-mountain-camp-dies/.

17 Martha Nakagawa, "Yosh Kuromiya, Who Resisted Wartime Draft from Heart Mountain Camp, Dies."

18 Reeve, *Infamy*, p. 157.

19 Ibid.

20 "In Memoriam: Yosh Kuromiya (1923–2018)," *Kokoro Kara: Heart Mountain Wyoming Foundation newsletter*, Summer 2018, p. 6.

CHAPTER 38: COMMONWEALTH CLUB

1 Ben's speech before the Commonwealth Club was widely covered by local newspapers and reporters for national radio networks and news agencies. Among the California papers carrying the Associated Press account were the *Modesto Bee* and the *Petaluma Argus-Courier*. See "Japanese American Sergeant's Tolerance Plea Is Applauded," *Modesto Bee*, February 4, 1944, p. 2, and "Jap American Sergeant Wins Big Ovation," *Petaluma Argus-Courier*, February 4, 1944, p. 5. The *Chicago Tribune* played coverage of Ben's speech on its front page. See "U.S. Jap Asks to Visit Tokio—in a Liberator," *Chicago Tribune*, February 5, 1944, p. 1.

CHAPTER 39: "NO TURNING BACK"

1 See Yoshito Kuromiya and Arthur A. Hansen, ed., *Beyond the Betrayal*, p. 63. Yosh also wrote about his decision to resist the draft in a July 2, 2000, essay titled "The Heart Mountain Fair Play Committee (A Resisters Account)," which was later incorporated in *Beyond the Betrayal*, pp. 59–63. Another account of Yosh Kuromiya's reaction to his draft notice is "In Memoriam: Yosh Kuromiya (1923–2018)," *Kokoro Kara: Heart Mountain Wyoming Foundation newsletter*, Summer 2018, p. 6.

2 Yosh Kuromiya, "The Heart Mountain Fair Play Committee (A Resisters Account)."

3 Ibid.

4 Ibid.

5 Ibid.

6 Susan Kamei, *When Can We Go Back to America?*, p. 216.

7 Frank Abe, *Conscience and the Constitution* documentary, 2000.

8 Yosh Kuromiya, "The Heart Mountain Fair Play Committee (A Resisters Account)."

9 Ibid.

CHAPTER 40: HEART MOUNTAIN

1 United Press dispatch, "Jap Air Hero Hitches Ride to Broadcast," *Oakland* (California) *Tribune*, February 23, 1944, p. 13.

2 Ben Kuroki interview with Bill Kubota, August 26–27, 1998.

3 Ibid.

4 Eichi Sakauye interview with Bill Kubota, December 6, 1998, *Most Honorable Son* documentary, unedited footage, Ben Kuroki Collection, KDN Films Archives.

5 Ben Kuroki interview with Bill Kubota, August 26–27, 1998.

6 Ibid.

7 James Sakoda interview with Bill Kubota, March 4, 2000, *Most Honorable Son* documentary, unedited footage, Ben Kuroki Collection, KDN Films Archives.

8 Jack Tono interview with Bill Kubota, n.d., *Most Honorable Son* documentary, unedited footage, Ben Kuroki Collection, KDN Films Archives.

9 Ibid.

10 Ben Kuroki interview with Bill Kubota, August 26–27, 1998.

11 Frank Abe, narration for *Conscience and the Constitution* documentary.

CHAPTER 41: A TURNING POINT

1 Brian Nilya, "James Sakoda," Densho Encylopedia entry, accessed at https://encyclopedia.densho.org/James_Sakoda/.

2 Ibid.

3 James Sakoda interview with Bill Kubota, March 4, 2000.

4 Ibid.

5 Ibid.

6 Ibid.

7 "Kuroki Arrives in Topaz," *Topaz* (Utah) *Times*, May 20, 1944, p. 1; "He's Human Too, He Keeps a Charm, Likes Steak, Played Center Field," *Topaz* (Utah) *Times*, May 19, 1944, p. 3.

8 "Sgt. Kuroki: Foremost An American," *Topaz* (Utah) *Times*, May 19, 1944, p. 2.

9 "Sgt. Kuroki: Foremost An American," *Topaz* (Utah) *Times*, May 19, 1944, p. 2.

10 "Residents Give Rousing Send-Off to Sgt. Kuroki," *Topaz* (Utah) *Times*, May 24, 1944, p. 1.

11 Ibid.

12 Dorothea Lange to My dear Mrs. Kuroki, handwritten letter dated February 7, 1944, Ben Kuroki collection, Military History, Smithsonian's National Museum of American History.

13 "Angelenos Polled on Postwar Views," *Los Angeles Times*, January 16, 1944, Part II (City News), pp. 1 and 3.

14 Ruth Kingman, February 1971 interviews, "Japanese American Relocation Reviewed, Volume II: The Internment," Earl Warren Oral History Project, University of California, accessed at https://oac.cdlib.org/view?docId=ft1290031s&brand=default&doc.view=entire_text.

CHAPTER 42: HONORABLE SAD SAKI

1 Gordon (Gordy) Jorgenson was killed in action on Biak Island on June 7, 1944, and the news was published in local newspapers later in the month. See "Two Lincoln County Boys Killed in Action," *Sutherland* (Nebraska) *Courier*, June 29,

1944, p. 2. Details of Gordy Jorgenson's death and the Hershey memorial service that followed can be found in "Hershey News," *Lincoln County* (Nebraska) *Tribune*, July 13, 1944, p. 4.

2   Ben told the story of the 1944 taxi incident a number of times over the years. With the passage of time, he sometimes recalled the incident as occurring in Salt Lake City rather than Denver. Ben's first recollection of the incident that I could find was published in a United Press dispatch in November 1945 and it fixed the location as Denver, so that's what I have used. The United Press dispatch was published as "Nisei Veteran Forbidden Taxi Ride in Denver," *Portage* (Wisconsin) *Daily Register and Democrat*, November 7, 1945, p. 8. In an essay for a 1985 book—Chester Marshall's *The Global Twentieth: An Anthology of the 20th AF in WW II*—Ben was quoted describing the incident as having occurred in Salt Lake City.

3   Carroll "Cal" Stewart, *Ben Kuroki: The Most Honorable Son*, short biography of Ben Kuroki, self-published and undated, p. 20.

4   Ken Neill interview with Bill Kubota, September 27, 1998, *Most Honorable Son* documentary, unedited footage, Ben Kuroki Collection, KDN Films Archives.

5   Colonel Warren L. Williams to Dear Sergeant, letter dated September 27, 1944, Ben Kuroki collection, Military History, Smithsonian's National Museum of American History.

6   Carl Curtis interview with Bill Kubota, September 3, 1998, and Ben Kuroki interview with Bill Kubota, August 26–27, 1998, *Most Honorable Son* documentary, unedited footage, Ben Kuroki Collection, KDN Films Archives.

7   Secretary of War Henry Stimson to My dear Mr. Deutsch, letter dated November 16, 1944, Ben Kuroki collection, Military History, Smithsonian's National Museum of American History.

8   Ben Kuroki oral history interview with Tom Gibbs, March 26, 2013, National WW2 Museum, and Ken Neill interview with Bill Kubota, September 27, 1998.

CHAPTER 43: TINIAN

1   Ben Kuroki interview with Bill Kubota, August 26–27, 1998.

2   Wesley Frank Craven and James Lea Cate, eds., *The Army Air Forces in World War II, Vol. 5. The Pacific: Matterhorn to Nagasaki, June 1944 to August 1945* (Washington, DC: Office of Air Force History, 1948), pp. 546–56; Charles Griffith, *The Quest: Haywood Hansell and American Strategic Bombing in World War II* (Maxwell Air Force Base, Alabama: Air University Press, 1999), pp. 167–74.

3   Craven and Cate, *The Pacific: Matterhorn to Nagasaki, June 1944 to August 1945*, pp. 558–60; Griffith. *The Quest*, pp. 176–77.

4   James M. Scott, *Black Snow: Curtis LeMay, the Firebombing of Tokyo, and the Road to the Atomic Bomb* (New York: W. W. Norton & Company, 2022), p. 133.

CHAPTER 44: DÉJÀ VU

1   Griffith, *The Quest*, p. 198.

2   Ben Kuroki letter from "Somewhere in the Marianas," published in "Ben Kuroki Writes," *Lincoln County Tribune*, North Platte, Nebraska, March 1, 1945, p. 2.

CHAPTER 45: FIREBOMBING TOKYO

1   Craven and Cate, *The Pacific: Matterhorn to Nagasaki, June 1944 to August 1945*, p. 614.

2   Ibid., pp. 615–17.

3   Ibid., p. 617.

4   Hap Arnold to Curtis LeMay, cable dated March 11, 1945, Henry H. Arnold Papers, Library of Congress, Manuscript Division, Washington, DC.

5   Ben Kuroki interview with Bill Kubota, August 26–27, 1998.

6   Ben Kuroki interview with Arthur A. Hansen, October 17, 1994, Center for Oral and Public History, California State University, Fullerton, Japanese American Oral History Project.

7   *Boy from Nebraska*, pp. 182–83.

8   Ibid.

9   Ibid., p. 183.

10 Ibid., p. 185.

11 Ibid., pp. 185–86.

CHAPTER 46: WOUNDED ENEMY

1   "Sergeant Ben Kuroki Returns After Taking Part in Bombing of Tokyo," *Honolulu Star-Bulletin*, April 23, 1945, p. 4.

2   "Sgt. Ben Kuroki B-29 Crewman in Raids on Tokyo," United Press dispatch, *McCook* (Nebraska) *Daily Gazette*, May 2, 1945, p. 5.

3   James M. Boyle, "How the Superfortress Paced the Attack Against Japan," *Air Force Magazine*, December 1964, pp. 63–69.

4   Ibid.

5   Ibid.

6   Ibid.

7   Craven and Cate, *The Pacific: Matterhorn to Nagasaki, June 1944 to August 1945*, p. 650.

8   Ibid., p. 636.

9   US Strategic Bombing Survey, *The Effects of Air Attack on the City of Nagoya* (Washington, DC: Urban Areas Division, June 1947), p. 12.

10 Craven and Cate. *The Pacific: Matterhorn to Nagasaki, June 1944 to August 1945*, p. 650.

CHAPTER 47: A WAR WITHOUT MERCY

1   John Glusman, *Conduct Under Fire: Four American Doctors and Their Fight for Life as Prisoners of the Japanese 1941–1945* (New York: Penguin Books, 2006), pp. 318–19.

2   Ibid., p. 401.

3   Citation of Distinguished Flying Cross with Oak Leaf Cluster awarded to Technical Sergeant Ben Kuroki, 680th Bombardment Squadron, 504th Bombardment Group, Air Corps, United States Army, General Orders No. 37, Aug. 19, 1946, 504th Bomb Group Records, Air Force Historical Research Agency, Maxwell Air Force Base, Alabama, Microfilm Reel B0674. The citation for this

DFC—Ben's third—reads in part: "The skill, airmanship, and accurate gunnery displayed by Sergeant KUROKI, veteran of repeated assaults against the Japanese homeland, reflect great credit on himself and the Army Air Forces."

4   Ibid.

5   Haywood S. Hansell, Jr., USAF Ret., *The Strategic Air War Against Germany and Japan: A Memoir* (Washington, DC: Office of Air Force History, US Air Force, 1986), p. 233.

6   Martin, *Boy from Nebraska*, pp. 189–90.

7   Ben Kuroki interview with Bill Kubota, August 26–27, 1998.

8   Glusman, *Conduct Under Fire*, p. 388.

9   Ibid., p. 403.

10   Ibid., p. 405.

11   The ten members of *Black Jack Too* who were executed on June 28, 1945, were: First Lieutenant Woodrow B. Palmer, pilot and aircraft commander; Second Lieutenant Owen P. Walls, copilot; Second Lieutenant Robert F. Dailey, navigator; First Lieutenant Don A. Coulter, bombardier; Sergeant Henry T. Farish, Jr., engineer; Master Sergeant Eugene J. Prouty, radar operator; Staff Sergeant Willard M. Chapman, radio operator; Staff Sergeant Cleveland T. Niles, gunner; Sergeant Peter Sabo, gunner; and Sergeant Charles A. Meisler, gunner. The crew member who died of injuries on the ground was Sergeant Joseph W. Romanelli, gunner. Also executed were two survivors of a 40th Bomb Group B-29 (42-24984) shot down on May 29, 1945: Lieutenant Richard M. Hurley, pilot, and Sergeant Elgie L. Robertson, gunner. More information on the executions, including photographs of the men as well as investigative reports and witness statements, can be found at the website of the 444th Bomb Group at https://www.444thbg.org/sabopete.htm.

12   The members of the *Indian Maid* crew were: Captain Edward Fishkin, aircraft commander, KIA; Flight Officer Alfred V. Boulton, copilot, KIA; Second Lieutenant Gerald J. McIntosh, bombardier, KIA; First Lieutenant John Meehan, navigator, POW, died in captivity; Staff Sergeant John Driapsa, engineer, KIA; Flight Officer William H. Moore, T-137750, radar operator, KIA; Sergeant Henry W. Sutherland, radio operator, POW, died in captivity; Sergeant Osmond J. Hannigan, central fire control, POW, died in captivity; Sergeant James N. Fitzgerald, right gunner, POW, executed on July 20, 1945; Sergeant Harvey B. Kennedy, Jr., left gunner, POW, executed July 20, 1945; and Sergeant Joseph G. Kanzler, tail gunner, POW, died in captivity. The source of this information is the Flight Safety Foundation's Aviation Safety Network website, https://aviation-safety.net/wikibase/162894; another source is the website of the Empire (Michigan) Area Museum Complex and the page dedicated to local native Warren Aylsworth, a B-29 pilot in World War II, http://empiremimuseum.org/docs/aylsworth.pdf.

CHAPTER 48: OUT OF LUCK

1   Craven and Cate, *The Pacific: Matterhorn to Nagasaki, June 1944 to August 1945*, pp. 641–42.

2   Ibid., p. 642.

3   Ibid., p. 642.

4   Ibid., p. 654.

5   Ibid.

6   Ronald Schaffer, *Wings of Judgment: American Bombing in World War II* (Oxford, England: Oxford University Press, 1985), p. 140. Schaffer carefully and powerfully explores the moral and ethical dimensions of the American bombing campaigns of World War II.

7   Craven and Cate, *The Pacific: Matterhorn to Nagasaki, June 1944 to August 1945*, pp. 654–55. Also see Schaffer, *Wings of Judgment*, pp. 140–41.

8   Biographical information on Technical Sergeant Harold J. (Hal) Brown is drawn from various sources, including "Broadcasting Goes on Combat Mission," *Broadcasting*, August 20, 1945, p. 68.

CHAPTER 49: UNSCRIPTED ENDING

1   Martin, *Boy from Nebraska*, p. 191.

2   Ibid.

3   Ben Kuroki interview with Bill Kubota, August 26–27, 1998.

4   Jim Jenkins interview with Bill Kubota, August 8, 1998.

5   President Harry S Truman radio statement announcing the atomic bomb strike on Hiroshima, Japan, August 6, 1945, RG 111, Records of the Office of the Chief Signal Officer, Moving Images Relating to Military Activities, NARA.

CHAPTER 50: A GREATER CAUSE

1   Martin, *Boy from Nebraska*, pp. 194–95.

2   Ben Kuroki interview with Arthur A. Hansen, October 17, 1994, Center for Oral and Public History, California State University, Fullerton, Japanese American Oral History Project.

3   Martin, *Boy from Nebraska*, p. 200.

4   Ibid., p. 201.

5   Ibid.

6   "Brushed-Off Japyank Seeks Own Vet Group," United Press dispatch dated November 4 and printed in the New York *Daily News* on November 5, 1945.

7   Ralph G. Martin would author or coauthor more than two dozen books over his career, but *Boy from Nebraska* was his first and it feels rushed and sloppy in places. Martin opens by describing Ben's postwar homecoming as occurring in January 1946. He ends the book with Ben's postwar homecoming occurring two months earlier, shortly after Ben's appearance on the *Report to the Nation* radio show—an event that occurred on Saturday night, November 3, 1945. Ben's military records, which I obtained from the National Personnel Records Center under the Freedom of Information Act, show he was discharged from the army on February 16, 1946. It's unlikely that Ben was in Hershey on a furlough in January 1946, only days before his discharge, as Martin writes. Indeed, all available evidence suggests that Ben's first trip home after his return from the Pacific took place sometime between November 5 and November 20, 1945.

8   Martin, *Boy from Nebraska*, p. 203.

9   "News Around the Clock," New York *Daily News*, November 23, 1945, p. 52.

CHAPTER 51: FIFTY-NINTH MISSION

1 Details about New York City's McBurney YMCA around the time that Ben lived there are drawn from "Takes New Post," *Eau Claire Leader*, Eau Claire, Wisconsin, December 17, 1944, p. 4.

2 Cal Stewart, "Ben Kuroki's 59th Mission," *Sunday World-Herald Magazine*, Omaha, Nebraska, February 24, 1946, p. 32.

3 Ibid.

4 Mike Masaoka with Bill Hosokawa, *They Call Me Moses Masaoka*, p. 157.

5 "Charge: Wounded Nisei Treated Like PWs: Japanese American Veterans Forced to Travel in Hold of Navy Transport Hayes," *Pacific Citizen*, March 23, 1946, p. 1.

6 "Nisei Veterans Will Speak at Salt Lake Fete," *Pacific Citizen*, Salt Lake City, Utah, March 23, 1946, p. 2.

7 Eric L. Muller, "Draft Resistance," Densho Encyclopedia, https://encyclopedia .densho.org/Draft_resistance.

8 "Nisei War Hero Hits Japanese Americans Who Fight the Draft," *Wyoming Tribune*, November 3, 1944.

9 "Segregated Veterans," *Pacific Citizen*, Salt Lake City, March 23, 1945, p. 4.

10 "Gen. Bradley to Issue Statement on Appointment of Minority Group Personnel in Regional Offices," *New York Age*, May 18, 1946, p. 3.

11 International News Service dispatch, "Women Are Urged to Lead in Rebirth of U.S. Democracy," *Buffalo* (New York) *News*, January 27, 1947, p. 7; and United Press dispatch, "Women Are Warned Radio, Movies Are Threat to U.S.," *Sacramento* (California) *Bee*, January 27, 1947, p. 4.

12 Westbrook Pegler, syndicated column, "American Veterans Committee Invites Watchful Attention," *Lancaster* (Pennsylvania) *New Era*, February 20, 1946, p. 6.

13 *Brooklyn Daily Eagle*, March 22, 1946, p. 24.

14 "Masaoka, Kuroki Will Speak Tuesday at New York JACL Meet," *Pacific Citizen*, March 23, 1946, p. 8.

15 For a fuller understanding of the work and impact of Pearl S. Buck and her East and West Association see Robert Shaffer, "Pearl S. Buck and the East and West Association: The Trajectory and Fate of 'Critical Internationalism,' 1940–1950," *Peace & Change* 28, no. 1 (January 2003).

CHAPTER 52: A PATH IN PEACE

1 Ben Kuroki–Shige Kuroki interview with Frank Abe and Frank Chin, January 31, 1998, Frank Abe Collection, Densho Digital Archive.

2 "Nisei from Nebraska," *New York Times*, November 3, 1946, p. 167.

3 "Greek Actress, Jap American to Give Education Week Talks," *Press and Sun-Bulletin*, Binghamton, New York, October 22, 1946, p. 3.

4 "Ben Kuroki, American, Visits O'Neill," *The Frontier*, O'Neill, Nebraska, December 12, 1946, p. 1.

5 "Senator Taylor Wants Law on Equal Rights," *Evening Star*, Washington, DC, February 3, 1947, p. 18.

6 "Nisei Hero Scores U.S. Intolerance," *Berkshire Evening Eagle*, Pittsfield, Massachusetts, February 17, 1947, p. 9.

7   "Haven't Killed Fascism, Jap-American Asserts," *Press and Sun-Bulletin*, Binghamton, New York, February 18, 1947, p. 5.

8   Ibid.

9   Ibid.

10 "Gettysburg Students Hear Nisei War Ace," *York* (Pennsylvania) *Daily Record*, March 10, 1947, p. 32.

11 "Says Yank Vets of Jap Ancestry Face Prejudice," *Gettysburg* (Pennsylvania) *Times*, March 4, 1947, pp. 1 and 4.

12 Ibid.

13 "Ben Kuroki, Nisei War Hero, Now G.I. Freshman at U. of N.," *Lincoln Evening Journal*, June 24, 1947, p. 3.

CHAPTER 53: PUBLISHER, REPORTER, EDITOR

1   *York* (Nebraska) *Republican*, June 8, 1950.

2   Dickson Terry, "Operation Democracy," *The Everyday Magazine, St. Louis Post-Dispatch*, June 18, 1950, Part 5, p. 1.

3   Ibid.

4   Ibid.

5   This account of the beginning of Ben's journalism career was drawn from several sources, starting with the Operation Democracy Edition of the *York Republican*, June 8, 1950. Also helpful was Cal Stewart's booklet-length biography of Ben Kuroki, *Ben Kuroki: The Most Honorable Son* (Lincoln, Nebraska: Nebraska Printing Center, 2010), pp. 26–27; other information was brought to my attention through the knowledge and generosity of Cal Stewart's son, Scott Stewart, beginning with a telephone conversation on July 24, 2023; finally, I found useful material in the article by Dickson Terry, "Operation Democracy," *The Everyday Magazine, St. Louis Post-Dispatch*, June 18, 1950, Part 5, p. 1. Terry garbles details about Ben's life before 1950, but his quotes from Ben and description of the events of Operation Democracy mesh with the accounts of Cal and Scott Stewart.

6   Associated Press dispatch published as "Floods Strike Southeast Nebr. After Heavy Rains," *Beatrice* (Nebraska) *Daily Sun*, July 10, 1950, p. 1; "Helps at York Flood," *Nebraska Signal*, Geneva, Nebraska, July 13, 1950, p. 1.

7   "Editors Again Go to Kuroki's Aid," *Lincoln* (Nebraska) *Journal Star*, July 14, 1950, p. 8.

8   Cal Stewart, *Ben Kuroki: The Most Honorable Son*, pp. 26–27.

9   "Ben Kuroki Sells York Republican," Omaha *Morning World-Herald*, January 12, 1952, p. 6

10 "He Writes His Editorials as He Fought—With Gusto," *Detroit Free Press*, May 6, 1960, p. 22.

11 "Williamston Editor Firm, Will Not Bow to Council," *Lansing State Journal*, October 21, 1960, p. 7.

12 "Japanese to Honor Brother Who Shot Down Bigotry," *Detroit Free Press*, June 29, 1964, p. 1.

13 Julie Kuroki, author interview, October 8, 2023. Based on her conversations with her mother, Julie had a different view of the financial success of her father's Michigan venture. For the growth and well-being of his daughters, "he literally gave up a flourishing publishing business that he owned and he had built from the ground up," Julie told me.

CHAPTER 54: HIDDEN HEROES

1 Julius Gius, "Editor's Notebook: Sad Farewell to the Herald-Trib," *Ventura County* (California) *Star-Free Press*, August 22, 1966, p. 22.

2 "They Made My Blood Boil," *Ventura County Star*, February 24, 1967, p. 19; also "The Day an Enemy Sub Shelled State Coast," *Ventura County Star*, February 24, 1967, p. 19.

3 Julie Kuroki, author interview, October 8, 2023.

4 Ibid.

5 "Congress Approves Payments to Japanese American Internees," Ben Kuroki letter to the editor published in the *Los Angeles Times*, August 13, 1988.

6 Charles F. Brannan to Col. Ray Ward, President, Air Force Association, letter dated March 24, 1990. Ben Kuroki papers, Military History, Smithsonian's National Museum of American History.

7 Fred Thomas, "War Hero Says Bigotry Fight Not Yet Won," *Omaha* (Nebraska) *World-Herald*, December 7, 1991, p. 3; "War Hero's Dogged Determination Pays Off," Associated Press dispatch, *Beatrice Daily Sun*, Beatrice, Nebraska, December 7, 1991, p. 3.

8 "The Hidden Heroes," *New York Times*, December 7, 1991, p. 22.

9 Stewart, *Ben Kuroki: The Most Honorable Son*, p. 28.

CHAPTER 55: RECKONING, REMEMBRANCE, AND REWARD

1 Arthur Hansen, author interview, August 23, 2023.

2 Ibid.

3 Ben Kuroki interview with Arthur A. Hansen, October 17, 1994, Center for Oral and Public History, California State University, Fullerton, Japanese American Oral History Project.

4 Scott Stewart, author interview, July 24, 2023.

5 The biographical material on Frank Abe and his father, George, is drawn from Frank Abe's interview with journalist Elaine Ikoma Ko. See Elaine Ikoma Ko, "Frank Abe's Search for an Authentic History," *North American Post*, November 14, 2021, https://napost.com/2021/frank-abes-search-for-an-authentic-history/. I also drew some background information from Frank Abe's curriculum vitae on his Resisters.com website.

6 Ben Kuroki and Shige Kuroki interview with Frank Abe and Frank Chin, January 31, 1998, Densho Digital Archive, Frank Abe Collection.

7 Ibid.

8 Frank Abe email to the author, October 17, 2023.

9 Carroll "Cal" Stewart, *Ben Kuroki: The Most Honorable Son*, p. 30.

10 "Text of speech by Ben Kuroki at the DSM ceremony, Cornhusker Hotel, Lincoln, Nebraska, August 12, 2005," Ben Kuroki collection, Military History, Smithsonian's National Museum of American History.

11 "Text of speech by Ben Kuroki at luncheon hosted by the University of Nebraska Journalism & Mass Communications Department, August 13, 2005," Ben Kuroki collection, Military History, Smithsonian's National Museum of American History.

12 Ben Kuroki's remarks at the Smithsonian National Air and Space Museum event are also preserved in the folder of speeches in the Ben Kuroki collection, Military History, Smithsonian's National Museum of American History.

13 Julie Kuroki, author interview, October 8, 2023.

14 Joe Avendano Duran, author interview, June 22, 2022.

15 Ibid.

EPILOGUE

1 Ben Kuroki to Noriko Sanefuji, October 23, 2013. Ben Kuroki collection, Military History, Smithsonian's National Museum of American History.

2 Julie Kuroki, author interview, October 8, 2023.

3 The history of the transformation of the Heart Mountain camp and the surrounding land is drawn from two sources: the website of the Heart Mountain Irrigation District at https://hmid.us, and Mieko Matsumoto, "Heart Mountain," Densho Encyclopedia, https://encyclopedia.densho.org/Heart_Mountain/.

SELECT BIBLIOGRAPHY

Air Force History Support Office. *The AAF in Northwest Africa: An Account of the Twelfth Air Force in the Northwest African Landings and the Battle for Tunisia. Wings at War Series, No. 6.* Washington, DC: Center for Air Force History, 1992.

Arnold, H. H. *Global Mission.* New York: Harper & Brothers, 1949.

Astor, Gerald. *The Mighty Eighth: The Air War in Europe as Told by the Men Who Fought It.* 1997. New York: Dell Publishing, 1998.

Atkinson, Rick. *An Army at Dawn: The War in North Africa, 1942–1943.* New York: Henry Holt and Company, 2002.

_____. *The Day of Battle: The War in Sicily and Italy, 1943–1944.* New York: Holt Paperbacks, 2007.

Baumbach, Werner. *The Life and Death of the Luftwaffe.* Costa Mesa, California: Noontide Press, 1991.

Beaulac, Willard L. *Franco: Silent Ally in World War II.* Carbondale, Illinois: Southern Illinois University Press, 1986.

Beckius, Jim. *North Platte: City Between Two Rivers.* Chicago: Arcadia Publishing, 2002.

Bekker, Cajus. *The Luftwaffe War Diaries.* New York: Ballantine Books, 1969.

Birdsall, Steve. *Log of the Liberators.* Garden City, New York: Doubleday & Company, 1973.

Bissinger, Buzz. *The Mosquito Bowl: A Game of Life and Death in World War II.* New York: HarperCollins, 2022.

Bowen, Wayne H. *Spain During World War II.* Columbia, Missouri: University of Missouri Press, 2006.

Bowman, Martin W. *Home By Christmas? The Story of US 8th/15th Air Force Airmen at War.* Wellingborough, Northamptonshire, United Kingdom: Patrick Stephens, 1987.

Bradley, James, with Ron Powers. *Flags of Our Fathers.* New York: Bantam Books, 2001.

Brereton, Lewis H., Lieutenant General, U.S.A. *The Brereton Diaries: The War in the Air in the Pacific, Middle East and Europe: 3 October 1941–8 May 1945.* New York, William Morrow and Company, 1946.

Brown, Daniel James. *Facing the Mountain: A True Story of Japanese American Heroes in World War II.* New York: Viking, 2021.

Burdick, Charles B. *Germany's Military Strategy and Spain in World War II.* Syracuse, New York: Syracuse University Press, 1968.

Caldwell, Donald L. *JG 26: Top Guns of the Luftwaffe.* New York: Ballantine Books, 1991.

Campbell, Richard H. *The Silverplate Bombers: A History and Registry of the Enola Gay and Other B-29s Configured to Carry Atomic Bombs*. Jefferson, North Carolina: McFarland, 2005.

Carigan, William. *Ad Lib: Flying the B-24 Liberator in World War II*. Manhattan, Kansas: Sunflower University Press, 1988.

Carter, Kit C., and Robert Mueller, eds. *U.S. Army Air Forces in World War II. Combat Chronology: 1941–1945*. Washington, DC: Center for Air Force History, 1991.

Childers, Thomas. *In the Shadows of War: An American Pilot's Odyssey Through Occupied France and the Camps of Nazi Germany*. New York: Henry Holt and Company, 2012.

_____. *Wings of Morning: The Story of the Last American Bomber Shot Down Over Germany in World War II*. Reading, Massachusetts: Addison-Wesley, 1996.

Coffey, Thomas. *Hap: The Story of the U.S. Air Force and the Man Who Built it: General Henry H. "Hap" Arnold*. New York: Viking, 1982.

Comer, John. *Combat Crew: A True Story of Flying and Fighting in World War II*. New York: Pocket Books, 1989.

Craven, Wesley Frank, and James Lea Cate, eds. *The Army Air Forces in World War II, Vol. 1. Plans and Early Operations, January 1939 to August 1942*. Washington, DC: Superintendent of Documents, 1948.

_____. *The Army Air Forces in World War II, Vol. 2. Europe, Torch to Pointblank, August 1942 to December 1943*. Washington, DC: Superintendent of Documents, 1948.

_____. *The Army Air Forces in World War II, Vol. 4. The Pacific, Guadalcanal to Saipan, August 1942 to July 1944*. Washington, DC: Office of Air Force History, 1948.

_____. *The Army Air Forces in World War II, Vol. 5. The Pacific, Matterhorn to Nagasaki*. Washington, DC: Office of Air Force History, 1948.

Crosby, Harry H. *A Wing and a Prayer: The "Bloody 100th" Bomb Group of the U.S. Eighth Air Force in Action Over Europe in World War II*. New York: Harper Paperbacks, 1994.

Dallek, Robert. *Franklin D. Roosevelt: A Political Life*. New York: Viking, 2017.

Daso, Dik Alan. *Hap Arnold and the Evolution of American Airpower*. Washington, DC: Smithsonian Institution Press, 2000.

Denman, Pauline A. *Letters from Tinian 1945*. United States: Xlibris, 2009.

Dorr, Robert F. *Mission to Tokyo: The American Airmen Who Took the War to the Heart of Japan*. Minneapolis: Zenith Press/MBI Pub, 2012.

Dower, John W. *War Without Mercy: Race and Power in the Pacific War*. New York: Pantheon Books, 1986.

Dugan, James, and Carroll Stewart. *Ploesti: The Great Ground-Air Battle of 1 August 1943*. New York: Random House, 1962.

Dupuy, Trevor Nevitt, Colonel, U.S. Army, Ret. *Land Battles: North Africa, Sicily, and Italy*, Volume 3 of *The Military History of World War II*. New York: Franklin Watts, 1962.

Edmundson, James V., and Celia Edmundson. *Letters to Lee: From Pearl Harbor to the War's Final Mission*. New York: Fordham University Press, 2010.

Eisenhower, David. *Eisenhower: At War 1943–1945.* New York: Vintage Books, 1987.

Eisenhower, Dwight D. *Crusade in Europe.* Garden City, New York: Doubleday, 1949.

Farrell, Don A. *Tinian: A Brief History.* Honolulu, Hawaii: Pacific Historical Parks, 2012.

Feis, Herbert. *The Spanish Story: Franco and the Nations at War.* New York: Alfred A. Knopf, 1948.

Fleming, Thomas. *The New Dealers' War: F.D.R. and the War Within World War II.* New York: Basic Books, 2001.

Freeman, Roger A. *The American Airman in Europe.* Osceola, Wisconsin: Motorbooks International, 1991.

Galland, Adolf. *The First and the Last: The Rise and Fall of the German Fighter Forces, 1938–1945.* 1954. Reprint. New York: Bantam Books, 1991.

Garland, Lieutenant Colonel Albert N., and Howard McGaw Smyth, *US Army in World War II: Mediterranean Theater of Operations: Sicily and the Surrender of Italy.* Washington, DC: Center of Military History, US Army, 1993.

Glusman, John A. *Conduct Under Fire: Four American Doctors and Their Fight for Life as Prisoners of the Japanese.* New York: Penguin, 2005.

Gordon, Linda. *Dorothea Lange: A Life Beyond Limits.* New York: W. W. Norton & Company, 2009.

Gordon, Linda, and Okihiro, Gary Y., eds. *Impounded: Dorothea Lange and the Censored Images of Japanese American Internment.* New York: W. W. Norton & Company, 2006.

Grayling, A. C. *Among the Dead Cities: The History and Moral Legacy of the WWII Bombing of Civilians in Germany and Japan.* New York: Walker & Company, 2006.

Greene, Bob. *Once Upon a Town: The Miracle of the North Platte Canteen.* New York: William Morrow, 2002.

Griffith, Charles. *The Quest: Haywood Hansell and American Strategic Bombing in World War II.* Maxwell Air Force Base, Alabama: Air University Press, 1999.

Hallas, James H. *Saipan: The Battle That Doomed Japan in World War II.* Guilford, Connecticut: Stackpole Books, 2019.

Hansell, Haywood S., Jr., USAF Ret. *The Strategic Air War Against Germany and Japan: A Memoir.* Washington, DC: Office of Air Force History, US Air Force, 1986.

Hansen, Arthur A. *Barbed Voices: Oral History, Resistance, and the World War II Japanese American Social Disaster.* Louisville, Colorado: University Press of Colorado, 2018.

Hansen, Randall. *Fire and Fury: The Allied Bombing of Germany, 1942–1945.* New York: NAL Caliber, 2008.

Hayes, Carlton J. H. *Wartime Mission in Spain 1942–1945.* New York: Macmillan Company 1945.

Hersey, John. *Hiroshima.* New York: Alfred A. Knopf, 1946.

Hill, Michael. *Black Sunday: Ploesti.* Atglen, Pennsylvania: Schiffer Military/Aviation History, 1993.

Hosokawa, Bill. *JACL in Quest of Justice: The History of the Japanese American Citizens League.* New York: William Morrow and Company, 1982.

Hoyt, Edwin P. *Angels of Death: Goering's Luftwaffe.* New York: Tom Doherty Associates, 1994.

_____. *The Death of the U-Boats.* New York: Warner Books, 1989.

_____. *U-Boats Offshore: When Hitler Struck America.* New York: Stein and Day, 1978.

Huston, Major General John W., USAF Retired, ed. *American Airpower Comes of Age: General Henry H. "Hap" Arnold's World War II Diaries.* Volumes 1 and 2. Maxwell Air Force Base, Alabama: Air University Press, 2002.

Hutton, Bud, and Andy Rooney. *Air Gunner.* New York: Farrar & Rinehart, 1944.

Jablonski, Edward. *Double Strike: The Epic Air Raids on Regensburg-Schweinfurt August 17, 1943.* Garden City, New York: Doubleday & Company, 1974.

_____. *Flying Fortress: The Illustrated Biography of the B-17s and the Men Who Flew Them.* Garden City, New York: Doubleday & Company, 1965.

Johnsen, Frederick A. *B-24 Liberator.* Osceola, Wisconsin: Motorbooks International Publishers, 1993.

Jordan, Jonathan W. *American Warlords: How Roosevelt's High Command Led America to Victory in World War II.* New York: NAL Caliber, 2015.

Kamei, Susan H. *When Can We Go Back to America? Voices of Japanese American Incarceration During WWII.* New York: Simon & Schuster, 2021.

Kuromiya, Yoshito, and Arthur A. Hansen, ed. *Beyond the Betrayal: The Memoir of a World War II Japanese American Draft Resister of Conscience.* Louisville, Colorado: University Press of Colorado, 2021.

Lyon, Cherstin. *Prisons and Patriots: Japanese American Wartime Citizenship, Civil Disobedience, and Historical Memory.* Philadelphia: Temple University Press, 2011.

Maharidge, Dale. *Bringing Mulligan Home: The Other Side of the Good War.* New York: Public Affairs, 2013.

Marshall, Chester, *The Global Twentieth—An Anthology of the 20th AF in WW II.* Winona, Minnesota: Apollo Books, 1985.

Martin, Ralph G. *Boy from Nebraska.* New York: Harper & Brothers, 1946.

Masaoka, Mike, and Bill Hosokawa. *They Call Me Moses Masaoka.* New York: Morrow, 1987.

McFarland, Stephen L. *America's Pursuit of Precision Bombing, 1910–1945.* Washington, DC: Smithsonian Institution Press, 1995.

Middlebrook, Martin. *The Schweinfurt-Regensburg Mission: American Raids on 17 August 1943.* New York: Penguin Books, 1985.

Miller, Donald L. *Masters of the Air: America's Bomber Boys Who Fought the Air War Against Nazi Germany.* Trade paperback edition. New York: Simon & Schuster, 2007.

Morison, Samuel Eliot. *Sicily-Salerno-Anzio: January 1943–June 1944. Vol. 9 of History of United States Naval Operations in World War II.* 1954. Reprint. Edison, New Jersey: Castle Books, 2001.

Muller, Eric L. *Free to Die for Their Country: The Story of the Japanese American Draft Resisters in World War II*. Chicago: University of Chicago Press, 2001.

Murray, Williamson. *The Luftwaffe 1933–45: Strategy for Defeat*. Washington, DC: Brassey's, 1996.

Neillands, Robin. *The Bomber War: The Allied Air Offensive Against Nazi Germany*. Woodstock, New York: Overlook Press, 2003.

Nelson, Douglas W. *Heart Mountain: The History of an American Concentration Camp*. Madison, Wisconsin: State Historical Society of Wisconsin, 1976.

Newby, Leroy W. *Into the Guns of Ploesti: The Human Drama of the Bomber War for Hitler's Oil, 1942–1944*. Osceola, Wisconsin: Motorbooks International, 1991.

Okada, John. *No-No Boy*. Seattle: University of Washington Press, 1976.

Overy, R. J. *The Air War: 1939–1945*. First Stein and Day paperback edition. New York: Stein and Day, 1985.

Paine, Wilmer H. *Flight Surgeon: The Journal of Maj. Wilmer H. Paine 93rd Bombardment Group Eighth Air Force*. W. Paine Jr., 2006.

Parton, James. *"Air Force Spoken Here." General Ira Eaker and the Command of the Air*. Bethesda, Maryland: Adler & Adler, 1986.

Pyle, Ernie. *Brave Men*. New York: Henry Holt, 1943.

_____. *Here Is Your War*. 1943. Reprint, Forum Books Edition. Cleveland, Ohio: World Publishing, 1945.

Reeves, Richard. *Infamy: The Shocking Story of the Japanese American Internment in World War II*. New York: Henry Holt and Company, 2015.

Rooney, Andy. *My War*. New York: Public Affairs, 2000.

Russell, Scott. *Tinian, the Final Chapter*. Washington, DC: CNMI Division of Historic Preservation, 1995.

Rust, Kenn C. *Eighth Air Force Story*. Terre Haute, Indiana: Sunshine House, 1978.

Schaffer, Ronald. *Wings of Judgment: American Bombing in World War II*. Oxford, England: Oxford University Press, 1985.

Scott, James M. *Black Snow: Curtis LeMay, the Firebombing of Tokyo, and the Road to the Atomic Bomb*. New York: W. W. Norton & Company, 2022.

Schultz, Duane. *Into the Fire: Ploesti: The Most Fateful Mission of World War II*. Yardley, Pennsylvania: Westholme, 2008.

Spector, Ronald H. *Eagle Against the Sun: The American War with Japan*. New York: Free Press, 1985.

Steinhoff, Johannes. *Messerschmitts Over Sicily: Diary of a Luftwaffe Fighter Commander*. Mechanicsburg, Pennsylvania: Stackpole Books, 2004.

Stewart, Carroll C. *Ben Kuroki: The Most Honorable Son*. Lincoln, Nebraska: Nebraska Printing Center, 2010.

_____. *Ted's Travelling Circus*. Lincoln, Nebraska: Sun/World Communication, 1996.

Stewart, John L. *The Forbidden Diary: A B-24 Navigator Remembers*. New York: McGraw-Hill, 1998.

Thomas, Lowell, and Edward Jablonski. *Doolittle: A Biography*. Garden City, New York: Doubleday & Company, 1976.

Weglyn, Michi. *Years of Infamy: The Untold Story of America's Concentration Camps.* New York: William Morrow and Company, 1976.

Yenne, Bill. *Rising Sons: The Japanese American GIs Who Fought for the United States in World War II.* New York: Thomas Dunne Books, 2007.

Zamperini, Louis, with David Rensin. *Devil at My Heels: A World War II Hero's Epic Saga of Torment, Survival, and Forgiveness.* New York: HarperCollins, 2003.

Ziegler, Philip. *London at War.* New York: Alfred A. Knopf, 1995.

INDEX